SECOND EDITION

Death Scene Investigation

Procedural Guide

D0479636

SECOND EDITION

Death Scene Investigation
Procedural Guide

MICHAEL S. MALONEY, MFS

CRC Press
Taylor & Francis Group
Boca Raton London New York

CRC Press is an imprint of the
Taylor & Francis Group, an **informa** business

CRC Press
Taylor & Francis Group
6000 Broken Sound Parkway NW, Suite 300
Boca Raton, FL 33487-2742

International Standard Book Number-13: 978-1-4987-5924-3 (Paperback)

Library of Congress Cataloging-in-Publication Data

Names: Maloney, Michael S., author.
Title: Death scene investigation : procedural guide / by Michael S. Maloney.
Description: Second edition. | Boca Raton : CRC Press, [2018] | Includes
bibliographical references and index.
Identifiers: LCCN 2017018789| ISBN 9781498759243 (pbk. : alk. paper) | ISBN
9781315107271 (ebook)
Subjects: LCSH: Forensic pathology. | Death--Causes.
Classification: LCC RA1063.4 .M338 2018 | DDC 614/.1--dc23
LC record available at https://lccn.loc.gov/2017018789

Visit the Taylor & Francis Web site at
http://www.taylorandfrancis.com

and the CRC Press Web site at
http://www.crcpress.com

Contents

Foreword xxix
Foreword, 1st Edition xxxi
Preface xxxiii
Acknowledgments xxxv
Author xxxvii

Section I

DEATH SCENE INVESTIGATION

1 Death Scene Response **3**

Initial Notification 3
Preparation 4
Coordination en Route 4
Arrival at the Scene 5
Establish a Perimeter 5
Immediate On-Scene Coordination 5
Initial Scene Evaluation: Walk-Through (with Preservation of Perishable Evidence) 6
Initial Approach to the Body 6
Preliminary Determination of Death 7
Documentation, Preservation, and/or Collection of Perishable Evidence 7
Document Postmortem Indicators 7
 Livor Mortis—Purplish Discoloration in Dependent Areas 7
 Rigor Mortis—Stiffening of Muscles and Joints 7
 Algor Mortis—Reduction in Body Temperature 8
Assessing and Establishing the Perimeter 8
 Primary Scene: Inner Perimeter 8
 Primary Scene: Outer Perimeter 8
Identifying Ancillary Scenes 9
Establishing Scene Controls 10
Scene Assessment, Planning, and Investigative Strategy 10

2   Natural Deaths   **13**

Definition of *Natural Death*   13
Worksheets and Documentation   13
Initial Scene Response   14
Scene Considerations   15
Death Scene Processing   15
   Identifying Primary and Secondary Death Scenes   15
      Primary Scene   15
      Secondary Scenes   16
   Take Control of Scene   16
   Scene Organization   16
   Legal Determination of Death   17
   Plan Development   17
   Conduct Team Briefing   18
   Scene Processing   18
   Processing the Body   19
   Photographing the Body   19
   Sketching the Body   19
   Examination of the Body   20
   Outdoor Death Scenes   20
   Common Indicators of Natural Death   21
   Related Searches   21
Death Scene Interviews   21
   First Responders   21
   Family Members   21
   Decedent's Physician   22
   Death Notification   22
General Guidelines   22
Notification Procedure   23

3   Accidental Deaths   **25**

Definition of *Accidental Death*   25
Worksheets and Documentation   25
Initial Scene Response   26
Scene Considerations   27
Death Scene Processing   27
   Identifying Primary and Secondary Death Scenes   28
      Primary Scene   28
      Secondary Scenes   28
   Take Control of Scene   28
   Scene Organization   29

Legal Determination of Death   29
   Plan Development   29
   Conduct Team Briefing   29
   Scene Processing   30
Processing: Examining the Mechanism of Death   31
   Processing   31
   Examination   31
   Documenting Scene Indicators   32
   Processing the Body   32
   Photographing the Body   32
   Sketching Body   33
   Documenting with Notes   33
   Examination of Body   34
Outdoor Death Scenes   34
Evidence Commonly Associated with Accidental Deaths   35
Related Searches   35
Review of Operator (Victim) Training and Certification   35
Death Scene Interviews   36
   First Responders   36
   Witnesses   36
   GSR Examination and Collection   36
Death Notification   37
General Guidelines   37
Notification Procedure   37

4   Suicidal Deaths   39

Definition of *Suicide*   39
Worksheets and Documentation   39
Initial Scene Response   40
Scene Considerations   41
Death Scene Processing   41
   Identifying Primary and Secondary Death Scenes   42
      Primary Scene   42
      Secondary Scenes   42
   Take Control of the Scene   42
   Scene Organization   42
Legal Determination of Death   43
Plan Development   43
Conduct Team Briefing   43
Scene Processing   44
Documenting Scene Indicators   45
Processing the Body   45

Photography and Videography of the Body   45
Sketching the Body   46
Documenting with Notes   46
Examination of the Body   46
Outdoor Death Scenes   48
Evidence Commonly Associated with Suicides   48
Related Searches   48
Death Scene Interviews   49
   First Responders   49
   GSR Examination and Collection   49
Death Notification   49
General Guidelines   50
Notification Procedure   50

5   Homicidal Deaths   53

Definition of *Homicide*   53
Worksheets and Documentation   53
Initial Scene Response   54
Scene Considerations   55
Death Scene Processing   55
   Identifying Primary and Secondary Death Scenes   55
      Primary Scene   56
      Secondary Scenes   56
   Take Control of the Scene   56
   Scene Organization   56
Legal Determination of Death   57
Plan Development   57
Conduct Team Briefing   57
Scene Processing   58
Document Scene Indicators   59
Processing Body   59
Photographing Body   59
Sketching the Body   60
Documenting with Notes   60
Examination of Body   62
Outdoor Death Scenes   62
Evidence Commonly Associated with Homicidal Deaths   62
Related Searches   63
Additional Functions Associated with the Death Scene   63
   Death Scene Interviews   63
      First Responders   63
      Witnesses   64

        GSR Examination and Collection Questions   64
    Death Notification   65
        General Guidelines   65
        Notification Procedure   65

Section II
THE MEDICOLEGAL DEATH INVESTIGATION

6   **The Role of the Medicolegal Death Investigator**   **69**

    Body and Scene Processing   70
    Transportation of Remains   70
    Death Notification   71
    General Guidelines   71
    Notification Procedure   71

7   **The Role of the Coroner**   **73**

    Establishing Identity   74
        Presumptive Identification   74
        Confirmatory Identification   74
    Establishing Cause of Death   74
    Establishing Manner of Death   75
    At the Death Scene   75
        Scene Considerations   75
        Death Notification   76
        General Guidelines   76
        Notification Procedure   76
    Coroner's Inquest   77

8   **The Role of the Medical Examiner**   **79**

    Establishing Identity   79
        Presumptive Identification   79
        Confirmatory Identification   79
    Establishing Cause of Death   80
    Establishing Manner of Death   80
    Establishing Postmortem Interval   81
    At the Death Scene   81
        Scene Considerations   81
        On-Scene Body Processing Procedures   81
        Circumstances Requiring Autopsy   82
        The Forensic Autopsy   82

Procedures in Lieu of Autopsy   84
Reports and Reporting   84
  Outbrief   84
  Preliminary Autopsy Report   84
  Toxicology Report   85
  Final Autopsy Report   85

9   Autopsy Protocol and the Investigator's Role   87

Circumstances Requiring Autopsy   87
Procedures in Lieu of Autopsy   87
Investigator's Responsibilities at Autopsy   88
  Equipment Required   88
  Arrival   88
  External Examination   89
  Internal Examination   90
  After Examination   90
Autopsy Photography Guidelines   92
  General   92
  ME Photographer   92
  Investigator   93
Body at Autopsy Photography   93
  Arrival   93
  Clothed   93
  Unclothed   94
  Identification   95
Photography of Injuries   96
  Injury Photography Guidelines   96
    Injuries   96
  Injuries (Injury Mapping)   96
Internal Examination Photographs   98
Evidence Photographs   100
Custody of Evidence from Autopsy   100
Outbrief with Medical Examiner   101

Section III
RECOVERY OF HUMAN REMAINS

10   Searching for Human Remains   105

Isolating a Search Area   105
Scientific Assistance   107
General Search Guidelines   108

Specific Search Guidelines   108
Point-to-Point Search   108
Line Search   108
Grid Search   110
Spiral Search   111

11 Surface Recovery of Human Remains: Open Field Recovery and Expedient Graves   113

General Principles   113
Worksheets and Documentation   113
Locating Remains   114
   Visual Techniques   114
   Cadaver Dogs   114
Forward-Looking Infrared and Thermal Tomography   115
NecroSearch International   115
Body Processing   116
Scene Processing   116
Establishing Datum   116
Establishing a Grid   117
Surface Documentation and Recovery of Evidence   119
Recovery of Remains   120
Sifting Soil   120
Soil Evidence   121
Scientific Assistance   121

12 Recovery of Buried Human Remains: Shallow Grave, Buried Remains, and Exhumation   123

General Principles   123
Worksheets and Documentation   123
Locating Remains   124
   Visual Methods   124
     Expedient Grave Indicators   124
     Shallow Grave Indicators   124
     Buried Remains Indicators   124
     Exhumation Site Location   125
   Probing Method   125
Cadaver Dogs   125
Technological Methods   126
Scientific Assistance   127
NecroSearch International   128
Recovery of Buried Remains   128
   Surface Documentation and Recovery of Evidence 128

Surface Preparation   128
  Establishing Datum   128
  Establishing Grid   129
  Preparing Sifting Site   130
Excavating the Grave   131
Sifting Soil   133
Impression Evidence   134
Soil Evidence   134
Exhumation of Remains   135

13 Aquatic Recovery of Human Remains   137

General Principles   137
Worksheets and Documentation   137
Locating Remains   138
  Surface Search   138
  Aerial Search   138
  Underwater Search   138
Drift   140
Computer Simulation Modeling   140
Cadaver Dogs   140
Technological Search   141
Processing the Scene   143
Processing the Body   145
  Documenting Recovery   145
  Remains Recovered from Predator   145

**14 Postmortem Changes: Estimating
Postmortem Interval (Time since Death)   147**

Worksheets and Documentation   147
  Determining Time Range   147
  Immediate Postmortem Changes   148
  Early Postmortem Changes   148
  Postmortem Lividity (Livor Mortis)   148
  Postmortem Rigidity (Rigor Mortis)   148
  Postmortem Cooling (Algor Mortis)   149
Late Postmortem Changes   150
  Decomposition   150
  Adipocere Development   150
  Mummification   151
  Skeletonization   151
Other Postmortem Factors   151
  Forensic Entomology   151

Stomach Contents	151
Scene Indicators	152
References	152

Section IV

WOUND DYNAMICS AND MECHANISM OF INJURY

15   Asphyxiation   **155**

Worksheets and Documentation	155
Strangulation	156
Manual Strangulation (Throttling)	156
General	156
Scene	156
Body	156
Ligature Strangulation (Garroting)	157
General	157
Scene	157
Body	158
Hanging	158
General	158
Scene	159
Body	160
Autoerotic Asphyxiation	161
General	161
Scene	161
Body	162
Choking	162
General	162
Scene	162
Body	162
Smothering	163
General	163
Scene	163
Body	163
Mechanical Asphyxia	164
General	164
Scene	165
Body	165
Chemical Asphyxia	165
General	165

Scene   166
Helium or Nitrogen Scene (Exit Bag or Exit Hood)   166
Carbon Monoxide Scene: Heater   167
Carbon Monoxide Scene: Vehicle   167
Body   167
Drowning   168
General   168
Scene   168
Scuba Scene   169
Body   169

16   Sharp Force Injuries   171

General   171
Worksheets and Documentation   171
Scene   172
Body   172

**17   Blunt Force Injuries: Blunt Instrument Blows,
       Fall from a Height, Collisions   177**

General   177
Worksheets and Documentation   177
Blunt Force Blows   178
Weapon or Striking Object   178
Body   178
Deceleration Injuries   179
Falls from a Height   179
Control Injuries   179
Automobile   180

18   Chopping Injuries   181

General   181
Worksheets and Documentation   181
Scene   182
Body   182

**19   Firearm Injuries: Pistols and Rifles
       (Rifled Bore Weapons)   183**

Gunshot Wounds   183
Worksheets and Documentation   183
Entrance Wounds   183

Effects of Distance on Gunshot Wounds   184
    Contact Gunshot Wounds   184
        Hard Contact Wounds   184
        Loose Contact Wounds   185
        Angled Contact Wounds   185
        Incomplete Contact Wounds   187
    Near Contact Wounds   187
    Intermediate Range Wounds   187
    Distant Wounds   188
    Rifle Entrance Wounds   189
    Exit Wounds   190

20 Firearm Injuries: Shotguns (Smooth Bore Weapons) — 191

Worksheets and Documentation   191
Shotgun Entrance Wounds   191
    Shotcup and Wadding Effect on Entrance Wound   191
    Shot Effect on Entrance Wound   193
Effects of Distance on Wounds   193
    Contact Wounds   193
        Stellate Wounds   193
        Hard Contact Head Wounds   193
        Intraoral Wounds   193
        Contact Wounds to Trunk   194
    Near Contact Wounds   194
    Close and Intermediate Range Wounds   194
    Distant Range Wounds   196
    Shotgun Exit Wounds   196

21 Explosive Injuries — 197

General Considerations   197
Worksheets and Documentation   197
    Scene   198
    Body   198
Mechanisms of Blast Injuries   199
    Primary   199
    Secondary   199
    Tertiary   199
    Quaternary   199
        Cautions   199

22   Thermal Injuries   **201**

General Considerations   201
Scene   201
Worksheets and Documentation   202
Body   202
First-Degree Burns   202
Second-Degree Burns   202
Third-Degree Burns   203
Fourth-Degree Burns   203
Deaths from Fire-Related Injuries   204

23   Electrical Injuries   **205**

Worksheets and Documentation   205
Commercial and Residential Power Sources   205
Scene   205
Body   206
Lightning Strikes   206
Direct Strike   206
Scene   206
Body   207
Side Flash (Splash)   208
Ground Strike   208
Scene   209
Body   209
Conduction   209
Streamers   209

24   Poisoning   **211**

General Considerations   211
Worksheets and Documentation   211
Methods of Exposure   212
Inhaled Poisons   212
Danger   212
Commonly Inhaled Poisons   212
Ingested Poisons   213
Danger   213
Commonly Ingested Poisons   213
Skin Exposure (Dermal Absorption)   214
Common Skin Absorption Poisons   214
Bites and Envenomation   214
Common Methods of Envenomation   214

The Body and Scene   214
    Accidental Poisonings   214
    Intentional Poisoning   215
The Body   215

25   Drug-Related Deaths   217

Worksheets and Documentation   217
Oral Ingestion   218
Intravenous, Subdermal, and Intramuscular Injection   218
Insufflation/Inhalation   219
Absorption   220
Drug-Related Death Scenes   220
Processing the Scene   221
Drug Scene Evidence   221
The Body at the Scene   221

Section V

SPECIAL DEATH INVESTIGATIONS

26   Infant Deaths   225

Worksheets and Documentation   225
Violent Death   226
Asphyxial   226
Asphyxial by Entrapment (Rollover)   226
    Shaken Baby Syndrome and Shaken Baby with
    Impact Syndrome   226
    Medical Findings   227
Failure to Thrive   227
    Organic Causes   227
    Neglect Causes   228
Sudden Unexplained Infant Death   228
Victim   229
Scene   230
Dietary History   231
Medical History   232
Mother's Pregnancy History   233

27   Child Deaths   235

Worksheets and Documentation   235
Physical Abuse and Violent Acts   236

The Scene   236
   Weapon or Item Used to Inflict Injury   236
   Burns, Scalds, Immersion Burns   236
   Falling Injuries and Staged Accidents   236
The Body   237
   Skeletal System Injuries   237
   Skin and Subcutaneous Tissue Injuries   237
   Immersion, Contact, and Cigarette Burns   238
   Head and Central Nervous System Injuries   239
   Chest and Abdominal Injuries   240
Medicolegal Autopsy   240
Additional Questions for Medical Examiner   241
   Medical Record Review   241
Munchausen Syndrome by Proxy   242
Scene Investigation   242
Neglect   243
The Scene   243
   General Living Conditions   243
   Child's Sleeping Area   243
   Food Preparation and Eating Area   243

28 Child Sexual Abduction and Murder   245

Worksheets and Documentation   245
Abduction   246
Missing Child Report   246
Missing Adolescent Report   247
Scene   248
Sexual Assault   248
Searches Related to Pedophilia   249
Murder   250
Body Recovery   251
   Evidence on Body   251
   Examination of Suspect   252

29 Sexual Activities Resulting in Death   253

Worksheets and Documentation   253
Death during Coitus   254
   The Scene   254
   The Victim   255
   The Intimate Partner   255
Hypoxic Deaths (Consensual, Breath Play)   255
   The Scene   255

The Victim   257
The Intimate Partner   257
Hypoxic Deaths (Nonconsensual)   257
The Scene   257
The Victim   259
The Intimate Partner   259
Autoerotic Asphyxiation   260
General   260
The Scene   260
The Victim   261

30   Rape and Sexual Assault Resulting in Death   263

Worksheets and Documentation   263
Scene Context and Considerations   264
Acquaintance Rape/Sexual Assault   264
Drug-Facilitated Rape/Sexual Assaults   265
Stranger Rape/Sexual Assault   265
Victim Control   266
Unique Scene Indicators   266
Examination of Victim   266
Sexual Assault Evidence   266
Physical Assault Evidence   267
Examination of Suspect   267
Examination of Intimate Partner   268
Scene Considerations   268

31   Multiple Victim Death Scenes   271

Serial Murders   271
Spree Killing   272
Scene Considerations   272
Mass Murder   273
Scene Considerations   273

Section VI

DEATH SCENE MANAGEMENT: TASKS AND RESPONSIBILITIES

32   Death Scene Management   277

Arrival and Initial Organization   277
Task Prioritization   277

Scene Coordination   278
Confirming the Scope of the Scene   279
  Primary Scene: Inner Perimeter   279
  Primary Scene: Outer Perimeter   279
Identifying Ancillary Scenes   279
Establishing Scene Controls   280
Major Scene Control Considerations   281
  Media Area   281
  Command Briefings   282
Legal Concerns   282
Scene Assessment, Planning, and Investigative Strategy   283
Scene Considerations   284
Available Personnel   284
Scene Documentation   285
Integrating with the Investigation (Information Flow)   285
Command Functions   285
Scene Completion and Post-Scene Activities   286
  Before Releasing the Scene   286
  Releasing the Scene   286
Post-Scene Activities   286
  Personnel Issues   286
  Evidence and Laboratory Issues   286
  Reports and Follow-Up Analysis   287

33 Death Scene Sketching   289

Rough Sketch   289
Finished Sketch (Final Diagram)   289
General Components of a Sketch   291
Depictions   292
Types of Sketches   292
The Body   293
Scene Measurements   295
Methods of Measuring   298
Evidence Identification   301

34 Death Scene Photography   303

Equipment   303
  Setup   304
  Technique   305
General Photography Guidelines   305
  Use of Flash   306
  Use of Filters   307

Scene Photography 308
Overlapping Method/Panographic 309
Progressive Method 309
Photographing Items of Evidence 309
Photographic Perspectives 309
Body at Scene Photography 311
  In-Scene Context 311
  Identification 312
  Overall 312
  Injuries 312
Body at Autopsy Photography 313

35 Death Scene Videography 315

WADI SAWABIN
Equipment 315
  Setup 316
  Technique 316
  Deep Focus 317
  Macro Focus 317
  Zoom 317
  Panorama Shot (Pan) 317
  Vertical Panorama Shot (Tilts) 318
  Use of Auxiliary Lighting 318
  Use of Filters 318
The Death Scene 318
  Record the Following 318
The Body at the Scene 319
  General 319
  Scene for Context 319
The Body (*In Situ*) 319
The Body at Autopsy 320
Bindings and Sequencing Issues 321

36 Death Scene Notes and Observation 323

Scene Observer Duties 323
Observations (Scene Indicators) for Indoor Scenes 324
  Structure Type/Location 324
  General Appearance 324
  Possible Related Video Coverage 324
  Entry/Exit 324
  Windows 324
  Kitchen and Dining Room 325

Environmental Controls   325
Laundry and Utility Areas   325
Lighting (In Each Room as well as Outside Lights)   325
Telephones and Cellular Phones   325
Mail   326
Contents of Wastebaskets and Ashtrays   326
Bath and Toilet Areas   326
Calendars and Planners   326
Computers and Internet   326
Observations for Outdoor Scenes   327
Environmental Conditions   327
Immediate Area of Crime Scene   327
Extended Area of Crime Scene   327
Observations for Motor Vehicle Scenes   327
Exterior   327
Interior   328

Section VII
DEATH SCENE EVIDENCE PROCESSING

37 Documenting and Processing Bloodstain Patterns at the Scene   331

Detection   331
Visual   331
Alternate Light Source   332
Infrared   332
Chemical Enhancement   332
Luminol   333
Modified Luminol Formulas (Such as BlueStar)   333
Fluorescein   334
Isolate and Identify Discrete Patterns   334
Spatter   334
Nonspatter Stains   335
Documentation through Mapping   336
Mapping   337
Mapping Large Area Patterns   338
Clothing   339
Photography   339
Sketching   340
Sampling and Collection   340

38 Documenting and Processing a Shooting Scene 341

Recovery of Firearms Evidence from the Scene 341
  The Weapon 341
    Weapons Safety Is of Paramount Concern 341
  Documenting the Firearm 342
  Make the Weapon Safe 342
  Processing the Weapon On-Scene 342
  Collecting and Packaging the Firearm 343
Recovery of a Firearm from Water 343
Recovery of Cartridges, Spent Bullet Cases, and Bullets 343
  Additional Analysis Considerations 344
  Documenting Bullet Defects 344
  Chemical Testing to Determine If It Is a Bullet Defect 347
  Testing for Copper 348
  Testing for Lead 349
Recovery of Firearms Evidence from the Victim 350
  Detection of Gunpowder Patterns 350
    Visual 350
  Infrared 351
  Collection and Packaging of Clothing 351
  Documentation and Collection of Gunshot Residue 352

39 Documenting and Processing Post-Blast (Explosive Incident) Scenes 355

Initial Actions 355
  Establishing a Perimeter 355
  Legal Concerns 355
  Establishing Context 356
Crime Scene Processing Guidelines 357
  Initial Briefing 357
  Initial Walk-Through 357
Blast Scene Mapping (Searching and Evidence Recovery) 358
  Procedure for Mapping 358
Collecting the Evidence 360
Commonly Encountered Evidence 360
  Identified Device and Component Parts 360
  Post-Blast Debris 360
Explosive Evidence Collection Guidelines 361
Sampling for Explosive Residue 361
Collecting and Packaging 361

| | Liquids | 361 |
| | Solids | 362 |

40 Entomological Evidence   363

DONALD HOUSMAN

Terminology	363
General Guidelines	364
Collection of Samples	365
Adult and Flying Insects	365
Crawling Adult Insects	365
Maggots, Pupae, and Other Immature Insect Forms	365
Insects in Soil	366
Documentation of Entomological Evidence	367
Contact with the Servicing Forensic Entomologist	367

41 Biological Evidence   369

Touch DNA	369
Detection	369
Preservation and Collection on Items of Evidence	370
Biological Fluids and Stains	370
Detection	370
The Body and Scene Analysis	371
Collection of Biological Stains	372
General	372
Dry Stains	374
The Body	374
The Scene	374
Wet Stains	375
The Body	375
The Scene	375
Liquid Stains	376
The Scene	376
Packaging	376

42 Trace Evidence   379

The Body	379
The Scene	380
General Processing Guidelines	380
Detection	380
General Collection	381
Packaging	382

Hairs   384
Fibers   384
Paint   384
  Collection   385
  Control Sample   385
  Known Sample   385
  Packaging   385
Glass   385
  On-Scene Examination   386
  Collection   387
  Known Sample   387
  Packaging   387
Building Materials   387
  Collection   387
  Known Sample   387
Soil Evidence   387
  Collection   388
  Known Sample   388
Alibi Sample   388
  Packaging   388
Trace Metals Evidence   389
  Field Testing for Lead and Copper for Bullet Defects   389
    Testing for Copper   389
    Testing for Lead   389
  Collection   390
  Control Sample   390
  Known Sample   390
  Packaging   390
Trace Explosives Evidence   390
  Collection of Explosives Residue Materials   391
  Collection of Trace Components Parts   391
Hazardous Materials Evidence   392

43   Friction Ridge Evidence   393

Prints on the Body/on Skin   393
  Patent (Visible) Prints on the Skin   393
  Latent Prints on the Skin   394
    Detection   394
Prints at the Scene   395
  General   395
  Detecting Prints   396
    Oblique Lighting   396

Reflected Ultraviolet Imaging System   396
Alternate Light Sources   396
Photography of Prints   397
DNA Considerations   398
Prints on Nonporous Surfaces   398
Print Stabilization with Superglue™ Fuming (Cyanoacrylate) 398
Developing   400
Recovering Latent Prints from Nonporous Surfaces   400
Packaging   401
Prints on Porous Surfaces   401
Packaging   401
Chemical Development of Latent Prints   401
Prints on Wet Surfaces   401
Prints in Blood   402
Amido Black   402
Hungarian Red   403
Leucocrystal Violet   403
Prints in Oil or Grease   404

44   Impression Evidence   407

The Body   407
Bite Marks in Skin   407
Photographing Bite Marks   407
Processing Bite Marks: Special Considerations   409
Tool Marks in Bone   409
Two-Dimensional Residue Impressions on Skin   410
Kick or Stomps to the Body   410
The Scene   411
Tool Marks (Three-Dimensional Impression Evidence)   411
General   411
Detection   411
Photography   411
Processing/Casting Tool Marks   412
Footwear and Tire Impressions (Three-Dimensional
Impression Evidence)   413
General   413
Detection   414
Photography   414
Processing/Casting   415

Casting Underwater   416
Impressions in Snow   417
Impressions in Sand/Dust   418
Special Considerations for Tire Marks   418
Packaging   419
Footwear and Tire Impressions
(Two-Dimensional Impression Evidence)   419
Detection   419
Oblique Lighting Visualization   419
Mirror and Oblique Lighting   419
Photography   420
Processing Dry Impressions   421
Processing Moist Impression   424
Packaging   425

Section VIII
DEATH INVESTIGATION CHECKLIST AND WORKSHEETS

Death Scene Investigation Check List Fill-In Forms   431

Death Scene Investigation Check List: Logs and Forms   463

Supplemental Death Scene Worksheets   481
Worksheet 1: Postmortem Indicator (PMI)   484
Worksheet 2: Death Scene Entry Log   485
Worksheet 3: Photographic Head Slate   486
Worksheet 4: Photography Log   487
Worksheet 5: Post-Blast Scene Management   488
Worksheet 6: Firearms Recovery Worksheet   489
Worksheet 7: Entomology Worksheet   490
Worksheet 8: Biological Evidence Notes   491
Worksheet 9: Trace Evidence Notes   492
Worksheet 10: Friction Ridge Evidence   493
Worksheet 11: Impression Evidence Notes   494
Worksheet 12: Immersion Burn Worksheet   495
Worksheet 13: SIDS/SUIDS (Sudden Infant Death)   496
Worksheet 14: Bullet Defect Worksheet   504
Worksheet 15: Bloodstain Pattern Worksheet   505

**Appendix A: Universal Precautions for
Bloodborne Pathogens**   507

Appendix B: Bloodstain Pattern Decision Tree   511

Appendix C: Druggist Fold   515

Death Scene Investigation Decision Tree   517

Index   519

Foreword

Every death scene tells a story. The scene must be properly and thoroughly examined, evidence collected, and everything carefully documented. The investigator(s) has (have) only one opportunity to properly process the death scene. Realizing that every investigation will involve a number of professionals from different disciplines (coroner, medical examiner, crime scene investigator, criminal investigator, etc.)—with varying levels of education and experience in death investigation—it is vitally important that all parties involved conduct the most complete and thorough scene examination and documentation as possible.

Michael Maloney, the author of the second edition of *Death Scene Investigation: Procedural Guide*, has used his vast experience to write a wholly comprehensive procedural guide to assist those involved in the profession of death investigation, whatever their role. This well-organized publication may be used as a field guide for all parties involved in an investigation. This guide will provide easy reference as to the proper procedures to follow in investigating all the various modes of death that will be encountered. With the addition of new chapters, it will also be a valuable study guide for all those planning to take the American Board of Medicolegal Death Investigators (ABMDI) Diplomat and Fellow certification examination for Medicolegal Death Investigator.

Coroner Lynn Reed, F-ABMDI
Moultrie County, Illinois and Director of Training, Illinois Coroners and Medical Examiners Association

Foreword, 1st Edition

Death Scene Investigation: Procedural Guide is the answer to a long recognized dilemma—how to have every death investigated by an experienced death investigator. Using his considerable experience in death investigations and forensics, Mr. Maloney has created a procedural guide that gives everyone, including the medical examiner's investigator, coroner, crime scene investigator, or detective, an on-scene guide for processing the death scene. This field guide will assist in understanding the story the scene tells as well as developing the investigative direction. The Death Investigation Decision Tree is an innovative, easy-to-use tool that ensures the scene investigation is focused, directed, and complete while prompting the investigator to see the "red flags" that are present but sometimes overlooked. This should be the first tool used on the scene after familiarization with the scene and basic facts. Easy-to-follow chapters and complete bulleted procedures are presented in a manner that minimizes the need to flip back and forth through the guide. The spiral bound format is designed to fit in a cargo pocket for easy access and transport to the scene. Unlike textbooks, this guide stands out because it is specifically designed for use in the field. The medical examiner, coroner, and homicide detective should not overlook this guide; it is a handy reference for proper procedures to employ in a wide variety of death scenes.

Tom Bevel
President of Bevel, Gardner & Associates, Inc.

Preface

This book is meant to be used at the scene as a practical field guide when responding to a death investigation. Some information in the various chapters of the guide may seem repetitious; this is meant to facilitate its field use by minimizing the need to flip back and forth for information while processing the scene. The guide is separated into the following sections for ease of use:

- *Section I*, Death Scene Investigations, includes procedures for preparing and responding to the scene. Chapter 1 provides for the initial response and evaluation required for all death scenes. The death scene investigation decision tree is provided as an easy-to-follow process to lead the investigator to a preliminary indication of manner of death. From there, the investigator goes to the specific chapter in Section I for accidental, natural, suicidal, or homicidal death to facilitate a thorough scene investigation.
- *Section II* covers the Medicolegal Death Investigation. This includes the roles of the medicolegal death investigator, coroner, and medical examiner. It covers the determination of identity, cause, and manner of death. The forensic autopsy as well as the investigator's role at the autopsy are discussed.
- *Section III* covers the Recovery of Human Remains from an open field, aquatic, expedient grave, sub-surface remains or the; exhumation of buried remains; as well as search techniques to locate clandestine graves.
- *Section IV* details Wound Dynamics and the evidence they may present at the scene and on the body.
- *Section V*, Special Death Scene Investigations, is used to supplement death investigations involving child or infant deaths, sexual deaths, or multiple victims.
- *Section VI*, Death Scene Management, Tasks, and Responsibilities, covers the responsibilities, duties, and necessary techniques to accomplish death scene management, documentation, evidence processing, and death scene procedures. This section serves as a ready reference for the death scene investigator assigned to photography, videography, sketching, and processing or as the scene observer.

- *Section VII*, Death Scene Evidence Processing, details the specific procedures to be followed when bloodstain patterns or a shooting scene are encountered, as well as in handling specific evidence types such as entomological, biological, trace, friction ridge, or impression evidence.
- *Section VIII*, Death Investigation Checklist and Worksheets, incorporates Dick Warrington's popular Death Scene Investigation Checklist with a supplemental series of customized checklists developed for this procedural guide. The checklists are also available in a digital form fill format through a download key offered with this text.

A note on additional content available: Dick Warrington's popular Death Scene Investigation Checklist is available in its entirety (over 30 pages of checklists to cover almost every conceivable scene!). With an additional 15 forms specific to documenting tasking suggested through this procedural guide, these forms have been made available for download to purchasers of this book. Purchasers of this book, and any agency individuals may work for, are free to use such forms in the course of their work and customize them for their purposes. You may go to the publisher's maintained Web site—and register to gain access to download the forms—here: www.crcpress.com/cw/maloney.

Acknowledgments

The foundation for the first edition of this procedural guide was established in 1996 while I was involved in co-authoring a government publication, *The Field Guide for Crime Scene Processing*, for the Naval Criminal Investigative Service (NCIS) with Special Agent Donald Housman. That guidebook covered not only basic crime scene investigation techniques but also chapters dealing with death investigations. My first edition, focusing on death investigations, was well received and used in a series of national and international death investigation seminars. The procedures laid out in the first edition were accepted as best practices by law enforcement and medical examiners offices both internationally and nationally. In the time since the first edition, there have been advances in the approach and processing of death scenes. Touch DNA and other advances in technology called for a second edition. In addition, this gave me the opportunity to incorporate suggestions, additional subjects, and techniques that had been suggested through training classes and seminars over the last several years. I would like to thank NCIS Special Agent (Retired) Donald Housman, NCIS Special Agent (Retired) William Herzig, NCIS Special Agent (Retired) Thomas Brady, Federal Law Enforcement Training Center (FLETC) Senior Instructor Ted McDonald, FLETC Senior Instructor Chris Stewart, FLETC Senior Instructor Michael Hulihan, Ms. Kim Duddy of the Washington State Patrol Laboratory, the membership of the Association for Crime Scene Reconstruction, the membership of the International Association of Bloodstain Pattern Analysts, and the countless students I have worked with that have contributed so greatly to the body of knowledge used in this procedural guide.

I would also like to thank Detective Lou Camelbeek, Tom Green County Sheriff's Office (Retired), for teaching me what it meant to be a law enforcement officer; Paul Susanbach of FLETC, who knows what he has done. I would also be remiss if I did not thank the special agents of the NCIS for the incredible professional relationship that I had as I worked among them on crime scenes throughout the world.

Last, but not least, I would like to thank my loving wife Maxine and my children Michael, Gabriel, and Tia, who put up with my frequent absences, no-notice deployments, and missed birthdays, anniversaries, basketball games, and soccer games during my career. I would also like to thank Michael, Gabe, and Tia, who, in whole or in body part, appear in various photographs in this book.

Author

Michael Maloney is an independent forensic consultant, trainer, and author. He holds a master of forensic science degree from George Washington University with a fellowship in forensic medicine from the Office of the Armed Forces Institute of Pathology. He has 20 years' experience as a special agent with the Naval Criminal Investigative Service and senior instructor at the Federal Law Enforcement Training Center for Death Investigations and Sex Crimes.

Mr. Maloney has undergone extensive training and is considered a subject matter expert in a variety of forensic disciplines including death/crime scene reconstruction, death/crime scene processing, wound dynamics/evidence of injury, shooting reconstruction, and bloodstain pattern analysis. He is the former president of the Association for Crime Scene Reconstruction and has held membership with the American Academy of Forensic Science, International Association of Bloodstain Pattern Analysts, International Crime Scene Investigators Association, and the International Association for Identification.

Mr. Maloney has been responsible for providing forensic investigation, coordination, and reconstruction for incidents involving death investigations, serial crimes, and crimes of extreme violence. He processed and reconstructed the terrorist attack on the North Arabian Gulf Oil platforms during Operation Iraqi Freedom. He served with the International War Crimes Tribunal for the former Yugoslavia in Bosnia, where he led the forensic processing and reconstruction on two sites of mass execution. He also served as an onsite forensic consultant to the Weapons of Mass Destruction Task Force at the Olympic Games in Atlanta, Georgia, and the Summit of Eight Conference in Denver, Colorado. He processed and reconstructed the events surrounding the deaths of 24 Iraqi citizens in Haditha, Iraq. He was recognized for his innovative approach to this scene as the 2008 co-recipient of the August Vollmer Award presented by the International Association of Chiefs of Police. He has served as a trainer for the South Africa Police Service

Forensic Laboratories on shooting scene response and served as the senior forensic advisor for the Justice Sector Project for the Palestinian Civil Police.

Mr. Maloney is a sought-after public speaker offering dynamic presentations to law enforcement, medical examiner, coroner, and forensic nursing groups on a wide variety of forensic topics. He provides training seminars and classes throughout the law enforcement community both nationally and internationally on death investigations, crime scene investigations, crime scene reconstruction, and shooting incident scenes and reconstruction.

New to the Second Edition of Death Scene Investigation Procedural Guide contains

- Dick Warrington's popular Death Investigation Checklist has been added to the second edition! This checklist has been the standard for many departments for the last decade and is now available in this guide in an updated format. The checklist has been supplemented with a series of worksheets for use while processing the scene. Readers are also provided with access to download these forms and all other worksheets in easy digital form fill formats.
- A sleeker format that allows for rapid assessment of the scene and seamless transition to the investigation at large, including a foldout Death Scene Investigation Decision Tree from the back cover.
- An expanded section on the medicolegal death investigation specifically addresses the role of the coroner, medical examiner, and medicolegal death investigator.
- Sections on death notification and the proper method to accomplish this often daunting task is now included.
- Chapters on drug-related deaths, poisoning, and sexual activities resulting in death (noncriminal) have been added.
- The "Recovery of Human Remains" section now includes guidance on grave exhumation.
- The very important skill of death scene videography has been moved to its own chapter and expanded considerably with the help of law enforcement video expert Wadi Sawabini.
- Revised and edited chapters based on feedback from readers and seminar students over the last 5 years!
- Lastly, Dick Warrington's popular Death Scene Investigation Checklist is available in its entirety (over 30 pages of checklists to cover almost every conceivable scene!), with an additional 15 forms specific to documenting tasking suggested through this procedural guide. These forms, presented in this edition, have

been made available for download to purchasers of this book. Purchasers of this book, and any agency individuals may work for, are free to use such forms in the course of their work and customize them for their purposes. You may go to the publisher's maintained Web site—and register to gain access to download the forms—here: www.crcpress.com/cw/maloney.

Death Scene Investigation

I

Death Scene Response 1

This chapter details the notification and response for the death scene investigator (DSI). The DSI may be a law enforcement crime scene investigator, detective, medical examiner's investigator, or coroner's investigator. No matter the title, how DSIs respond to and handle the death scene is a reflection on their agency's professionalism. Though it is recognized that at routine death scenes or in smaller departments DSIs may also serve as the on-site manager/supervisor, the duties specific to managing the death scene have been explained in Chapter 32, "Death Scene Management." This chapter will focus solely on the procedural aspects of the death scene response.

Initial Notification

The first receipt of information of a death or possible death by a DSI formally begins the death scene investigation. Death scenes are documented through notes, photography, and sketching. Documentation begins with note taking—the Death Scene Investigation Checklist included as Section VIII provides a template for thorough death scene documentation. The checklist may be downloaded from the publisher's website at (www.crcpress.com/cw/maloney) as a digital fill-in form for tablets and PCs or may be printed as hard copy forms. Information initially documented will include the following:

- Method of notification.
- Person making notification.
- Time of notification.
- Description of death scene (outdoor, indoor, residential, commercial area, etc.).
- Who will have investigative jurisdiction, or lead, in a multiagency response?
- People present at death scene (law enforcement, medical, coroner, family, etc.).
- Reported crime (suspicious death, murder, sex crime, child abuse, burglary, etc.).

- Identification and security of scene (agency currently in charge).
- Body at scene (if not at scene, where is it?).
- Authority who pronounced victim dead.
- Safety hazards or unique considerations at scene (electrocution, poisonous gases, unstable terrain, civil insurrection, etc.).
- Information about suspects and witnesses still in area.
- Other agencies notified and responding.

Preparation

- Initial information will almost certainly be wrong or incomplete. Expect this when you arrive at the scene.
- Get mentally prepared. No matter how seasoned you may be, you may encounter a scene that you find disturbing.
- Get yourself ready for what you are about to do. The time to get focused and oriented is *not* at a scene with witnesses, bystanders, and perhaps suspects standing around.

Coordination en Route

It may be possible en route to determine the following or make the following notifications. If not, complete this list as soon as possible after your initial actions. Coordination efforts are more thoroughly detailed in Chapter 32.

- Who has jurisdiction and will be lead on the investigation?
- Will other jurisdictions be responding to assist? If so, what assets are they sending?
- Who is in charge of the scene now?
- Has the medical examiner's office or coroner been notified? Are they sending investigators or responding?
- Is the victim still at the scene? If not, where have they been transported to? Ensure a response to the body.
- Does the initial scope and description of the death scene indicate a need for external or interagency assistance?
  - Is there a need for auxiliary lighting?
  - Is there building or structural instability?
  - Is this an aquatic scene requiring boats or divers?
  - Did the death occur in a fatal fire?

Arrival at the Scene

Initial arrival at the scene may often be chaotic. The presence of first responders, law enforcement, fire or rescue, emergency medical services, and agencies from multiple jurisdictions will impact order at a scene. During the
initial response, the primary concerns are as follows:

- Mitigate any immediate threat to victims, bystanders, or first
  responders.
  - Tactical threats
  - Scene hazards
  - Toxic environment
- Render aid to those injured to the ability of your training while
  summoning emergency care if needed.
- Get a briefing from whoever controls the scene.
- Identify witnesses.

NOTE: If emergency medical services are present on scene and treating the
victim(s), immediately photograph the location and position of the injured.
Take immediate steps to document and collect perishable items of evidence
that may be disturbed through their lifesaving efforts.

Establish a Perimeter

- If the first responders have established a perimeter, quickly assess it
  to determine if it needs to be expanded.
- The perimeter should include all areas associated with the primary
  scene in which evidence is expected to be found.

Immediate On-Scene Coordination

Receive a brief from whoever controls the scene. Coordinate with the following agencies if represented:

- Law enforcement agencies
- Emergency medical services
- Fire department
- Security agencies

Identify everyone who has entered the scene. Determine if they have
changed the conditions within the scene (lights, doors, etc.), if they have safed

or unloaded any weapons, what they have touched, and where they have walked. Photograph footwear patterns if appropriate.

Initial Scene Evaluation: Walk-Through (with Preservation of Perishable Evidence)

After establishing death scene perimeters and ensuring death scene security, the DSI should take the opportunity to walk through the scene and examine the body to become familiar with the evidence present and its interrelationship to the scene.

- The walk-through should be conducted with personal protective equipment (PPE) appropriate to the scene—at a minimum, gloves and shoe covers.
- Paths of travel should be those least likely to have been traversed by the perpetrator or victim.
- It is appropriate to videotape, digitally record, or take general photographs during the initial walk-through. The recording may be accomplished by the death scene photographer or videographer accompanying the lead DSI on the walk-through.
- It is also appropriate to note observations of scene conditions that may have been, or could be, changed inadvertently, for example, doors that were opened or closed, locked or not locked, lights on or off, and other general conditions.
- If during the walk-through an item of perishable evidence is discovered (a hair on a broken window, a footwear impression outside when inclement weather is likely, etc.), the item should be immediately safeguarded or expeditiously documented and processed.

Initial Approach to the Body

- Within the scene, determine a path of approach that is least likely to disturb evidence associated with the body.
  - Avoid, if possible, entering or exiting through the doors a perpetrator may have used.
  - Avoid, if possible, any path of travel that may have been used by a perpetrator.
- Rapidly conduct a point-to-point search along the determined path while marking and safeguarding physical evidence. Conduct of a point-to-point search is detailed in Chapter 10.

Preliminary Determination of Death

If not already established, determine that the decedent is in fact dead and does not require emergency medical care. Some physical signs indicating that death is presumed (until legal determination) are:

- Absence of pulse and respiration
- Fixed and dilated pupils that are unresponsive to light
- No signs that indicate cardiopulmonary resuscitation is required
- Obvious injury inconsistent with life such as decapitation, traumatic head injury with evacuation of brain content, massive blood loss, body cut in two or more pieces, and obvious decomposition

Documentation, Preservation, and/or Collection of Perishable Evidence

- Photograph discrete bloodstain patterns on the victim's body, clothing, or adjacent to the body before they are obscured by further blood flow.
- Collect hairs and fibers on the victim's clothing or body that may be lost through air movement or exposure to the elements.
- Collect foreign fluids or stains (such as semen) on the body may be obscured by blood flow.

Document Postmortem Indicators

Examine the body and document the stage of development of livor, rigor, and algor mortis as soon as practical. The status of these indicators should be noted every hour while the body remains at the scene. Chapter 14 provides guidance. A Postmortem Indicator (PMI) worksheet is provided as Supplemental Worksheet 1.

Livor Mortis—Purplish Discoloration in Dependent Areas

- Is livor mortis present?
- Is its location consistent with the body position?
- Is the livor mortis fixed or fluid?
  - Can it be blanched with the pressure of a gloved finger?

Rigor Mortis—Stiffening of Muscles and Joints

- Is rigor mortis present?
- Is it consistent with the body position?

- Is it partially or fully developed in all muscles and joints of the body?
  - Check fingers and jaw for partial development.
  - Check leg at hip and knee for full development.

Algor Mortis—Reduction in Body Temperature

- Is the body warm or cool to the touch?
- Record body temperature via method authorized by medical examiner.
  - Digital thermal scan of forehead.
  - Digital thermal scan of tympanic membrane (eardrum).
  - Digital or mercury thermometer temperature of armpit.
  - Temperature of liver (invasive procedure to be used only by properly trained practitioners and authorized by medical examiner).
- Record ambient temperature at elevation of the body.
- Record temperature of surface on which the body rests.
- Repeat all recordings hourly until the body is removed from the scene.

NOTE: Further processing of the body should be held in abeyance until all physical evidence surrounding the body and in a clear path leading to the body has been documented, preserved, and collected.

Assessing and Establishing the Perimeter

Primary Scene: Inner Perimeter

- The inner perimeter should be extended to include all areas associated with the primary scene in which evidence is expected to be found. Determine if the scene has been adequately identified and its perimeter secured. If not, enlarge perimeter as necessary (Figure 1.1).
- Determine the likely areas through which a perpetrator would have entered or exited the scene and any subsequent paths of travel. If noted, ensure they are within the inner perimeter.

Primary Scene: Outer Perimeter

- This is a clearly marked border around the inner perimeter that allows access to locations within the inner perimeter without having to constantly traverse the scene.
- This includes a DSI staging area for donning Tyvek suits and gathering equipment if needed (Figure 1.2).

Figure 1.1 Establishing death scene inner perimeter.

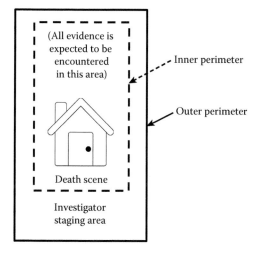

Figure 1.2 Establish death scene outer perimeter.

Identifying Ancillary Scenes

- Determine if the initial information would indicate the possibility of ancillary, or secondary, death scenes.
- See specific guidance under chapters 2. natural death, 3. accidental death, 4. suicide, and 5. homicide.
- Properly secure these areas until they can be processed.

Establishing Scene Controls

- Identify a point of entry and exit for those working the scene and establish an entry control point and a controller (preferably someone from law enforcement) using a Death Scene Entry Log, provided as Supplemental Worksheet 2.
- Determine the level of security required and task appropriate personnel.
- Determine what level of PPE is required for the scene and establish PPE guidelines for entry (Appendix A).
- Once a scene's perimeter is established, designate an area outside the perimeter for DSIs to work in (e.g., sketching, processing scene evidence, changing PPE, trash collection, or for breaks) (Figure 1.2).
- DSIs or other law enforcement personnel should never take food, drinks, or tobacco products into a death scene area!

Legal Concerns

The initial response to the call and determination that there is no one that requires aid and that there is no threat present are typically covered under a search exception called *exigent circumstances*. Once the threat is removed and aid has been rendered, the presence of law enforcement moves from the public safety realm (exigent circumstances) to the investigative realm. Under the investigative realm, it is important to ensure you have the authority to search for and seize evidence. Chapter 32 provides a detailed explanation of search and processing legal concerns.

Scene Assessment, Planning, and Investigative Strategy

At the conclusion of the walk-through, the evidence and body are assessed within the context of the scene. The videotape from the walk-through (or pictures) may be helpful during this process. The Death Scene Investigation Decision Tree (inside of back cover) will aid the investigator in making an evidence-based decision on initially handling the scene as a homicide, suicide, accident, or natural death. This method defaults in ambiguous situations to the more conservative investigative approach.

Scene processing steps are continued in the following chapters:

- For investigations of suspected *natural death*, refer to Chapter 2 for detailed processing guidance.
- For investigations of suspected *accidental death*, refer to Chapter 3 for detailed processing guidance.

- For investigations of suspected *suicidal death*, refer to Chapter 4 for detailed processing guidance.
- For investigations of suspected *homicidal death*, refer to Chapter 5 for detailed processing guidance.

This is an opportunity to *slow down* and determine investigative priorities, tasking, and assignments. Once an investigative direction is developed, it should remain sufficiently flexible to allow for unforeseen developments.

Natural Deaths

2

Natural deaths are often indicated through scene findings but not confirmed until the autopsy is complete. This poses a special challenge to the DSI to thoroughly document the scene and carefully look for red flags that might move the death toward a homicide, suicide, or accident.

The following considerations and activities are listed in an order conducive to efficiently processing a death scene. Individual circumstances may dictate a different order. This procedure should be used when the Death Scene Investigation Decision Tree (inside of back cover) indicates a preliminary investigative direction for natural death.

NOTE: The procedures and steps that allowed the DSI to identify, secure, and perform the initial walk-through of the scene were covered in Chapter 1, "Death Scene Response." The analysis from the evidence within the context of the scene allowed for the investigative direction to be established. If this initial assessment has not been completed, return to the procedures detailed in Chapter 1, "Death Scene Response," and the Death Scene Investigation Decision Tree (inside of back cover).

Definition of *Natural Death*

A natural death results from a medically observable disease or medical condition for which the expected outcome is death.

Worksheets and Documentation

The following documentation guides, forms, logs, and worksheets are provided in Section VIII, "Death Scene Investigation Checklist and Worksheets," and may be used in documenting this scene. Additional forms, other than those noted, may also be used as dictated by your scene. These forms may be preprinted from the publisher's website (www.crcpress.com/cw/maloney) or photocopied from this procedural guide.

- *Death Investigation Checklist*
  - Section 1: Death Scene Information

- Section 2: Civilians Who Entered the Death Scene
- Section 3: Death Scene
- Section 4: Coroner/Medical Examiner Notification
- Sections 5–8: Appropriate Body Location When Discovered
- Section 10: Identification/Notification
- Section 11: Scene Processing
- Section 12: Death Scene Release Information
- Section 13: Narrative Report
- Section 14: (appropriate forms and logs)
- *Worksheets*
  - Worksheet 1: Postmortem Indicators
  - Worksheet 2: Death Scene Entry Log
  - Worksheet 3: Photography Head Slate
  - Worksheet 4: Photography Log

Initial Scene Response

The following tasks should have already been completed; if not, please see Chapter 1, "Death Scene Response."

- Initial notification
- Initial scene coordination
- Arrival at the scene
- Establishing a perimeter
- Initial scene evaluation—walk-through
- Initial examination of the deceased
- Scene assessment, planning, and investigative strategy

Legal Concerns

The initial response to the call and determination that there is no one that requires aid and that there is no threat present are typically covered under a search exception called "exigent circumstances." Once the threat is removed and aid has been rendered, the presence of law enforcement moves from the public safety realm (exigent circumstances) to the investigative realm. Under the investigative realm, it is important to ensure you have the authority to search for and seize evidence. Chapter 1, "Death Scene Response," provides a detailed explanation of search and processing concerns.

Scene Considerations

Although a death may initially appear natural, the circumstances as ascertained through a thorough and complete investigation may indicate that the cause was an accident, suicide, or homicide. Examples include suicide by overmedication, accidental death due to unintentional overmedication, and physician- or medical professional–assisted suicide.

- The medical examiner or coroner who has jurisdiction for the body should be notified as soon as possible. The intent is to inform authorities of the investigation and coordinate any on-scene responses, not request removal of the body.
- Except to protect fragile evidence from potential destruction, there is no need to rush the processing of a death scene without first establishing a plan.
- If the body has already been removed to a medical facility or funeral home, an investigator should respond to the receiving facility to gather physical evidence and process the body.

Death Scene Processing

Death scenes are often highly complex and require skilled care and methodical processing. There is no requirement to have a body removed immediately from a scene, and removal may be detrimental if it occurs before a scene is thoroughly examined for evidence. The steps are detailed below.

Identifying Primary and Secondary Death Scenes

Reassess the original scene perimeter to determine if it is adequate. This inner perimeter should contain all items of evidence or expected items of evidence or evidentiary areas within the scene. The outer perimeter is established to allow access to all areas within the inner perimeter without having to excessively traverse the inner perimeter. It also includes staging areas for DSIs working the scene. These are established as applicable to all primary and secondary scenes.

Primary Scene
- The body of the deceased generally constitutes the primary death scene.
- The area directly around the body or room in which it is discovered also becomes part of the primary death scene.

- Any medicines or medical paraphernalia/equipment attached to, adjacent to, or near the body should also be considered part of the primary scene.

NOTE: Any indication of forced entry or a violent struggle should move this investigation to Chapter 5, "Homicidal Deaths."

Secondary Scenes
- All areas where medicine and medical supplies are kept
- Victim's in-home medical records, medical appointment records, and treatment notes
- Smartphone, tablet, computer containing Internet searches on medical equipment, maintenance issues, etc.
- Social media accounts containing images or entries involving medical treatment or end-of-life considerations
- Social media accounts containing images or entries involving termination of life, suicide, and/or assisted suicide
- Social media accounts containing indications of depression or suicidal ideation

NOTE: Any indication of suicide, suicidal ideation, or suicide attempt should move this investigation to Chapter 4, "Suicidal Deaths."

NOTE: Any indication of assisted suicide or medically assisted suicide should move this investigation to Chapter 5, "Homicidal Deaths."

Take Control of Scene

- Start documentation of the scene via notes, sketching, and photography. Documentation is an ongoing process.
- Establish an investigators/DSI staging area.
- Extend death scene perimeter if necessary. Consider media presence and ranges of lenses (see Figure 2.1).
- Establish log of all persons entering or exiting death scene (Supplemental Worksheet 2, "Death Scene Entry Log").

Scene Organization

- Use protective booties, gloves, and mask at a minimum. Full PPE may be appropriate (Appendix A).

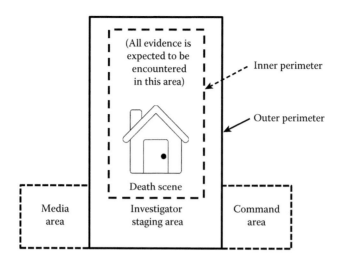

Figure 2.1 Establish locations for death scene command and control functions.

- Establish investigator paths of entry and exit separate from those used by the victim.
- Establish investigator path of travel to and from the body. Use the point-to-point search method to clear the path of evidence and avoid both the victim and perpetrators route of ingress or egress.
- Document and safeguard perishable evidence.

Legal Determination of Death

If not already accomplished, have the body pronounced dead by the proper legal authority.

Plan Development

- Evaluate results of walk-through.
- Evaluate available assets.
- Determine whether additional or specialized personnel are required, for example, a medical examiner, sexual assault response team, explosive ordnance disposal (EOD), forensic anthropologist, or scuba divers.
- Determine whether additional or specialized equipment is required, for example, lighting, ladders, evidence collection supplies, and metal detectors
- Formulate a processing plan.

Conduct Team Briefing

A team briefing is only one aspect of death scene management. See Chapter 32 for a detailed discussion of death scene management.

- Assign duties to team members.
- Ensure team members understand their roles.
- Explain the level of biological hazard and PPE required for personnel entering a scene or specific parts of a scene (see Appendix A).
- Provide a thorough briefing of death scene details to all team members. Discuss the evidence expected to be encountered.

Scene Processing

- Preserve as best as practical the paths of entry, exit, and the area of the incident for two- and three-dimensional footwear and/or tire impressions (Chapter 44).
- Document all lighting, heating, and security conditions at the scene and note other scene markers that may indicate times of activities.
- Photograph the scene (see Chapter 34).
- Sketch the scene (see Chapter 33).

NOTE
1. Any indication of forced entry (beyond that caused by first responders) or criminal activity within the scene should move this investigation to Chapter 5, "Homicidal Deaths."
2. If bloodstain patterns at the scene are not directly attributed to purge from the body or as a result of decomposition, move this investigation to Chapter 5, "Homicidal Deaths."

- Locations of all medical debris should be documented.

NOTE
1. If there are indications of despondency, anger, or rage at the scene, this investigation should be moved to Chapter 4, "Suicidal Deaths," or Chapter 5, "Homicidal Deaths," as indicated.
2. If a weapon (gun, knife, etc.) is associated with the body, reassess the scene indicators and move the investigation to Chapter 4, "Suicidal Deaths," or Chapter 5, "Homicidal Deaths."

Processing the Body

The medical examiner, coroner, or their representatives may wish to be present at the scene during the processing of the body or to conduct examinations. Gloves and appropriate PPE should be worn during processing.

- External injury (with the exception of artifacts associated with medical treatment, or wounds associated with the disease) should not be present.
- Some diseases may make bruising or fragile bones far more likely; their presence needs to be thoroughly documented and investigated.
- Contact and coordination with the medical examiner, or the medical examiner's response to the scene, may be called for.
- Remember, natural death will only be determined after autopsy or medical records review by treating physician.

Photographing the Body

See Chapter 34, "Death Scene Photography," for specific guidance. The body should be photographed as it was found (prior to moving it). Detailed note-taking and photography should continue during processing of the body. Specific areas to be photographed include the following:

- Face
- Head and upper torso
- Hands (detailed, all surfaces)
- Lower torso and legs
- Feet (detailed, including soles)
- Entire body
- Right and left profiles

Sketching the Body

See Chapter 33, "Death Scene Sketching," for specific guidance. Draw the body and clearly show its position. Fix the position by triangulating (or another method of measurement if indicated) the positions of the following:

- Head (nose)
- Torso (umbilicus)
- Arms (shoulder, elbow, and wrist joint)
- Legs (hip, knee, and ankle joint)

Examination of the Body

- Fully document the appearance of the body (sex, skin color, clothing, disarray of clothing, jewelry, etc.).
- Fully document obvious injuries, decomposition changes (Chapter 14), insect activity (Chapter 40), presence of blood and state of coagulation (Chapter 37), open or closed eyes, etc.

NOTE: Injury inconsistent with the illness or bloodstain patterns on the body that are not directly attributed to purge from the body, or as a result of decomposition move this investigation to Chapter 5, "Homicidal Deaths."

- Continue hourly postmortem indicator data collection using Worksheet 1, "Postmortem Indicator (PMI)."
- Note apparent activity at time of death, such as sleeping, eating, and bathing
- Examine and empty pockets that are accessible without moving the body. The contents of pockets should be documented and placed in separate containers and labeled as to pocket location.
- Roll the body onto a clean sheet and examine the clothing and pockets on the underside.
- The body, wrapped in the sheet, should be placed in a body bag in the original position in which it was found, if practical.
- The body bag should be sealed with a tamperproof device. If the security of the body in transit is questionable, it should be escorted to the place where the autopsy will take place.
- After removal of the body, the area from which the body was removed should be thoroughly examined for additional evidence and trace evidence.

Outdoor Death Scenes

- Consider using clean tarps or similar devices to shield bodies from onlookers while the scene is processed.
- If needed for expediency in adverse weather conditions, a body may be covered by a clean tarp or sheet, which should be collected later because it may contain trace evidence.
- Take soil samples beneath and around the body (Chapter 42).
- Sift the soil beneath the body for evidence.
- Collect appropriate entomological evidence (Chapter 40).

Common Indicators of Natural Death

- Prescription and other medicines
- Medical alert bracelet or pendant
- Indications of medical care or treatment
- Names of treating physicians and contact information

Related Searches

- Medicine cabinets
- Kitchen cabinets (for medicines)
- Nightstand (for medicines)
- Refrigerator (for medicines)
- Medical records
- Medical insurance documentation
- Disease-related literature

Death Scene Interviews

First Responders

- Who reported the death? How and to whom was it reported? Review and, if appropriate, obtain copies or transcripts of notification calls to public safety agencies (i.e., 911 calls in the United States).
- Who discovered the body and under what circumstances? What triggered the discovery?
- Where and when was the body found?
- How was the body positioned? Was it moved or altered in any way?
- When was the last time the person was seen alive? What was he or she doing?
- Was the victim infected with a contagious disease such as hepatitis and HIV?
- How did the responders (police, EMS, etc.) gain access to the scene?
- What were the circumstances surrounding the death?

Family Members

- Was the decedent being treated for any known medical conditions or diseases?
- Was the decedent diagnosed with an illness or disease that was expected to be fatal?

- Was the death unexpected?
- Who is the decedent's physician and how can he or she be contacted?
- Was the decedent taking prescribed medications? Obtain a list.

Decedent's Physician

- Was the decedent being treated for a disease or illness expected to lead to death?
- Is there any reason we should believe his or her death was not natural?
- Will you sign a death certificate or coordinate with the local medical examiner to issue a death certificate citing a natural death?
- Are all of the medications found consistent with the decedent's treatment plan?

Death Notification[1]

One of the least enviable tasks of the death investigator is the necessity to make death notification to the deceased's next of kin. Though unenviable, if accomplished with professional, calm, quiet dignity, it can make all of the difference to the deceased's survivors.

In the case of homicide, the police investigator or detective should make the notification if there is an expectation of a spontaneous exclamation. Exclamations, such as "I knew she would kill him one day" or "We told him to stay off of those drugs," may be crucial for identifying a perpetrator or motive.

General Guidelines

- Death notifications may be a physically and emotionally draining task.
- Notification should be done in as timely a manner as possible; get there before the press or the neighbors!
- Notification should be done in person.
- Notification should be done with a partner.

---

[1] Information for this section was derived in part from Douglas Page's *Death Notification: Breaking the Bad News*, written in 1981 and published on the Officer.com website, and informal conversations with Chris Stewart, a senior instructor with the FLETC as well as serving as a deputy coroner for Glynn County, Georgia.

Notification Procedure

- In a calm, businesslike manner, show credentials, identify yourself, and request to come inside to speak privately. Ask to sit with them. *Move steadfastly toward the notification: the family is as alarmed as possible at this point—do not prevaricate!*
- Determine if they have a support team (spouse, partner, clergy, close friend) who could join them. This allows for emotional support and physical reassurance. If not readily available, move forward and be prepared for an emotional hurricane.
- Be empathetic but direct; do not use euphemisms such as *passed on* or *expired*. Instead, use *died, dead,* and *death*.
  - "I am sorry, but your mother died in her sleep last night."
  - "I am sorry, but your husband died this morning."
- Pause now and allow for them to process the information.
  - Do not flood them with details or questions.
  - Do not be surprised if there is an emotional outburst.
- Be prepared for follow-on questions. Remember the information is often sketchy and details are either insufficient, unknown, or wrong at this point. Do not provide information that you will have to walk back later! Assure them that more information will be forthcoming.
- Let them know what will happen next.
  - "You can get in touch with me later today." (Provide contact number.) "I know this will take some time to process; we can further discuss arrangements then."
  - "You may contact the coroner." (Provide contact number.) "I know this will take some time to process; we can further discuss arrangements then."
- If they are alone, ask if there is anyone you could call to come over and be with them.
- Leave as soon as practical.

Accidental Deaths

3

Accidental deaths pose unique challenges to the DSI. The subtleties between an accidental death and an accident orchestrated for the purpose of murder or an accident that is the result of negligence may be easy to miss.

The following considerations and activities are listed in an order conducive to efficiently processing a death scene. Individual circumstances may dictate a different order. This procedure should be used when the Death Scene Investigation Decision Tree (inside back cover) indicates a preliminary investigative direction for accidental death.

NOTE: The procedures and steps that allowed the DSI to identify, secure, and perform the initial walk-through of the scene were covered in Chapter 1, "Death Scene Response." The analysis from the evidence within the context of the scene allowed for the investigative direction to be established. If this initial assessment has not been completed, return to the procedures detailed in Chapter 1, "Death Scene Response," and the Death Scene Investigation Decision Tree (inside back cover)

Definition of *Accidental Death*

An accidental death results from an act or activity whose outcome is *not* expected to cause death.

Worksheets and Documentation

The following documentation guides, forms, logs, and worksheets are provided in Section VIII, "Death Investigation Checklist and Worksheets," and may be used in documenting this scene. Additional forms, other than those noted, may also be used as dictated by your scene. These forms may be preprinted from the publisher's website (www.crcpress.com/cw/maloney) or photocopied from this procedural guide.

- *Death Investigation Checklist*
  - Section 1: Death Scene Information
  - Section 2: Civilians Who Entered the Death Scene

- Section 3: Death Scene
- Section 4: Coroner/Medical Examiner Notification
- Sections 5–8: Appropriate Body Location When Discovered
- Section 9: Wounds/Weapons/Drugs/Medications
- Section 10: Identification/Notification
- Section 11: Scene Processing
- Section 12: Death Scene Release Information
- Section 13: Narrative Report
- Section 14: (appropriate forms and logs)
- *Worksheets*
  - Worksheet 1: Postmortem Indicator (PMI)
  - Worksheet 2: Death Scene Entry Log
  - Worksheet 3: Photography Head Slate
  - Worksheet 4: Photography Log
  - Worksheet 5: Post-Blast Scene Management
  - Worksheet 6: Firearms Recovery
  - Worksheet 7: Entomology Recovery
  - Worksheet 8: Biological Evidence Worksheet
  - Worksheet 9: Trace Evidence
  - Worksheet 10: Friction Ridge Evidence
  - Worksheet 11: Impression Evidence
  - Worksheet 12: Immersion Burn
  - Worksheet 13: SIDS/SUIDS (Sudden Infant Death)
  - Worksheet 14: Bullet Defects
  - Worksheet 15: Bloodstain Patterns

Initial Scene Response

The following tasks should have already been completed; if not, please see Chapter 1, "Death Scene Response."

- Initial notification
- Initial scene coordination
- Arrival at the scene
- Establishing a perimeter
- Initial scene evaluation—walk-through
- Initial examination of the deceased
- Scene assessment, planning, and investigative strategy

Legal Concerns

The initial response to the call and determination that there is no one that requires aid and that there is no threat present are typically covered under a search exception called "exigent circumstances." Once the threat is removed and aid has been rendered, the presence of law enforcement moves from the public safety realm (exigent circumstances) to the investigative realm. Under the investigative realm, it is important to ensure you have the authority to search for and seize evidence. Chapter 1, "Death Scene Response," provides a detailed explanation of search and processing concerns.

Scene Considerations

Although a death may initially appear accidental, the circumstances as ascertained through a thorough and complete investigation may indicate that the cause was natural or that it was a suicide or homicide. Examples include a suicide staged to look like an accident, a homicide staged to look like an accident, or an accident secondary to natural death (victim had a heart attack, collapsed, car veered off the road and into an embankment).

- Caution must be exercised when responding to all accidental deaths, because the conditions that precipitated the accident may still exist.
- The medical examiner or coroner who has jurisdiction for the body should be notified as soon as possible. The intent is to inform authorities of the investigation and coordinate any on-scene responses, not request removal of the body.
- Except to protect fragile evidence from potential destruction, there is no need to rush the processing of a death scene without first establishing a plan.
- If the body has already been removed to a medical facility or funeral home, an investigator must respond to the receiving facility to gather physical evidence and process the body.
- If the exact location of the body is unknown, Section II provides specific guidance on search techniques.
  - Surface recovery of remains is covered in Chapter 11.
  - Recovery of buried remains is discussed in Chapter 12.
  - Recovery of remains from water is covered in Chapter 13.

Death Scene Processing

Death scenes are often highly complex and require skilled care and methodical processing. There is no requirement to have a body removed immediately from a scene, and removal may be detrimental if it occurs before a scene is thoroughly examined for evidence. The steps are detailed below.

Identifying Primary and Secondary Death Scenes

Reassess the original scene perimeter to determine if it is adequate. This inner perimeter should contain all items of evidence or expected items of evidence or evidentiary areas within the scene. The outer perimeter is established to allow access to all areas within the inner perimeter without having to excessively traverse the inner perimeter. It also includes staging areas for DSIs working the scene. These are established as applicable to all primary and secondary scenes.

Primary Scene
- The body of the deceased generally constitutes the primary death scene.
- The area directly around the body or room in which it is discovered also becomes part of the primary death scene.
- Any machinery or equipment believed to be causal in the accident is a part of the primary scene.
- Any adjacent areas with evidence, bloodstains, bullet defects, indications of violent altercation, or with signs of forced entry are also a part of the primary scene.

NOTE: Any indication of forced entry or a violent struggle should move this investigation to Chapter 5, "Homicidal Deaths."

Secondary Scenes
- Equipment maintenance records
- Victim training records with equipment
- Smartphone, tablet, computer for Internet searches on equipment, maintenance issues, etc.
- Social media accounts for images or entries involving accident activity
- Social media accounts for indications of depression or suicidal ideation
- Other logical areas suggested by the instrumentality of death

Take Control of Scene
- Start documentation of the scene via notes, sketching, and photography. Documentation is an ongoing process.
- Extend the death scene perimeter if necessary. Consider media presence and ranges of lenses.
- Establish a log of all persons entering or exiting the death scene.
- Establish an investigator/DSI staging area.

Scene Organization

- Use protective booties, gloves, and mask at a minimum. Full PPE may be appropriate (Appendix A).
- Establish investigator paths of entry and exit separate from those used by the victim.
- Establish investigator path of travel to and from the body. Use the point-to-point search method to clear the path of evidence and avoid the victim and perpetrators path of ingress or egress.
- Document and safeguard perishable evidence.

Legal Determination of Death

If not already accomplished, have the body pronounced dead by the proper legal authority.

Plan Development

- Evaluate results of walk-through.
- Evaluate available assets.
- Determine whether additional or specialized personnel are required, for example, a medical examiner, sexual assault response team, EOD, forensic anthropologist, or scuba divers.
- Determine whether additional or specialized equipment is required, for example, lighting, ladders, evidence collection supplies, metal detectors, etc.
- Formulate a processing plan.

Conduct Team Briefing

A team briefing is only one aspect of death scene management. See Chapter 32 for a detailed discussion.

- Assign duties to team members.
- Ensure team members understand their roles.
- Explain the level of biological hazard and PPE required for personnel entering a scene or specific parts of a scene (see Appendix A).
- Provide a thorough briefing of death scene details to all team members. Discuss the evidence expected to be encountered.
- For specific evidence and indicators associated with various types of death (gunshot wounds, hangings, stabbings, etc.), see the appropriate chapter in Section IV, "Wound Dynamics and Mechanism of Injury."

Scene Processing

- Examine and process the paths of entry, exit, and the area of the incident for two- and three-dimensional footwear and/or tire impressions (Chapter 44, "Impression Evidence"). Avoid areas containing biological evidence.
- Document all lighting, heating, and security conditions at the scene and note other scene markers that may indicate times of activities.
- If forced entry is evident, the case may not be accidental.

NOTE: Any indication of forced entry (beyond that caused by first responders) should move this investigation to Chapter 5, "Homicidal Deaths."

- Process for biological and trace evidence (Chapter 41, "Biological Evidence," and Chapter 42, "Trace Evidence").
- Locations of all medical debris should be documented.
- Document bloodstain patterns (Chapter 37, "Documenting and Processing Bloodstain Patterns at the Scene")
- Note any items that may relate to motive or intent.
- Seize and protect all writing paper and tablets. They may be examined later for latent prints and indented writing and subjected to handwriting analysis.
- Note and seize any indicators of despondency or anger (torn photos, letters, items of symbolic or sentimental value, etc.). If such items are present, the case may not be accidental.

NOTE: If there are indications of despondency, anger, or rage at the scene, this investigation should be moved to Chapter 5, "Homicidal Deaths."

- Secure all video, audio, digital, computer, and other media for determination of possible motive for the death.
- Consider which items of evidence may require special handling, processing, or preservation to safeguard any friction ridge on fingerprints, latent prints, or other evidence (Chapter 43, "Friction Ridge Evidence").
- If a gunshot was fired as the result of an "accidental" discharge, the gun should be in a logical position/location for the circumstances reported in the accident.

NOTE: If the gun is not in a logical position/location for the reported accident, or if an individual other than the victim wielded the weapon, this investigation should move to Chapter 5, "Homicidal Deaths."

- Search for, examine, and recover items associated with the weapon such as cases and bullets.
- Search for, examine, and recover any other items that may link a suspect to a crime and/or death scene.

Processing: Examining the Mechanism of Death

The machinery, equipment, or device that failed to operate, operated incorrectly, or was incorrectly operated and led to the death must be fully processed prior to examination for functionality. The functionality checks, when conducted, must be accomplished by an industry expert on the operation and mechanical function of that equipment/device.

Processing

- The hand control surfaces of the device should be processed for the presence of friction ridge evidence (prints) and touch DNA (Chapter 41, "Biological Evidence").
- The foot control surfaces should be processed for two-dimensional footwear impressions and then compared to the footwear of the victim (Chapter 44, "Impression Evidence").
- A foot on the accelerator rather than the brake may indicate this is not a motor vehicle accident but a suicide.
- Control injuries in deceleration deaths should match the logical controls for avoiding a collision (Chapter 17, "Blunt Force Injuries").

NOTE: Control injuries or other indicators that demonstrate the victim was not trying to avoid collision/impact may indicate suicide rather than an accidental death.

Examination

An expert in the use and function of the device must conduct the examination.

- Is the device functioning within its described parameters?
- Are any and all safety devices on the device functioning?
- Did the device fail?
- Are there circumstances in which the device can be forced to failure?
- Can the failure that resulted in death be replicated?
- Does this forced failure indicate operator error?

Documenting Scene Indicators

- Note any indicators of activity of the decedent at the time of the accident. Specifically, could the decedent have been distracted while operating the equipment?
  - Texting
  - Phone conversation
  - Posting/reading social media
  - Viewing video feed, movies, etc.
  - Eating
  - Distracted by activities of a passenger
  - Distracted by passenger interaction
- Note any indicators of activity of the decedent prior to death, for example, meal preparation, telephone calls (note time made and to whom), computer and Internet activities, postings to social media accounts, etc.
- Note any indicators of industrial activity that could have led to an accidental death.
  - Ladders
  - Step stools
  - Expedient step stools (standing on rolling chair)
  - Power tools
  - Tools
  - Cleaning chemicals
- Note any indications of sporting activities that may have led to an accidental death.
  - Climbing gear
  - SCUBA gear
  - Padding, boxing gloves, contact gear
  - Other

Processing the Body

The medical examiner, coroner, or their representative may wish to be present at the scene during the processing of the body or to conduct examinations. For specific signs of physical trauma and evidence associated with various types of death (gunshot wounds, hangings, stabbings, etc.), see the applicable chapter in Section IV, "Wound Dynamics and Mechanism of Injury." Gloves and appropriate PPE gear should be worn during processing.

Photographing the Body

See Chapter 34, "Death Scene Photography," and Chapter 35, "Death Scene Videography," for specific guidance. The body should be photographed as it was found (prior to moving it). Detailed note-taking and photography should continue during body processing. Specific areas to be photographed include the following:

- Orientation and spatial relationship between the body and the equipment whose use or failure may have had a role in the accident, for example, a vehicle.
- Face
- Head and upper torso
- Hands (detailed, all surfaces)
- Lower torso and legs
- Feet (detailed, including soles)
- Entire body
- Right and left profiles

Sketching Body

See Chapter 33, "Death Scene Sketching," for specific guidance. Draw the body and clearly show its position. Fix the position by triangulating (or another method of measurement if indicated) the positions of the following:

- Head (nose)
- Torso (umbilicus)
- Arms (shoulder, elbow, and wrist joint)
- Legs (hip, knee, and ankle joint)
- Distances and relationship of body to equipment in the immediate vicinity of the body that may have played a role in the death

Documenting with Notes

- Fully describe the appearance of the body (sex, skin color, and clothing, disarray of clothing, jewelry, etc.).
- Fully document obvious injuries, decomposition changes (Chapter 14), insect activity (Chapter 40), presence of blood and state of coagulation, open or closed eyes, etc.
- Continue hourly postmortem indicator data collection using Worksheet 1, "Postmortem Indicator (PMI)."
- Note the apparent activity at time of death, such as sleeping, eating, and bathing.
- If blood is present at the scene, note the presence or absence of blood on the hands, feet, and soles of the shoes. Fully document all bloodstain patterns on and near the victim (Chapter 37, "Documenting and Processing Bloodstain Patterns at the Scene").

Examination of Body

- Examine the clothing for evidence of struggle or damage caused by weapons.

NOTE: If there is evidence of a struggle, this investigation should be moved to Chapter 5, "Homicidal Deaths."

- If restraints are present (ropes, belts, tape, clothing, etc.) to bind the victim, do not remove them. Knots and overlapped areas of tape should not be cut through or untied.

NOTE: If restraints are present and could not have been self-tied, this investigation should be moved to Chapter 5, "Homicidal Deaths." (The application of self-tied restraints may be present in suicides and autoerotic asphyxia, an accidental death.)

- Place the hands in small paper (not plastic) bags and seal them with tape at the wrists. This is not just for gunshot residue (GSR) but will protect other trace evidence that may be on the hands or beneath the fingernails.
- Consider the possibility of developing latent fingerprints on the skin or sampling for touch DNA if it is believed the body was handled (Chapter 43, "Friction Ridge Evidence").
- Examine the clothing, body, and immediate surrounding area for trace evidence. Consider the use of ultraviolet light or an alternate light source; see Chapter 42, "Trace Evidence."
- Examine and empty the pockets that are accessible without moving the body. The contents of pockets should be placed in separate containers and labeled as to pocket location.
- Roll the body onto a clean sheet and examine the clothing and pockets on the underside.
- The body, wrapped in the sheet, should be placed in a body bag in the original position in which it was found, if practical.
- The body bag should be sealed with a tamperproof device. If the security of the body in transit is questionable, it should be escorted to the place where the autopsy will take place.
- After removal of the body, the areas from which the body was removed should be thoroughly examined for additional evidence and trace evidence.

Outdoor Death Scenes

- Consider using clean tarps or similar devices to shield bodies from onlookers while the scene is processed.

- If needed for expediency in adverse weather conditions, the body may be covered by a clean tarp or sheet that should be collected later because it may contain trace evidence.
- Take soil samples beneath and around body (Chapter 42, "Trace Evidence").
- Sift the soil beneath the body for evidence.
- Collect appropriate entomological evidence (Chapter 40, "Entomological Evidence").

Evidence Commonly Associated with Accidental Deaths

- Tools and machinery
- Ladders
- Scaffolding
- Industrial equipment
- Sporting and recreational equipment
- Automobiles

Related Searches

- Equipment maintenance and repair records
- Equipment storage area
- Operator manuals for associated equipment
- Operator training records

Review of Operator (Victim) Training and Certification

A thorough examination of the training records, certifications, and history of the victim with the device must be completed.

- Was the victim authorized to operate the device?
- Was the victim trained to operate the device?
- Was the victim's training current?
- Did the victim hold a certification to operate this device (if required)?
- Was the victim licensed to operate this device? (if required)?
- Did the victim's training include any modifications to this specific device?
- Was the victim operating the device for its intended purpose?
- Did the victim exceed the device's operation parameters?

Death Scene Interviews

First Responders

- Who reported the death? How and to whom was it reported? Review and, if appropriate, obtain copies or transcripts of notification calls to public safety agencies (i.e., 911 calls in the United States).
- Who discovered the body and under what circumstances was it discovered? What triggered the discovery?
- Where and when was the body found?
- How was the body positioned? Was it moved or altered in any way?
- When was the last time the person was seen alive? What was he or she doing?
- Was the victim infected with a contagious disease such as hepatitis and HIV?
- How did the responders (police, EMS, etc.) gain access to the scene?
- What were the circumstances surrounding the death?

Witnesses

- What did you observe happen?
- What was the deceased doing just prior to the accident?
- Did you observe anything unusual in the activities of the deceased right before or at the time of the accident?
- Did you observe anything unusual in the activities of those around the deceased right before or at the time of the accident?
- Did the equipment or gear used by the deceased at the time of the accident appear to be working properly?
- Do you have any reason to believe the death was not an accident? What is that reason?

GSR Examination and Collection

- When was the last time you handled a firearm?
- When was the last time you fired a weapon?
- When was the last time you were present when a weapon was fired? What was your proximity to the weapon?
- When was the last time you washed your hands?
- Are you right- or left-handed?

Death Notification[1]

One of the least enviable tasks of the death investigator is the necessity to make death notification to the deceased's next of kin. Though unenviable, if accomplished with professional, calm, quiet dignity, it can make all of the difference to the deceased survivors.

In the case of homicide, the police investigator or detective should make the notification if there is an expectation of a spontaneous exclamation. Exclamations, such as "I knew she would kill him one day" or "We told him to stay off of those drugs," may be crucial for identifying a perpetrator or motive.

General Guidelines

- Death notification may be a physically and emotionally draining task.
- Notification should be done in as timely a manner as possible; get there before the press or the neighbors!
- Notification should be done in person.
- Notification should be done with a partner.

Notification Procedure

- In a calm, businesslike manner, show credentials, identify yourself, and request to come inside to speak privately. Ask to sit with them. *Move steadfastly toward the notification: the family is as alarmed as possible at this point—do not prevaricate!*
- Determine if they have a support team (spouse, partner, clergy, close friend) who could join them. This allows for emotional support and physical reassurance. If not readily available, move forward and be prepared for an emotional hurricane.
- Be empathetic but direct; do not use euphemisms such as *passed on* and *expired*; use *died*, *dead*, and *death*.
  - "I am sorry, but your daughter was involved in an automobile accident and died while paramedics were attempting to revive her."

---

[1] Information for this section was derived in part from Douglas Page's *Death Notification: Breaking the Bad News*, written in 1981 and published on the Officer.com website, and informal conversations with Chris Stewart, a senior instructor with the FLETC as well as serving as a deputy coroner for Glynn County, Georgia.

- "I am sorry, but your husband was involved in an industrial accident and he died in the hospital emergency room."
- "I am sorry, but your son was involved in a shooting tonight and died at the scene."
- Pause now and allow for them to process the information.
  - Do not flood them with details or questions.
  - Expect an emotional outburst that may cast blame, including on the messenger.
- Be prepared for follow-on questions. Remember the information is often sketchy and details are either insufficient, unknown, or wrong at this point. Do not provide information that you will have to walk back later! Assure them the incident is being thoroughly investigated.
- Let them know what will happen next.
  - "You can get in touch with me later today." (Provide contact number.) "I know this will take some time to process; we can further discuss arrangements then."
  - "You may contact the coroner." (Provide contact number.) "I know this will take some time to process; we can further discuss arrangements then."
- If they are alone, ask if there is anyone you could call to come over and be with them.
- Leave as soon as practical.

Suicidal Deaths

4

Suicide investigations are among the most difficult and most often challenged investigations that face the DSI. Traditionally, suicide involves both intent and the action that led to an individual taking his or her own life. A challenge within the investigation of a suicide is the intent qualifier. Intent cannot be established by a crime scene examination, though there may be a note (fewer than 10% of suicides) that when authenticated may indicate intent. The physical examination of the scene will focus on determining if the mechanism of death was self-inflicted or self-initiated.

The following considerations and activities are listed in an order conducive to efficiently processing a death scene. Individual circumstances may dictate a different order. This procedure should be used when a Death Scene Investigation Decision Tree (inside back cover) indicates a preliminary investigative direction for suicidal death.

NOTE: The procedures and steps that allowed the DSI to identify, secure, and perform the initial walk-through of the scene were covered in Chapter 1, "Death Scene Response." The analysis from the evidence within the context of the scene allowed for the investigative direction to be established. If this initial assessment has not been completed, return to the procedures detailed in Chapter 1, "Death Scene Response," and the Death Scene Investigation Decision Tree (inside of back cover)

Definition of *Suicide*

Suicide occurs when an individual desires to die and initiates an action that intentionally results in the loss of his or her life.

Worksheets and Documentation

The following documentation guides, forms, logs, and worksheets are provided in Section VIII, "Death Investigation Checklist and Worksheets," and may be used in documenting this scene. Additional forms, other than those noted, may also be used as dictated by your scene. These forms may be preprinted from the publisher's website (www.crcpress.com/cw/maloney) or photocopied from this procedural guide.

- *Death Investigation Checklist*
  - Section 1: Death Scene Information
  - Section 2: Civilians Who Entered the Death Scene
  - Section 3: Death Scene
  - Section 4: Coroner/Medical Examiner Notification
  - Sections 5–8: Appropriate Body Location When Discovered
  - Section 9: Wounds/Weapons/Drugs/Medications
  - Section 10: Identification/Notification
  - Section 11: Scene Processing
  - Section 12: Death Scene Release Information
  - Section 13: Narrative Report
  - Section 14: (appropriate forms and logs)
- *Worksheets*
  - Worksheet 1: Postmortem Indicator (PMI)
  - Worksheet 2: Death Scene Entry Log
  - Worksheet 3: Photography Head Slate
  - Worksheet 4: Photography Log
  - Worksheet 5: Post-Blast
  - Worksheet 6: Firearms Recovery
  - Worksheet 7: Entomology Recovery
  - Worksheet 8: Biological Evidence Worksheet
  - Worksheet 9: Trace Evidence
  - Worksheet 10: Friction Ridge Evidence
  - Worksheet 11: Impression Evidence
  - Worksheet 14: Bullet Defects
  - Worksheet 15: Bloodstain Patterns

Initial Scene Response

The following tasks should have already been completed; if not, please see Chapter 1, "Death Scene Response."

- Initial notification
- Initial scene coordination
- Arrival at the scene
- Establishing a perimeter
- Initial scene evaluation—walk-through
- Initial examination of the deceased
- Scene assessment, planning, and investigative strategy

Legal Concerns

The initial response to the call and determination that there is no one that requires aid and that there is no threat present are typically covered under a search exception called "exigent circumstances." Once the threat is removed and aid has been rendered, the presence of law enforcement moves from the public safety realm (exigent circumstances) to the investigative realm. Under the investigative realm, it is important to ensure you have the authority to search for and seize evidence. Chapter 1, "Death Scene Response," provides a detailed explanation of search and processing concerns.

Scene Considerations

Although a death may initially appear suicidal, the circumstances as ascertained through a thorough and complete investigation may indicate that the death was natural or the result of an accident or homicide.

- The medical examiner or coroner who has jurisdiction for the body should be notified as soon as possible. The intent is to inform authorities of the investigation and coordinate any on-scene responses, not to request removal of the body.
- Except to protect fragile evidence from potential destruction, there is no need to rush the processing of a death scene without first establishing a plan.
- If the body has already been removed to a medical facility or funeral home, an investigator must respond to the receiving facility to gather physical evidence and process the body.
- If the exact location of the body is unknown, Section II provides specific guidance on search techniques.
  - Surface recovery of remains is covered in Chapter 11.
  - Recovery of buried remains is discussed in Chapter 12.
  - Recovery of remains from water is covered in Chapter 13.

Death Scene Processing

Death scenes are often highly complex and require skilled care and methodical processing. There is no requirement to have a body removed immediately from the scene, and removal can be detrimental if it occurs before a scene is thoroughly examined for evidence. The steps are detailed below.

Identifying Primary and Secondary Death Scenes

Reassess the original scene perimeter to determine if it is adequate. This inner perimeter should contain all items of evidence or expected items of evidence or evidentiary areas within the scene. The outer perimeter is established to allow access to all areas within the inner perimeter without having to excessively traverse the inner perimeter. It also includes staging areas for DSIs working the scene. These are established as applicable to all primary and secondary scenes.

Primary Scene

- The body of the deceased generally constitutes the primary death scene.
- The area directly around the body or the room in which it is discovered also become part of the primary death scene.
- Any adjacent areas with evidence, bloodstains, bullet defects, indications of violent altercation, or with signs of forced entry are also a part of the primary scene.

NOTE: Any indication of forced entry or a violent struggle should move this investigation to Chapter 5, "Homicidal Deaths."

Secondary Scenes

- Medicine cabinets, if pill- or drug-related
- Gun safe or storage area, if a gun was used
- Kitchen cabinets, knife block, etc., if sharp force was used
- Smartphone, tablet, computer for Internet searches on suicide
- Social media accounts for indications of depression or suicidal ideation
- Other logical areas suggested by the instrumentality of death

Take Control of the Scene

- Start documentation of the scene via notes, sketching, and photography. Documentation is an ongoing process.
- Extend the death scene perimeter if necessary. Consider media presence and ranges of lenses.
- Establish a log of all persons entering or exiting the death scene.
- Establish an investigator/DSI staging area.

Scene Organization

- Use protective booties, gloves, and mask at a minimum. Full PPE may be appropriate (Appendix A).

- Establish investigator paths of entry and exit separate from those used by the victim.
- Establish investigator path of travel to and from the body. Use the point-to-point search method to clear the path of evidence and avoid the victim and perpetrators path of ingress or egress.
- Document and safeguard perishable evidence.

Legal Determination of Death

If not already accomplished, have the body pronounced dead by the proper legal authority.

Plan Development

- Evaluate results of walk-through.
- Evaluate available assets.
- Determine whether additional or specialized personnel are required, for example, a medical examiner, sexual assault response team, EOD, forensic anthropologist, or scuba divers.
- Determine whether additional or specialized equipment is required, for example, lighting, ladders, evidence collection supplies, metal detectors, etc.
- Formulate a processing plan.

Conduct Team Briefing

A team briefing is only one aspect of death scene management. See Chapter 32 for a detailed discussion.

- Assign duties to team members.
- Ensure team members understand their roles.
- Explain the level of biological hazard and PPE required for personnel entering a scene or specific parts of a scene (see Appendix A).
- Provide a thorough briefing of death scene details to all team members. Discuss the evidence expected to be encountered.
- For specific evidence and indicators associated with various types of death (gunshot wounds, hangings, stabbings, etc.), see the appropriate chapter in Section IV, "Wound Dynamics and Mechanism of Injury." An evaluation of the injury through Section III may indicate the injury could not be self-inflicted.

NOTE: If it is indicated that the injuries could not have been self-inflicted, this investigation should be moved to Chapter 5, "Homicidal Deaths."

Scene Processing

- Overall photography (Chapter 34) and videography (Chapter 35) of the scene may be the next step. The photographer must avoid likely paths of travel by the victim and physical evidence still at the scene.
- Examine and process the paths of entry, exit, and the area of the incident for two- and three-dimensional footwear and/or tire impressions (Chapter 44, "Impression Evidence"). Avoid areas containing biological evidence.
- Document all lighting, heating, and security conditions at the scene and note other scene markers that may indicate times of activities.
- If forced entry is evident, the case may not be a suicide.

NOTE: Any indication of forced entry should move this investigation to Chapter 5, "Homicidal Deaths."

- Process for biological and trace evidence (Chapter 41, "Biological Evidence" and Chapter 42, "Trace Evidence").
- Locations of all medical debris should be documented.
- Document bloodstain patterns (Chapter 37, "Documenting and Processing Bloodstain Patterns at the Scene").
- Note any items that may relate to motive or intent.
- Seize and protect all writing paper and tablets. They may be examined later for latent prints and indented writing and subjected to handwriting analysis.
- Note and seize any indicators of despondency or anger (torn photos, letters, items of symbolic or sentimental value, etc.). If such items are present, the case may not be a suicide.
- Secure all video, audio, digital, computer, and other media for determination of possible motive for the death.
- Consider which items of evidence may require special handling, processing, or preservation to safeguard any friction ridge on fingerprints, latent prints, or other evidence (Chapter 43, "Friction Ridge Evidence").
- Search for, examine, and recover any weapons or possible instruments of death. If such items are present and not in a position as to have been wielded by the victim, the case may not be a suicide.
- If a weapon was likely used and cannot be found, conduct an expanded search of the area focusing on the likely path of retreat, particularly dumpsters, bodies of water, and roofs of buildings.

NOTE: If the weapon cannot be located or is not in a location where it could have been associated with or discarded by the victim after inflicting the injury, this investigation should move to Chapter 5, "Homicidal Deaths."

- Search for, examine, and recover items associated with the weapon, such as cases and bullets.
- Search for, examine, and recover any other items that may link a suspect to a crime and/or death scene.

Documenting Scene Indicators

- Note any indicators of activity of the decedent prior to death, for example, meal preparation, telephone calls (note time made and to whom), computer and Internet activities, postings to social media accounts, etc.
- Note any indicators of industrial, sporting, or other activity that may have led to an accidental death, for example, ladders, tools, parachutes, etc.
- Note any indications of planning for activities that would have occurred after death, for example, food thawing or in preparation, alarm set, and appointments.

Processing the Body

The medical examiner, coroner, or their representative may wish to be present at the scene during the processing of the body, or to conduct examinations. For specific signs of physical trauma and evidence associated with various types of death (gunshot wounds, hangings, stabbings, etc.), see the applicable chapter in Section IV, "Wound Dynamics and Mechanism of Injury." Gloves and appropriate PPE gear should be worn during processing.

Photography and Videography of the Body

See Chapter 34, "Death Scene Photography" and Chapter 35, "Death Scene Videography" for specific guidance. The body should be photographed/video recorded as it was found (prior to moving it). Detailed note-taking and photography should continue during body processing. Specific areas to be photographed include the following:

- Orientation and spatial relationship between the body and equipment whose use or failure may have had a role in the suicide, for example, a vehicle.

- Face
- Head and upper torso
- Hands (detailed, all surfaces)
- Lower torso and legs
- Feet (detailed, including soles)
- Entire body
- Right and left profiles

Sketching the Body

See Chapter 33, "Death Scene Sketching" for specific guidance. Draw the body and clearly show its position. Fix the position by triangulating (or another method of measurement if indicated) the positions of the following:

- Head (nose)
- Torso (umbilicus)
- Arms (shoulder, elbow, and wrist joint)
- Legs (hip, knee, and ankle joint)
- Distances and relationship of body to equipment in the immediate vicinity of the body that may have played a role in the death

Documenting with Notes

- Fully describe the appearance of the body (sex, skin color, and clothing, disarray of clothing, jewelry, etc.).
- Fully document obvious injuries, decomposition changes (Chapter 14, "Post mortem Changes"), insect activity (Chapter 40, "Entomological Evidence"), presence of blood, and state of coagulation, open or closed eyes, etc.
- Continue hourly postmortem indicator data collection using Worksheet 1, "Postmortem Indicator (PMI)."
- Note the apparent activity at time of death, such as sleeping, eating, and bathing.
- If blood is present at the scene, note the presence or absence of blood on the hands, feet, and soles of the shoes. Fully document all bloodstain patterns on and near the victim (Chapter 37, "Documenting and Processing Bloodstain Patterns at the Scene").

Examination of the Body

- Examine the clothing for evidence of struggle or damage caused by weapons.

NOTE: If there is evidence of a struggle, this investigation should be moved to Chapter 5, "Homicidal Deaths."

- If restraints were used (ropes, belts, tape, clothing, etc.) to bind the victim, do not remove them. Knots and overlapped areas of tape should not be cut through or untied.

NOTE: If restraints are present and have not been self-tied, this investigation should be moved to Chapter 5, "Homicidal Deaths."

- Place the hands in small paper (not plastic) bags and seal them with tape at the wrists. This is not just for GSR but will protect other trace evidence that may be on the hands or beneath the fingernails (Figure 4.1).
- Consider the possibility of developing latent fingerprints on the skin or sampling for touch DNA if it is believed the body was handled (Chapter 41, "Biological Evidence").
- Examine the clothing, body, and immediate surrounding area for trace evidence. Consider the use of ultraviolet light or an alternate light source; see Chapter 42, "Trace Evidence."
- Examine and empty pockets that are accessible without moving the body. The contents of pockets should be placed in separate containers and labeled as to pocket location.
- Roll the body onto a clean sheet and examine the clothing and pockets on the underside.

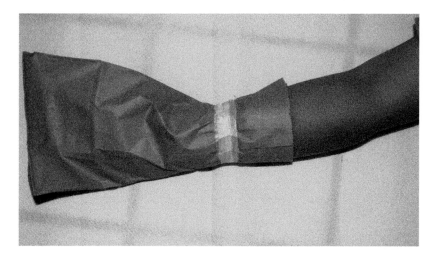

Figure 4.1 Bagging the hands at the scene.

- The body, wrapped in the sheet, should be placed in a body bag in the original position in which it was found, if practical.
- The body bag should be sealed with a tamperproof device. If the security of the body in transit is questionable, it should be escorted to the place where the autopsy will take place.
- After removal of the body, the areas from which the body was removed should be thoroughly examined for additional evidence and trace evidence.

Outdoor Death Scenes

- Consider using clean tarps or similar devices to shield bodies from onlookers while the scene is processed.
- If needed for expediency in adverse weather conditions, the body may be covered by a clean tarp or sheet, which should be collected later because it may contain trace evidence.
- Take soil samples beneath and around body (Chapter 42, "Trace Evidence").
- Sift the soil beneath the body for evidence.
- Collect appropriate entomological evidence (Chapter 40, "Entomological Evidence").

Evidence Commonly Associated with Suicides

- Weapons
- Medications
- Ligatures, ropes
- Suicide note (fewer than 10% of cases)
- Evidence of arranging final affairs
- Internet searches on suicide

Related Searches

- Smart phone
- Tablet
- Digital devices
- Social media pages
- Computer
- Desk
- Safety deposit box

Death Scene Interviews

First Responders

- Who reported the death? How and to whom was it reported? Always review and, if appropriate, obtain copies or transcripts of notification calls to public safety agencies (i.e., 911 calls in the United States).
- Who discovered the body and under what circumstances? What triggered the discovery?
- Where and when was the body found?
- How was the body positioned? Was it moved or altered in any way?
- When was the last time the person was seen alive? What was he or she doing?
- Was the victim infected with a contagious disease such as hepatitis or HIV?
- How did the responders (police, EMS, etc.) gain access to the scene?
- What were the circumstances surrounding death?

GSR Examination and Collection

- "When was the last time you handled a firearm?"
- "When was the last time you fired a weapon?"
- "When was the last time you were present when a weapon was fired? What was your proximity to the weapon?"
- "When was the last time you washed your hands?"
- "Are you right- or left-handed?"

Death Notification[1]

One of the least enviable tasks of the death investigator is the necessity to make death notification to the deceased's next of kin. Though unenviable, if accomplished with professional, calm, quiet dignity, it can make all the difference to the deceased's survivors.

In the case of homicide, the police investigator or detective should make the notification if there is an expectation of a spontaneous exclamation. Exclamations, such as "I knew she would kill him one day," or "We told him to stay off of those drugs," may be crucial for identifying a perpetrator or motive.

[1] Information for this section was derived in part from Douglas Page's *Death Notification: Breaking the Bad News*, written in 1981 and published on the Officer.com website, and informal conversations with Chris Stewart, a senior instructor with the FLETC as well as serving as a deputy coroner for Glynn County, Georgia.

General Guidelines

- Death notification may be a physically and emotionally draining task.
- Notification should be done in as timely a manner as possible; get there before the press or the neighbors!
- Notification should be done in person.
- Notification should be done with a partner.

Notification Procedure

- In a calm, businesslike manner, show credentials, identify yourself, and request to come inside to speak privately. Ask to sit with them. *Move steadfastly toward the notification: the family is as alarmed as possible at this point—do not prevaricate!*
- Determine if they have a support team (spouse, partner, clergy, close friend) who could join them. This allows for emotional support and physical reassurance. If not readily available, move forward and be prepared for an emotional hurricane.
- Be empathetic but direct; do not use euphemisms such as *passed on* or *expired*; use *died*, *dead*, and *death*.
  - "I am sorry, but your daughter was involved in a shooting incident and died while paramedics were attempting to revive her."
  - "I am sorry, but your husband was the victim of a stab wound he died in the hospital emergency room."
  - "I am sorry, but your son was involved in a shooting tonight and died at the scene."
- Pause now and allow for them to process the information.
  - Do not flood them with details or questions.
  - Expect an emotional outburst that may cast blame, including to the messenger.
- Be prepared for follow-on questions. Remember the information is often sketchy and details are either insufficient, unknown, or wrong at this point. Do not provide information that you will have to walk back later! Assure them the incident is being thoroughly investigated.
- Let them know what will happen next.
  - "You can get in touch with me later today." (Provide contact number.) "I know this will take some time to process; we can further discuss arrangements then."

- "You may contact the coroner." (Provide contact number.) "I know this will take some time to process; we can further discuss arrangements then."
- If they are alone, ask if there is anyone you could call to come over and be with them.
- Leave as soon as practical.

Homicidal Deaths

5

In a death investigation, the default investigative direction is always homicide. The investigation may eventually lead to the conclusion that the death was natural, accidental, or suicidal. The Death Scene Investigation Decision Tree (inside back cover) will, by design, default to the more suspicious investigative direction if questions arise. If progress along the Death Scene Investigation Decision Tree does not allow continuation down a certain decision branch, move to the homicide branch and evaluate from there.

NOTE: The procedures and steps that allow the DSI to identify, secure, and perform the initial walk-through of the scene were covered in Chapter 1, "Death Scene Response." The analysis from the evidence within the context of the scene allow for the investigative direction to be established. If this initial assessment has not been completed, return to the procedures detailed in Chapter 1, "Death Scene Response," and the Death Scene Investigation Decision Tree (inside back cover).

Definition of *Homicide*

Homicide is an action or inaction (where action is required) that results in the death of another. Homicidal deaths may or may not be criminal.

Worksheets and Documentation

The following documentation guides, forms, logs, and worksheets are provided in Section VIII, "Death Investigation Checklist and Worksheets," and may be used in documenting this scene. Additional forms, other than those noted, may also be used as dictated by your scene. These forms may be preprinted from the publisher's website (www.crcpress.com/cw/maloney) or photocopied from this procedural guide.

- *Death Investigation Checklist*
  - Section 1: Death Scene Information
  - Section 2: Civilians Who Entered the Death Scene

- Section 3: Death Scene
- Section 4: Coroner/Medical Examiner Notification
- Sections 5–8: Appropriate Body Location When Discovered
- Section 9: Wounds/Weapons/Drugs/Medications
- Section 10: Identification/Notification
- Section 11: Scene Processing
- Section 12: Death Scene Release Information
- Section 13: Narrative Report
- Section 14: (appropriate forms and logs)
- *Worksheets*
  - Worksheet 1: Postmortem Indicator (PMI)
  - Worksheet 2: Death Scene Entry Log
  - Worksheet 3: Photography Head Slate
  - Worksheet 4: Photography Log
  - Worksheet 6: Firearms Recovery Worksheet
  - Worksheet 7: Entomology Worksheet
  - Worksheet 8: Biological Evidence Notes
  - Worksheet 9: Trace Evidence Notes
  - Worksheet 10: Friction Ridge Evidence
  - Worksheet 11: Impression Evidence Notes
  - Worksheet 14: Bullet Defect Worksheet
  - Worksheet 15: Bloodstain Pattern Worksheet

Initial Scene Response

The following tasks should have already been completed; if not, please see Chapter 1, "Death Scene Response."

- Initial notification
- Initial scene coordination
- Arrival at scene
- Establishing a perimeter
- Initial scene evaluation—walk-through
- Initial examination of the deceased
- Scene assessment, planning, and investigative strategy

Legal Concerns

The initial response to the call and determination that there is no one that requires aid and that there is no threat present are typically covered under a search exception called "exigent circumstances." Once the threat is removed and aid has been rendered, the presence of law enforcement moves from the public safety realm (exigent circumstances) to the investigative realm. Under the investigative realm, it is important to ensure you have the authority to search for and seize evidence. Chapter 1, "Death Scene Response," provides a detailed explanation of search and processing concerns.

Scene Considerations

- Caution must be exercised when responding to all homicide scenes. Perpetrators may still be at or near the scene. The incident may still be dynamic and there may be additional victims.
- Except to protect fragile evidence from potential destruction, there is no need to rush the processing of a death scene without first establishing a plan.
- If the body has already been removed to a medical facility or funeral home, an investigator must respond to the receiving facility to gather physical evidence and process the body.
- The medical examiner or coroner who has jurisdiction for the body should be notified as soon as possible. The intent is to inform authorities of the investigation and coordinate any on-scene responses, not to request removal of the body.
- If the exact location of the body is unknown, Section II provides specific guidance on search techniques.
  - Surface recovery of remains is covered in Chapter 11.
  - Recovery of buried remains is discussed in Chapter 12.
  - Recovery of remains from water is covered in Chapter 13.

Death Scene Processing

Homicide scenes are highly complex and require skilled care and methodical documentation and processing. There is no requirement to have a body removed immediately from a scene, and removal may be detrimental if it occurs before a scene is thoroughly examined for evidence and its relationship in the context of the scene.

Identifying Primary and Secondary Death Scenes

Reassess the original scene perimeter to determine if it is adequate. This inner perimeter should contain all items of evidence or expected items of evidence or evidentiary areas within the scene. The outer perimeter is established to allow access to all areas within the inner perimeter without having to excessively traverse the inner perimeter. It also includes staging areas for DSIs working the scene. These are established as applicable to all primary and secondary scenes.

Primary Scene
- The body of the deceased generally constitutes the primary death scene.
- The area directly around the body or room in which it is discovered also becomes part of the primary death scene.
- Any adjacent areas with evidence, bloodstains, bullet defects, indications of violent altercation, or with signs of forced entry are also a part of the primary scene.

Secondary Scenes
- Location used by perpetrator for surveillance of victim and planning the murder
- Location where the perpetrator would have lain in wait for the victim
- Area where initial contact between suspect and victim and/or the assault occurred
- Area where the victim was killed
- Path along which the body was moved
- Vehicle or other conveyance used to transport the body
- Any area the perpetrator may have "cleaned up" after the event
- Area where perpetrator discarded weapons or other items

Take Control of the Scene

- Start documentation of the scene via notes, sketching, and photography. Documentation is an ongoing process.
- Extend the death scene perimeter if necessary. Consider media presence and ranges of lenses.
- Establish a log of all persons entering or exiting the death scene.
- Establish a command post outside the death scene perimeter.

Scene Organization

- Use protective booties, gloves, and mask at a minimum. Full PPE may be appropriate (see Appendix A).
- Establish investigator paths of entry and exit separate from those used by suspected perpetrators.
- Establish investigator path of travel to and from the body. Use the point-to-point search method to clear the path of evidence and avoid the suspected path of ingress or egress of the perpetrator.

- Document and safeguard perishable evidence encountered.
- Establish an investigator's staging area.
- Establish secondary perimeter and media/command briefing areas if necessary.

Legal Determination of Death

If not already accomplished by initial responders, have the body pronounced dead by the proper legal authority.

Plan Development

- Consider the use of a video walk-through for briefings.
- Evaluate results of walk-through.
- Evaluate available assets.
- Determine whether additional or specialized personnel are required, for example, a medical examiner, sexual assault response team, EOD, forensic anthropologist, or scuba divers.
- Determine whether additional or specialized equipment is required, for example, lighting, ladders, evidence collection supplies, and metal detectors.
- Formulate a scene plan.

Conduct Team Briefing

A team briefing is only one aspect of death scene management. See Chapter 32, "Death Scene Management," for a detailed discussion.

- Assign duties to team members.
- Ensure team members understand their roles.
- Explain the level of biological hazard and PPE required for personnel entering a scene or specific parts of a scene (Appendix A).
- Provide a thorough briefing of death scene details to all team members. Discuss the evidence expected to be encountered.
- For specific evidence and indicators associated with various types of death (gunshot wounds, hangings, stabbings, etc.), see the appropriate chapter in Section IV, "Wound Dynamics and Mechanism of Injury."

Scene Processing

- Overall photography (Chapter 34, "Death Scene Photography") and videography (Chapter 35, "Death Scene Videography") of the scene may be the next step. The photographer must avoid likely paths of travel by the perpetrators and physical evidence still at the scene.
- Examine and process the paths of entry, exit, and the area of the incident for two- and three-dimensional footwear and/or tire impressions (Chapter 44, "Impression Evidence"). Avoid areas containing biological evidence.
- Document all lighting, heating, and security conditions at the scene and note other scene markers that may indicate times of activities.
- If forced entry was used, process appropriately for burglary and housebreaking.
- Process for biological and trace evidence (Chapter 41, "Biological Evidence," and Chapter 42, "Trace Evidence").
- Locations of all medical debris should be documented.
- Document bloodstain patterns (Chapter 37, "Documenting and Processing Bloodstain Patterns at the Scene").
- Note any items that may relate to motive or intent.
- Seize and protect all writing paper and tablets. They may be examined later for latent prints and indented writing and subjected to handwriting analysis.
- Secure all video, audio, digital, computer, and other media for determination of possible motive for the death.
- Consider which items of evidence may require special handling, processing, or preservation to safeguard any friction ridges on fingerprints, latent prints, or other evidence (Section VII, "Death Scene Evidence Processing").
- Search for, examine, and recover any weapons or possible instruments of death.
- If a weapon was likely used and cannot be found, conduct an expanded search of the area focusing upon the likely path of retreat. Search dumpsters, bodies of water, roofs of neighboring structures, and other items along the suspected egress route of the perpetrator.
- Search for, examine, and recover items associated with the weapon, such as spent bullet cases and bullets.
- Search for, examine, and recover other items that may link a suspect to the crime and/or death scene.

Document Scene Indicators

- Note if lights are on, doors are locked, or other indicators that may show time of day during last active period.
- Note any indicators of activity of the decedent prior to death, for example, meal preparation, telephone calls (note time made and to whom), computer and Internet activities, etc.
- Note any dated material (digital or print) that would indicate when the victim was still alive.
- Note any social media postings that would indicate when the victim was still alive.
- Note any indications of planning for activities that would have occurred after death, for example, food thawing or in preparation, alarm set, and appointments.

Processing Body

The medical examiner, coroner, or their representative may wish to be present at the scene during the processing of the body or to conduct an examination. For specific signs of physical trauma and evidence associated with various types of death (gunshot wounds, hangings, stabbings, etc.), see the appropriate chapter in Section IV, "Wound Dynamics and Mechanism of Death." Gloves and appropriate PPE gear should be worn.

Photographing Body

See Chapter 34, "Death Scene Photography," and Chapter 35, "Death Scene Videography," for specific guidance. The body should be photographed and video recorded as it was found (prior to moving it). Detailed note-taking and photography should continue throughout processing. Specific areas to be photographed include the following:

- Orientation and spatial relationship between the body and the scene, weapons, and any instruments of death that may be present
- Face
- Head and upper torso
- Hands (detailed, all surfaces)
- Lower torso and legs
- Feet (detailed, including soles)
- Entire body

- Right and left profiles
- Close-up shots of relationships of wounds and damage to clothing indicative of injury. Use the mapping technique (Figure 5.1) to depict clothing damage.

Sketching the Body

Draw the body and clearly show its position (Figure 5.2). Fix the position by triangulating (or another method of measurement if indicated) the positions of the following:

- Head (nose)
- Torso (umbilicus)
- Arms (shoulder, elbow, and wrist joint)
- Legs (hip, knee, and ankle joint)
- Note distances and relationships to any object in the immediate vicinity of the body that may have played a role in the death.

Documenting with Notes

- Fully describe the appearance of the body (sex, skin color, clothing, disarray of clothing, jewelry, etc.).
- Fully document obvious injuries, decomposition changes (Chapter 14, "Postmortem Changes"), insect activity (Chapter 40, "Entomological Evidence"), presence of blood and state of coagulation (Chapter 37,

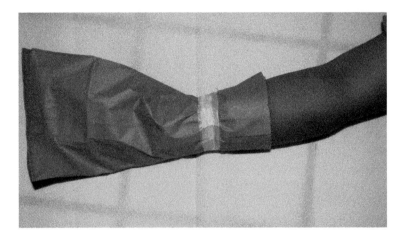

Figure 5.1 Bagging the hands at the scene.

Figure 5.2 Scene security privacy shield. Photograph courtesy of "SRN, Inc. Stop Rubbernecking."

"Documenting and Processing Bloodstain Patterns at the Scene"), open or closed eyes, etc.

- Continue hourly postmortem indicator data collection Worksheet 1, "Postmortem Indicator (PMI)."
- Note apparent activity at time of death, such as sleeping, eating, and bathing.
- If blood is present at the scene, note its presence or absence on the hands, feet, and soles of the shoes. Fully document all bloodstain patterns on and near the victim.
- Examine the clothing for evidence of struggle or damage caused by weapons.
- If restraints (ropes, belts, tape, clothing) were used to bind the victim, do not remove them. Knots and overlapped areas of tape should not be cut through or untied.
- If authorized and indicated, collect GSR from victim's hands.
- Place the hands in small paper (not plastic) bags and seal them with tape at the wrists. This will protect GSR and other trace evidence that may be on the hands or beneath the fingernails (Figure 5.1).
- Consider the possibility of developing latent fingerprints on the skin or sampling for touch DNA if it is believed the body was handled (Chapter 43, "Friction Ridge Evidence," and Chapter 41, "Biological Evidence").
- Examine the clothing, body, and immediate surrounding area for trace evidence. Consider the use of ultraviolet (UV) light or an alternate light source (ALS); see Chapter 42, "Trace Evidence."
- Examine and empty pockets that are accessible without moving the body. The contents of pockets should be placed in separate containers and labeled as to pocket location.

Examination of Body

- Examine the clothing for evidence of struggle or damage caused by weapons.
- Examine the clothing, body, and immediate surrounding area for trace evidence. Consider the use of UV light or an ALS; see Chapter 42, "Trace Evidence."
- Examine and empty pockets that are accessible without moving the body. The contents of pockets should be documented and placed in separate containers and labeled as to pocket location.
- Roll the body onto a clean sheet and examine the clothing and pockets on the underside.
- The body, wrapped in the sheet, should be placed in a body bag in the original position in which it was found, if practical.
- The body bag should be sealed with a tamperproof device. If the security of the body in transit is questionable, the body should be escorted to the place where the autopsy will take place.
- The area beneath where the body lay should be thoroughly examined for additional evidence and trace evidence.

Outdoor Death Scenes

- Consider using visual barriers to shield the body from onlookers while the scene is processed (Figure 5.2).
- Consider the use of a pop-up–style shelter to shield the body from the elements (Figure 5.3)
- If needed for expediency in adverse weather conditions, the body may be directly covered by a clean tarp or sheet, which should be collected later because it may contain trace evidence.
- Take soil samples beneath and around body (Chapter 42, "Trace Evidence").
- Sift the soil beneath the body for evidence.
- Collect appropriate entomological evidence (Chapter 40, "Entomological Evidence").

Evidence Commonly Associated with Homicidal Deaths

- Weapons
- Bloodstain pattern evidence
- Gunshot residue
- Ropes and ligatures

Figure 5.3 Pop-up shelter. Photograph courtesy of Arrowhead Forensics.

- Friction ridge evidence
- Biological and trace evidence
- Impression evidence

Related Searches

- Paths of access and egress used by the perpetrator
- All surveillance cameras footage covering the scene and paths of access and egress
- All secondary crime scenes
- Smart phone, tablets, etc., of the victim
- Smart phone, tablets, etc., of the suspect
- Social media accounts of the victim and suspect

Additional Functions Associated with the Death Scene

Death Scene Interviews

First Responders

- Has the suspected perpetrator been identified? Is the suspect in custody?
- Is the scene secure?
- Has the scene been searched for other victims or suspects?
- Who reported the death? How and to whom was it reported? Review and, if appropriate, obtain copies or transcripts of notification calls to public safety agencies (i.e., 911 calls in the United States).

- Who discovered the body and under what circumstances? What triggered the discovery?
- Where and when was the body found?
- How was the body positioned? Was it moved or altered in any way?
- When was the last time the decedent was seen alive? What was he or she doing?
- Was the victim infected with any contagious diseases, such as hepatitis and HIV?
- How did the responders (police, EMS, etc.) gain access to the scene?
- What were the circumstances surrounding the death?

Witnesses

Be sure to obtain identifying and contact information for each witness before you ask the following questions.

- "Who was at the scene when this incident happened?"
- "When did you arrive?"
- "How did you arrive?"
- "When did the others arrive?"
- "How did they arrive?"
- "What was each person at the scene doing when the incident happened?"
- "What were you doing when the incident happened?"
- "Where were you positioned when the incident happened?"
- "Where were others at the scene positioned when the incident happened?"
- "What happened?"
- "Where did others at the scene move as the incident happened?"
- "Where did they go after the incident?"
- "When did they leave?"
- "How did they leave?"
- "What happened to the weapon?"
- "What have you touched or handled in the scene?"

GSR Examination and Collection Questions

- "When was the last time you handled a firearm?"
- "When was the last time you fired a weapon?"
- "When was the last time you were present when a weapon was fired? What was your proximity to the weapon?"
- "When was the last time you washed your hands?"
- "Are you right- or left-handed?"

Death Notification[1]

One of the least enviable tasks of the death investigator is the necessity to make death notification to the deceased's next of kin. Though unenviable, if accomplished with professional, calm, quiet dignity, it can make all of the difference to the deceased's survivors.

In the case of homicide, the police investigator or detective should make the notification if there is an expectation of a spontaneous exclamation. Exclamations, such as "I knew she would kill him one day," or, "We told him to stay off of those drugs," may be crucial for identifying a perpetrator or motive.

General Guidelines
- Death notification may be a physically and emotionally draining task.
- Notification should be done in as timely a manner as possible; get there before the press or the neighbors!
- Notification should be done in person.
- Notification should be done with a partner.

Notification Procedure
- In a calm, businesslike manner, show credentials, identify yourself, and request to come inside to speak privately. Ask to sit with them. *At this point, move steadfastly toward the notification; the family is as alarmed as possible—do not prevaricate!*
- Determine if they have a support team (spouse, partner, clergy, close friend) who could join them. This allows for emotional support and physical reassurance. If not readily available, move forward and be prepared for an emotional hurricane.
- Be empathetic but direct; do not use euphemisms such as *passed on* and *expired*; use *died*, *dead*, and *death*.
  - "I am sorry, but your daughter was in an automobile accident this afternoon and died while paramedics were attempting to revive her."
  - "I am sorry, but your husband was the victim of a robbery tonight and was shot; he died in the hospital emergency room."
  - "I am sorry, but your son was involved in a shooting tonight and died at the scene."

---

[1] Information for this section was derived in part from Douglas Page's *Death Notification: Breaking the Bad News*, written in 1981 and published on the Officer.com website, and informal conversations with Chris Stewart, a senior instructor with the FLETC as well as serving as a deputy coroner for Glynn County, Georgia.

- Pause now and allow for them to process the information.
  - Do not flood them with details or questions.
  - Expect an emotional outburst that may cast blame, including on the messenger.
- Be prepared for follow-on questions. Remember the information is often sketchy and details are either insufficient, unknown, or wrong at this point. Do not provide information that you will have to walk back later! Assure them the incident is being thoroughly investigated.
- Let them know what will happen next.
  - "You can get in touch with me later today." (Provide contact number.) "I know this will take some time to process; we can further discuss arrangements then."
  - "You may contact the coroner." (Provide contact number.) "I know this will take some time to process; we can further discuss arrangements then."
- If they are alone, ask if there is anyone you could call to come over and be with them.
- Leave as soon as practical.

The Medicolegal Death Investigation

II

The Role of the Medicolegal Death Investigator

6

Medicolegal death investigators are generally in the employ of the medical examiner or coroner (ME/C) for a given jurisdiction. They generally do not hold law enforcement or police powers nor do they become involved in criminal investigations at large. Rather, they are specialized in death investigations and serve as the ME/C's on-scene asset to ensure the scene and body are documented with the specific needs of the ME/C in mind and to complete the necessary on-scene examination, processing of the body, and facilitate transportation. The medicolegal death investigator differs dramatically from the body transportation services used in some jurisdictions. The American Board of Medicolegal Death Investigators offers Registry Certification (Basic) and Board Certification (Advanced). Their current requirements (2016) are summarized below:

- Registry Certification (Basic) requires over 640 hours of verifiable death investigation experience, completion of a 52-skill performance checklist, professional recommendations, and completion of a written examination.
- Board Certification (Advanced) requires Basic Registry Certification, over 4,000 verifiable hours of death investigation experience, professional recommendations, and successful completion of a board certification examination.

In short, the certified medicolegal death investigator is a highly trained and experienced professional that is the extension of the ME/C at the scene and a valuable resource to law enforcement at the scene.

The medicolegal death investigator typically

- Responds to the scene as the ME/C representative
- Interacts with law enforcement and other first responders present
- Establishes jurisdiction, certifies the death
- Determines the scope of ME/C response
  - Determines if the ME/C will be required at the scene
  - Determines in coordination with law enforcement if this will be a combined investigative effort or if the circumstances dictate that it will fall solely under the scope of the ME/C

- Interacts with the family of the deceased
- Interviews witnesses as required within the scope of the investigation
- Serves as an on-scene resource/consultant to law enforcement personnel
- Documents and processes the scene in accordance with established procedure
- Documents postmortem indicators—livor, rigor, and algor mortis
- Makes preliminary identification of the remains, if possible
- Identifies and preserves evidence
- Makes appropriate written reports
- Makes death notifications when required

Body and Scene Processing

The process for conducting an examination of deaths scenes and the body are thoroughly covered as follows:

- Initial assessment (Chapter 1) is conducted and the Death Investigation Decision Matrix (inside back cover) is used to determine the investigative direction.
- Chapter 2, "Natural Deaths"
- Chapter 3, "Accidental Deaths"
- Chapter 4, "Suicidal Deaths"
- Chapter 5, "Homicidal Deaths"

Transportation of Remains

Whether the ME/C representative or a contract carrier transports the body, the following must be ensured.

- Any personal effects that were removed from the body or clothing at scene are inventoried, placed in a moisture-resistant tamperproof envelope, and placed within the body bag or remain in the custody of the death investigator.
- The body bag zipper is secured with a serialized tamperproof seal.
- Photograph the seal in place.
- The body is transported to the morgue facility.
- The serialized seal is verified on intake to the morgue.
- The serialized seal is verified again on removal from refrigeration for autopsy.

Death Notification[1]

One of the least enviable tasks of the death investigator is the necessity to make death notification to the deceased's next of kin. Though unenviable, if accomplished with professional, calm, quiet dignity, it can make all of the difference to the deceased's survivors.

One of the factors that determines who makes the death notification is the type of death and circumstances involved. In the case of homicide, it may be beneficial to have the police investigator or detective make the notification, especially if there is an expectation of a spontaneous exclamation, such as "I knew she would kill him one day" or "We told him to stay off of those drugs".

General Guidelines

- Death notification may be a physically and emotionally draining task.
- Notification should be done in as timely a manner as possible; get there before the press or the neighbors!
- Notification should be done in person.
- Notification should be done with a partner.

Notification Procedure

- In a calm, businesslike manner, show credentials, identify yourself, and request to come inside to speak privately. Ask to sit with them. *At this point move steadfastly toward the notification: the family is as alarmed as possible—do not prevaricate!*
- Determine if they have a support team (spouse, partner, clergy, close friend) who could join them. This allows for emotional support and physical reassurance. If not readily available, move forward and be prepared for an emotional hurricane.
- Be empathetic but direct; do not use euphemisms such as *passed on* and *expired*; use the words dead, death, and died.
  - "I am sorry, but your daughter was in an automobile accident this afternoon and died while paramedics were attempting to revive her."

[1] Information for this section was derived in part from Douglas Page's *Death Notification: Breaking the Bad News*, written in 1981 and published on the Officer.com website, and informal conversations with Chris Stewart, a senior instructor with the FLETC as well as serving as a deputy coroner for Glynn County, Georgia.

- "I am sorry, but your husband was the victim of a robbery tonight and was shot; he died in the hospital emergency room."
- "I am sorry, but your son was involved in a shooting tonight and died at the scene."
- Pause now and allow for them to process the information.
  - Do not flood them with details or questions.
  - Expect an emotional outburst that may cast blame, including on the messenger.
- Be prepared for follow-on questions. Remember the information is often sketchy and details are either insufficient, unknown, or wrong at this point. Do not provide information that you will have to walk back later!
- Let them know what will happen next.
  - "The police will be in touch with you." Provide them a contact number of the investigator assigned if at all possible.
  - "You can get in touch with me later today." (Provide contact number.) "I know this will take some time to process; we can further discuss arrangements then."
  - "You may contact the coroner." (Provide contact number.) "I know this will take some time to process; we can further discuss arrangements then."
- If they are alone, ask if there is anyone you could call to come over and be with them.
- Leave as soon as practical.

The Role of the Coroner 7

Many areas use a coroner's system to legally investigate deaths. Generally, their role is to provide a lawful determination as to pronouncing death, the identity of the deceased, and the cause and manner of death. These systems vary widely from jurisdiction to jurisdiction.

- Appointed coroner who is a medical doctor
- Appointed coroner who has medical or investigative training and certifications
- Elected official who has met requirements for medical or investigative training
- Elected official with no investigative or medical requirements

To clarify discussions on the types of deaths investigated, the following terms will be used:

- *Medically attended death*: A medically attended death is one in which the decedent has been diagnosed and is under the treatment of a physician for a disease or illness for which the expected outcomes include death. The attending physician agrees to sign the death certificate and certify the cause of death as that diagnosed illness/illness and the manner of death as natural.
- *Medically unattended death*: A medically unattended death is any death that falls outside of the scope of the medical diagnoses described above. *Note*: Having a medical doctor at the scene of the death does not make it medically attended; it is the existence of a condition that is being medically attended to and for which the outcome includes death. Medically unattended deaths include accidental deaths, suicides, and homicides.

Additionally, the duties or scope of duties for coroners may vary greatly from jurisdiction to jurisdiction.

- Covers all medically unattended deaths
- Often uses either state/regional services or contract services of a forensic pathologist in cases of homicide or in other cases they feel warrant an autopsy

- May issue death certificate or the state may issue the death certificate if a state medical examiner is used
- Covers only natural deaths and issues death certificates
- Covers only natural and accidental deaths and issues death certificates

Clearly, the wide variance in these coroner qualifications may lead to a similar variance in abilities and investigative thoroughness. It is incumbent upon the DSI to be familiar with the system in place and capabilities of the system used within the local jurisdiction.

A coroner may be trained in death investigations and certified by an organization such as the American Board of Medicolegal Death Investigators or may employ deputy coroners or coroner's investigators with such training and certification.

Establishing Identity

The coroner confirms the identity of the deceased. Typically, the coroner determines identity in those cases where identity is clear using presumptive identification methods.

Presumptive Identification

- Physical identification by next of kin
- Identification of personal effects associated with the body

In those instances where identity is questioned or difficult to establish, the coroner may have to contract for scientific analysis to determine identity.

Confirmatory Identification

- Fingerprints
- DNA
- Dental records
- Radiological (x-ray comparison)

Establishing Cause of Death

The cause of death is the underlying injury or illness that starts the cascade of events leading to the victim's demise. Examples are gunshot wounds, stab wounds, blunt force trauma, myocardial infarction (heart attack), cerebrovascular accident (stroke), and a myriad of other possibilities. Cardiac and respiratory arrests are conditions that *define* death; they are *not* causes of death.

As stated above, the cause of death is the initiating injury or illness that leads to the cascade of events resulting in death. An example would be an individual who is shot, resulting in continuing surgeries and infections. Though they may die sometime later as a result of these surgeries and infections, the initiating event was the gunshot wound; thus, it is the primary cause of death.

Establishing Manner of Death

Manner of death describes one of four circumstances that result in death: natural cause, accident, suicide, or homicide. A manner of death may also be categorized as *undetermined*.

- *Natural*: Result of natural process of a disease whose expected outcome is death.
- *Accident*: Result of activity or action that is not intended or expected to lead to death.
- *Suicide*: The taking of one's own life through deliberate action with the intent to die.
- *Homicide*: The taking of another's life by an action or inaction (if action is required); may or may not be a criminal act.
  - *Noncriminal* homicides may include justifiable situations such as self-defense, war, and law enforcement killings.
  - *Criminal* homicides range from negligent homicide to manslaughter to murder.
- *Undetermined*: This classification may be temporary or long term. It is used when information about the nature of death is insufficient, for example:
  - Determination awaiting toxicology results.
  - Bones recovered show no indications of trauma.
  - Manner of death cannot be medically determined.

At the Death Scene

Scene Considerations

- Considerations vary widely based on local coroner requirements.
- Know the capabilities of coroner's investigators in your area. Are they trained and skilled medicolegal investigators or simply transportation providers?
- The coroner (or representative) will respond to a scene and examine the body *in situ* (in its original position).

Death Notification[1]

One of the least enviable tasks of the coroner is the necessity to make death notification to the deceased's next of kin. Though unenviable, if accomplished with professional, calm, quiet dignity, it can make all of the difference to the deceased's survivors.

One of the factors that determines who makes the death notification is the type of death and circumstances involved. In suspicious or ambiguous deaths Coroners may request that the investigating officer or his or her law enforcement representative perform the task if criminal culpability is expected. If there is an expectation of a spontaneous exclamation, such as "I knew she would kill him one day" or "We told him to stay off of those drugs," it may be beneficial to have law enforcement document and conduct the notification.

General Guidelines

- Death notification may be a physically and emotionally draining task.
- Notification should be done in as timely a manner as possible; get there before the press or the neighbors!
- Notification should be done in person.
- Notification should be done with a partner.

Notification Procedure

- In a calm, businesslike manner, show credentials, identify yourself, and request to come inside to speak privately. Ask to sit with them. *At this point, move steadfastly toward the notification: the family is as alarmed as possible—do not prevaricate!*
- Determine if they have a support team (spouse, partner, clergy, close friend) who could join them. This allows for emotional support and physical reassurance. If not readily available, move forward and be prepared for an emotional hurricane.
- Be empathetic but direct. Do not use euphemisms such as *passed on* or *expired*; use the words dead, death and died.
  - "I am sorry, but your daughter was in an automobile accident this afternoon and died while paramedics were attempting to revive her."
  - "I am sorry, but your husband was the victim of a robbery tonight and was shot; he died in the hospital emergency room."

---

[1] Information for this section was derived in part from Douglas Page's *Death Notification: Breaking the Bad News*, written in 1981 and published on the Officer.com website, and informal conversations with Chris Stewart, a senior instructor with the FLETC as well as serving as a deputy coroner for Glynn County, Georgia.

- "I am sorry, but your son was involved in a shooting tonight and died at the scene."
- Pause now and allow for them to process the information.
  - Do not flood them with details or questions.
  - Expect an emotional outburst that may cast blame, including on the messenger.
- Be prepared for follow-on questions. Remember the information is often sketchy and details are either insufficient, unknown, or wrong at this point. Do not provide information that you will have to walk back later!
- Let them know what will happen next.
  - "The police will be in touch with you." Provide them a contact number for the investigator assigned if at all possible.
  - "You can get in touch with me later today." (Provide contact number.) "I know this will take some time to process; we can further discuss arrangements then."
- If they are alone, ask if there is anyone you could call to come over and be with them.
- Leave as soon as practical.

Coroner's Inquest

The coroner may hold an inquest. This is a legal proceeding often held in front of a jury or judge. It allows for the presentation of evidence and the testimony of witnesses. The coroner may use this tool to determine the identity of the deceased or the cause and manner of death. If the death is suspicious and the suspect known, the suspect in most jurisdictions does not testify before the inquest. The results of the inquest may be used to further criminal prosecution or aid in civil cases by legally identifying the deceased and the circumstances of his or her death. The coroner in most jurisdictions has the ability to call this inquest independent of law enforcement or judicial review or approval.

The Role of the Medical Examiner

8

The role of the medical examiner (ME) is to serve as a medicolegal expert investigating the cause and manner of death in suspicious, unexplained, and unnatural deaths. The forensic autopsy is a unique tool in the ME's arsenal. The scientific and systematic examination of the body and its vital systems allows for the death and any injuries associated with the body to be placed into context concerning the events and processes that led to the deceased's demise. The ME may choose to be present at the scene of certain deaths in order to better place the deceased within the context of the circumstances surrounding his or her death. The ME will often depend on the crime scene investigator, DSI, or their own ME's investigator to respond to the scene and record the information of the decedent *in situ* and present this contextual information back to them.

MEs may be in the public employ serving a given jurisdiction (state, county, or city) or geographic region. They are to serve as independent and unbiased scientific investigators; they are seldom in the employ of the police or an investigative agency.

Private MEs are independent (free from a jurisdiction or government appointment) and provide contract services. They may serve to provide contract autopsies in areas serviced by a coroner's system or provide services to families or attorneys when questions still exist in a death after a government investigation.

Establishing Identity

The ME establishes and confirms the identity of the deceased.

Presumptive Identification

- Physical identification by next of kin
- Identification of personal effects associated with the body

Confirmatory Identification

- Fingerprints
- DNA

- Dental records
- Radiological (x-ray comparison)

Establishing Cause of Death

The cause of death is the underlying injury or illness that starts the cascade of events leading to the victim's demise. Examples are gunshot wounds, stab wounds, blunt force trauma, myocardial infarction (heart attack), cerebrovascular accident (stroke), and a myriad of other possibilities. Cardiac and respiratory arrests are conditions that *define* death; they are *not* causes of death.

As stated above, the cause of death is the initiating injury or illness that leads to the cascade of events resulting in death. An example would be an individual who is shot, resulting in continuing surgeries and infections. Though the individual may die sometime later as a result of these surgeries and infections, the initiating event was the gunshot wound; thus, it is the primary cause of death.

Establishing Manner of Death

Manner of death describes one of four circumstances that result in death: natural cause, accident, suicide, or homicide. A manner of death may also be categorized as *undetermined*.

- *Natural*: Result of natural process of a disease whose expected outcome is death.
- *Accident*: Result of activity or action that is not intended or expected to lead to death.
- *Suicide*: The taking of one's own life through deliberate action with the intent to die.
- *Homicide*: The taking of another's life by an action or inaction (if action is required); may or may not be a criminal act.
  - *Non-criminal* homicides may include justifiable situations such as self-defense, war, and law enforcement killings.
  - *Criminal* homicides range from negligent homicide to manslaughter to murder.
- *Undetermined*: This classification may be temporary or long term. It is used when information about the nature of death is insufficient, for example:
  - Determination awaiting toxicology results.
  - Bones recovered show no indications of trauma.
  - Manner of death cannot be medically determined.

Establishing Postmortem Interval

The ME may render an opinion as to the time since death, also known as the *postmortem interval*. The only accurate method of determining the time of death is observation by a reliable witness. Physiological changes since death may be observed at a scene and generally indicate the time since death. Careful observations of these changes should be recorded at the scene and presented to the ME, who may be able to determine a far more accurate postmortem interval than could be determined from scene indicators alone. The ME may also use the stomach contents of the deceased and the passage of food through the bowel to help determine the postmortem interval. A forensic entomologist or anthropologist may also be called in to consult on bodies in a more advanced stage of decomposition. A description of and process for documentation/observation of postmortem indicators is thoroughly covered in Chapter 14, "Postmortem Changes."

At the Death Scene

Scene Considerations

- Considerations vary widely based on local ME requirements.
- Know the capabilities of ME investigators in your area. Are they trained and skilled medicolegal investigators or simply transportation providers?
- Under certain circumstances, the ME may choose to respond to a scene and examine the body *in situ* (in its original position).

On-Scene Body Processing Procedures

- Certain on-scene body processing steps *require* the ME's permission. The permission may be a blanket authorization or a special authorization for a unique situation.
- The clothing of a victim is usually removed at autopsy. In special circumstances such as possible obliteration of critical bloodstain spatters, the ME should be contacted.
- GSR testing should be arranged immediately for anyone believed to have handled a firearm, including the victim. Do not wait for the victim's arrival at the morgue. With the ME's permission, the victim's hands should be thoroughly documented by photography and the GSR kit used as nonintrusively as possible. The hands should be bagged before the body is moved from the scene (Figure 8.1).

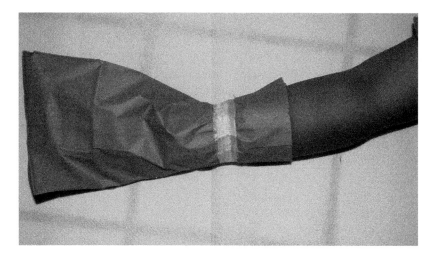

Figure 8.1 Bagging the hands at the scene.

- The most accurate method of recording body temperature at a scene is taking the temperature of the liver. This requires making a small incision with a scalpel about 0.5 cm below the rib margin of the right side of the body and inserting a thermometer through the incision and into the liver (Figure 8.2).

Circumstances Requiring Autopsy

The autopsy and role of the investigator at autopsy is covered thoroughly in Chapter 9. An autopsy is warranted when

- Circumstances of death suggest a crime, suicide, or other act requiring investigation.
- Death is medically unattended.
- The cause of death may constitute a menace to public health.
- A physician is unable to establish the cause of death.
- The decedent was in law enforcement custody at the time of death.

The Forensic Autopsy

Autopsies are generally conducted under the auspices of an ME who has jurisdiction where the body was found. An ME is a medical doctor, usually a pathologist and preferably a board-certified forensic pathologist. Board certification as a forensic pathologist requires a minimum of 11 years of specialized medical training after earning a 4-year college degree. MEs are masters of their craft.

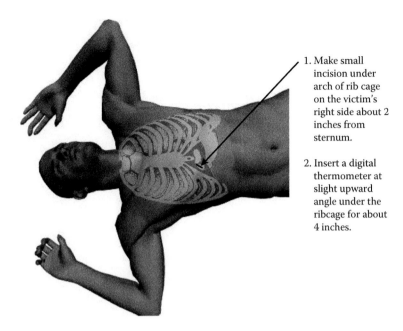

1. Make small incision under arch of rib cage on the victim's right side about 2 inches from sternum.

2. Insert a digital thermometer at slight upward angle under the ribcage for about 4 inches.

Figure 8.2 Incision location for liver temperature.

An autopsy conducted by a trained forensic pathologist is critical for establishing the cause and manner of death and also to place injuries within the context of a scene and investigation. Although the DSI is charged with investigating the scene of death, the ME usually exercises control of the body and determines the cause and manner of death.

The ME documents and collects physical evidence from the body, determines wound dynamics and mechanisms of injury, and provides vital information that may be used to reconstruct the scene. The DSI's role at autopsy is thoroughly discussed in Chapter 9. The DSI's documentation, notes, and observations at the scene help the ME identify the victim, determine the cause and manner of death, and detail the mechanisms of the fatal injuries and dynamics of that event. That information travels full circle back to the DSI, who integrates it into the context of the scene to develop investigative directions and identify those responsible for the death. The ME should

- Legally pronounce the victim deceased, if this has not already been done.
- Establish the legal identity of the victim.
- Conduct an autopsy or inspection of the remains based upon the circumstances presented.
- Establish the legal cause and manner of death based on information from the scene and results of autopsy.

- Establish approximate time since death, if possible, using information from the scene and the results of autopsy.
- Properly collect and safeguard items of evidence associated with or within the body.

Procedures in Lieu of Autopsy

If an autopsy will not be required, ensure that needed evidence and documentation are still collected. In some circumstances, this limited analysis and collection of evidence from the body constitutes an "inspection" and may entail the following:

- Documenting all injuries.
- Swabbing for gunshot residue.
- Taking fingerprints.
- Taking x-rays.
- Collecting blood and urine samples at the hospital or funeral home.
- A virtual autopsy may be performed using computerized tomography and magnetic resonance imaging to demonstrate wound tracks, depths of injuries, and impacts on various internal organs. This procedure is completely noninvasive.

Reports and Reporting

Outbrief

The outbrief is an opportunity to confirm opinions the ME may have voiced during the autopsy. This is the time to request copies of photographs and be listed to receive the preliminary and final autopsy reports. Request a copy of the diagram the ME used to indicate external injuries. Ask specific questions about the ME's opinions.

Preliminary Autopsy Report

The preliminary report, if used by your ME, is usually issued within a week of the autopsy and confirms findings discussed at the outbrief. The preliminary report may provide justification for the issue of warrants to search for weapons and other forensic evidence that may be associated with an identified perpetrator.

Toxicology Report

Toxicology testing and reporting may take several weeks. The report will detail levels of alcohol, drugs, or poisons found in fluids collected from the body.

Final Autopsy Report

The final report will mirror the preliminary autopsy report, along with additional forensic testing results based on the toxicology report.

Autopsy Protocol and the Investigator's Role

9

The autopsy suite and the body constitute the absolute domain of an ME. The ME usually has at least one assistant, who is commonly called a *diener* (German for "servant," a traditional term used in autopsy protocols). A diener is responsible for handling, moving, and cleaning the corpse and assisting with the autopsy. The ME may also employ a medical photographer to document the autopsy and significant findings. The ME is a medical doctor, usually a pathologist, and in the most desirable circumstances a board-certified forensic pathologist. Board certification in forensic pathology requires a minimum of 11 years of specialized medical training, after earning a 4-year college degree. Recognizing this expertise will go a long way toward cementing a long-term working relationship with an ME.

- Establish a relationship with your local ME and staff *before* you need them for an investigation.
- Request training and to attend an autopsy or two to become familiar with ME policies and procedures.
- During an autopsy, get as close to the evidence (the body) as the ME allows and demonstrate your willingness to learn.
- Arrive early. The body may be out of the bag, undressed, rinsed, and waiting for the pathologist by the announced autopsy time.

Circumstances Requiring Autopsy

- A suspicious death.
- A death suggesting a crime, suicide, or other act requiring investigation.
- A death is medically unattended.
- The cause of death may constitute a menace to public health.
- A physician is unable to establish cause of death.
- The decedent was in law enforcement custody at the time of death.

Procedures in Lieu of Autopsy

If an autopsy is not going to be conducted, ensure that needed evidence and documentation are still collected. In some circumstances, this limited analysis and collection of evidence from the body may constitute an "inspection" and may entail the following:

- Externally documenting all injuries.
- Swabbing for gunshot residue.
- Taking fingerprints.
- Taking x-rays.
- Collecting blood and urine samples at the hospital or funeral home.
- A virtual autopsy may be performed using computerized tomography and magnetic resonance imaging to demonstrate wound tracks, depths of injuries, and impacts on other internal organs. This procedure is completely noninvasive.

Investigator's Responsibilities at Autopsy

Equipment Required

Camera gear with off-camera flash capability, flash, and close-up lenses or attachments

- Postmortem fingerprint kit
- GSR kit, if applicable
- Sexual assault evidence recovery kit, if applicable
- Evidence collection and packaging supplies
- Medical and/or dental records of decedent
- PPE (Tyvek® suit, gloves, etc.) if not provided

Arrival

It is incumbent upon a DSI to represent the scene at the autopsy. Arrive early.

- Be prepared to brief the ME about the death scene using photographs or video. Make any special autopsy requests suggested by conditions at the scene.
- Draw the ME into the investigative process beyond examination of the body.
- Discuss any particular needs that may be resolved by autopsy: for example, ask which injury was most likely fatal, whether multiple weapons were used, whether the position of the victim at the time of injury can be determined.
- Take full advantage of PPE offered by the ME staff because certain activities require an investigator's proximity to the body during the autopsy.

- Identify the pathologist and all others present at the autopsy.
- Fully document by notes and photographs your observations and actions of ME staff during the autopsy.
- Request permission to take photographs if a forensically trained photographer is not present. Even then, backup photography is recommended.
- Discuss the need for full body and dental x-rays to identify the victim. Bone surveys may be required to document prior injuries in fatal child abuse cases.
- Discuss the procedure for recovery of evidence (such as bullets) from the body and custody of evidence after autopsy.

External Examination

- Note method of positive identification.
- Note and document external injuries, scars, marks, and tattoos. Ensure they are consistent with pathologist's findings. It may be more effective to ask if the ME's diagrams of external injuries and scars/marks/tattoos will be available to the investigator.
- Specific photographs to be taken are covered later in this chapter. See Chapter 34, "Death Scene Photography," for specific guidance.
- Apply UV light or ALS to body and clothing to reveal trace and fiber evidence (Chapter 42, "Trace Evidence").
- Take GSR samples if appropriate before the hands are disturbed. Ensure hands are thoroughly photographed before GSR testing.
- Take fingernail scrapings and clippings, if appropriate.
- Consider latent prints on the body if the perpetrator may have handled the body. Finding these prints will require the ME's approval and a special technique to perform the procedure (Chapter 43, "Friction Ridge Evidence").
- Consider a "touch DNA" swab if the perpetrator is believed to have handled the body (Chapter 41, "Biological Evidence").
- Each layer of clothing should be photographed as it is removed.
- Personal effects should be removed, inventoried, and photographed.
- Collect the clothing as it is removed and package each item separately.
- Take entomological (insect and larva) samples if evident on body and not taken at the scene (Chapter 40, "Entomological Evidence").
- Consider the use of UV light or ALS to detect trace evidence, bruising, dried body fluids, and fiber evidence before and after the clothing is removed (Chapter 42, "Trace Evidence").
- Take photographs of the front and back of the body; take individual photographs of all scars, marks, tattoos, and injuries.

- Ask the ME to utilize a sexual assault evidence recovery kit if indicated. A sexual assault kit may provide standards and samples for other crimes such as aggravated assault.

Internal Examination

- Photograph all external and internal injuries and other anomalies noted by the ME.
- Ensure any severed body parts are rearticulated and photographed in place if possible.
- Consider asking the ME to use a probe to demonstrate any wound tracks present and photograph them.
- Take into custody any additional evidence removed from the body (bullets, knife blades, etc.). Close-up photography of these items is important.
- After examining and collecting trace and biological evidence (Chapters 41 and 42), consider rinsing bullets or fragments removed from the body in clean water before collection. Blood remaining on bullets or fragments may be corrosive enough to deteriorate firearm markings.

After Examination

- Obtain a good quality 10-fingerprint card from the deceased. This may be left until the end of the autopsy if evidence on the hands and wrists dictates. If the fingertips are not accessible due to rigor, consider splaying the fingers before moving to harsher measures (Figure 9.1).
- If suicide or homicide is suspected or the victim is a suspect in another crime such as a suicide–murder, take major case prints (10-print card, palm, knife edge, web between thumb and index finger, full finger length roll, finger tips). These may be recorded by the direct ink method or by the powder and tape lift method (Figures 9.2 and 9.3). This is best accomplished when the autopsy is complete and the body has warmed to ambient temperature; the hands must be free of all moisture.
- Discuss preliminary autopsy findings concerning cause and manner of death with the ME. Clearly note them as preliminary findings.
- Leave a business card and ask to be notified when the final autopsy results are available. A preliminary report may be available quickly but you must also obtain a final report of an autopsy.

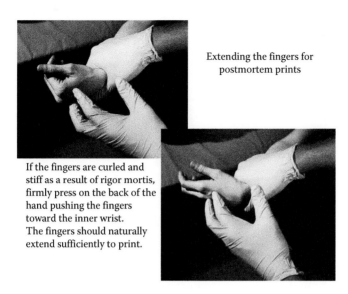

Extending the fingers for postmortem prints

If the fingers are curled and stiff as a result of rigor mortis, firmly press on the back of the hand pushing the fingers toward the inner wrist.
The fingers should naturally extend sufficiently to print.

Figure 9.1 Splaying the fingers for easier fingerprinting of cadavers.

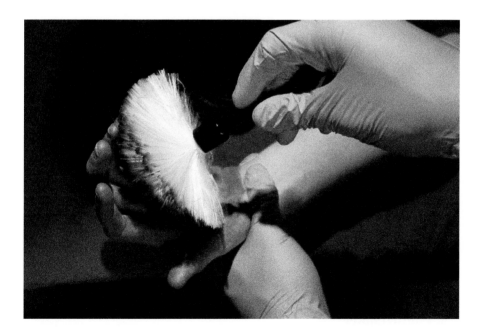

Figure 9.2 Powdering the palm for major case prints on a cadaver. The print may then be recovered by rolling the palm with a gelatin lifter. The rolling technique for lifting the prints is demonstrated in Figure 9.3.

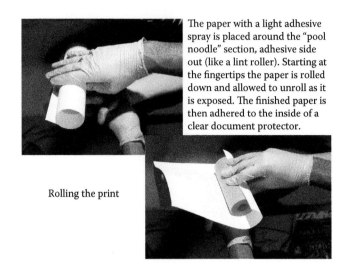

The paper with a light adhesive spray is placed around the "pool noodle" section, adhesive side out (like a lint roller). Starting at the fingertips the paper is rolled down and allowed to unroll as it is exposed. The finished paper is then adhered to the inside of a clear document protector.

Rolling the print

Figure 9.3 Rolling the fingers and palm using a "pool noodle" to facilitate a smooth roll and complete coverage.

Autopsy Photography Guidelines

General

- The bright reflective surfaces in an autopsy suite pose unique photography conditions. Tungsten surgical lamps generally provide the lighting. Ask that they be turned off or temporarily directed away from the photographic field before photography is started. Tungsten lights will cast a yellow tint to all photographs taken with standard daylight film or digital media if not compensated for through white balance.
- A color chart should be included as the first photograph on each series or roll of film and taken under the same lighting conditions as the remainder of the roll (Worksheet 3, "Photography Head Slate").
- A photography log should be kept (Worksheet 4, "Photography Log").

ME Photographer

- Discuss specific shots required for your investigation, such as close-ups of back-spatter on hands after a self-inflicted gunshot wound.
- Discuss injury-mapping technique the ME will use or suggest one. Mapping will aid subsequent use of photographs.
- Discuss how and when you will receive *all* the images. You may need to take some duplicate photographs.

Investigator

- Discuss your photography plans with ME.
- See note above regarding tungsten surgical lighting; set auto white balance.
- Because of many highly reflective surfaces in autopsy suites, watch for flash hotspots and your own reflection.

Body at Autopsy Photography

Arrival

- A close-up of the identification tag and seal
- The body in body bag demonstrating the integrity of seals
- A view of the bag unzipped with the body in the bag

Clothed

Photograph the body as it lies from as high an angle as possible (overhead view).

- Upper half of body
- Face, front, right profile, left profile
- Head and shoulders
- Chest and abdomen
- Right upper arm
- Right lower arm
- Right hand (palm and back)
- Left upper arm
- Left lower arm
- Left hand (palm and back)
- Lower half of body
- Abdomen and pelvis
- Right upper leg
- Right lower leg
- Right foot/footwear (upper surface and sole)
- Left upper leg
- Left lower leg
- Left foot/footwear (upper surface and sole)
- Any bloodstain pattern on clothing using mapping technique (Figure 9.4)
  - Orientation photograph of discrete bloodstain patterns on clothing
  - Close-ups, with and without scale, of discrete bloodstain patterns on clothing

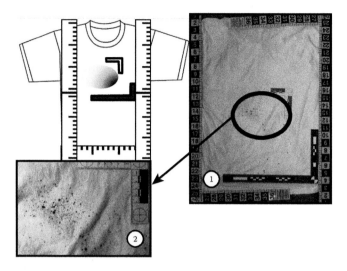

Figure 9.4 Bloodstain pattern mapping on clothing.

- Any damage to clothing
  - Orientation photograph of damage to clothing
  - Close-ups, with and without scale, of damage to clothing
- Roll the body onto its side and repeat photographs from the back

Unclothed

Photograph the body as it lies from as high an angle as possible (overhead view).

- Upper half of body
- Face, front, right profile, left profile
- Head and shoulders
- Chest and abdomen
- Right upper arm
- Right lower arm
- Right hand (palm and back)
- Left upper arm
- Left lower arm
- Left hand (palm and back)
- Lower half of body
- Abdomen and pelvis
- Right upper leg
- Right lower leg

- Right foot (upper surface and sole)
- Left upper leg
- Left lower leg
- Left foot (upper surface and sole)
- Any bloodstain pattern on body using mapping technique (Figure 9.5)
  - Orientation photograph of discrete bloodstain patterns on clothing
  - Close-ups, with and without scale, of discrete bloodstain patterns on clothing
- Roll the body onto its side and repeat photographs from the back

Identification

Identification photographs should be taken after the associated area is cleaned.

- Photograph of the face.
  - Front
  - Right profile
  - Left profile
- Photograph any obvious scars, marks, or tattoos.
  - All scars, marks, and tattoos should be photographed using the mapping technique described below.
  - All scars, marks, and tattoos should be photographed examination quality.

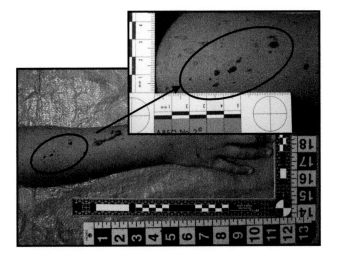

Figure 9.5 Bloodstain pattern mapping on skin.

Photography of Injuries

Injury Photography Guidelines

Injuries

- All injuries are photographed without scale and with scale. No alterations to the injury or clothing are made at this point. Only what is visible is photographed.
- Each injury is photographed in a mapping technique.
- Each injury is photographed in as much detail as possible with an emphasis on demonstrating associated defects, bloodstain flow patterns, bruising, or powder residues and their alignment/ association with the wound.
- Each injury is photographed again when the clothing is removed.
    - Without scale
    - Mapping photography
    - Examination quality
- Each injury is photographed again when the surrounding skin has been cleaned.
    - Examination quality
    - With sharp force injuries, after wound is gently closed to demonstrate size and shape when inflicted

Injuries (Injury Mapping)

Injury mapping involves taking a series of photographs from a general area to detailed examination quality, each with a marker in place from the previous exposure (Figure 9.6). This allows for the body location and wound orientation to be accurately recorded.

- Overall body region with anatomical markers visible (ankle, knee, umbilicus, ear, etc.)
- Overall body region with scale framing body with "zero" oriented towards top of head.
- Body region with ABFO® (American Board of Forensic Odontology) scale framing injury. One arm of the scale should be parallel to the body's midline, the other parallel with the feet.
- Use multiple scales to demonstrate wound clusters (Figure 9.7).
- Sequence shots from general body region to specific body area and then close-up of the injury.
    - Photograph each cluster or individual wound to show its relationship to the body.

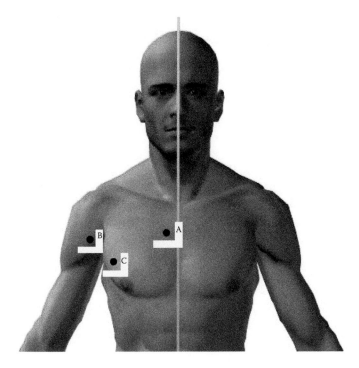

Figure 9.6 Injury mapping. "L"-shaped scales are placed with one arm toward midline, the other toward the feet.

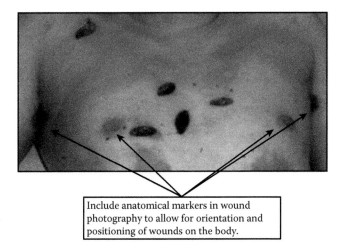

Include anatomical markers in wound photography to allow for orientation and positioning of wounds on the body.

Figure 9.7 Photographing wound clusters. The injuries are photographed in clusters with an anatomical marker visible.

- Photograph each cluster or individual wound to show its relationship to an anatomical marker (umbilicus, nipple, ankle, nose, ear, etc.).
  - Photograph each individual wound using an examination quality photograph. Fill the frame with the wound, orienting the ABFO scale to the edge of the frame (square) (Figure 9.8).
- Lastly, take examination quality photographs with the injury both as it lies and with the edges of a sharp force injury reapproximated (Figure 9.9).

Internal Examination Photographs

- Photograph any areas or organs relating to the cause and manner of death.
- Injuries to internal organs (with and without scale).
- Organs in place within body cavity.
- Organs outside body cavity against clean background (Figure 9.10).
- Wound tracks if ME considers appropriate. Multicolored fiberglass knitting needles serve as effective wound probes and are very easy to clean.
- Frame and compose photographs with minimal extraneous views of blood and internal organs. One objective may be to get a clean, detailed photograph of the injury that will be admissible in court. Excessive blood or views of the body cavity may preclude that.

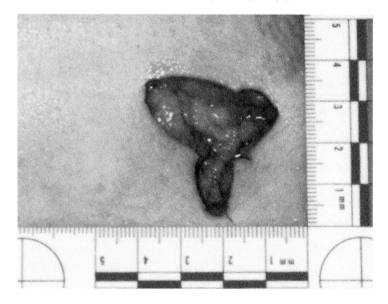

Figure 9.8 Examination quality photograph of wound. The injuries are photographed close-up, framed by the "L"-shaped scale (stab wound to abdomen).

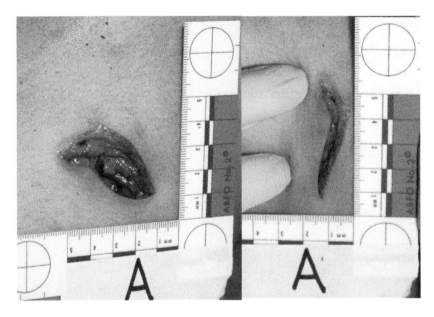

Figure 9.9 Photographing sharp force injury after re-approximating wound edges (stab wound to abdomen).

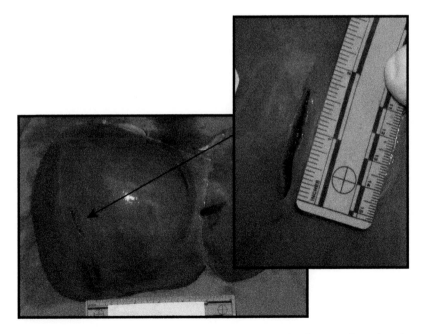

Figure 9.10 Photographing injury to internal organs (stab wounds to liver).

Evidence Photographs

- All clothing of the deceased
- All clothing items and personal effects showing bloodstains, bullet defects, sharp force defects, or other forensic evidence (using mapping technique)
- All personal effects of the deceased (Figure 9.11)
- Items of evidence removed from the body, in place if possible, and close-up

Custody of Evidence from Autopsy

Evidence to be taken into custody must be documented on the required chain-of-custody document and properly packaged and sealed.

- Evidence items that are wet or contain biological stains may be temporarily protected by butcher paper and packaged in plastic (no more than 2 hours) until they can be properly dried.
- Avoid taking custody personal effects of the deceased that have no bearing on the investigation, for example, wedding ring, watch,

Figure 9.11 Photograph of clothing and personal affects.

wallet, and jewelry. Entering them into the evidence custody system may prevent their timely return to the family or availability for interment with the deceased.

Outbrief with Medical Examiner

Discuss time frame for receiving photographs and preliminary and final autopsy results. Ask specific questions:

- What is the preliminary determination of cause and manner of death?
- Is there anything unique about the wound dynamics to indicate whether the perpetrator was right- or left-handed? Can you tell what hand the perpetrator used to wield the weapon?
- Can the wounds identify the weapon?
- If injuries are sharp, blunt, or indicate chopping, can the general type of weapon be identified? Can specific physical characteristics of the perpetrator be determined?
- If a firearm was involved, can the type of firearm and caliber or ammunition type be identified?
- Can the muzzle-to-victim distance be determined by the wound characteristics?
- Was the victim capable of purposeful movement after the injury?
- Could the victim have moved or continued to respond to the attack after injury?
- Can the victim's proximity to the suspect at the time of wounding be determined? Was the victim's back turned? Was he or she on the ground?
- Prepare other questions that may assist in identifying a perpetrator or weapon.

Recovery of Human Remains III

Searching for Human Remains

10

This chapter deals with ground searches for human remains. It covers general search techniques and guidelines for searches of open ground and wooded areas. Detailed guidance for surface recoveries, buried remains, and aquatic recoveries are provided in subsequent chapters.

Isolating a Search Area

Prior to searching for human remains, the area in which to search must be established. This may be dictated by the investigation, statements, or confessions or may be left to the deductive ability of the investigator.

- Insects drawn to the decomposing body may indicate the search area in a heavily wooded or overgrown area. As an example, a swarm of flies in an area may indicate a logical search area.
- Scavenger activities may aid in location of a body.
  - Vultures or other carrion eaters either circling in the air or on the ground may indicate a logical search area.
  - In wilderness areas, fire watch personnel may be asked to assist in spotting circling scavengers.
- If the body is believed to have been disposed of in a wilderness area, investigate the point of origin of any wildfires.
- Cadaver dogs are trained to recognize scents from early decomposition through skeletonization. They are effective for searching large areas for surface remains or expedient burial sites (Figure 10.1).
- Forward-looking infrared allows an area to be scanned to detect differences in temperature that may identify human remains (Figure 10.2).
  - Typically mounted on a helicopter or fixed-wing aircraft or drone.
  - Detects the elevated temperature of a body during decomposition.
  - Entomological activity, particularly the presence of maggot masses, may increase the temperature of areas of the body even to the point of mid-decomposition changes.

Figure 10.1 K9 Panda with handler Ronda Bowser. Cadaver dogs are capable of searching over both land and water.

Figure 10.2 Forward-looking infrared (FLIR) unit attached to a drone allows for economical deployment technology. Photograph courtesy of dronenerds.com.

- Thermal tomography units also detect temperature differences (Figure 10.3).
    - Typically portable or handheld units may also be mounted on an aircraft or drone.
    - Detects the elevated temperature of a body during decomposition.
    - Entomological activity, particularly the presence of maggot masses, may increase the temperature of areas of the body even to the point of mid-decomposition changes.
- NecroSearch International is a volunteer multidisciplinary team dedicated to assisting law enforcement to locate clandestine graves and recover evidence (including human remains) from them. Its website is www.necrosearch.com.

Scientific Assistance

- *Forensic anthropologist*: These specialists may be sufficiently familiar with an area to advise on unmarked graves, historical graves, or native burial mounds. Storms, erosion, and construction may cause disinterment of these and other remains. Forensic anthropologists can advise on appropriate search methodologies. When an area containing scattered remains is located, they can expertly guide

Figure 10.3 M12 thermal imaging unit. Photograph courtesy of L-3 Wescam.

the recovery while ensuring appropriate methods and complete documentation. They can determine whether scattered remains are human or nonhuman.

- *Botanist*: A botanist from a local university may be able to determine how long flora may have taken to become established within an area. They may be able to note differences or disturbances in the vegetative life cycle that might indicate buried remains.

General Search Guidelines

- The most time-consuming search is generally the most thorough one.
- All items that may have evidentiary value should be noted.
- Items that you would expect to see and are not present should also be noted.
- The search method or pattern chosen must be methodical.
- The most logical method should adapt to the unique aspects of the search area.

Specific Search Guidelines

- For guidance on surface recoveries, refer to Chapter 11.
- For guidance on recovering buried remains, refer to Chapter 12.
- For guidance on aquatic recoveries, refer to Chapter 13.

Point-to-Point Search

- Use this technique as soon as a body is discovered to search the area between first observation and location of the body.
- Direct movement to the body while searching and clearing a path along the way.
- The path cleared should avoid the perpetrator's suspected path of travel, both ingress and egress (Figure 10.4).

Line Search

- A group of searchers in line and standing slightly closer than arm's width apart methodically move through the area to be searched in a straight line (Figure 10.5).

Figure 10.4 Point-to-point search pattern. Allows the investigator to clear a working path of travel to the body with the least likelihood of disturbing evidence.

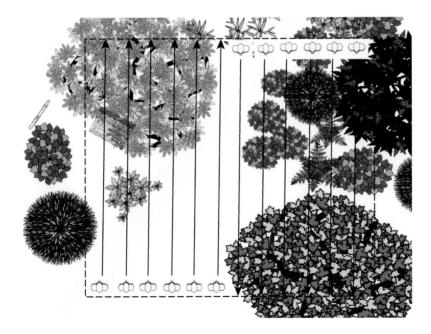

Figure 10.5 Line search patterns.

- After an initial search, it may be necessary to repeat the process on hands and knees.
- A third search may be necessary to clear the ground in front of the searchers to bare earth as they move forward.

Grid Search

- This is the most effective visual search technique.
- A line search doubles back over itself at right angles to the first search (Figure 10.6).
- The search may be repeated with an increased degree of scrutiny on each pass.

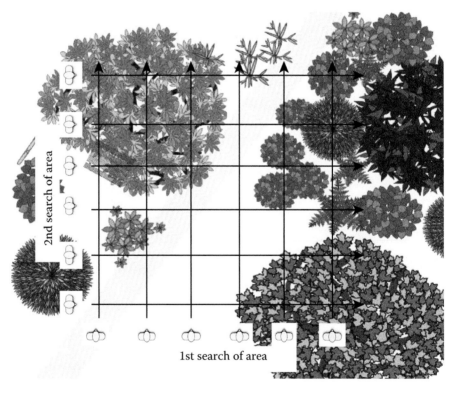

Figure 10.6 Grid search pattern.

Spiral Search

- The search is conducted by spiraling out from a central area of interest.
- It may be effective underwater or when moving from an area of known evidence in an unconfined space (Figure 10.7).

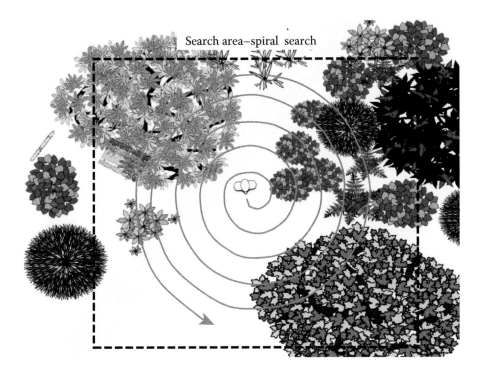

Figure 10.7 Spiral search method.

Surface Recovery of Human Remains

Open Field Recovery and Expedient Graves

11

General Principles

The recovery of human remains from an expedient grave or surface find is a time-consuming and exacting task. Rather than being confined within a grave, the body is left on the surface of the ground or loosely covered with soil, brush, or other items and allowed to decompose. This may be intentional—the result of "dumping" a body; accidental, for example, resulting from an undiscovered aircraft accident; or simply the result of a natural death in an isolated location. Usually the discovery of the body is delayed.

If decomposition is minimal, a body may remain relatively articulated and confined to a small area. Through skeletonization, animal predation, and other events, the body may become disarticulated and spread over a considerable area.

Worksheets and Documentation

The following documentation guides, forms, logs, and worksheets are provided in Section VIII, "Death Investigation Checklist and Worksheets," and may be used in documenting this scene. Additional forms, other than those noted, may also be used, as dictated by your scene. These forms may be preprinted from the publisher's website (www.crcpress.com/cw/maloney) or photocopied from this procedural guide.

- *Death Investigation Checklist*
  - Section 1: Crime Scene Information
  - Section 2: Civilians Who Entered the Death Scene
  - Section 3: Death Scene
  - Section 4: Coroner/Medical Examiner Notification
  - Section 8: Body Found in Open Area
  - Section 10: Identification/Notification
  - Section 11: Scene Processing
  - Section 12: Death Scene Release Information
  - Section 13: Narrative Report
  - Section 14: (appropriate forms and logs)

- *Worksheets*
  - Worksheet 1: Postmortem Indicator (PMI)
  - Worksheet 2: Death Scene Entry Log
  - Worksheet 3: Photography Head Slate
  - Worksheet 4: Photography Log
  - Worksheet 7: Entomology Worksheet
  - Worksheet 9: Trace Evidence Notes

Locating Remains

Visual Techniques

- Insect and scavenger activities may aid in location of a body, for example, a swarm of flies over an area or the presence of turkey vultures or other carrion eaters.
- A grid search pattern is effective for locating body parts or skeletal remains.
- Remember, the body was transported where it was found. Follow foot and vehicle paths and concentrate on areas off the paths because it is difficult to carry a body a great distance from a trail or road.
- Remains may be scattered or concentrated based on the extent of decomposition and animal predation.
- A skull may be disassociated from its body if a canine moves it to chew or play with it. Search windfalls and other areas where a canine can protect its back while chewing.
- In parks or areas near residences, consider searching neighborhood yards, especially those where dogs are unattended and allowed to run off leash.
- Other methods will be discussed below.

Cadaver Dogs

Cadaver dogs undergo highly specialized training. They differ from search-and-rescue dogs and bloodhounds in that they are trained to detect human body decomposition, not follow living human scents (Figure 11.1).

- Cadaver dogs are trained to recognize scents from early decomposition through skeletonization.
- Cadaver dogs are effective for searching large areas for surface remains.
- When selecting a cadaver dog team, it is important to ensure they have proper training and review their training records.

Figure 11.1 K9 Nexus, trained by handler Scott Lee, conducting an open-ground/buried remains search after the Oso, Washington, mud slide in 2014.

Forward-Looking Infrared and Thermal Tomography

Forward-looking infrared (FLIR) allows an area to be scanned to detect differences in temperature that may identify human remains. Decomposition of the body and entomological activity, particularly the presence of maggot masses, may increase the temperature of areas of the body even to the point of mid-decomposition changes. The temperature of a body during decomposition is elevated above the ambient temperature and may be detected by FLIR (often mounted on a helicopter or fixed-wing aircraft) or via a portable thermography unit. This technique is most effective for surface recoveries and expedient graves.

NecroSearch International

NecroSearch International is a volunteer multidisciplinary team dedicated to assisting law enforcement to locate clandestine graves and recover evidence (including human remains) from them. Its website is www.necrosearch.com.

Body Processing

- If a body is not yet skeletonized and scattered, process it based on the manner of death as described in Chapters 2 through 5.
- Ensure that entomological evidence is collected.
- Preserve impression evidence leading to or from the body location.
- Collect, sift, and collect any evidence from beneath the body.

Scene Processing

- When the body location is discovered, all efforts to minimize foot and vehicle traffic should be made until a search for footwear impressions and tire tracks are made.
- A safe path to the body should be established and marked for access to the body.
- A safe site for soil sifting and debris staging should be established close to the body but far enough removed to protect any evidence associated with the site.

Establishing Datum

- A site datum is a known location in three-dimensional space established to serve as a reference point for all horizontal and vertical measurements taken at the scene.
- Establish the datum at the southwest limit of a site (Figure 11.2).

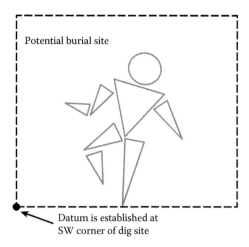

Potential burial site

Datum is established at
SW corner of dig site

Figure 11.2 Establishing a datum reference point.

- Mark the datum by driving a piece of rebar or other marker into the ground, leaving at least a foot of the material above the surface. When the site is completely measured, the rebar may be driven completely into the ground for later relocation with a metal detector.
- Fix the location of the datum with GPS coordinates or by association with fixed references.
- Mark a reference elevation height on the datum. The reference should be leveled with the highest ground in the search area (Figure 11.3).

For Expedient Graves

- Each layer of brush or refuse covering the body must be documented as it is removed.
- Each item composing the layer should be considered for fingerprints, touch DNA, and two-dimensional footwear impressions. If detected, process accordingly.
- When the body has been exposed or is only covered by a shallow layer of soil, move to the next section to establish a grid.

Establishing a Grid

- Use a compass to establish a north–south line from the datum. Stake this line at the northernmost part of the recovery area.
- Use a compass to establish an east–west line from the datum. Stake this line at the easternmost part of the recovery area.
- Build out the square for the grid, ensuring that all corners are 90 degrees and based on the north–south line (Figure 11.4).
- Divide the grid into logically sized squares. Squares should be large enough to allow movement within them as the evidence is recovered and documented. It is recommended that squares measure 3 feet on each side (Figure 11.5).

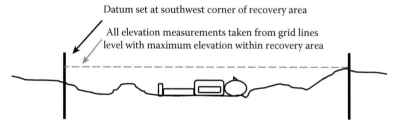

Datum set at southwest corner of recovery area

All elevation measurements taken from grid lines level with maximum elevation within recovery area

Figure 11.3 Establishing elevation for recovery documentation.

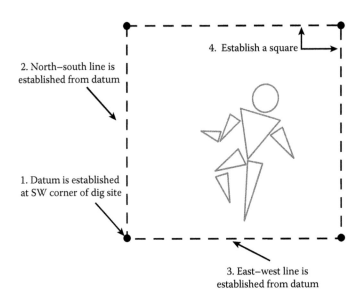

Figure 11.4 Establishing a square by running north–south and east–west lines from the datum point.

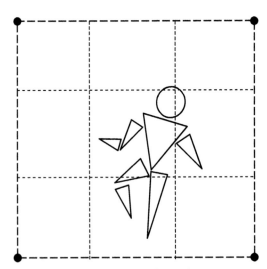

Establish a grid system. Three-foot grid squares are recommended though the size may be adjusted to the search area and terrain.

Figure 11.5 Establishing grid squares.

- When attaching the surveyor's string to the grid stakes, the string should be hung level with the initial mark on the datum indicating the highest point of ground at the site. This may be accomplished with a simple line level.
- Grid squares are identified from the datum by the number of squares north followed by the number of squares east (Figure 11.6).

Surface Documentation and Recovery of Evidence

- Conduct a thorough surface search using the grid method if practical.
- Initial search may involve flagging and documenting all obvious remains or items of evidentiary value. Care must be taken to locate footwear and tire impressions (the body had to be moved to the site and the perpetrator had to leave it).
- Conduct a secondary search on hands and knees to flag and document any remains or items of evidentiary value not revealed during the initial standing search.
- A tertiary search on hands and knees involves removing all vegetation, clearing the ground to bare soil, and flagging and documenting remains or evidence revealed.

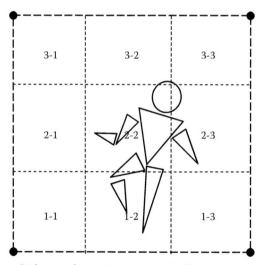

Grid square designations are numerically assigned: The first number reflects the number of grid squares north from the datum and the second number reflects the number of grid squares east of the datum.

Figure 11.6 Designating grid squares.

- Vegetation grows at predictable rates in a given area. Consider documenting plant growth and roots that have grown over the surface remains.
- A botanist familiar with the area to be searched may be able to tell you how long a surface find remained undisturbed.

Recovery of Remains

- All skeletal or body parts should be flagged.
- If a body part is found outside the central search grid, the grid may be extended (if not isolated and disassociated) or the find may be marked by GPS and/or measured by polar coordinates to the datum.
- The body part is photographed in place.
- Loose debris on top of the part should be removed.
- The body part is photographed again, without and with scale.
- The body part location is noted on the overall sketch.
- The body part should be described only in general terms (e.g., small bone fragment, long bone, flat bone, rib bone). Do not be more specific at this stage.
- Note and photograph any obvious defects. Do not attempt to differentiate animal chew marks, cut marks, skull fractures, or bullet holes at this stage. Note their presence; they will require follow-up after examination of the remains by a medical examiner or forensic anthropologist.
- Body parts should be packaged in appropriate containers.

Sifting Soil

- Soil beneath where the body was found should be sifted. The area is easily identified by the presence of grouped vertebrae, ribs, scapula, pelvis, and other bones. Some animal predation may have disassociated bones from the grouping.
- The sifting area should be close enough to the discovery site to allow easy transport of material and communications between team members (Figure 11.7).
- Sifting should be accomplished with successively finer mesh sieves; 1/2, 1/4, and 1/8 inch meshes are most often used.
- Always sift over a clean tarp. Soil should be sifted through progressively finer meshes.

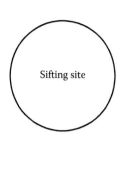

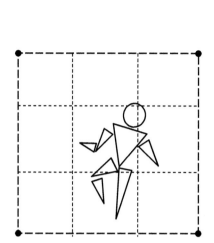

Figure 11.7 Setting up sifting site.

Soil Evidence

- Soil samples may be used to link a suspect with a burial scene. Soil samples from the suspect's shoes, tires, wheel wells, or clothing may be examined and compared to the samples taken from the scene.
- Soil samples should be taken from the beneath the body once the body is removed.
- Soil samples should be taken from the area surrounding the gravesite.

Scientific Assistance

Forensic anthropologist: This expert is invaluable for examining buried remains. He or she can quickly determine the sex, approximate age, and general characteristics of a victim. These specialists may be sufficiently familiar with an area to advise on unmarked graves, historical graves, or native burial mounds. Storms, erosion, and construction may cause disinterment of these and other remains. Forensic anthropologists can advise on appropriate search methodologies. When an area containing scattered remains is located, they can expertly guide the recovery while ensuring appropriate methods and complete documentation. They can determine whether scattered remains are human or nonhuman.

Botanist: A botanist from a local university may be able to determine how long flora may have taken to become established within remains. For instance, a vine growing through the eye orbit of a skull that indicates 3 months of growth means the skull was completely skeletonized at least 3 months earlier. A botanist may assist in determining postmortem intervals for skeletonized remains. It is important to engage an appropriately qualified professional who can testify in court if necessary.

Ornithologist: An individual who studies birds may help recover biological evidence. Birds may have used the hair from a victim to line their nests. An ornithologist familiar with the area will be able to guide an investigator to the types of bird likely to build such nests and locate nests within the area. He or she should have appropriate qualifications and be capable of testifying in court if necessary.

Mammalogist or zoologist: Someone familiar with the behavior of small animals indigenous to the discovery site can help locate and explore small rodent holes that are excellent hiding places for rings, small bones, or other artifacts of a crime. Again, you should locate an appropriately trained professional who can appear in court if necessary.

Recovery of Buried Human Remains

12

Shallow Grave, Buried Remains, and Exhumation

General Principles

The location of clandestine graves and recovery of human remains are time-consuming tasks that often require specialized assistance and equipment. Buried remains may be classified as follows:

- *Expedient graves*: Often located in natural or man-made shallow depressions and loosely covered with soil scraped from the surface. They are often hastily covered with vegetation, leaves, and limbs from the immediate area. Covered in Chapter 11, "Surface Recovery of Human Remains."
- *Shallow graves*: Hastily dug shallow depressions; only inches of soil cover the remains.
- *Buried remains*: Characterized by depth. No exact depth determines the difference between a shallow grave and a burial, but the depth and corresponding effort required to reach buried remains call for an approach different from uncovering a shallow grave. The significant digging by hand or machine required to bury the body requires similar effort by investigators.
- *Interment of remains*: This differs from even deep burial, as it is formalized and part of the death ritual within a society as compared to disposing of the body from a crime. It involves a casket and often a vault and may occur subsurface or on the surface in a mausoleum or lawn crypt.
- *Exhumation*: The removal of remains, usually under court order, from a cemetery or formal burial site. This burial includes a casket and vault buried beneath the earth at a depth prescribed by local law or custom or within an above ground, mausoleum or lawn crypt.

Worksheets and Documentation

The following documentation guides, forms, logs, and worksheets are provided in Section VIII, "Death Investigation Checklist and Worksheets," and may be used in documenting this scene. Additional forms, other than those noted, may also be used as dictated by your scene. These forms may be pre-printed from the publisher's website (www.crcpress.com/cw/maloney) or photocopied from this procedural guide.

- *Death Investigation Checklist*
  - Section 1: Death Scene Information
  - Section 2: Civilians Who Entered the Death Scene
  - Section 3: Death Scene
  - Section 4: Coroner/Medical Examiner Notification
  - Section 8: Body Found in Open Area
  - Section 10: Identification/Notification
  - Section 11: Scene Processing
  - Section 12: Death Scene Release Information
  - Section 13: Narrative Report
  - Section 14: (appropriate forms and logs)
- *Worksheets*
  - Worksheet 1: Postmortem Indicator (PMI)
  - Worksheet 2: Death Scene Entry Log
  - Worksheet 3: Photography Head Slate
  - Worksheet 4: Photography Log
  - Worksheet 7: Entomology Worksheet
  - Worksheet 8: Biological Evidence Notes
  - Worksheet 9: Trace Evidence Notes
  - Worksheet 11: Impression Evidence Notes

Locating Remains

Visual Methods

Expedient Grave Indicators
- Insect and scavenger activities, for example, swarms of flies over an area or circling of turkey vultures or other carrion eaters at the site
- Dead or dying vegetation that was pulled to cover a grave

Shallow Grave Indicators
- Disturbed vegetation and soil
- Color change of grass or other vegetation over a grave
- Depressed area in the soil caused by decomposition of the abdomen and subsequent caving in of soil

Buried Remains Indicators
- Indications of disturbed vegetation and soil
- Mounded soil over a relatively fresh grave

- Depressed area of an older grave caused by soil settling and compaction
- Inconsistent vegetation growth

Exhumation Site Location

- The exhumation of human remains is accomplished from a formal grave or internment site.
- Typically, public records are available to identify the exact location of the grave.
- These records should be thoroughly researched for accuracy, as the site will most likely be specified on the legal order for exhumation.

Probing Method

- A T-shaped metal or fiberglass-probing rod is used. Caution must be exercised at a shallow grave to prevent damage to the body when the rod is inserted (Figure 12.1).
- Several investigators with probing rods should stand shoulder width apart and position themselves in a line that will move forward over the suspected gravesite.
- Starting well before the expected gravesite (in order to get the feel of the soil resistance), they insert the probe into the soil at the toe of their left shoe, then the center of their body, and then the toe of their right shoe. They then step forward as a unit (Figure 12.2).
- They repeat this process, probing the soil as they move forward.
- When they note a change in the soil's resistance to probing (less resistance; the probe will slip into the soil more easily), they should stop and observe the ground features to determine whether the grave exhibits a natural outline.
- They should use the probes to gently determine the borders of the grave and use marker flags to clearly demarcate the borders until the outline of the entire grave is marked.

Cadaver Dogs

Cadaver dogs undergo highly specialized training. They differ from search-and-rescue dogs and bloodhounds in that they are trained to detect human body decomposition, not follow living human scents.

- Cadaver dogs are trained to recognize scents from early decomposition through skeletonization.

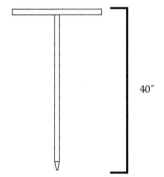

40″

Figure 12.1 "T" probe.

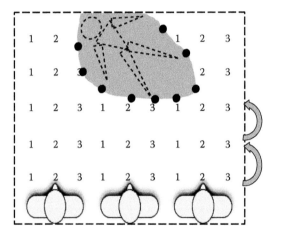

Align the team each with a probe in a line search pattern.
In unison probe left (1), center (2), and right (3).
Then step forward repeating the probing sequence.

Probing straight down
"feeling" for change in
resistance or looser soil.

Figure 12.2 "T"-probe technique.

- Cadaver dogs are effective for searching for expedient, shallow, buried, or submerged remains.
- When selecting a cadaver dog team, it is important to ensure proper training and review training records.

Technological Methods

Methane gas detection: A body produces methane gas as it decomposes. In a clandestine grave, the gas is trapped beneath the ground or slowly leaches up through the ground. The leaching gas may be located by a methane

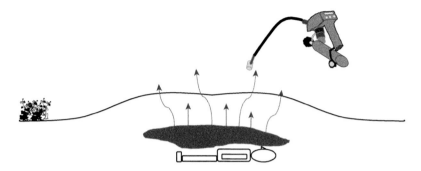

Figure 12.3 Methane gas detector.

detector (Figure 12.3) used with a probing rod slipped beneath the surface at a suspected clandestine grave. Care should always be taken to avoid damaging the body by overly aggressive insertion of a probe.

FLIR and thermal tomography: FLIR allows an area to be scanned to detect differences in temperature that may identify human remains. Decomposition of the body and entomological activity, particularly the presence of maggot masses, may increase the temperature of areas of the body even to the point of mid-decomposition changes. The temperature of a body during decomposition is elevated above the ambient temperature and may be detected by FLIR (often mounted on a helicopter or fixed-wing aircraft) or via a portable thermography unit. This technique is most effective for surface recoveries and expedient graves.

Magnetometry: A magnetometer detects the magnetic fields of buried ferrous (iron-containing) objects. While magnetometry will not detect a body in a grave, it may reveal ferrous artifacts buried with the body, for example, zippers, shoe eyelets, belt buckles, snaps, and weapons containing iron.

Electrical resistivity: As fluids from a body leach into the surrounding soil as a natural result of decomposition, they alter the ability for an electrical current to pass through the ground. A survey of the level of electrical resistance in the soil of an area suspected to contain a clandestine grave may indicate decomposition. This method is best used when late decomposition changes are present.

Scientific Assistance

Forensic anthropologist: This expert is invaluable for examining buried remains. He or she can determine the sex, approximate age, and general characteristics of a victim. These specialists may be sufficiently familiar with an area to advise about unmarked graves, historical graves, or native burial mounds. Storms, erosion, and construction may cause disinterment of these and other remains. Forensic anthropologists can advise on appropriate search methodologies. When an area containing scattered remains is located, they can expertly guide the recovery while ensuring appropriate methods and complete documentation.

Botanist: A botanist from a local university may be able to determine how long flora may have taken to become established over a burial site. Additionally, he or she may be able to assist in determining the amount of time it would have taken for root intrusion into a burial site. A botanist may assist in determining interment intervals for buried remains. It is important to engage an appropriately qualified professional who can testify in court if necessary.

NecroSearch International

This voluntary multidisciplinary team is dedicated to assisting law enforcement in locating clandestine graves and recovering evidence (including human remains) from them. Its website is www.necrosearch.com.

Recovery of Buried Remains

Surface Documentation and Recovery of Evidence

- Conduct a thorough surface search using the grid method if practical.
- The initial search on foot involves flagging and documenting all obvious remains and items of evidentiary value. Care must be taken to locate any footwear or tire impressions (the body had to be moved to the site and the perpetrator had to leave it).
- A secondary search is conducted on hands and knees, while also flagging and documenting all obvious remains and items of evidentiary value.
- A tertiary search is also conducted on hands and knees. Vegetation must be removed to reveal bare soil. All obvious remains and items of evidentiary value should be flagged and documented.
- Vegetation grows at predictable rates in a given area. Consider documenting plant growth and roots encountered during excavation at a gravesite.
- A botanist familiar with the area to be searched may be able to tell you how long a grave remained undisturbed.

Surface Preparation

Establishing Datum

- A site datum is a known location in three-dimensional space established to serve as a reference point for all horizontal and vertical measurements taken at the scene.

- Establish the datum at the southwest limit of a site (Figure 12.4).
- Mark the datum by driving a piece of rebar or other marker into the ground, leaving at least a foot of the material above the surface. When the site is completely measured, the rebar may be driven completely into the ground for later relocation with a metal detector.
- Fix the location of the datum with GPS coordinates or by association with fixed references.
- Mark a reference elevation height on the datum. The reference should be level with the highest ground in the search area (Figure 12.5).

Establishing Grid

- Use a compass to establish a north–south line from the datum. Stake this line at the northernmost part of the recovery area (Figure 12.6).
- Use a compass to establish an east–west line from the datum. Stake this line at the easternmost part of the recovery area (Figure 12.6).

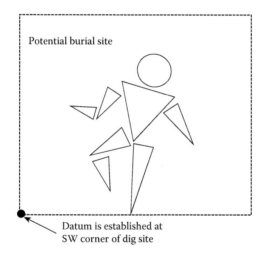

Figure 12.4 Establishing a datum reference point.

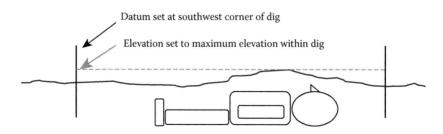

Figure 12.5 Establishing elevation for recovery documentation.

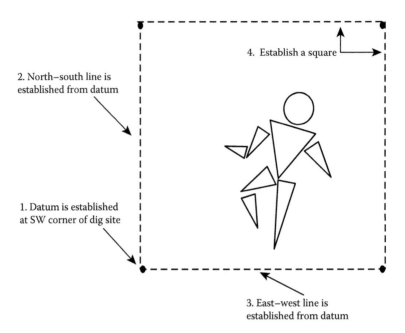

Figure 12.6 Establishing a square by running north–south and east–west lines from the datum point.

- Build out the square for the grid, ensuring that all corners are 90 degrees and based on the north–south line.
- Divide the grid into logically sized squares. Squares should be large enough to allow movement within them as the earth is excavated. It is recommended that squares at a subsurface measure 3 feet on each side (Figure 12.7).
- When attaching the surveyor's string to the stakes, the string should be hung level with the initial mark on the datum indicating the highest point of ground at the site. This may be accomplished with a simple line level (Figure 12.8).
- Grid squares are identified from the datum by the number of squares north followed by the number of squares east (Figure 12.9).

Preparing Sifting Site

- The sifting area should be close enough to the discovery site to allow easy transport of material and communications between team members (Figure 12.10).
- Sifting should be accomplished with successively finer mesh sieves; 1/2, 1/4, and 1/8 inch meshes are most often used.
- Always sift over a clean tarp. Soil should be sifted through progressively finer meshes.

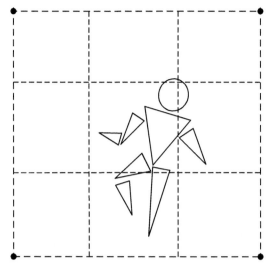

Establish a grid system. Three-foot grid squares are
recommended though the size may be adjusted
to the search area and terrain.

Figure 12.7 Establishing grid squares.

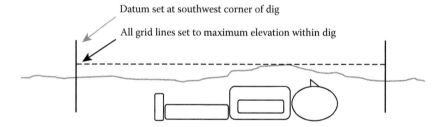

Datum set at southwest corner of dig

All grid lines set to maximum elevation within dig

Figure 12.8 Setting the grid to the elevation.

Excavating the Grave

- Excavating should start only after ground search and preparation
  are complete. Do not rush this phase. Ensure that you have prepared
  the site properly and have the proper equipment and personnel to
  perform the excavation.
- All vegetation should have been removed during ground preparation. Soil is then removed in thin layers (no more than an inch deep)
  from the target grid squares. The soil should be removed using a
  masonry trowel, placed into a scoop, and transported for sifting.
- When troweling, keep the trowel edge at a low angle to the ground to
  prevent gouging the floor of the unit.

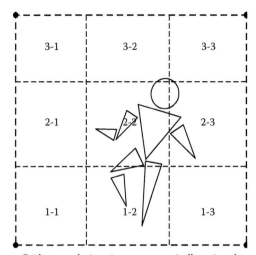

Grid square designations are numerically assigned:
The first number reflects the number of grid squares
north from the datum and the second number
reflects the number of grid squares east of the datum

Figure 12.9 Designating grid squares.

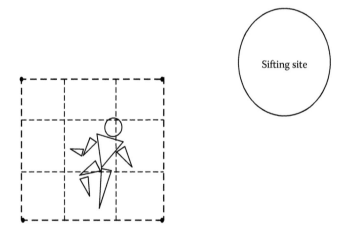

Figure 12.10 Locating and setting up a sifting site.

- Work carefully to remove thin layers of soil to preserve natural margins or edges of the grave.
- As soon as a body part, bone, or other evidence item is discovered in a grid square, digging must stop. Photograph the item *in situ*. The soil around the find and additional soil from the grid square should be removed with a whiskbroom and swept into a scoop.
- Reveal the bone or body part by removing the soil around it.

- As you approach the bone or other item, replace the whiskbroom with a paintbrush to allow careful excavation around the item.
- The item should be maximally or fully exposed and photographed again. Measurements within the grid square and depth of the recovery as measured from the datum point should be recorded (Figure 12.11).
- The find area should be extended into adjacent grid squares. Follow the procedure of completely excavating to one depth across the find area before excavating deeper.
- Additional finds should be photographed and documented as well. Their spatial relationships to other finds should be clearly shown and documented.
- When it becomes necessary to remove a bone or other item, it may be helpful to place it on a Tyvek suit that has been spread out next to the excavation. This is a very effective way to allow anyone with even a rudimentary understanding of anatomy to see what body parts and items have been recovered and which ones have not been found (Figure 12.12).

Sifting Soil

- All sifted excavated material must be identified by its grid square.
- Material is placed in the sieve and shaken until only refuse remains. The refuse is examined for evidentiary value.
- The process is repeated using progressively smaller mesh sieves.
- All items of evidentiary value are documented and associated with the grid square and depth from which the excavated material came.

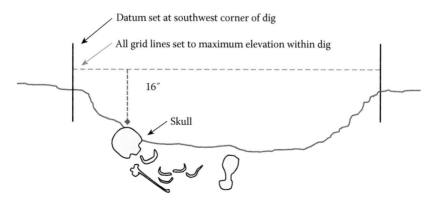

Figure 12.11 Documenting the depth of recovery.

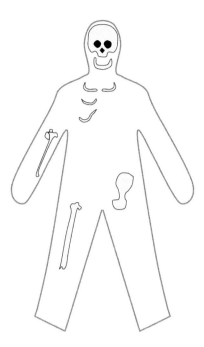

Figure 12.12 Using a protective suite as a template for bone inventory.

Impression Evidence

- A person who places a body in a shallow or deep grave may find it necessary to stand in the grave while digging or manipulating the body. Footwear impressions may be left on the floor of the grave, perhaps under the body. Careful excavation may reveal these impressions.
- Digging creates multiple tool marks. The shape of a shovel, spade, or other digging tool may be impressed and left at the margins or walls of a grave. This area is the interface between the harder compacted soil external to the grave and the softer soil that was removed and replaced into the grave. The shape of the tool used to dig may be apparent on the walls at this margin.
- Additional tool marks may be present where a digging tool cut through roots. These marks should be preserved if indicated.

Soil Evidence

- Soil samples may be used to link a suspect with a burial scene. Soil samples from the suspect's shoes, tires, wheel wells, or clothing may be examined and compared to the samples taken from the scene.
- Soil samples should be taken from the area surrounding the gravesite.
- Soil samples should be taken from the bottom or floor of the gravesite.

Exhumation of Remains

- General considerations
  - Consider planning the exhumation as early as possible during a weekday to limit outside interest (including that of the media).
  - Know what you are looking for prior to exhumation.
  - Know what samples you will need and ensure you have the proper equipment to collect and preserve them.
  - Expect unique circumstances due to degradation and decomposition.
  - Ensure you coordinate with laboratories to ensure the samples you seize are collected in a manner such that they can be tested.
  - Based upon body processing during embalming or other processes, anticipate the condition of the body.
  - Based upon the interment site, anticipate grave wax, water intrusion into vault, etc., and its effect on the body.
- Administrative
  - Ensure you have the proper legal authority for the exhumation of the body. This may mean a court order and/or permission from the family.
  - Ensure you have proper passage documents if the body is to be moved through another ME's jurisdiction.
  - Arrange with the ME for reautopsy and collection of evidence.
  - Arrange for transportation of the body to the ME's facility and for return and reinterment.
  - Coordinate with local law enforcement if the body is out of your jurisdiction.
  - Coordinate with the proprietors of the burial site to determine what equipment is available, what functions will be accomplished by their staff, and what costs may be incurred.
  - Obtain dental records of deceased, if available, for ease of dental identification at autopsy.
  - Optional confirmatory identification methods may involve available x-rays, known tattoos, and DNA samples from immediate family members.
  - Coordinate to have a forensic odontologist available at the autopsy for identification.
- Scene
  - Locate grave site.
  - Confirm gravesite. It is highly recommended that cemetery records be reviewed and confirmed with any grave marker.
  - Document site prior to digging.

- Document each stage of the exterment.
- Document removal of the coffin from the vault.
- If looking for heavy metal poisoning or natural poisons, consider soil samples from the grave depth to prove that the poisons were present in the tissue at death and did not leach in from soil or groundwater contamination.
- Autopsy
  - Document breaking of the seal of the coffin (preferred to be done at ME's office).
  - Using prepopulated dental records, have the forensic odontologist identify the remains.
  - If dental identification is not possible, consider identification through radiographic comparison with predeath radiographs, if available.
  - Latent fingerprint comparison with premortem records may be possible with a skilled print examiner.
  - Advanced techniques may be employed to maximize the potential recovery of prints from the deceased.
  - These techniques often have the potential to degrade the skin and limit the possibility of second or third attempts using different techniques.
  - Coordination between the ME and an advanced latent print specialist with experience in this type of recovery is recommended.
- Document as standard autopsy (Chapter 9, "Autopsy Protocol and the Investigator's Role").

Aquatic Recovery of Human Remains

13

General Principles

This chapter focuses on search and recovery techniques when a body is in water. In most cases, a body is submerged in a pond, lake, river, or saltwater environment. Under no circumstances should anyone without proper training attempt an aquatic search or recovery mission. A well-equipped aquatic search team is required to ensure the safety of the members of the operation and achieve a successful recovery that is appropriately documented.

A DSI must be versed in the techniques employed in water recovery and play a part in the effort. A submerged body will often hold valuable evidence that must be properly handled upon recovery. A DSI who is familiar with the techniques and technology of water recovery may also help narrow the team's search focus.

Worksheets and Documentation

The following documentation guides, forms, logs, and worksheets are provided in Section VIII, "Death Investigation Checklist and Worksheets," and may be used in documenting this scene. Additional forms, other than those noted, may also be used as dictated by your scene. These forms may be preprinted from the publisher's website (www.crcpress.com/cw/maloney) or photocopied from this procedural guide.

- *Death Investigation Checklist*
  - Section 1: Death Scene Information
  - Section 2: Civilians Who Entered the Death Scene
  - Section 3: Death Scene
  - Section 4: Coroner/Medical Examiner Notification
  - Section 6: Body Found in Water
  - Section 10: Identification/Notification
  - Section 11: Scene Processing
  - Section 12: Death Scene Release Information
  - Section 13: Narrative Report
  - Section 14: (appropriate forms and logs)

- *Worksheets*
  - Worksheet 1: Postmortem Indicator (PMI)
  - Worksheet 2: Death Scene Entry Log
  - Worksheet 3: Photography Head Slate
  - Worksheet 4: Photography Log
  - Worksheet 7: Entomology Worksheet
  - Worksheet 8: Biological Evidence Notes
  - Worksheet 9: Trace Evidence Notes
  - Worksheet 14: Bullet Defect Worksheet
  - Worksheet 15: Bloodstain Pattern Worksheet

Locating Remains

Surface Search

- Visual location of remains by scanning the surface of the water is often very difficult. Unless the body is snagged on a limb, rocky prominence, or other feature, it will likely remain submerged early during the search.
- For surface searches from boats or from shore, polarized sunglasses may provide better visualization just below the surface.
- As a body decomposes, subsequent gas formation may cause it to become buoyant and float near the surface. This does not occur until decomposition has progressed and may take days or weeks, depending on the water temperature. The body may return to the surface in a facedown position, with the arms, legs, and head dangling into the water. Often only the shoulder blades and upper back are visible at or near the surface (Figure 13.1).

Aerial Search

- The use of helicopters or other platforms that allow observation by looking down at the surface of the water is very effective and should be employed as soon as practical.
- If a drowning or water burial occurs near a boat ramp or dock with sufficient access, a fire department ladder truck may be helpful for searching the area around the dock.

Underwater Search

Underwater recovery requires specialized training, certification, proper equipment, and familiarity with a specific aquatic environment. It should

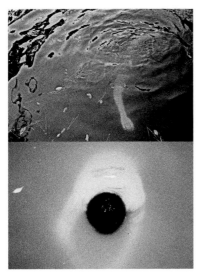

Body floating at surface. Viewed without polarizing lens (sunglasses or camera filter). Note that the reflection from the surface of the water obscures most of the body from view.

Body floating at surface. Viewed with polarizing lens. The reflection from the surface of the water has been eliminated and the body is easier to view.

Figure 13.1 Using a polarizing filter in aquatic recoveries.

never be attempted by sports divers. An underwater search for a body may be conducted by a dive search team and is often most effective if a body is believed to be in or near a submerged vehicle or other container (Figure 13.2).

Benton County Arkansas
Dive/Rescue Team

Figure 13.2 Underwater and aquatic recovery of remains/evidence should be conducted by a trained and properly equipped dive recovery team. Photograph courtesy of Chris Perry, Benton County Arkansas Dive and Rescue Team.

- To search a bottom with multiple snags and other features that may entrap a body, a dive team may be effective for an early search when movement of the body is minimal. Divers must be cautious around the snags and entrapments.
- Open bottom searches may be conducted by a dive team, although they are often less effective unless the search field is limited by observation from a helicopter or by technological methods such as side scanning sonar.
- Underwater visual searches may also be made by video taken from a remote operated vehicle. Such vehicles are portable and controlled by cables. They may be available from local harbor or ship inspection and marine construction facilities.

Drift

- An expert familiar with local waterways such as a marine and fisheries officer, ranger, or marine patrol should be contacted to help determine normal or expected drift from the suspected location of the drowning or submersion.
- Drift may also be observed from the surface, although it is important to remember that currents and water movements may be different beneath the surface at depths where they will affect the body.
- By maintaining neutral buoyancy just above the bottom, search divers may quickly be able to determine the direction or likely movement or drift of a body.

Computer Simulation Modeling

Many navigable waterways and other water bodies supported by the US Army Corps of Engineers, Coast Guard, and state agencies may have computer simulation models available. Although these models were not developed for the recovery of human remains, an adept operator may be able to simulate the conditions from the time since drowning or submersion and the submersion point and greatly narrow the potential search area.

Modeling may also be helpful in cold case recoveries—if a body is believed to have been submerged in a vehicle or other container and a significant amount of time has passed since submersion.

Cadaver Dogs

Cadaver dogs undergo highly specialized training. They differ from search-and-rescue dogs and bloodhounds in that they are trained to detect human

Figure 13.3 K9 Lopez trained by his handler Scott Lee conducts a search for a drowning victim from the prow of a boat.

body decomposition, not follow living human scents. Properly trained cadaver dogs may be used to locate submerged remains. The dog and its boat handler should complete joint training. The dog typically remains at the bow of the boat and alerts the handler when decomposition gases from a body percolate to the surface (Figure 13.3).

Technological Search

Methane gas detection: A body produces methane gas during decomposition. In an aquatic environment, methane will percolate up through the water to the surface and the gas release may be located by a methane detector.

FLIR and thermal tomography: FLIR allows an area to be scanned for differences in temperature that may identify human remains even in water (if at surface). The temperature of a recently drowned body will be higher than the temperature of the surrounding water for some time and it may be possible to detect the body using FLIR mounted on a helicopter or fixed-wing aircraft.

Scanning sonar: The equipment is mounted on a tripod on the bottom of a boat or mounted on a remotely operated vehicle and submerged. Sonar is used to search smaller bodies of water such as ponds, where side scanning sonar equipment could not be effectively towed (Figure 13.4). Sonar provides a 360-degree view of the bottom regardless of water visibility (Figure 13.5).

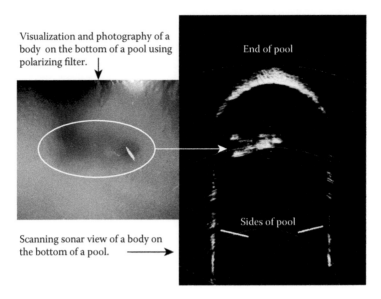

Visualization and photography of a body on the bottom of a pool using polarizing filter.

End of pool

Scanning sonar view of a body on the bottom of a pool.

Sides of pool

Figure 13.4 Body in pool. Sonar image courtesy of Jack Fisher, JW Fishers Underwater Search Equipment.

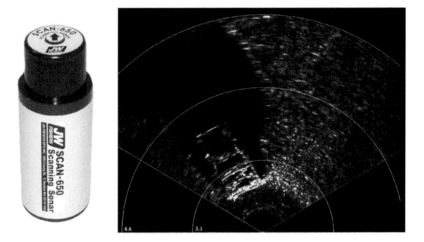

Figure 13.5 Search image from sonar. Photograph and image courtesy of Jack Fisher, JW Fishers Underwater Search Equipment.

Side scanning sonar: The equipment is submerged and towed behind a boat. It emits sonar waves that strike objects and return to the device. The returning waves reveal details of a lake, river, or ocean bottom. Side scanning sonar is useful for finding remains that rest on the bottom. It is not very effective for locating remains along a very rocky or irregular bottom surface or remains covered by silt or debris (Figure 13.6).

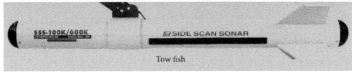

Figure 13.6 Side-scanning sonar. Photograph and image courtesy of Jack Fisher, JW Fishers Underwater Search Equipment.

Magnetometry: A magnetometer detects the magnetic fields of buried ferrous (iron-containing) objects. Magnetometry will not detect a body. It is used to find ferrous artifacts associated with the body (e.g., belt buckle). The technique is very useful if a body may be in or near a submerged vehicle or ferrous container.

Processing the Scene

- If possible, the body should be placed into the body bag at the depth and location of its recovery. This will prevent the loss of associated evidence. Special mesh body bags are available for this purpose (Figure 13.7).
- A recovered body may be moved onto a floating recovery board or basket for removal from the water (Figure 13.7).
- The body should be processed by the standard methods used for nonaquatic recoveries.

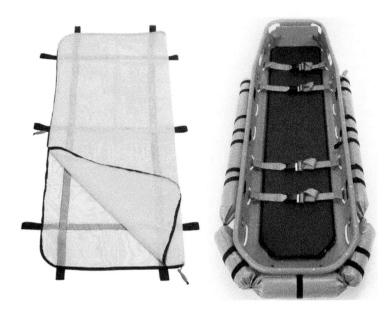

Figure 13.7 Mesh body bag for underwater recovery of remains and rescue basket with floatation collar for removal from water. Body bag photograph courtesy of Extra Packaging, LLC and www.thebodybagstore.com. Basket with floatation collar courtesy of FERNO-Washington.

- Samples of water from the recovery site should be taken.
- If the body is in a submerged vehicle, do not rush recovery! Plan, prepare for, and set up the recovery of the body and vehicle. Both may reveal valuable forensic evidence.
- A body associated with a submerged vehicle or container must be fully documented photographically *before recovery* to the extent visibility allows.
- The process of lifting a submerged vehicle from the bottom will cause many items to shift. To the extent possible, fully photograph a submerged vehicle or container before it is moved.
- Using underwater metal detectors, magnetometers, and visual search techniques, search the area beneath and adjacent to a submerged vehicle or container.
- If a complex recovery of a body in a submerged vehicle or container is required, videotape the recovery with an underwater camera system.
- Any metallic item submerged in water may rapidly oxidize (rust) when exposed to air. Weapons and other vital metallic evidence should be secured while still submerged and placed in a container of the same water without exposure to air. This step may be safely accomplished in shallow water or on a recovery platform over a catch net to prevent loss of items like bullets and cases (Figure 13.8).

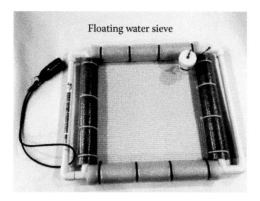

Figure 13.8 Aquatic evidence recovery using a floating water sieve. Photograph courtesy of Sharktoothsifter.com.

Processing the Body

Documenting Recovery

- Record the name of the individual who discovered the body and the names of all those involved in the recovery.
- Obtain a detailed statement from the individual who discovered the body. Record details of the body's position, condition, and location (including depth) where found.
- Photograph the recovery process from the surface.
- If the body is in a vehicle or container or trapped in some way, make every effort to document with underwater photography prior to recovery.

Remains Recovered from Predator

- Human remains have been recovered from the stomachs of marine predators such as sharks.
- If this occurs, immediately coordinate with the ME to attempt to determine whether bite injuries are premortem or postmortem.
- Coordinate with a knowledgeable marine biologist to determine the hunting area of the predator in relation to the location where it was captured.

Postmortem Changes Estimating Postmortem Interval (Time since Death)

14

The only accurate method of determining the time of death is observation by a reliable witness. Evaluating the changes that occur in a body after death may help you estimate the time since death, also known as the *postmortem interval*. Physiological changes since death may be observed at a scene and generally indicate the time since death. Careful observations of these changes should be recorded at the scene and presented to the ME, who may be able to determine a far more accurate postmortem interval than could be determined from scene indicators alone.

Rigor mortis (stiffening of the body) and livor mortis (purple discoloration) may also indicate if a body was moved after death and after the onset of these two physiological changes. If the body is stiffened in a manner that is inconsistent with the position it was found in or if the discoloration does not match the body position, it is likely the body has been repositioned or moved.

Worksheets and Documentation

The following documentation guides, forms, logs, and worksheets are provided in Section VIII, "Death Investigation Checklist and Worksheets," and may be used in documenting this scene. Additional forms, other than those noted, may also be used as dictated by your scene. These forms may be preprinted from the publisher's website (www.crcpress.com/cw/maloney) or photocopied from this procedural guide.

- *Worksheets*
  - Worksheet 1: Postmortem Indicator (PMI)

Determining Time Range

First, ascertain when the body was discovered, then work backward to determine when the deceased was last seen alive. That will provide a range of time that can be narrowed based on receipt of other information.

Immediate Postmortem Changes

Immediate postmortem changes are the body changes that occur at the time of death and within the minutes after death.

- Cessation of respiration
- Cessation of circulation
- Pale skin
- Muscular relaxation
- Contact flattening
- Fixed and dilated pupils

Early Postmortem Changes

Early postmortem changes mark the physiological changes that occur to the body within the first 36 hours from time of death.

Postmortem Lividity (Livor Mortis)

- Lividity can appear within 30 minutes; full development (fixed lividity takes 6–12 hours.[1,2]
- Evaluate the extent of lividity. Is it present? Is it fixed?
- Apply pressure with a gloved finger to an area of lividity. If the lividity disappears under pressure, it is not fixed. The disappearance of the purplish discoloration is called *blanching*.
- Describe the color and location of discoloration.
- Lividity should be consistent with body position.
- Lividity should be more prominent in body areas nearest the ground but not in contact with a surface.
- The location of lividity will shift if a body is moved before the lividity is fixed.

Postmortem Rigidity (Rigor Mortis)[3]

- Rigidity of the muscles is first apparent in smaller muscles, such as the fingers, neck, and jaw.
- Rigidity can appear in 2–4 hours.
- It is generally fully developed between 6 and 12 hours.
- It is sustained in the fully developed state for an additional 12 hours.
- It disappears over the next 12 hours.

Rule of Twelves

Rigor mortis takes 12 hours to build to full, remains at full for 12 hours, and disappears over the next 12 hours.

- *Factors that delay onset*: cold environment, asphyxial death (CO poisoning, hanging), hemorrhage, arsenic poisoning.
- *Factors that hasten onset:* rigorous exertion prior to death; death in a warm, moist environment; certain diseases; poisoning by alkaloids.
- Postmortem rigidity may not be as prominent in very young and very old decedents.

Postmortem Cooling (Algor Mortis)

- Algor mortis is determined by on-scene recording of body temperature.
- Consideration should be given to the effect of taking a rectal temperature on physical evidence found within the rectum in sodomy cases.
- Examination for algor mortis is normally done or not done in accordance with the local ME's policy.
- The decedent's temperature is most accurately taken at the liver (Figure 14.1). This requires that a small incision be made and the thermometer inserted into the liver. **Note:** *This is only done with the ME's approval!*
- Temperatures should be taken at least twice and at least 1 hour interval.
- If no thermometer is available, describe the decedent's temperature as *hot*, *warm*, *cool*, or *cold to touch*.
- As a guide, the rate of body cooling is approximately 1.5°F–2°F per hour for the first 12 hours.[4,5]

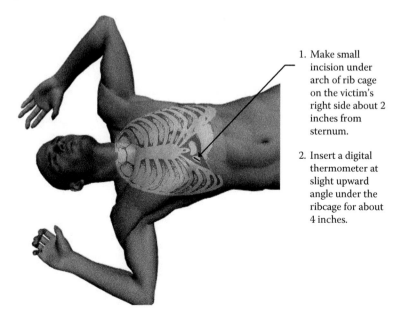

1. Make small incision under arch of rib cage on the victim's right side about 2 inches from sternum.

2. Insert a digital thermometer at slight upward angle under the ribcage for about 4 inches.

Figure 14.1 Taking the liver temperature.

- Describe any factors that may affect the rate of cooling.
  - A body may not necessarily cool if the ambient temperature exceeds normal body temperature; it will warm to ambient temperature (desert environment, sauna, etc.).
  - Cold temperatures, winds, and drafts affect the rate of temperature change.
  - Position affects temperature. A body in a spread-eagle position will cool faster than one in the fetal position due to the greater body surface exposure.
  - Physical activity prior to death may affect temperature change.
  - Physique: a large, obese body cools slowly. Bodies of infants and children cool faster.
  - Contact with warm or cold objects.
  - Body temperature at death (fever or hypothermia).
  - A body covered with clothing or blankets cools slower.
  - Location within structure (basement versus upstairs bedroom).

Late Postmortem Changes

Late postmortem changes are those that are generally observed after 24 hours from time of death.

Decomposition

Decomposition depends more on the environment of the body than the passage of time. Knowledge of decomposition changes may determine early investigative directions. The following are very general guidelines:

- Blue-green abdominal discoloration occurs in 24–36 hours.
- Bloating occurs in 36–48 hours.
- Marbling appears in 2–3 days.
- Skin blistering appears in 3 days.
- Skin slippage occurs from 4 to 7 days.

Adipocere Development

- A soapy white substance covering a body
- Most often encountered in moist conditions with little air movement
- May take months to form
- Also referred to as "grave wax"

Mummification

- Complete dehydration of skin, organs, and other tissues
- Leathery, dry, shriveled appearance
- Most often encountered in dry environments
- May take weeks to years to form

Skeletonization

- Removal of all soft tissues from bones
- Depends on exposure to environment and scavenger activity
- Completion takes weeks to years

Other Postmortem Factors

Forensic Entomology

Insect infestation generally follows a specific order. Flies may begin to lay eggs on the body within minutes of death (under the right conditions); this will be followed by the larval, pupal, and adult stages, which are predictable based upon the species and ambient weather conditions. The flies are followed in succession by those that feed on the fly larvae and ultimately those that feed on the desiccated tissue. For details about collection and processing of insect evidence, see Chapter 40, "Entomological Evidence."

- Flies are usually the first insects to infest a body.
- Flies lay eggs in open, moist areas such as the mouth, nose, eyes, rectum, vagina, and open wounds.
- A maggot mass on the chest, abdomen, or other body area that does not contain a natural opening may be indicative of an injury (gunshot wound, stab wound, etc.) associated with the death.

Stomach Contents

- Stomach contents are determined at autopsy.
- The condition and location of the food within the digestive system may indicate how long before death the victim ate.
- Specific foods may be identifiable.
  - The foods may be unique enough to indicate an origin (hamburgers, fries, steak, etc.).
  - If a serving restaurant or fast food establishment is indicated, surveillance tapes may show the victim and anyone accompanying or associating with them.
- Pill fragments or other substances of investigative interest may be noted.

Scene Indicators

Scene indicators are items of evidence at a death scene that may indicate the time a victim was still alive or indicate a time after they died. (See complete details in Chapter 36, "Death Scene Notes and Observations," as well as the individual chapters on natural, accidental, suicidal and homicidal deaths.)

- Telephone calls made, received, and answered
- Text messages sent, received, and answered
- Social media posts made or comments made to posts
- Mail opened, brought in, still in mail receptacle compared with postmark
- Newspapers read or those still at delivery point
- Meal preparation (breakfast, lunch, dinner) and state of decomposition
- Meal cleanup, what dishes have been cleaned, waiting to be cleaned.
- Expiration date of foodstuff in refrigerator
- Date of receipts for purchases, at scene, in pockets, in wallet or purse or vehicle
- Daily medications taken or waiting/prepared to be taken
- Most recent year of pocket coins for remains or scene of indeterminate age

References

1. Dimaio, V.J. and Dimaio, D. 2001. *Forensic pathology.* 2nd edition. CRC Press, Boca Raton, FL.
2. Froede, R.C. 2003. *Handbook of Forensic pathology.* College of American Pathologists, Northfield, IL.
3. Dimaio, V.J. and Dimaio, D. 2001. *Forensic pathology.* 2nd edition. CRC Press, Boca Raton, FL.
4. Dimaio, V.J. and Dimaio, D. 2001. *Forensic pathology.* 2nd edition. CRC Press, Boca Raton, FL.
5. Spitz, W.U., Spitz, D.J. and Fisher, R.S. 2006. *Spitz and Fisher's Fisher's medico-legal investigation of death: Guidelines for the application of pathology to crime investigation.* Charles C. Thomas, Springfield, IL.

Wound Dynamics and Mechanism of Injury

IV

Asphyxiation

15

Asphyxia occurs when oxygenated blood cannot reach the brain. A variety of mechanisms can cause asphyxiation. Oxygenated blood cannot reach the lungs if the air passage is blocked through choking or suffocation. Preventing the chest from expanding to bring in oxygen is considered *mechanical asphyxia*. The obstruction of blood and airflow occurs in *ligature strangulations* and *hangings*. When the oxygen in the air is replaced with another gas such as carbon dioxide, *chemical asphyxia* occurs. All these conditions deprive the body and particularly the brain of oxygen. Partial oxygen deprivation causes unconsciousness. Total oxygen deprivation may result in death.

Worksheets and Documentation

The following documentation guides, forms, logs, and worksheets are provided in Section VIII, "Death Investigation Checklist and Worksheets," and may be used in documenting this scene. Additional forms, other than those noted, may also be used as dictated by your scene. These forms may be preprinted from the publisher's website (www.crcpress.com/cw/maloney) or photocopied from this procedural guide.

- *Death Investigation Checklist*
  - Section 9: Wounds/Weapons/Drugs/Medications
- *Worksheets*
  - Worksheet 1: Postmortem Indicator (PMI)
  - Worksheet 2: Death Scene Entry Log
  - Worksheet 3: Photography Head Slate
  - Worksheet 4: Photography Log
  - Worksheet 8: Biological Evidence Notes
  - Worksheet 9: Trace Evidence Notes
  - Worksheet 10: Friction Ridge Evidence
  - Worksheet 11: Impression Evidence Notes

Strangulation

Strangulation is caused by constriction or compression of the neck, resulting in the obstruction of blood and oxygen reaching the brain. There are three types of strangulation.

Manual Strangulation (Throttling)

This type of strangulation results from pressure of a hand, arm, or other limb against the victim's neck that causes compression.

General

- Throttling is usually homicidal. It may be accidental if death occurs from sexual activities involving consensual hypoxyphilia.
- Manual strangulation cannot be self-inflicted. When a person loses consciousness, his or her hands will relax and blood will return to the brain.
- Generally, there is a disparity in strength between the assailant and the victim or the victim was incapacitated prior to strangling.
- Look for evidence of a struggle (moved or damaged furniture, etc.).

Scene

- Look for signs of a struggle. Manual strangulation does not instantly incapacitate a victim.
- A rug under a victim's feet may have been displaced during strangulation and other items within reach may have been disturbed.

Body

- The skin of a victim may take on a bluish hue due to an increase of poorly oxygenated blood in the circulatory system.
- Evidence of a struggle may be evident, for example, bruising and defensive scratches around the neck if a victim attempted to break an attacker's hold. Scrapings found under the nails of the deceased may provide useful information about the attacker that can link him or her to the deceased.
- Fingernail marks, abrasions, and contusions on a victim's neck are common. They may have been caused as the victim struggled against the assailant or when the assailant fought against the victim (Figure 15.1).
- Cyanosis and petechial hemorrhages of the face and eyes will usually be present.

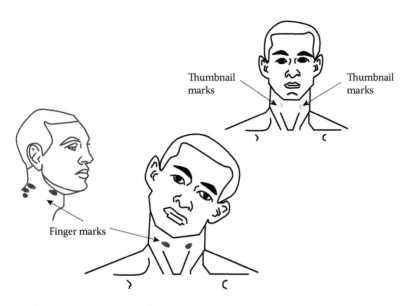

Figure 15.1 Manual strangulation.

Ligature Strangulation (Garroting)

This type of strangulation involves pressure on the neck caused by a constricting band that is tightened by a force other than body weight (Figure 15.2).

General
- Most garroting cases are homicides.
- Suicides and accidental deaths by garroting have been known to occur.

Scene
- An expedient ligature is usually a common object such as a necktie, stocking, belt, or rope.
- When planned, a garrote is generally a short cord or wire with a wooden handle at each end.
- The ligature may be missing. Expand the search area accordingly.
- Examination of the ligature mark may show a pattern consistent with the design of the ligature.
- Look for signs of a struggle.
- The ligature may contain trace evidence such as skin cells, blood, and clothing fibers from the perpetrator.

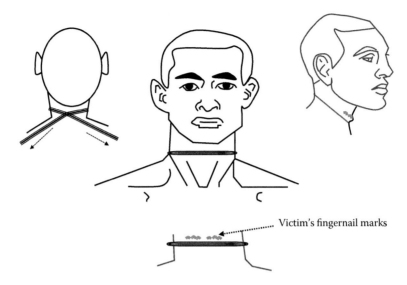

Figure 15.2 Ligature strangulation (garroting).

Body

- The decedent's face and upper chest may show a dusky purple discoloration. Petechial hemorrhages may be present in the whites of the eyes and skin.
- A ligature mark is usually horizontal, completely encircling the neck below the larynx (unlike a V-shaped mark on a hanging victim).
- A ligature will often leave a pattern abrasion on the neck.
- Do not remove the ligature from the body at the scene.
- Fibers may be present in the ligature mark even if the ligature is missing.

Hanging

Hanging is strangulation by means of a rope, cord, or similar ligature tightened by the weight of the body (Figure 15.3).

General

- Most hangings are self-inflicted, but foul play should not be ruled out until an autopsy and full examination of the death scene are completed.
- Homicidal hangings are rare. Simulating a hanging to disguise a homicide should be considered when injuries could not have been self-inflicted or evidence indicates the cause of death was not asphyxia.

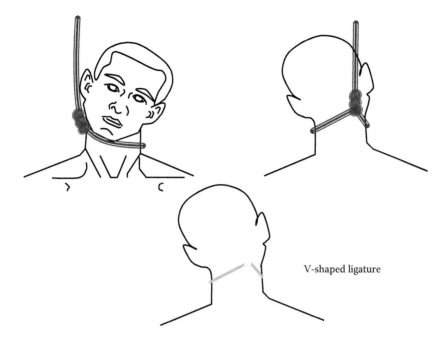

Figure 15.3 Hanging.

- The decedent can be in any position, provided that the pressure on the neck is sufficient to block the blood vessels in the neck.
- Small quantities of blood and other fluids may purge from body openings and collect on clothing or beneath the body.

Scene

- The body may be partially or fully suspended.
- Note the position of the body, composition of the ligature, position of the knot, course and level of the ligature, point of suspension, and method of attachment.
- If the ligature is thrown over a suspension point and not tied to it, the ligature should be further examined. Examine both sides of the suspension point. An abraded area on the side opposite the body may indicate the hanging was not a suicide.
- A ligature on a body should be removed by the pathologist at the time of the autopsy.
- If ligature material must be cut at the scene, find the midway point between the suspension point and noose and wrap electrical tape around the line. Cut through the center of the taped section to prevent the line from fraying or unraveling (Figure 15.4).
- If possible, remove the knot from the suspension point without cutting the line or untying the knot.

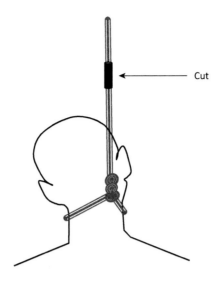

Figure 15.4 Identify mid-way point, tape, and cut.

- If you must untie the knot, photograph it completely before you untie it. Videotape the untying. This may help reconstruct a complex knot. Take the rope or material used to tie the knot and the video to the autopsy for examination by the pathologist.
- Leave the noose and remaining ligature material attached to the body.

Body
- The face of a hanging victim may appear congested. The tongue may protrude and turn dark from drying.
- Lividity will appear in the lower parts of the arms and legs. If lividity appears in an area inconsistent with the position of a hanging body, the victim may have been hanged after death.
- The ligature groove is deepest and narrowest at the point of greatest pressure. The ligature takes an upward course in the region of the knot to form an inverted V.
- The ligature almost always lies above the Adam's apple.
- A furrow will usually remain on the neck even if the hanging victim has been cut down and moved to suggest another manner of death.
- If the ligature is not present, examine the furrow with an alternate light source to find embedded trace evidence. Consider tape lifting the ligature mark for trace evidence.
- A pattern present on a noose or rope is often transferred to the neck as pattern abrasions. Both the furrow and the line should be documented with scale.

Autoerotic Asphyxiation

This is an accidental death from self-inflicted asphyxia as the victim induces a hypoxic state to increase sexual excitement and the intensity of orgasm during masturbation.

General

- Autoerotic asphyxiation is typically a male masturbation practice, although female autoerotic deaths have been documented.
- Autoerotic asphyxia is typically done in a place that affords great privacy.
- Death may involve ligature strangulation, hanging, asphyxiating gases, or suffocation.
- Death results when unconsciousness occurs before the victim releases the asphyxiating device.
- These deaths are distinguished from suicides by the presence of an escape mechanism and/or indications of repeated practice.

Scene

- Document scene indicators that show the victim sought privacy (closed blinds, locked doors, remote location, etc.).
- Any of the following indicators may be present at the scene: nudity, cross-dressing, pornographic materials, lubricants, receptacle for ejaculate (rag or tissue), strategically placed mirrors for self-viewing, cameras, and bondage paraphernalia.
- Search for a cache of sexual paraphernalia or clothing associated with autoerotic practices.
- A scene may be altered by those who discovered the body due to the implications of this type of death.
- Bindings, suspension mechanisms, and escape mechanisms must be thoroughly examined and documented. They may initially appear too elaborate or complex to have been self-applied.
- The escape mechanism, its location relative to the body, and its failure or inability to be reached or employed must be thoroughly documented.
- The location may indicate signs of repeated autoerotic activity such as hooks or areas worn smooth from repeated rope passage.
- Do not underestimate the creativity of a practitioner of autoerotic hypoxyphilia in devising complex self-bondage and asphyxiating devices.
- A ligature may be wide or padded to prevent marks or contusions.
- Look for signs of repeated activity, such as multiple abraded areas at the suspension point and elsewhere. Examine fixed suspension points such as anchor points in overhead beams.

Body

Appearance will be consistent with suffocation, hanging, ligature, or other strangulation death.

- A ligature may be wide or padded to prevent marks or contusions.
- The body may have a variety of sexual devices associated with it and its openings. These should be thoroughly documented through photography and maintained in or on the body until autopsy if possible.
- The body should be carefully documented photographically and through video as clothing, bindings, and devices are removed. It must be demonstrated that the victim was capable of applying all clothing, devices, and bindings without assistance.

Choking

Choking is caused by obstruction of the internal airway.

General

Death is generally accidental. Homicidal choking is rare. However, choking can occur if a victim is gagged and the gag becomes so saturated with saliva that air can no longer pass through the material.

Scene

- The scene should be examined to ensure consistency with witness statements.
- The decedent's location and activity prior to death should be noted.

Body

- If choking was caused by a visible object, leave the object where found for removal at autopsy.
- The signs and symptoms noted by a witness may have been attributed to a heart attack. A blockage of the airway may be discovered at autopsy, indicating a "cafe coronary."
- If homicidal choking is suspected, a thorough examination of the mouth and airway should be made for fibers and other trace evidence.

Smothering

A smothering death is caused by obstruction of the external airway. This may be accomplished by a hand, cloth, pillow, plastic bag, or any other object that prevents air from entering through the mouth and nose.

General

- Children may accidentally smother if they play with plastic bags or similar objects.
- Placing hands, a pillow, or a cushion over another person's nose and mouth or placing a plastic bag over his or her head may cause homicidal smothering.
- An adult can obstruct an infant or child's airway by placing the child against his or her chest. A "soft suffocation" may be accomplished with a pillow.

Scene

- Smothering scenes rarely reveal evidence to assist in determining the method used unless the device was left at the scene.
- Look for signs of a struggle.
- Any object that may have been used to smother a victim should be examined under an alternate light source for the presence of the victim's saliva.
- Any object that may have been used and also the victim's saliva should be collected and processed for trace evidence.

Body

- Smothering may leave no external signs of injury, particularly on an infant.
- A pattern injury of bruising on the face may be consistent with the pattern of an item used to smother, such as a hand (Figure 15.5).
- Trace evidence may be detected around the nose and mouth.
- The frenulum (thin tissue that holds the lips to the gums) may be cut or abrasions may appear around, under, and between the lips and gums (Figure 15.6).
- Look for signs of physical trauma resulting from a struggle (trace evidence under victim's fingernails).

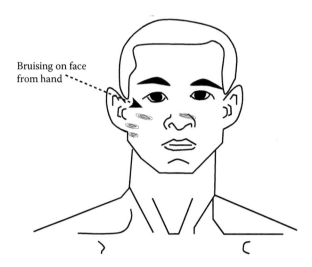

Figure 15.5 A pattern injury may result from smothering.

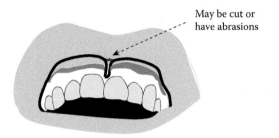

Figure 15.6 The frenulum anchoring the upper and lower lip may be abraded or torn.

Mechanical Asphyxia

Death results from manual compression of the chest by a heavy weight or the anatomical positioning of a victim that prevents respiration. This may be accomplished by an intoxicated person collapsing to a position where their chest is compressed or diaphragm compromised in such a way that they cannot draw breath. Additionally, mechanical asphyxia may occur in industrial or mechanical accidents such as an automobile slipping from its jack and compressing the chest of the individual performing maintenance beneath it.

General

- Mechanical asphyxia is almost always accidental.
- It may occur during auto repair when a jack slips and the weight of the vehicle rests on the victim's chest.

- As a result of drug or alcohol intoxication, a person may stumble or fall into a position that restricts breathing.
- During hypoxic sexual activities, death may accidentally result from bondage-related face or chest sitting that restricts airflow. See Chapter 29, "Sexual Activities Resulting in Death."

Scene

- Fully document the object causing the compression, its weight, and any safety measures or devices in place.
- Fully document any failure of safety devices or the lack of common sense safety procedures.
- Consider consulting a safety engineer.

Body

- Fully document the position of the body when discovered.
- Document any pattern injuries to the chest along with objects at the scene that may have created the patterns.
- Document any injuries to the hands or arms that indicate the victim may have attempted to remove the compressing object.

Chemical Asphyxia

This occurs when the atmosphere breathed lacks sufficient oxygen to support life or contains a chemical that prevents oxygen intake. The manner of death may be accident, suicide, or homicide.

General

- *Never* enter a chemical scene until the source of the chemical has been identified and secured.
- Deaths from chemical asphyxia are usually accidents or suicides.
- Chlorine gas and the mixture of bleach with cleaning agents may cause the accidental release of toxic fumes in a pool environment.
- An increasingly popular form of suicide involves posting a sign (such as "Caution: Poisonous Gas") outside a vehicle or bathroom, then mixing chlorine bleach and detergent cleanser to release toxic gas inside the vehicle or room (Figure 15.7).
- Death may occur from "huffing" (inhaling fumes that produce a "high").
- Carbon monoxide is the most common chemical asphyxiate.

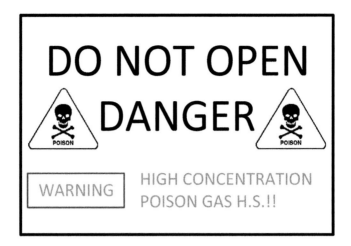

Figure 15.7 Victim placed warning sign for poisonous gas suicide.

- The use of helium in a hood is a method of suicide (exit hood) that is gaining more widespread usage as it is publicized through the Internet, publications, and commercial outlets.
- Carbon monoxide poisoning has been associated with homicides, suicides, and accidental deaths.

Scene

- Note the probable source of the asphyxiate.
- Note the exact position of the body.
- Note indications that the victim may have attempted to escape.
- Note indications of alcohol or drug use that may have prevented the victim from attempting to escape.
- Note any safety measures or equipment in place or available and their functionalities.

Helium or Nitrogen Scene (Exit Bag or Exit Hood)

- Widely publicized method in right-to-die literature and on websites.
- Considered painless. The inert gases reportedly suppress the panicky need-to-breathe feeling associated with suffocation.
- Generally requires 5 minutes or less exposure.
- Requires a plastic bag fitted over the head and sealed at the neck with a drawstring or other device, a helium tank, and plastic tubing extending from a tank valve regulator to the hood.
- Not indicated through standard toxicology testing. Death may appear natural if the equipment is removed.

- If suicide is criminally assisted, the equipment may contain latent prints or DNA of individuals who assisted.
- Kits may be commercially obtained. Search for packing and wrapping materials, address labels, and credit card records.

Carbon Monoxide Scene: Heater

- Determine that the area is safe to enter.
- Determine probable source of gas.
- Charcoal grills used indoors produce significant levels of carbon monoxide and may cause accidental deaths.
- Fossil fuel heaters that are not properly vented will emit carbon dioxide into a home. They should be made safe by the fire department or a competent heating technician. While heater-caused deaths are usually accidental, look for evidence of tampering. Only a trained technician should test a heater.

Carbon Monoxide Scene: Vehicle

- Determine whether vehicle was still running when discovered. Carbon monoxide deaths may be accidental (running a vehicle in a garage with inadequate ventilation) or suicidal (sealing windows and channeling exhaust into the passenger compartment).
- Determine the location of the keys and position of the ignition.
- Determine the gas gauge level. If the key is in the "run" position and the engine is not running, the gas gauge should read empty if death was suicidal.
- Search for a device such as a hose used to transport exhaust emissions to the passenger compartment.
- Determine whether and how the windows were sealed; search for tape, rags, and other materials.
- If the vehicle was in a locked garage, determine position of the garage door and whether attempts were made to seal it.
- Collect hoses, tape, and other items used to channel the exhaust or seal the doors; preserve them for fingerprint and DNA analysis.

Body

- Note the position of the body and whether lividity is present.
  - In persons with darker complexions, lividity may be difficult to determine.
  - Lividity and coloration changes may be seen at the nail beds.
- Determine if lividity is fixed.
- Determine if the lividity is consistent with the body position.

- Lividity associated with carbon monoxide poisoning is generally bright and cherry red.
- Lividity associated with cyanide is generally pink.
- Lividity associated with nitrites is generally brown.

Drowning

Drowning is usually a diagnosis of exclusion after a body is found in or near water and no other cause of death is determined.

General

- There is no reliable test that specifically determines death from drowning.
- It is important at autopsy to determine whether the victim was alive at the time of submersion.
- Since most drowning victims swallow water prior to death, a lack of water in the stomach of a person found in still water (bathtub, pond, etc.) suggests death may have occurred prior to submersion. In fast moving water, the lungs may fill after death.
- Most drowning involves inhalation of water. "Dry drowning" or "dry lungs" indicate the larynx closed by spasm and prevented water from entering the lungs.
- Death may be greatly delayed from a near-drowning incident when a small amount of water was inhaled, causing a cascade of events within the lungs that eventually may lead to the victim's demise.
  - Repeated cough increasing in intensity
  - Late-stage frothy sputum from productive cough

Scene

- Quickly secure the scene and body, documenting all items relative to the incident.
- Removal of the body from the water after a long submersion may cause rapid decomposition. Thorough photography of the face and body is very important.
- Metal objects removed from or associated with the body may quickly corrode when removed from the water. Place such items into a container filled with water from the scene.
- Fully document all rescue and resuscitation attempts.
- Record weather conditions, depth of water, water currents, water condition (rough, smooth), and other pertinent factors.

- A sample of water may be taken for comparison with water and contaminants obtained from the lungs.
- Broaden the scene of an outdoor drowning. Find and document any signs that the victim walked, slipped, fell, or was carried into the water.
- Search for missing clothing and other items belonging to victim.

Scuba Scene

- Any equipment such as scuba gear involved in the incident should be seized for expert examination for functionality.
- A dive computer (console or wristwatch) at the scene must be seized. It will contain the information about the fatal dive and previous dives. Data from the dive computer should be recovered and logged by someone very familiar with its operation.
- In a scuba-related diving death, determine the depths of the dives, the number of dives, time at depth for each dive, and the intervals on the surface between dives.

Body

- Note the exact location and depth where found using GPS coordinates if possible. This information may become important for drift studies to determine point or location of immersion.
- Note any unusual findings associated with the body such as bindings and weights.
- Note specific body conditions, particularly rigor, livor, and algor mortis. The intense physical activity associated with drowning may often dramatically accelerate the onset of rigor mortis.
- Note any signs of struggle, scratches, bruising, or marks that may have been self-inflicted during drowning.
- Note any objects clutched in the hands, for example, weeds or other flora from the water where the drowning occurred.
- Note any frothy sputum in the mouth or nose.
- Note injuries to the head, back, or shoulders that may be consistent with impact by a boat or propeller.

Sharp Force Injuries

16

A sharp force injury results from cutting and stabbing and may be associated with chopping injuries. In sharp force injuries, the skin and tissue are cleanly separated by the cutting edge (incised wounds). This can also be accomplished by the plunging action of the cutting edge when forcefully inserted point first in a stabbing. These incised wounds differ from skin and tissue that is torn open (lacerated) in blunt force trauma. Chopping injuries may have aspects of both sharp force and blunt force based upon the sharpness of the cutting edge.

General

- Evaluation of a wound may provide information about the type of weapon used.
- Bloodstain pattern analysis, if conducted from a properly documented scene and body, may be used to reconstruct the movements and positions within the dynamic event around the incident.
- Wound patterns and their frequencies may help determine motive.

Worksheets and Documentation

The following documentation guides, forms, logs, and worksheets are provided in Section VIII, "Death Investigation Checklist and Worksheets," and may be used in documenting this scene. Additional forms, other than those noted, may also be used as dictated by your scene. These forms may be preprinted from the publisher's website (www.crcpress.com/cw/maloney) or photocopied from this procedural guide.

- *Death Investigation Checklist*
  - Section 9: Wounds/Weapons/Drugs/Medications
- *Worksheet*
  - Worksheet 15: Bloodstain Pattern Worksheet

Scene

- A recovered weapon may yield fingerprints, hairs, fibers, and blood and tissue evidence.
- The gripping surface of the weapon or implement should be considered for touch DNA processing.
- If the weapon has a broken or chipped tip or edge, the broken piece may be lodged in the victim's body. Inform the ME who will perform the autopsy.
- Suspect and victim's clothing may provide blood spatter, trace, and serological evidence.
  - The victim's clothing may no longer be at the scene; it may have accompanied the victim to the hospital or have been removed and discarded within the ambulance or trauma center.
  - The suspect's clothing should be obtained as soon as possible before he or she has an opportunity to discard or wash it.
- Bloodstain evidence should be thoroughly documented.
- Every attempt should be made to recover the weapon. If not with the suspect or discarded at the scene, a thorough search of trash receptacles, drains, and rooftops along the likely egress route should be made.
- If the type of weapon used is not obvious, the wounds may indicate the type of weapon used.

Body

- The length and depth of an incised wound will not provide specific information about the weapon but may provide general information (Figure 16.1).

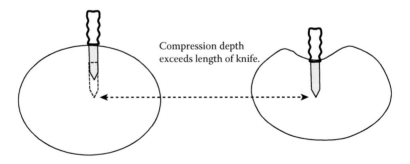

Figure 16.1 The length of the blade cannot accurately be determined through measuring the depth of the wound track.

- The injury must be carefully documented through the injury mapping technique. See Chapter 9, "Autopsy Protocol and the Investigator's Role," and Chapter 34, "Death Scene Photography."
  - An overall photograph of the body region without scale or indicator.
  - Place ABFO scale bracketing injury site with one scale arm toward centerline and the other toward the feet.
  - Place an identification marker (1, 2, 3, ... , A, B, C,...) close to the injury.
  - Rephotograph body region.
  - Take a close-up photograph of injury.
  - Take an examination quality photograph with the ABFO scale bracketing the frame.
  - Close-up photography of injuries is essential to the proper evaluation of wounds.
- Persons defending themselves from knife attacks often sustain incised wounds. These wounds are most common on the forearms, palms, fingers, and backs of the hands and can be severe. They are known as *defensive injuries*.
- Hesitation wounds are usually seen in suicides and suicide attempts as the victim gathers the courage to complete the act. They are usually multiple, parallel, incised wounds found on the wrists and neck. Hesitation wounds on the wrists are usually found between the base of the palm and the elbow.
- The exact length of a blade or cutting instrument cannot be determined from a wound track. The wounded area may have been compressed when injured.
- "Hilt" marks where the handle of the knife impacted the skin may be evident in cases where the blade fully penetrated the body (Figure 16.2).
- The width of a blade (measured across from sharp edge to dull edge) cannot be measured exactly from a wound because the knife may have been drawn through the injured tissues (Figure 16.3).
- The shape of a stab wound depends on the shape of the instrument and Langer's lines—elastic fibers in the skin that run in the direction in which skin is stretched (Figure 16.4).
- Stab wounds will gape if the stab is across or perpendicular to Langer's lines; they will gape less if the stab is parallel to the lines.

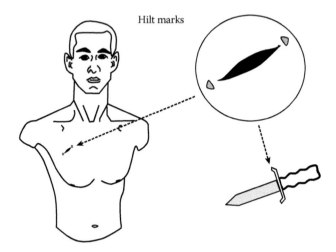

Figure 16.2 "Hilt" marks may leave a pattern injury on the skin.

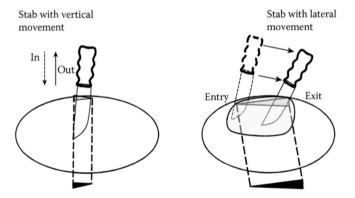

Figure 16.3 The width of the blade cannot be accurately determined through measuring the wound as portrayed here.

- After a knife has been shoved into the body, the twisting of the knife or the struggling of the victim when it is removed can cause Y- or L-shaped wounds.

- Stab wounds in pairs (or other multiples) may be caused by scissors or forks (Figure 16.5). A fork will create a consistent distance between paired stabs. Varied distances between paired stabs indicate a weapon like scissors.

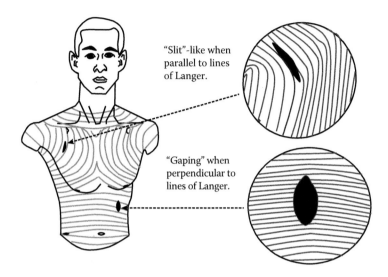

"Slit"-like when parallel to lines of Langer.

"Gaping" when perpendicular to lines of Langer.

Figure 16.4 Lines of Langer.

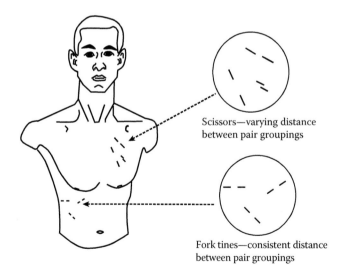

Scissors—varying distance between pair groupings

Fork tines—consistent distance between pair groupings

Figure 16.5 Paired stab wounds.

Blunt Force Injuries
Blunt Instrument Blows, Fall from a Height, Collisions

17

Blunt force injuries may be produced by a variety of mechanisms. The striking object may be in motion such as in the case of injuries sustained by being struck with a baseball bat. Conversely, the body itself may be in motion, such as deceleration injuries when falling from a height or when involved in a collision. Such injuries result in abrasions, contusions, lacerations, and fractures.

General

- Blunt forces tear, crush, and shear tissues. Blunt forces are transmitted by objects with relatively broad or rounded edges.
- The pattern and appearance of a blunt force injury varies, depending on the amount of force, the location of the wound, and the type of weapon.
- Blunt force trauma can also cause fractures if sufficient force is used.
- Abrasions, contusions, and lacerations are the three general types of blunt force injuries. A blunt force can cause any combination of these types of injuries.
- Deaths from blunt force injuries may occur in child abuse, assault, falls, collisions, and accident cases.

Worksheets and Documentation

The following documentation guides, forms, logs, and worksheets are provided in Section VIII, "Death Investigation Checklist and Worksheets," and may be used in documenting this scene. Additional forms, other than those noted, may also be used as dictated by your scene. These forms may be preprinted from the publisher's website (www.crcpress.com/cw/maloney) or photocopied from this procedural guide.

- *Death Investigation Checklist*
  - Section 9: Wounds/Weapons/Drugs/Medications

- *Worksheets*
  - Worksheet 9: Trace Evidence Notes
  - Worksheet 10: Friction Ridge Evidence
  - Worksheet 11: Impression Evidence Notes
  - Worksheet 15: Bloodstain Pattern Worksheet

Blunt Force Blows

Weapon or Striking Object

- Weapons may have fingerprint, blood, hair, or tissue evidence on their surfaces.
- The handle or gripping surface of the implement should be considered for touch DNA.
- Blood spatter evidence should be thoroughly documented.

Body

- Weapons may leave identifiable injury patterns (Figure 17.1).
- Injury pattern may suggest the type of weapon used.
- Close-up photography of injuries with and without scales is essential for proper evaluation of wounds. Consider ultraviolet and infrared photography.

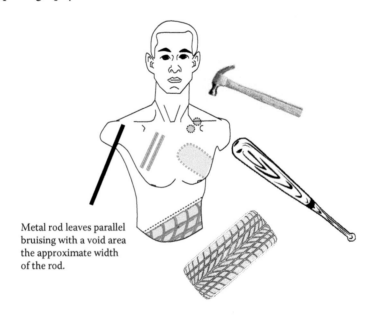

Metal rod leaves parallel bruising with a void area the approximate width of the rod.

Figure 17.1 Pattern injury from blunt force trauma.

- While an abrasion may be the only visible injury, significant internal injuries may be present.
- Patterns on the weapon may be imparted to the skin and called *pattern abrasions.*
- Contusions (bruises) do not necessarily reflect the intensity of a blow. Bruises may or may not transmit patterns from the object that caused them.
- Lacerations may be external or internal and involve tearing of organ tissues.
- Trace evidence transfer between weapon and victim is possible. Paint, debris, or fragments of the weapon may be found in a wound. Hair, blood, or fibers from the victim's clothing may be found on the weapon.
- The size and shape of the laceration may suggest the type of weapon used.

Deceleration Injuries

In falls from a height or rapid deceleration in automobile or other conveyance collisions, deceleration injuries are often noted.

Falls from a Height

- When falling from a height, the rapid deceleration and the space within the thoracic cavity may allow the heart to shift within the body a sufficient distance that the aorta is severed.
- If the body strikes the surface feet first, the heels often sustain fractures, the pelvis may be fractured from the impact with the head of the femur, and the skull may be fractured at its base in a concentric ring pattern from the impact of the first vertebrae.
- From a height, water is not a yielding surface unless entry is made deliberately and with skill; deceleration injuries may be noted.
- Ensure that you record the vertical distance fallen as well as the horizontal distance traveled during the fall. These measurements may be critical in later reconstruction efforts to determine the mechanism of the fall.

Control Injuries

Control injuries generally refer to the injuries to the body inflicted through rapid deceleration from the control surfaces of the vehicle (automobile, airplane, ATV, etc.). This category has also been adapted to include the interaction with safety devices such as lap and shoulder restraints and airbags. Control injuries allow the reconstructionist to determine the driver/pilot as compared to the passengers in a conveyance.

Automobile

- The driver may have dislocations and fractures of the hands with laceration/separation of the skin between the thumb and forefinger where the hands were gripping the steering wheel.
- The driver may have fractures of the ball area of the foot and/or toes from contact with the control pedals.
    - The bottom of the driver's footwear should be photographically recorded.
    - The control pedals (gas, brake, clutch) should be photographed.
    - An electrostatic dust print lift of the pedals and footwear should be made. This may indicate if the foot was on the gas or brake at the time of the incident and may be critical in potential suicides (Chapter 44, "Impression Evidence").
- If the driver had no restraints in place and no airbag was present, there may be a flail chest (multiple fractures of the ribs caused by steering wheel impact) and the steering wheel pattern may be visible.
- The driver or passengers may exhibit diagonal bruising pattern on the appropriate shoulder and the lower abdomen from shoulder/lap restraints. This pattern should be on the appropriate shoulder for their stated position in the vehicle.
- Pattern injuries may be visible on the face and upper body from airbag inflation. This should be consistent with the airbag for the driver's side of the vehicle.
- Dicing injuries to the left side of the face and neck from the driver's side window or right side of the face for the passenger side of the vehicle may be present from shattered side windows (left-hand drive vehicles, the opposite for right hand drive vehicles)
- Impact with the windshield should be correlated to appropriate head injuries to determine positions within the vehicle.

Chopping Injuries

18

Chopping wounds demonstrate a combination of both blunt and sharp force injuries. A typical weapon used to inflict a chopping injury might be an axe, hatchet, or machete. The sharp cutting edge coupled with the weight of the cutting blade results in a combination of lacerations, incisions, and blunt force trauma.

General

- The scene and body will exhibit combinations of conditions expected from sharp force and blunt force injuries.
- Refer to the appropriate guidelines in Chapters 16 and 17 for processing incidents involving these types of injuries.

Worksheets and Documentation

The following documentation guides, forms, logs, and worksheets are provided in Section VIII, "Death Investigation Checklist and Worksheets," and may be used in documenting this scene. Additional forms, other than those noted, may also be used as dictated by your scene. These forms may be preprinted from the publisher's website (www.crcpress.com/cw/maloney) or photocopied from this procedural guide.

- *Death Investigation Checklist*
  - Section 9: Wounds/Weapons/Drugs/Medications
- *Worksheets*
  - Worksheet 9: Trace Evidence Notes
  - Worksheet 11: Impression Evidence Notes
  - Worksheet 15: Bloodstain Pattern Worksheet

Scene

- These wounds are usually caused by common objects that are sharper and heavier than household knives. Look for an ax, machete, meat cleaver, boat propeller, or similar item at the scene.
- The handle or gripping surface of the implement should be considered for touch DNA.
- Blood spatter evidence should be thoroughly documented.

Body

- Weapons may leave identifiable injury patterns.
- Injury pattern may suggest the type of weapon used.
- Close-up photography of injuries with and without scales is essential for proper evaluation of wounds. Consider ultraviolet and infrared photography.
- While an abrasion may be the only visible injury, significant internal injuries may be present.
- Patterns from the weapon may be imparted to the skin and called *pattern abrasions.*
- Contusions (bruises) do not necessarily reflect the intensity of a blow. Bruises may or may not transmit a pattern from the object that caused them.
- Lacerations may be external or internal and involve the tearing of organ tissues.
- Trace evidence transfer is possible between the weapon and the victim. Paint, debris, or fragments of the weapon may be found in a wound. Hair, blood, or fibers from the victim's clothing may be found on a weapon.
- The size and shape of the laceration may suggest the type of weapon used.

Firearm Injuries
Pistols and Rifles
(Rifled Bore Weapons)

19

Gunshot Wounds

When a handgun or rifle is discharged, flame, smoke, a bullet, and burned and unburned powder exit the barrel. Gunshot wounds exhibit different appearances that depend on the proximity of the weapon to the target and the bullet's direction of travel. This chapter describes common characteristics of handgun and rifle wounds. Shotgun wounds are discussed in Chapter 20.

Worksheets and Documentation

The following documentation guides, forms, logs, and worksheets are provided in Section VIII, "Death Investigation Checklist and Worksheets," and may be used in documenting this scene. Additional forms, other than those noted, may also be used as dictated by your scene. These forms may be pre-printed from the publisher's website (www.crcpress.com/cw/maloney) or photocopied from this procedural guide.

- *Death Investigation Checklist*
  - Section 9: Wounds/Weapons/Drugs/Medications
- *Worksheets*
  - Worksheet 6: Firearms Recovery Worksheet
  - Worksheet 14: Bullet Defect Worksheet
  - Worksheet 15: Bloodstain Pattern Worksheet

Entrance Wounds

- Most entrance wounds are surrounded by reddish zones of abraded skin, regardless of firing distance. This is referred to as a *margin abrasion.*
- Fibers from clothing may be driven into a wound.

- Entrance wounds resulting from a ricochet or a bullet striking an intermediary target may be shaped irregularly.
- For more details of entrance wounds, see the descriptions based on the effects of distance detailed below.
- It is not possible to determine a bullet's trajectory through the body from examination of the entrance wound alone.

Effects of Distance on Gunshot Wounds

Contact Gunshot Wounds

When the muzzle of a gun is held against a body at the time of firing, gas, soot, powder, and metallic particles from the bullet are forced into the wound track with the bullet. Because a gun can be held against a body in several ways, contact wounds are further classified as *hard*, *loose*, *angled*, or *incomplete* (variation of angled).

Hard Contact Wounds
- The muzzle of the gun is pushed against the skin, indenting the skin so that it wraps around the muzzle (Figure 19.1).
- A hard contact wound is burned by hot gases and blackened by soot. Soot can be washed off. It differs from *stippling*—burned and unburned powder lodged into the skin that cannot be washed off.
- All the material emerging from the muzzle will be driven into the wound, often leaving very little external evidence of a contact wound. In cases where no soot can be seen, autopsy analysis may reveal microscopic soot and powder grains.

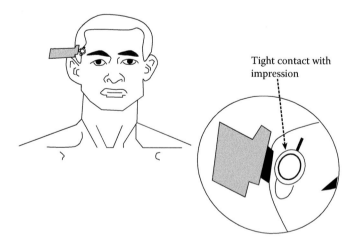

Figure 19.1 Muzzle impression from hard contact wound.

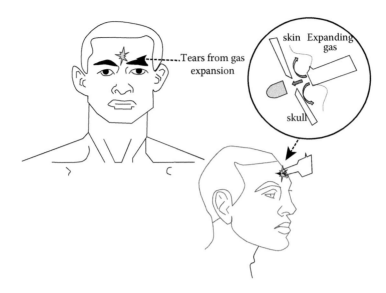

Figure 19.2 Hard contact wound over flat bone.

- Muscle surrounding an entrance wound may turn cherry red due to carboxyhemoglobin formation from the carbon monoxide in the muzzle gas.
- Hard contact wounds over areas of the body where the skin is supported by flat underlying bone are usually star-shaped or stellate. They are caused by the energy of the gases escaping from the gun barrel. The gases have little room to expand between the skin and the bone, causing the skin to balloon and lacerate. Soot, smoke, and powder are blown into the wound (Figure 19.2). These wounds are typically found on the skull. Small-caliber, low-energy weapons may not always produce enough energy to cause stellate wounds.

Loose Contact Wounds

- These wounds result when a gun muzzle is in contact with the skin but is not pushed firmly against the body at the time of discharge.
- Since the skin does not create a seal around the muzzle, hot gases can escape and form a circle of soot around the wound. Soot, smoke, and powder will be present inside the wound. Most of this soot can be wiped away easily (Figure 19.3).

Angled Contact Wounds

- An angled contact wound is created when the gun barrel is held at an angle to the skin. The complete circumference of the muzzle does not make contact with the skin.

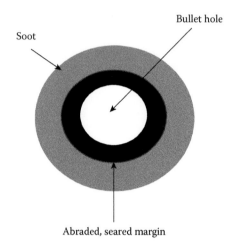

Figure 19.3 Loose contact wound.

- Gas and soot escaping from the space between the muzzle and the skin radiate outward, causing two patterns of soot. The first pattern is a blackened, seared zone that may be pear-shaped, circular, or oval. The second pattern is usually light gray and fan-shaped. The entrance wound is often located at the base of the blackened, seared zone (Figure 19.4).
- As the angle between the gun and skin increases, the entrance hole will be found more toward the center of the blackened zone. Most of the blackened, seared zone will appear opposite where the muzzle

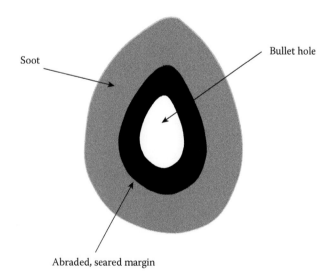

Figure 19.4 Angled contact wound.

made contact with the skin. This indicates the angle from which the gun was fired.

Incomplete Contact Wounds

- Incomplete contact wounds are variations of angled contact wounds. They occur over body surfaces that are rounded or not completely flat.
- The weapon is held against the skin, but a gap exists between the muzzle and the uneven skin surface. Hot gases escape from the gap, forming an area of blackened, seared skin.
- Incomplete contact wounds are often seen on the head.

Near Contact Wounds

- Near contact wounds fall between contact and intermediate range wounds. The muzzle of the weapon is not in contact with the skin; it is held a short distance away.
- A near contact entrance wound is surrounded by a wide zone of powder and soot, overlying blackened, seared skin. The zone of searing is wider than zones resulting from loose contact wounds. The soot in the seared zone penetrates the skin and cannot be completely wiped away.
- Since near and loose contact wounds have similar characteristics, it is not always possible to distinguish them, especially if the muzzle is held perpendicular to the skin.
- With handguns, small clumps of unburned powder may accumulate at the edges of the entrance in the seared zone of the skin.
- Near contact wounds with handguns usually occur at ranges less than 1/2 inch. Distance will vary based on caliber, ammunition, and barrel length.

Intermediate Range Wounds

- A wound is considered intermediate when the distance from the muzzle is sufficient that the soot no longer reaches the target surface but the particals of burning and unburned powder do.
- Stippling (tattooing) is produced by the penetration of the burning and unburned powder grains into the skin. Stippling consists of the dark colored lodged powder surrounded by reddish-brown to orange-red punctate (small dot or point) lesions surrounding the entrance wound (Figure 19.5).

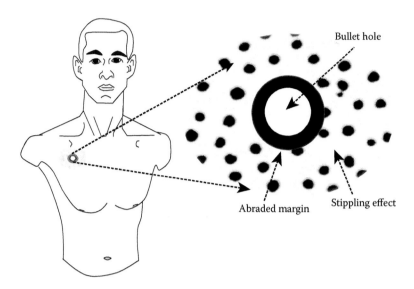

Figure 19.5 Intermediate range gunshot wound.

- Stippling may take a circular or oval shape around the entrance wound, depending on the angle of the gun to the target at firing, the shape of the target (flat or rounded), and the presence of clothing or hair (that may keep powder grains from reaching the skin).
- Vital reaction (the reddish-orange discoloration) surrounding powder tattooing indicates a victim was alive at the time of the shooting. The presence of the vital reaction must be confirmed by a pathologist.
- The distance between the muzzle of the gun and the target is important because it affects the appearance of the powder particle distribution. As the range between the muzzle and the target increases, the size of stippling increases and the density of the stippling pattern on the body decreases until it is no longer present.
- As the distance between the gun muzzle and target increases, the density of the powder particles will decrease until few particles adhere to the target surface.

Distant Wounds

- When a gun is fired from a distance, the only marks on the target are produced when the bullet penetrates the skin. The muzzle of the weapon is too far from the target to deposit soot and unburned powder on the target. Soot and powder particles serve as indicators of distance between the gun and target. They are absent on a distant wound (Figure 19.6).

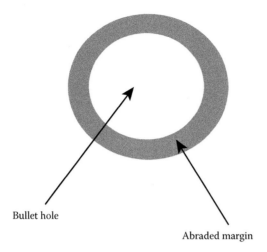

Bullet hole

Abraded margin

Figure 19.6 Distant wound.

- The only visible characteristics may be an abrasion ring and defect.
- A distant range wound may be difficult to distinguish from an intermediate range wound. For instance, an intermediate range gunshot wound may look like a distant range wound if clothing or another object comes between the gun and the body, preventing soot and unburned powder from reaching the skin. Only careful examination of the facts (e.g., was the victim clothed at the time of the shooting?) will allow correct identification of this type of gunshot wound.

Rifle Entrance Wounds

Rifle wounds have similar characteristics to wounds caused by handguns. However, rifle shots usually involve much more energy.

- A handgun placed in the mouth and fired may produce relatively little structural damage from expanding gases. However, a rifle shot will usually cause more damage to the mouth and head. The damage is even greater if the victim closes his mouth around the muzzle of the rifle.
- When studying self-inflicted rifle wounds, care should be taken to determine whether the victim was capable of firing the weapon without help. The person's reach should be measured and compared with the reach required to fire the rifle.

Exit Wounds

- Exit wounds are usually more irregularly shaped than entrance wounds.
- Exit wounds are usually larger and usually do not exhibit abrasion rings.
- As a bullet travels through a body, it may tumble, deform as it strikes objects, or tumble *and* deform, in which case the exit wound will often appear larger and more irregular than an entrance wound.
- The size and shape of the exit wound is often dependent on the body area where it exits. In slack skin, a wound tends to appear smaller and slit-shaped. In areas where the skin is stretched across a hard surface such as bone, the exit wound may appear larger and more irregular.
- In some circumstances, an exit wound may exhibit an abrasion ring and a regular shape. This occurs when the victim was against a hard surface such as a wall or floor or wore constrictive clothing such as a bra or belt. In such cases, the hard surface or clothing supports the skin, keeping it from tearing into irregular shape and is called a *shored exit wound*.
- As the skin dries, an exit wound may look more like an entrance wound. The absence of gunshot powder residue on the surrounding skin or clothing (in cases of close range gunshot wounds) may help identify an injury as an exit wound.
- Bullets may be found just under the skin, partly protruding from the skin, or loose in the clothing around an exit wound.

Firearm Injuries
Shotguns (Smooth Bore Weapons)

20

Wounds produced by shotguns and smooth bore weapons typically appear very different from wounds caused by rifles and handguns. This distinctive appearance results from several differences between these weapons. A shotgun disperses one large or many smaller projectiles with a single shot. The number of projectiles and distance from muzzle to target contribute to a distinct but more variable shot pattern when compared to a single projectile from a rifle or handgun.

Worksheets and Documentation

The following documentation guides, forms, logs, and worksheets are provided in Section VIII, "Death Investigation Checklist and Worksheets," and may be used in documenting this scene. Additional forms, other than those noted, may also be used as dictated by your scene. These forms may be preprinted from the publisher's website (www.crcpress.com/cw/maloney) or photocopied from this procedural guide.

- *Death Investigation Checklist*
  - Section 9: Wounds/Weapons/Drugs/Medications
- *Worksheets*
  - Worksheet 6: Firearms Recovery Worksheet
  - Worksheet 14: Bullet Defect Worksheet
  - Worksheet 15: Bloodstain Pattern Worksheet

Shotgun Entrance Wounds

Shotcup and Wadding Effect on Entrance Wound

Both the shot cup and wadding (if present in the shotshell) exit the muzzle of the shotgun and leave with an initial velocity sufficient to penetrate skin; as the distance increases, their velocity decreases, and the shot cup and wadding will have less of a penetrating effect but may still mark the skin (Figure 20.1).

- The wadding and shot cup travel a much shorter distance than the shot.

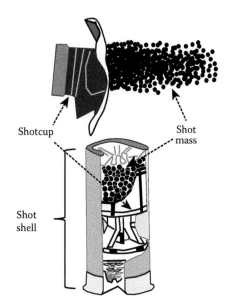

Figure 20.1 Shotshell, shotcup, and shot mass.

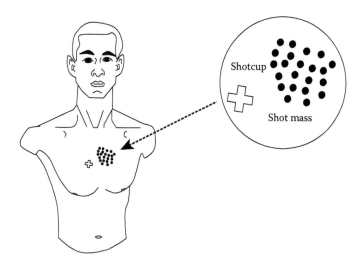

Figure 20.2 Shotcup strikes off center from shot mass.

- At close range, they enter the central defect with the mass of shot.
- As distance increases, they strike (and often leave a mark) off-center from the shot mass (Figure 20.2).
- Eventually the shot cup and wadding lose sufficient force to make marks or they fall to the ground before reaching the target.

Shot Effect on Entrance Wound

The physical attributes of the entrance wound defect are dependent upon the shot load fired (birdshot, 00 buckshot, slugs), as well as the distance or range from the muzzle to the body. The effects of distance are covered in the following section.

- Entrance wounds generally exhibit margin abrasions for each individual shot pellet.
- Entrance wounds may range from a neat circle to dispersed individual shot defects dependent on range of fire (see Section "Effects of Distance on Wounds").
- The shot size from the shotshell will correlate with individual defects.
- Contact wounds may include considerable tearing at the entrance site due to massive gas expansion from the muzzle.

Effects of Distance on Wounds

Contact Wounds

- Characterized by burning, soot, powder, and a margin abrasion around the entry wound.
- The shot cup and wadding (if present in shotshell) will be lodged within the wound or have exited the body through the exit wound.

Stellate Wounds

- These may be present on hard and soft surfaces because of the highly pressurized gases that exit the muzzle of the shotgun.

Hard Contact Head Wounds

- These wounds cause massive fragmentation to the skull and brain. Large fragments of the skull and the brain may be found many feet away from the body or imbedded in or adhering to walls or ceilings.
- The face of the decedent may be completely unrecognizable. It is important to collect tissue and bone fragments because a pathologist may be able to reconstruct portions of the face.

Intraoral Wounds

- May be characterized by soot on the palate, tongue, and sometimes the lips.

- The intraoral discharge of shotguns often creates stretch-mark changes radiating from the mouth and extensive damage to the brain and skull.

Contact Wounds to Trunk

- Wounds are usually circular; diameter is approximately equal to the diameter of the bore of the weapon.
- Soot is not usually visible around the margins of contact wounds. The edges of wounds are burned and blackened by the hot gases.
- The front sight or muzzle may leave an imprint on the skin.
- The entrance wound may be surrounded by a large area of abraded skin.

Near Contact Wounds

- The entrance wound is described as "cookie cutter" shaped. The shot enters as a single mass, making a circular defect.
- A circular area of soot is deposited upon the skin immediately surrounding the entrance wound (Figure 20.3).
- As the distance between the shotgun muzzle and the target increases, the diameter of the soot deposit increases and the density decreases.

Close and Intermediate Range Wounds

- An abrasion ring may be present because the shot tends to enter the body as a mass.
- When the distance between the shotgun muzzle and the target increases beyond an inch or two, faint powder tattooing may occur. It may be less pronounced than tattooing resulting from other gunshot wounds.
- Range affects wound pattern. At close range, shot pellets enter the body as a group.
- As the muzzle of the shotgun is moved away from the body, the diameter of a shotgun entrance wound increases until individual pellets separate from the main mass. This creates a scalloped edge to the wound (Figure 20.4).
- The size of the shot pattern on the body should be measured to assist in determining range. Remember: even the best range determination is only an estimate.
- As the range increases, the wadding will separate from the main shot mass and may impact the side of the entrance wound before entering

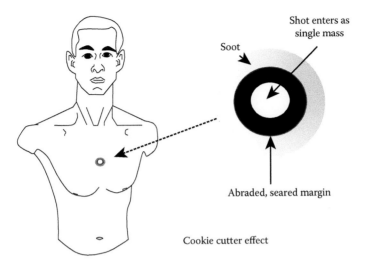

Figure 20.3 Contact shotgun wound.

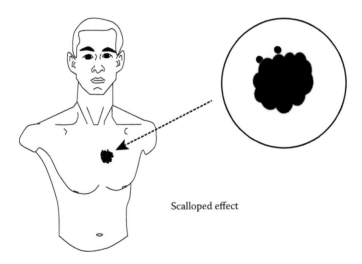

Figure 20.4 Intermediate shotgun wound.

the body at relatively close ranges. This may create an irregular abraded margin on one side of the entrance wound.

- Beyond a range of 5–8 feet, the wadding will drift to one side of the discharge until it impacts the skin adjacent to the entrance site but does not penetrate the skin. At this range, the wadding may leave an imprint (usually circular or oval) on the skin.

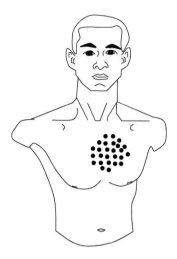

Each shot
(or almost all shots)
makes separate
entrance wounds

Figure 20.5 Distant shotgun wound.

Distant Range Wounds

- As shot is fired from a shotgun over a distance, it separates, no longer forming a mass; it impacts as individual shot and may be very dispersed (Figure 20.5).
- Defects created in the skin are dependent on the size of the shot. Defects caused by birdshot are small and round, with tiny margin abrasions. Buckshot produces defects that are large enough to resemble bullet wounds.
- If shot strikes an intermediate target (door, tree, heavy clothing) before impacting the victim, range estimates from the shot pattern on the body will not be accurate.

Shotgun Exit Wounds

- Individual exit wounds attributable to the separate projectiles are not common.
- If the shot is at relatively close range, the individual shot does not have the distance necessary to significantly spread. This results in the shot mass exiting the body, leaving an exit area of massive tissue loss.
- If the shot comes from a range where there is sufficient distance for the shot pattern to spread, the individual pellets generally do not exit the body but rather may be discovered within the body tissues or just underneath the skin on the side of the body opposite the entrance wound.

Explosive Injuries

21

Explosive injuries are generally generated from a blast wave or its effects on structures and other objects.[1] The concussive force of the blast wave may be responsible for blunt force trauma. Additionally, sharp force and blunt force may also result from a device designed to produce fragmentation. Incidental fragmentation may occur and cause blunt force trauma. Victims may be injured by objects thrown by a blast wave or as a result of structural collapse. Explosive injuries may be accompanied by thermal injuries, depending on a victim's proximity to the device or secondary fire or heat from items ignited by the explosion.

General Considerations

- Have an EOD team clear the area to ensure safety prior to scene examination.
- If fire accompanied the explosion, consider the appropriate steps detailed in Chapter 22 ("Thermal Injuries").
- Need for further investigation is based on the cause of death determined by an autopsy. Do not release the scene until the autopsy is completed.

Worksheets and Documentation

The following documentation guides, forms, logs, and worksheets are provided in Section VIII, "Death Investigation Checklist and Worksheets," and may be used in documenting this scene. Additional forms, other than those noted, may also be used as dictated by your scene. These forms may be preprinted from the publisher's website (www.crcpress.com/cw/maloney) or photocopied from this procedural guide.

- *Death Investigation Checklist*
  - Section 9: Wounds/Weapons/Drugs/Medications

---

[1] Information in chapter taken from *Explosion and Blast Injuries: A Primer for Clinicians*, Centers for Disease Control, www.bt.cdc.gov/masscasualties/explosions.asp

- *Worksheets*
  - Worksheet 5: Post-Blast Scene Management
  - Worksheet 8: Biological Evidence Notes
  - Worksheet 9: Trace Evidence Notes
  - Worksheet 10: Friction Ridge Evidence
  - Worksheet 11: Impression Evidence Notes
  - Worksheet 15: Bloodstain Pattern Worksheet

Scene

- Safety is always the paramount concern. Consider the possibility that secondary explosive devices were set to kill or injure responders to the scene.
- Structural collapses, stray electrical lines, and venting natural gas are potential hazards at a blast scene.
- The perimeter of an explosion scene should be at least one and one half times the distance from the center of the explosion to the most distant debris.
- Coordinate a death scene response with organizations that specialize in post-blast investigations. These may include local, state, or federal assets.
- Searches involving explosion victims should be as thorough as possible. Small bone and tissue fragments may be the only remains found but may be sufficient for DNA identification. Special collection techniques may be required.
- Teeth are especially important items. Dental identification may be possible if enough teeth are recovered.
- Worksheet 12, "Post-Blast Scene Management," can be used to document a post-blast scene and recovery of remains using the polar coordinate method.

Body

A fatal injury depends on a number of factors: size of the blast, degree of containment, distances of victims from the blast, intermediate or barriers between the victim and the blast, and susceptibility to secondary collapse of structures associated with the victim. In all cases, it is important to identify to the extent possible the pre- and post-blast locations of bodies and body parts.

Mechanisms of Blast Injuries

Primary

- Caused by blast wave effect; unique to high explosives (military-grade demolition explosives).
- Primary effect on gas-filled structures of the body such as the lungs, gastrointestinal tract, and middle ear.
- Blast lung (pulmonary barotrauma) is caused by overpressurization from forced air embolism or air outside the lung forced into the space between the lung and chest wall (pneumothorax).
- Abdominal bleeding and perforation of the gastrointestinal tract.
- Traumatic brain injury without external evidence of impact.

Secondary

- Caused by penetrating and blunt force injury from flying debris, shrapnel, and bomb parts.
- Penetrating injuries from foreign objects.
- Blunt force trauma from items striking the victim.

Tertiary

- Caused when a victim is thrown by a blast.
- Fractures or amputations of extremities.
- Fractures of trunk or skull.
- Brain injuries associated with falls.

Quaternary

- Category includes all other blast-related injuries.
- Flash burns from initial blast effect.
- Partial and full thickness burns from fires associated with blast.
- Crushing injuries.

Cautions

- All fatal explosion victims should receive full body x-rays prior to autopsy.
- Bomb parts or unexploded munitions parts may have penetrated victims' bodies and pose a threat to investigators.

Thermal Injuries

22

Thermal injuries result from heat and direct flame impingement upon the skin, underlying tissue, and mucosa.

General Considerations

- Most injuries and deaths caused by fire are accidental.
- Fire may be used to mask the results of other crimes and causes or manners of death.
- Most fire victims die of carbon monoxide poisoning. Thermal injury, if present, is often secondary.

Scene

A fatal fire may require processing of both a death scene and a fire scene. A fire death scene involves specific issues.

- A fire scene is an extremely dangerous area to work. Consider having a firefighter assigned to your team for the sole purpose of ensuring safety at scenes.
- Need for further investigation is based on the autopsy determination of cause of death. Do not release the scene until the autopsy results are issued.
- Examine the scene to determine whether the immediate area around the victim was consumed by fire. An area of destruction not in proportion to the rest of a fire scene may indicate an attempt to burn the body or a fire started by the victim.
- Photograph the removal of the debris atop the body in detail, layer by layer.
- All debris removed from the area atop and beneath the body should be sifted for evidence of another possible cause of death (gunshot, knife, ligature, etc.).
- Thoroughly photograph and document the exposed body. Photography of burned remains is very difficult due to the lack of contrast.

- Complete body processing steps described in Chapters 3 through 5.
- After the body is removed, photograph the area from which it was removed.
- Collect samples below and immediately adjacent to the body for accelerant detection.
- Document locations of all exits and potential exit routes and their conditions (locked, unlocked). Note indications that an escape route may have been blocked.

Worksheets and Documentation

The following documentation guides, forms, logs, and worksheets are provided in Section VIII, "Death Investigation Checklist and Worksheets," and may be used in documenting this scene. Additional forms, other than those noted, may also be used as dictated by your scene. These forms may be preprinted from the publisher's website (www.crcpress.com/cw/maloney) or photocopied from this procedural guide.

- *Death Investigation Checklist*
  - Section 9: Wounds/Weapons/Drugs/Medications
- *Worksheet*
  - Worksheet 12: Immersion Burn Worksheet

Body

Burns are classified according to the depth of tissue damage.

First-Degree Burns

- First-degree burns are superficial (Figure 22.1).
- Damage is limited to the outer layer of skin and has a reddish appearance.

Second-Degree Burns

- Second-degree burns are red and often show blistering (Figure 22.2).
- The upper layers of the skin are damaged.
- These burns usually heal without scarring.

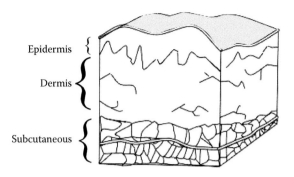

Figure 22.1 First-degree burn.

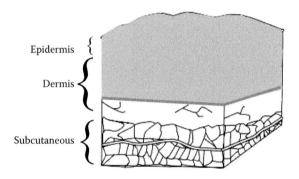

Figure 22.2 Second-degree burn.

Third-Degree Burns

- Third-degree burns damage the entire thickness of the skin (Figure 22.3).
- The skin may appear white and leathery or black and burned.
- These burns heal with scarring.

Fourth-Degree Burns

- Fourth-degree burns extend beyond the skin into the tissues below.
- Complete charring of tissue and destruction of skin and underlying tissue occur.

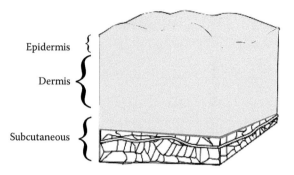

Epidermis {

Dermis {

Subcutaneous {

Figure 22.3 Third-degree burn.

Deaths from Fire-Related Injuries

- If a body is not burned, proceed as you would with any other type of death.
- Deaths attributed to fire are caused by asphyxia due to smoke inhalation and thermal tissue injuries. Death may be immediate or delayed.
- Immediate deaths are the results of burns or smoke inhalation.
- Delayed deaths may occur even months after the fire and are usually caused by shock, fluid loss, infection, or respiratory failure.
- A fire victim may appear in a defensive posture like a boxer—arms in front of the chest and face. The position is called the *pugilistic stance* and results from muscle reactions to extreme heat. It is a natural characteristic of death by fire, not an indicator that the victim was trying to protect himself or herself before death.
- Fractures of the extremities of fire victims may be caused by excessive shrinking of the muscles.
- Heat fractures of the skull can appear as cracks on both sides of the head above the temples.
- Steam pressure in the cranial vault may cause breakage of the skull and the protrusion of brain tissue.
- At autopsy, the presence of soot inside the airway is an indicator that the person was alive at the time of the fire.
- X-rays should be taken of burned bodies before autopsy.
- Blood samples must be taken to establish carbon monoxide concentration in the blood.

Electrical Injuries 23

Electrocution is death or injury resulting from contact with an electrical source that transmits a flow of electricity through the body. Deaths and injuries caused by electricity are rare and usually accidental. However, safety concerns often require thorough investigations of the circumstances that caused deaths and injuries.

Worksheets and Documentation

The following documentation guides, forms, logs, and worksheets are provided in Section VIII, "Death Investigation Checklist and Worksheets," and may be used in documenting this scene. Additional forms, other than those noted, may also be used as dictated by your scene. These forms may be preprinted from the publisher's website (www.crcpress.com/cw/maloney) or photocopied from this procedural guide.

- *Death Investigation Checklist*
  - Section 9: Wounds/Weapons/Drugs/Medications
- *Worksheet*
  - Worksheet 9: Trace Evidence Notes

Commercial and Residential Power Sources

Scene

- Ensure that the power source is turned off before you approach an electrocution scene. This is best accomplished by trained electrical personnel.
- Process the scene in accordance with the guidelines in Chapters 3 through 5.
- Low-voltage cases usually involve household appliances or electrical cords. An examination of the suspect device is essential for a thorough investigation. Some cases may require a team approach involving an assisting pathologist, investigator, and a qualified electrician.

Body

- High-voltage electrocutions (those involving more than 1,000 volts) usually present extensive burns and are relatively easy to identify.
- Low-voltage electrocutions (fewer than 1,000 volts) often result from contact with household current (110–120 volts). No visible injury may be evident.
- A lightning strike may cause a noticeable fern-like pattern on the skin.
- The path of electricity through a body runs from the point of contact to the point of grounding. For example, if a person handles a live wire, the electricity will run from the hand, through the body along the major arteries, and exit at a foot or both feet.
- The presence of electrical burns depends on the voltage, amount of current flow, area of contact, and duration of contact. Burns may be present at both the entry and exit points of the current. Electrical burns often appear round, whitish, and crater-like, or may resemble second- or third-degree burns.

Lightning Strikes[1]

Direct Strike

- Entrance defect will show indications of severe burning, charred skin.
- Entrance defect is typically small but may be more diffuse if conductive surface is present at strike site.
- Exit defect (if present) will generally indicate the point on the body in contact with a grounded surface.
- Exit defect may be larger than the entrance and include what would appear to be blown-out tissue.
- If the victim is wearing a metal chain, watch, bracelet, or piercing, they may heat to the level of causing contact burns.
- Between the entrance and exit, the surface of the skin may exhibit a fern-like pattern called a *Lichtenberg figure* (Figure 23.1).

Scene

- If an exit injury is present at ground, there may be significant damage to the grounding surface.
- A road surface or soil surface may have an area of disturbance similar to the crater at the seat of a blast.

---

[1] Information on lightning strikes derived in part from the National Weather Service Lightening Safety website: http://www.lightningsafety.noaa.gov/struck.shtml

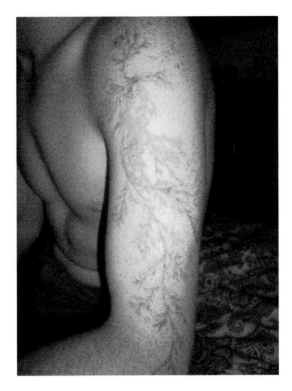

Figure 23.1 Fern pattern (Lichtenberg figure) as a result of lightning strike. Photograph provided courtesy of Judie Stanford. Photograph originally appeared in http://geardiary.com/2011/06/17/meet-winston-kemp-lightning-strike-survivor-and-lichtenberg-figure-owner/.

- If on sandy soil, the lightning may have turned the sand components to glass, which will resemble the root pattern of a small tree and will be uncovered beneath the sandy soil at the strike area. They are very fragile, as they are glass tubes formed by the strike. This is known as *fulgurate* (Figure 23.2).

Body
- The body may be unremarkable other than the burn marks and any trauma associated with a fall after the strike.
- The mechanism of death is most often asystole or fatal heart arrhythmia as a result of the electrical current passing through the body.
- Additionally a strike to the head may cause fatal damage to the brain.
- The clothing of the deceased may be charred at entrance and exit. If through the foot, the shoe may be blown out.

Figure 23.2 Fulgurite formation recovered from the sand at the base of a lightning strike. Specimen and photograph provided courtesy of Eric Greene, TreasureMountainMining.com.

Side Flash (Splash)

- A side flash occurs when a taller object is struck by lightning and the charge jumps to the victim.
- The victim is generally only 2 or 3 feet from the object struck by lightning.

Ground Strike

- When lightning strikes a tree or other object, the charge goes to ground and is greatly dispersed.
- The charge may travel a great distance and can even travel through concrete floors (rebar).
- Though often fatal to animals, many people are insulated through their footwear. Golfers and other with metal spikes may be at risk as the charge travels through the spike and causes death.
- Additionally, near lakes and swimming areas, people are often barefoot and also at risk for fatal consequences from a ground strike.

Scene

- The scene may involve multiple victims as they unknowingly gather under trees or other objects to get out of a thunderstorm.
- The original strike location must be documented.
- If on sandy soil, the lightning may have turned the sand components to glass, which will resemble the root pattern of a small tree and will be uncovered beneath the sandy soil at the strike area. This is known as *fulgurate*.

Body

- The path of travel of the current travels from the foot or ground contact point and an opposing ground contact point. This may be a hand on the ground or leaning against a tree.
- If the path from contact to ground travels through the heart, there is the possibility of fatal arrhythmia.

Conduction

- Anyone in contact with metal objects, including wiring that is in contact with an object struck by lightning, may receive fatal current through the contact point.
- If the current's path to ground is through the heart, a fatal arrhythmia may develop.
- Contact burn at entrance.
- Possible burning at point of ground.
- Must demonstrate lightning strike up line from the contact point.

Streamers

- As the downward moving leader approaches the ground, streamers develop. Typically, the downward leader connects with a single streamer and the return flash is seen.
- When the main streamer discharges, so do all of the other streamers. If a person is in contact with one of the other streamers, he or she may receive fatal current.

Poisoning

24

General Considerations

In the United States alone there are over 2 million human poisoning incidents a year; of these, over 15% are intentional.[1]

- About 3% are unintentional adverse reactions to commonly ingested/encountered items.
- In children younger than 6, almost all poisonings are unintentional. The investigator must still consider intentional poisonings to include such issues as Munchausen syndrome by proxy incidents (Chapter 27).
- In teens, 37% of poisonings are unintentional.
- In adults, 61% of poisonings are unintentional.
- Intentional poisonings may be suicidal, homicidal, and accidental (recreational drugs intentionally ingested with fatal results).

Intentional, unintentional, and adverse reaction poisonings may be difficult to distinguish from one another. The poisoner often chooses this method because of its difficulty to detect and not having to be physically present for the death. The investigator must thoroughly analyze the scene and the body within the scene context while working with the medical examiner and toxicologist to ensure the proper resolution of the investigation.

Worksheets and Documentation

The following documentation guides, forms, logs, and worksheets are provided in Section VIII, "Death Investigation Checklist and Worksheets," and may be used in documenting this scene. Additional forms, other than those noted, may also be used as dictated by your scene. These forms may be

---

[1] Statistical information taken from 2014 data reported by Poison Control—National Capital Poison Center website: http://www.poison.org/poison-statistics-national

preprinted from the publisher's website (www.crcpress.com/cw/maloney) or photocopied from this procedural guide.

- *Death Investigation Checklist*
  - Section 9: Wounds/Weapons/Drugs/Medications
- *Worksheets*
  - Worksheet 9: Trace Evidence Notes

Methods of Exposure

Inhaled Poisons

These are poisons in a gaseous, atomized, or aerosol powder form that are breathed in and transmitted through the mucus lining of the respiratory system or through the alveoli.

They may be intentionally inhaled for recreational purposes or suicide. They may also be accidentally inhaled in industrial accidents, or they may be used in intentional exposure in homicide.

Danger

For inhaled poison, ensure that the scene has been cleared of all toxic fumes prior to entry. *Do not* enter a gaseous poison scene without proper equipment and training!

Commonly Inhaled Poisons
- Carbon monoxide
  - Automobile exhaust
  - Charcoal fire for heat in home
  - Poorly vented furnace
- Carbon dioxide
  - Dry ice (rapidly warmed)
  - Fire extinguisher
- Helium
  - Party balloons
  - Exit hood
- Chlorine
  - Commercial pool/spa gas system
  - Home pool or spa
- Hydrogen sulfide
  - Chemical detergent suicide
  - Swamp gas/sewer gas

- Solvents (huffing and industrial exposure)
  - Gasoline
  - Paint thinners
  - Degreasers
- Huffing (recreational)
  - Nail polish remover
  - Aerosol sprays
  - Compressed gases (for cleaning, whipping, etc.)

Ingested Poisons

Poisons in a solid, semisolid, or liquid form may be ingested, where they are absorbed through the mucus lining of the digestive tract.

They may be intentionally ingested (suicide), accidentally ingested or intentionally administered (homicide).

Danger

Some ingested poisons may vent toxic fumes or may be able to be absorbed through the skin. Ensure that the scene has been cleared of all toxic fumes prior to entry. Wear proper barrier protection when handling poisons!

Commonly Ingested Poisons

- Children
  - Medicines
  - Button batteries
  - Iron pills
  - Cleaning products
  - Pesticides
  - Antifreeze
  - Wild mushrooms
  - Alcohol
  - Drain cleaners
  - Topical anesthetics
- Adults
  - Pain medicines
  - Sedatives
  - Cardiovascular drugs
  - Cleaning substances

- Alcohols
- Pesticides

Skin Exposure (Dermal Absorption)

Some poisons in powder or liquid form may be absorbed through the skin. This type of poisoning is most often suicide or homicide.

Common Skin Absorption Poisons

- Arsenic
- Many pesticides

Bites and Envenomation

Poisonous spiders, fish, coral, and venomous spiders may all expose the victim to poison through their bite, envenomation, or contact with poisoned barbs.

These exposures are most often accidental but may be homicidal if the poisonous animal was intentionally introduced to a setting where they would envenomate the victim.

Common Methods of Envenomation

- Snakes
- Spiders
- Scorpions
- Ticks
- Bees

The Body and Scene

Accidental Poisonings

Children under 6: almost always unintentional
Adults: feeble mental status

- Cosmetics and personal care products
  - Traces of agent around mouth or on hands
  - Odor of agent lingers on victim
  - Container or packaging from agent removed from usual storage space

- Pain or other medications
  - Medicine bottles, prescription bottles, or drug packaging removed from usual storage space
  - Partial pills or capsule remnants in vomitus near body
- Cleaning substances
  - Cleaning agents accessible to victim. Spilled cleaning agents or bottles, packaging near victim.
  - Odor of cleaning agent lingers on body.
  - Chemical burns around the mouth.

Intentional Poisoning

- Medications
  - Medicine bottles, prescription bottles, or drug packaging removed from usual storage space
  - Partial pills or capsule remnants in vomitus near body
  - Pill count from "prescription filled" date—overdose
- Drugs are covered in Chapter 25.
- Other (such as antifreeze, arsenic, cyanide): scene indicators and autopsy will lead to specialized toxicology.

The Body

The symptoms of some poisons are similar to the symptoms of some natural diseases. Consequently, toxicology of the affected person's body fluids or tissues is absolutely necessary to determine if the person has been poisoned.

- The biological sample (usually blood) should be taken as soon as possible after the suspected poisoning incident, regardless of whether the victim is alive or dead.
- If the person is alive, the poison must be identified as soon as possible because an antidote may exist.
- A scene investigation and a history of what the person has had to eat or drink should be obtained from the victim or the victim's family, friends, or coworkers. Provide this information to the attending medical physician or examiner as soon as possible.
- A thorough examination of the workspace and living space of the victim may reveal the presence of toxins that could be responsible for the poisoning. Environmental contaminants, stored household or commercial contaminants, and environmental contamination by exposure to pesticides must all be considered.

Drug-Related Deaths[1] 25

Drug-related deaths resulting from overdose, unexpected fatal toxicity due to purity of the drug, and asphyxia (positional or vomitus obstructed airway as a result of acute drug intoxication) are often classified as accidental, though they may be homicidal due to the context of their administration and procurement. Suicidal overdose is also possible but is difficult to distinguish from accidental overdose.

All drug-related deaths will require a thorough medicolegal autopsy and toxicology screen.

For the purposes of this chapter, drugs of abuse will be classified by their method of administration, as the method tends to dictate the findings at the scene and on the body.

- *Oral ingestion* is the swallowing of drugs, most commonly pills, mushrooms, or marijuana.
- *Intravenous injection* involves a hypodermic syringe and introducing the drug in a liquid form directly into the bloodstream. This frequently requires an intermediate step to heat the drug to a liquid form and is common with heroin administration.
- *Insufflation/inhalation* includes smoking, snorting, and huffing drugs to introduce them by absorption through either the mucus membranes of the airway passages or through alveolar transfer in the lungs. This includes smoking marijuana, crack cocaine, snorting cocaine, and huffing gases.
- *Dermal Absorption* of drugs may be accomplished through the dermis (skin) or through the mucus membranes including sublingual (under the tongue) and through the colon by enema. This may be done with LSD and cocaine.

Worksheets and Documentation

The following documentation guides, forms, logs, and worksheets are provided in Section VIII, "Death Investigation Checklist and Worksheets,"

---

[1] Information on specific drugs of abuse are taken from the National Institutes of Health National Institute on Drug Abuse website: drugabuse.gov.

and may be used in documenting this scene. Additional forms, other than those noted, may also be used as dictated by your scene. These forms may be preprinted from the publisher's website (www.crcpress.com/cw/maloney) or photocopied from this procedural guide.

- *Death Investigation Checklist*
  - Section 9: Wounds/Weapons/Drugs/Medications

Oral Ingestion

Oral ingestion is the swallowing of drugs, most commonly pills, mushrooms, or marijuana.
- Prescription pill abuse (painkillers, muscle relaxants, etc.) are easily swallowed and ingested.
- Chewing or crushing the pill prior to ingestion speeds the effect and intensity of the drug.
- Often pill capsules, plant husk, or partially chewed remnants of the ingested item may be found in the stomach contents or vomitus.

Intravenous, Subdermal, and Intramuscular Injection

Injection involves using a hypodermic syringe and introducing the drug in a liquid form directly into the body. This frequently requires an intermediate step to heat the drug to a liquid form and is common with heroin administration. Intravenous injection allows for the most rapid and intense high. Steroids are often injected directly into the muscle.

- The most frequently injected drug is heroin.
- All opiates may be liquefied and injected, including prescription drugs like oxycontin.
- Methamphetamine, ketamine, cocaine, and morphine are also frequently injected.
- Intravenous injections go directly into the bloodstream.
  - A rubber constricting tube, belt, or piece of cord is often used as a tourniquet.
  - A spoon and lighter are used to liquefy the drug.
  - Needles are often difficult to obtain, so they are frequently reused and present with the drug kit.
  - Track marks are frequently seen along the major veins of the inner arm. Additionally, needle marks may be found in more discreet places such as between the toes.

Insufflation/Inhalation

Inhalation is the breathing in of a substance. This includes smoking, snorting, and huffing drugs such as smoking marijuana, crack cocaine, snorting cocaine, and huffing gases.

- Smoking is a common way to burn drugs within a rolled cigarette or pipe and draw the smoke directly into the lungs.
  - A "bong" using water or juice may be used to cool and flavor the smoke prior to inhalation.
  - The pipe, rolling papers, or other expedient pipes are often present in the area.
  - The substance itself is often in a plastic bag that should be preserved for prints.
- Snorting is drawing the drug in powder form through a straw (or expedient straw made from a rolled bill) directly into the nasal passages.
  - The drug is usually cut to a fine powder if necessary and drawn into lines on a solid surface, which the user then snorts through the straw, down the line.
  - A razor blade and expedient straw are often present at the scene.
  - The victim may have a single long fingernail, generally the little finger; this is often an indication that they snort this in a snuff-like fashion. The nail should be swabbed and tested.
- Huffing is accomplished by inhaling the fumes that naturally emanate from certain substances.
  - Acrylic paint, model glue, aerosol paints, aerosol air fresheners, and whipping cream gas cylinders all release toxic gases that give the user a high.
  - Frequently, the substance is sprayed into a bag or on a cloth and held against the mouth and nose. The substances frequently stain the mouth and nose.
  - Bags, clothes, expended and partially full aerosol canisters, etc., should all be seized from the scene and preserved for prints.
- Insufflation is the act of blowing a gas, powder, or vapor into a body cavity. This is most often accomplished through the mouth and nose. Technically differs from inhalation as the airflow used to introduce them originates external to the user. "Shotgunning" is an example where marijuana (or any smoked or vaporized drug) is forced into person's lungs by the forceful exhalation of another person.
  - This practice generally indicates a level of sexual familiarity between the two parties.

- If direct mouth-to-mouth contact is suspected to have been made, DNA swabs of the victim's lips should be taken. This may be useful in identifying whom they were with.

Absorption

Absorption of drugs may be accomplished through the dermis (skin) or through the mucus membranes including sublingual (under the tongue) and through the colon by suppository or enema.

- Suppository administration is fairly uncommon but has been seen with LSD, cocaine, and ecstasy.
- Sublingual absorption is generally used when drugs are permeated into or dried onto the surface of a strip of blotter-type paper. LSD and heroin are examples of these drugs. The blotter typically is a larger piece of paper with repeating designs, logos, or images containing the drug. *Caution: With damp, unprotected hands, fingertip absorption is a possibility when handling these.*
- Dermal absorption may be accomplished with LSD in its blotter form.
- Dermal absorption may be accomplished with almost any drug when a transdermal medical path is subverted for this cause.

Drug-Related Death Scenes

The drug-related death scene contains many hazards.

- If it is suspected that you are dealing with a clandestine drug lab, have an appropriate team from the DEA (Drug Enforcement Agency) or other agency conduct the search. Clandestine drug labs pose a unique hazard with explosive and volatile chemicals, as well as the potential for booby traps.
- IV needles and the presence of drugs and various constituents that may be absorbed through the skin pose a potential hazard to the investigator.
- Due to their lifestyle, drug users may be infected with HIV, hepatitis B, and other communicable diseases, and the appropriate PPE should be worn.

Processing the Scene

- A methodical search for drugs and their associated paraphernalia should be undertaken. In addition, personal telephone number books and other storage mediums may be of value to the investigator.
- Locate, fully document, and seize all prescription medications, alcohol, and other drugs present.

Drug Scene Evidence

The following evidence is commonly found at drug and drug distribution scenes:

- Illegal drugs
- Computer evidence
- Smart phones (recent calls, texts, etc.)
- Drug paraphernalia
- Packaging material
- Weapons
- Currency

The Body at the Scene

- The abuse of most drugs does not usually create visible external injury on the body.
- Exceptions include track marks and injection marks from intravenously injected drugs and broken and cracked teeth from the heat effect of smoking crack.
- Prolonged drug abuse can cause disease and infection.
- The key to any drug-related injury or death is the toxicology of the victim's body fluids.

Special Death Investigations

V

Infant Deaths

26

Infants die from diseases, metabolic disorders, accidents, neglect, injuries, and intentional acts of violence and neglect. Any of these reported incidents require thorough scene documentation, processing, and analysis following the procedures established in Chapter 5 ("Homicidal Deaths"), along with the guidelines below. This chapter focuses on violent death, fatal malnourishment, and other intentional acts that take infants' lives. For more specific guidance on cases where fatal physical abuse or neglect are suspected, see Chapter 27.

Worksheets and Documentation

The following documentation guides, forms, logs, and worksheets are provided in Section VIII, "Death Investigation Checklist and Worksheets," and may be used in documenting this scene. Additional forms, other than those noted, may also be used as dictated by your scene. These forms may be preprinted from the publisher's website (www.crcpress.com/cw/maloney) or photocopied from this procedural guide.

- *Death Investigation Checklist*
  - Section 1: Crime Scene Information
  - Section 2: Civilians Who Entered the Death Scene
  - Section 3: Death Scene
  - Section 4: Coroner/Medical Examiner Notification
  - Section 9: Wounds/Weapons/Drugs/Medications
  - Section 10: Identification/Notification
  - Section 11: Scene Processing
  - Section 12: Death Scene Release Information
  - Section 13: Narrative Report
  - Section 14: (appropriate forms and logs)
- *Worksheets*
  - Worksheet 1: Postmortem Indicator (PMI)
  - Worksheet 2: Death Scene Entry Log
  - Worksheet 3: Photography Head Slate
  - Worksheet 4: Photography Log

- Worksheet 7: Entomology Worksheet
- Worksheet 8: Biological Evidence Notes
- Worksheet 9: Trace Evidence Notes
- Worksheet 10: Friction Ridge Evidence
- Worksheet 11: Impression Evidence Notes
- Worksheet 12: Immersion Burn Worksheet
- Worksheet 13: SIDS/SUIDI (Sudden Infant Death)
- Worksheet 15: Bloodstain Pattern Worksheet

Violent Death

The signs of violent death in an infant, particularly by suffocation or shaken baby syndrome, may be very subtle. Violent deaths are classified separately from deaths resulting from the intentional withholding of nourishment or sudden unexplained infant death (SUID) syndrome.

Asphyxial

- Caused by "soft" suffocation.
- Victim may exhibit bruised or torn frenulum.
- Pattern injuries on mouth and nose may be visible under alternate light sources.
- A pillow or other soft object may show significant saliva staining under ultraviolet or alternate light sources.

Asphyxial by Entrapment (Rollover)

- Infant entrapment (rollover) by a parent sleeping next to an infant is very rare.
- If suspected, investigate possible obese caregiver or drug or alcohol intoxication.

Shaken Baby Syndrome and Shaken Baby with Impact Syndrome

Shaken baby syndrome describes a variety of findings that result when an infant is forcibly shaken. The medical examiner community does not agree on the activities that cause it. Some believe the shaking must be accompanied by the impact of an infant's head on some surface. Others believe that shaking alone is sufficient. In suspected cases, coordinate the scene analysis and additional searches with the guidance of the medical examiner.

- Death is usually the result when a frustrated caregiver is unable to settle a crying or screaming infant.
- Death is not instantaneous. A period of listlessness during which the brain reacts to traumatic injury is followed by the critical cascade of events that lead to death.
- Medical treatment is often sought when an infant appears listless or cannot be awakened.

Medical Findings

- Retinal hemorrhages are small bleeding events seen on the surface of the retina of the eye. They are often medically documented during treatment of injuries before the victim's demise.
- Subdural or subarachnoid hemorrhages occur when blood escapes into the layer between protective coverings of the brain or between the brain and its closest protective layer.
- Edema (swelling) of the brain.
- Cerebral contusions (bruises) of the brain.
- Cerebral infarction, deprivation of blood to an area of the brain due to a disturbance in blood flow.
- These injuries may exist despite few or no external signs of trauma.
- Bruising to the chest and back may occur from the fingertips of the perpetrator as he or she gripped and shook the infant. Consider swabbing the bruises for touch DNA and measuring their orientation to each other and the body to determine the finger spread. Suspects may be eliminated by not meeting the finger-spread measurements.
- Rib fractures may accompany the event as the infant's chest is most often encircled by the perpetrator's hands and forcefully shaken.
- Injuries resulting from violent shaking or pulling of the limbs may be present.

Failure to Thrive

Organic Causes

- Certain diseases and hereditary conditions prevent an infant from being able to metabolize nutrients.
- Infant may have a diagnosed medical condition.

- Medical records will indicate failure of the infant to thrive under medically supervised feeding.
- Home will reveal evidence of medical treatment, records, and attempts at intervention.
- No indications of neglect will be present.
- Infant will present as emaciated and clean.
- Living conditions will not reflect neglect (may reflect poverty).
- Typically, the death will occur under medical supervision and be certified as natural by the treating physician.
- Autopsy may reveal a physical condition, disease, or deformity inhibiting the infant's ability to metabolize age-appropriate food.

Neglect Causes

Fatal child neglect requires extensive documentation of the conditions in the home. Scene documentation is covered in great detail in the next chapter.

- Failure to meet base level of nutritional needs of an infant.
- Seldom affects toddlers. A child who can move about often develops foraging skills.
- Often demonstrated by infant's ability to thrive in a medical environment.
- May also result from a caregiver with diminished capacity or a failure to understand and/or follow nutritional guidance.
- Failure to thrive from withholding of nutrition is rarely an isolated behavior; search for other indications of neglect.
- Infant will present as emaciated and most likely show other physical signs of neglect. The infant may be filthy, have severe diaper rash, or other signs not consistent with a nurturing environment.
- Living conditions will often demonstrate neglect.
- Few or no age-appropriate foods or nutritional supplements will be present in the home.
- Autopsy will reveal no medical condition that would inhibit the infant's ability to metabolize age-appropriate food.

Sudden Unexplained Infant Death[1]

SUIDs are cases in which no cause of death was obvious at the time of the demise. SUID occurs in infants under 1 year of age and remains unexplained

---

[1] Information on investigative procedures taken in part from the Centers for Disease Control reporting form: https://www.cdc.gov/sids/suidrf.htm.

after a thorough investigation. The risk for SUID peaks at 2–4 months of age and 90% of SUID deaths occur in children younger than 6 months. For investigative purposes, SUID deaths are handled as homicides (Chapter 5). Special guidance is provided below. SUIDs may only be diagnosed after the following:

- Performance of a complete autopsy that rules out all other causes
- A thorough death scene examination
- A complete review of the infant's medical and clinical history

Appendix E is an SUID scene worksheet. The form is not copyrighted and is available electronically from the Centers for Disease Control: www.cdc.gov/SIDS/SUIDIRF-EV.htm.

The worksheet covers investigative details, witness interviews, infant medical and dietary histories, mother's pregnancy history, incident scene investigation, investigator's summary and diagrams, and a pathologist's summary section. Risk factors associated with SUIDS include the following:

- Breastfeeding
- Exposure to tobacco smoke
- Sleeping prone
- Male gender
- Low maternal education
- Young maternal age
- Single mother
- Late or no prenatal care

Victim

Specific information should be obtained related to circumstances surrounding a suspected death from SUID:

- Age of victim.
- Race of victim.
- Ethnicity of victim.
- Date and time of notification of emergency personnel.
- Person or organization that notified emergency personnel.
- Condition of infant when discovered (dead, unconscious, in distress).
- Sequence of events before death.
- Evidence of injury.
- Position of infant when found.
- Position of infant when last seen alive.

- Resuscitation attempts made by relatives, EMS, others.
- If injury is noted, consider utilizing scene procedures from Chapter 15 ("Asphyxiation") and Chapter 17 ("Blunt Force Injuries").
- Document scene in accordance with Chapter 5, "Homicidal Death."

It is also essential to obtain a complete medical history and copies of appropriate documentation to ascertain the following:

- Problems during labor or delivery
- Maternal illness or complications during pregnancy
- Major birth defects
- Hospitalization of infant after initial discharge
- Emergency room visits in 2 weeks preceding death
- Known allergies
- Whether growth and weight gain were considered normal
- Exposure to contagious diseases in 2 weeks preceding death
- Illnesses in 2 weeks preceding death
- Whether infant ever stopped breathing or turned blue
- Whether the infant was breastfed
- Vaccinations in 72 hours preceding death
- Deceased siblings and circumstances of their deaths
- Medication history
- Number of smokers in household

Scene

The death scene is an essential component of a thorough investigation of SUIDs. Information gathered during the scene investigation augments information obtained from an autopsy and review of clinical and medical history and aids the medical examiner to determine the cause and manner of death.

- Is the death scene the primary residence of the infant?
- If the infant was discovered after being put down to sleep, was he or she sleeping in a primary or usual sleeping location?
- Is the death scene a day-care or childcare setting?
- How many children were in the care of the provider at the time of the death?
- How many adults were supervising the children?
- Were any youth supervising the children? How old were they?

Fully describe and document the following at the scene:

- Heating and cooling sources. Were they operating? What were their settings?
- Were windows open or closed? Was a fan operating in or near a window?
- The temperature of the room where the infant was found. Determine thermostat setting, thermostat reading, room temperature, and outside temperature.
- Any observed mold growth, excessive dampness, or standing or dripping water. Preserve samples of mold, standing water, and dripping water.
- Indications of insect or vermin infestation.
- Peeling paint.
- Odor of cigarette smoke.
- Unusual smells or fumes.
- Electrical cords or wires near or contacting crib or sleeping surface. Exercise extreme caution; check for stray voltage and ensure breaker has not tripped.
- Was the room recently painted? Have all associated fumes dissipated?
- Are alcoholic beverage containers or drug paraphernalia present?
- Determine source of drinking water at scene and preserve a sample.

Fully describe, document, and collect the following items of evidence:

- Sleeping or supporting surface
- Clothing, including diapers
- Other items in contact with infant (pacifiers, dangling toys, bumper guards, etc.)
- Items in crib or immediate environment
- Electrical and mechanical devices operating in room
- Room temperature; cooling and heat sources

Dietary History

- Who was the last person to feed the infant? Collect remaining food or formula.
- What is the relationship of the feeding person to the infant?
- What foods and liquids were fed in the last 24 hours? Collect samples of all foods and liquids if possible, for example:
  - Breast milk
  - Formula

- Cow's milk
- Water
- Juices or teas
- Solids
- Other
- Were any new foods introduced in the last 24 hours? Describe them and collect samples.
- Was the infant last placed to sleep with a bottle? Collect bottle and contents.
- Was the bottle propped? If so, what was used to prop the bottle?
- Did death occur during breastfeeding? Bottle-feeding? Eating solid foods?

Medical History

- In the 72 hours before death, did the infant have any of the following:
  - Fever
  - Excessive sweating
  - Lethargy or sleeping more than usual
  - Decrease in appetite
  - Vomiting
  - Choking
  - Diarrhea
  - Stool changes
  - Difficulty breathing
  - Apnea (stopped breathing)
  - Cyanosis (skin turned blue or gray)
  - Seizures or convulsions
  - Other medical condition
- In the 72 hours prior to death, was the infant injured?
- In the 72 hours prior to death, was the infant given vaccinations or medications?
- Did the infant have a history of:
  - Allergies (foods, medications, other)
  - Abnormal growth or weight gain or loss
  - Apnea (stopped breathing)
  - Cyanosis (skin turned blue or gray)
  - Seizures or convulsions
  - Cardiac (heart) abnormalities
  - Metabolic disorders
  - Other observed medical condition

- Describe the infant's two most recent visits to a physician or health care provider.
- Record the following birth data:
  - What were the infant's length and weight at birth?
  - Was the infant born early, late, or when expected?
  - Was the infant a singleton, twin, triplet, or other multiple births?
  - Did any complications occur during delivery or at birth?
  - Have there been previous infant deaths in the family?

Mother's Pregnancy History

- Is mother of the infant his or her birth mother? If she is not, attempt to find and interview the birth mother and/or review her pregnancy medical history.
- For how many weeks or months did the mother participate in prenatal care?
- Where did the mother receive prenatal care?
- During pregnancy or birth, did the mother suffer any complications?
- Was the mother injured during pregnancy?
- During pregnancy, did the mother use any of the following:
  - Over-the-counter medications
  - Prescription medications
  - Herbal remedies
  - Cigarettes
  - Alcohol
  - Other
- Did the mother or other caregiver at the time of the death use any of the following:
  - Over-the-counter medications
  - Prescription medications
  - Herbal remedies
  - Cigarettes
  - Alcohol

Child Deaths

27

Children die from diseases, accidents, neglect, injuries, and intentional acts of violence and neglect. Any of these reported incidents require thorough scene documentation, processing, and analysis following the procedures established in Chapter 5 ("Homicidal Deaths"), along with the guidelines below. This chapter focuses on violent death, fatal malnourishment, and other intentional acts that take a child's life. For more specific guidance on cases where fatal physical abuse or violence is associated with sexual abuse, see Chapter 28.

Worksheets and Documentation

The following documentation guides, forms, logs, and worksheets are provided in Section VIII, "Death Investigation Checklist and Worksheets," and may be used in documenting this scene. Additional forms, other than those noted, may also be used as dictated by your scene. These forms may be preprinted from the publisher's website (www.crcpress.com/cw/maloney) or photocopied from this procedural guide.

- *Death Investigation Checklist*
  - Section 1: Crime Scene Information
  - Section 2: Civilians Who Entered the Death Scene
  - Section 3: Death Scene
  - Section 4: Coroner/Medical Examiner Notification
  - Section 9: Wounds/Weapons/Drugs/Medications
  - Section 10: Identification/Notification
  - Section 11: Scene Processing
  - Section 12: Death Scene Release Information
  - Section 13: Narrative Report
  - Section 14: (appropriate forms and logs)
- *Worksheets*
  - Worksheet 1: Postmortem Indicator(PMI)
  - Worksheet 2: Death Scene Entry Log
  - Worksheet 3: Photography Head Slate
  - Worksheet 4: Photography Log

- Worksheet 7: Entomology Worksheet
- Worksheet 8: Biological Evidence Notes
- Worksheet 9: Trace Evidence Notes
- Worksheet 10: Friction Ridge Evidence
- Worksheet 11: Impression Evidence Notes
- Worksheet 12: Immersion Burn Worksheet
- Worksheet 15: Bloodstain Pattern Worksheet

Physical Abuse and Violent Acts

The Scene

Weapon or Item Used to Inflict Injury

- Seize any items that may have been used to inflict injury: weapons, belts, coat hangers, wires, cords, etc. These items often leave distinct pattern injuries on the victim's body.
- If the object associated with the injury cannot be found, conduct an expanded search of the area. Focus on the likely paths of travel by the perpetrator and nearby dumpsters, bodies of water, and roofs of buildings.
- If restraints were used (ropes, belts, tape, clothing, etc.) to bind the victim, seize the items and protect them for the recovery of trace and other evidence. Knots and overlapped areas of tape should not be cut through or untied.
- Search for, examine, and recover other items that may link a suspect to the crime and/or death scene or corroborate the reports of the event by victims, suspects, and witnesses.

Burns, Scalds, Immersion Burns

- Consider taking the temperature of hot water from the faucet in cases involving scalds, splash burns, or immersion burns. Also note the temperature setting of the hot water heater. These procedures and steps are detailed in Worksheet 12, "Immersion Burns."
- Look for items that are consistent with pattern burn injuries on the child.
- Look for skin on the surfaces of objects used to dry-burn the victim.

Falling Injuries and Staged Accidents

- Take measurements of furniture, stairs, and equipment if a case involves falling-type injuries or claims that the victim fell accidentally.
- Check for indications that a death scene accident was staged.

The Body

Because of the undeveloped nature of children's skeletal and muscular systems, child injuries often manifest differently than injuries to adults. Certain types of injuries are common to child abuse cases and should be considered suspicious, especially in the absence of clinical history or when the history given is inconsistent with the injury.

Skeletal System Injuries

- Bone injuries that appear out of proportion to the clinical history provided, especially rib fractures, skull fractures, and long bone fractures
- Multiple fractures at different stages of healing that may indicate multiple incidents of physical abuse over time
- Combination of skeletal and soft tissue injuries

Skin and Subcutaneous Tissue Injuries

- Abusive injuries commonly appear in areas not usually involved in accidental falls of childhood—fleshy body parts such as the arms or legs, buttocks, abdomen, inner thighs, face, mouth, cheeks, genitals, or the back above the buttocks (Figure 27.1).
- Multiple injuries in various stages of healing may indicate repeated beatings. Children who fall and injure themselves accidentally

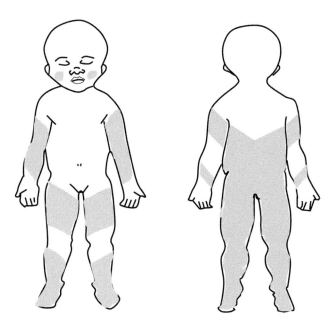

Figure 27.1 Suspicious location for "accidental" injuries.

usually have bruises on the bony prominences—chin, forehead, elbows, knees, and shins.

- Insect or other bites indicative of infestation of the living environment.
- Severe diaper rash; uncleaned, untreated sores; and other indicators of failure to provide basic hygiene.
- Examine contents of soiled diapers, training pants, or underwear worn. If insect eggs or maggots are present or associated with injuries, collect the entomological evidence (Chapter 40). It may provide an indication of the duration of neglect.

Immersion, Contact, and Cigarette Burns

- The shapes and locations of these injuries are important for distinguishing accidental and nonaccidental burns.
- Accidental burns are usually asymmetrical, random, and most often on the hands, chest, and legs. They usually are devoid of patterns and poorly defined. Inflicted burns are usually well defined and symmetrical (Figure 27.2).
- Immersion burns frequently occur over both legs and can extend to the abdomen. The burn pattern may resemble a glove over the hands or a sock over the feet. The knees and popliteal spaces (areas behind the knees) are typically spared as the child may flex his legs when contact is made with the hot water (Figure 27.3).

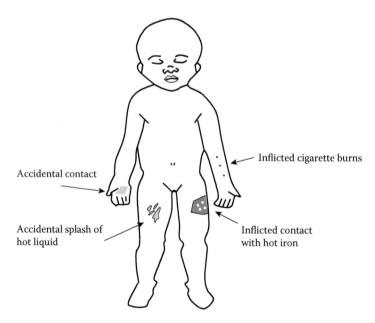

Figure 27.2 Accidental versus inflicted burns.

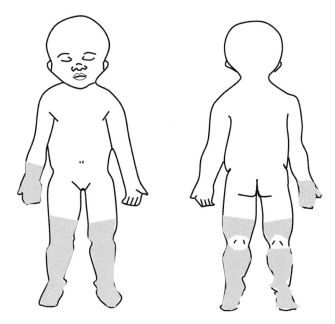

Figure 27.3 Immersion burns.

- Pattern burns result from contact with hot surfaces such as stove burners and irons. Typical locations are the back, forearms, and buttocks. During scene examination, search for an object that may have produced the pattern.
- Accidental cigarette burns are not uncommon. However, multiple cigarette burns and burns in various stages of healing are almost always indicative of abuse.

Head and Central Nervous System Injuries
- A torn frenulum in the mouth may be indicative of abuse and occurs from the forcible insertion of an object into the mouth, striking the child across the face, or smothering (Figure 27.4). The frenulum may also be torn when a child falls with an object in their mouth such as a spoon. The frenulum is the small fold of tissue between the gums and lip that prevents the lips from extending too far away from the mouth (you can easily observe your frenulum in a mirror by raising your upper lip).
- Have the victim examined for the presence of retinal hemorrhages to determine the possibility of forcible repeated shaking prior to death. At autopsy, the pathologist should investigate possible detached retinas.
- Scalp bruises and bald patches on the head are common signs of abuse.

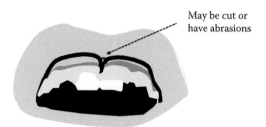

May be cut or
have abrasions

Figure 27.4 A torn frenulum is almost always indicative of abuse.

- *Shaken baby syndrome* is a general term that covers a variety of findings: retinal hemorrhage, subdural or subarachnoid hemorrhage, edema, cerebral contusion, cerebral infarction, rib fractures, and injuries resulting from violent shaking or pulling of the limbs. Despite these injuries, the victim may show few or no external signs of trauma.
- The medical examiner community continues to disagree about shaken baby syndrome. Some believe it must be accompanied by impact of the victim's head on some surface during the shaking episode. Others believe that shaking alone is sufficient. Coordinate scene analysis and search details with the guidance of the local medical examiner.

Chest and Abdominal Injuries
- *Rib fractures*: Significant force is needed to fracture the ribs of infants and children. Rib fractures should be considered suspicious.
- *Abdominal injuries*: Bruises over the abdomen are uncommon even in cases of major abdominal injuries.

Medicolegal Autopsy

In addition to standard autopsy documentation, photography, and evidence collection, consider the following:

- Full body x-rays (bone survey) should be requested for any suspected physical child abuse death.
- During close-up photography of injuries, white balance and a color card should be used to ensure the most accurate color rendition on final prints.
- Consider requesting ultraviolet or infrared photography to enhance the visibility of pattern injuries or older bruising.
- Bruises and bite marks should be photographed several times over several hours with and without ultraviolet and infrared light to maximize possible pattern recognition.

- Bite marks should be processed as soon as possible (Chapter 44, "Impression Evidence"). Preservation of bite marks should be discussed with the medical examiner.
- Fully describe and collect the victim's clothing.

Additional Questions for Medical Examiner

- What type of weapon may have caused the injuries?
- Are injuries consistent with the care provider's account of the incident?
- Are the injuries likely to have resulted from accidental or inflicted trauma?
- If weapons or items suspected of having inflicted the injuries are available, ask the physician to compare them with the injuries. If they are not immediately available, return to the medical examiner for an opinion after the weapon or implement is discovered. Ensure the item is protected to preserve friction ridge and touch DNA evidence before handling!
- Is it possible to date (even approximately) fractures and bruising? If not, can the medical examiner determine whether they occurred at different times?
- Ask for an opinion about the causes of injuries. Determine what weapons, if any, may have inflicted the injuries. Determine whether the injuries are consistent with the history given by care providers, family members, suspects, and witnesses. Ask the physician whether the injuries are consistent with accidental or nonaccidental trauma.
- Request a specific opinion about indications of physical child abuse. If abuse is indicated, are the injuries associated with the abuse fatal or did they lead to death?

Medical Record Review

A thorough review of all medical records must be conducted in any case where physical child abuse is suspected.

- Any statements made to medical providers by parents or care providers about recent or past injuries should be thoroughly documented.
- To avoid detection of multiple incidents of abuse, a caregiver may have used different medical facilities. Insurance records, Medicaid records, and medical bills found at the scene may provide names of relevant health care providers.
- Injuries documented during autopsy, healing burns, and old fractures may not be covered in medical records. Failure of a caregiver to seek treatment may have been an attempt to avoid detection.

Munchausen Syndrome by Proxy

Munchausen syndrome by proxy is the result of a caregiver (most often the mother of the child) fabricating the symptoms of or inducing a life-threatening medical condition in the child in their care. It is believed that they seek the continual attention that comes from an ongoing medical crisis with the child.

- The caregiver most often begins by inducing a poison or foreign substance into the child that causes unexplained illness.
- The caregiver may also start the behavior with a child having a natural disease or illness that is beginning to get better.
- The caregiver often continues to introduce the foreign substance even while the child is undergoing medical treatment to include in hospital medical care.
- The caregiver will often increase their efforts at inducing illness if the child is scheduled for hospital release.

Common actions causing injury include

- Repeated near suffocations
- Repeated suppositories

Common poisons or contaminants include

- Excess salt ingestion
- Insulin injections
- Laxatives
- Injecting urine
- Rubbing or contaminating wounds with feces

Scene Investigation

Munchausen syndrome by proxy is most often brought to the attention of law enforcement by medical personnel or a concerned family member. An effective method of detecting Munchausen actions is through coordination with hospital administration for the installation of surveillance equipment in the hospital room and its bathroom. Once suspected, medical waste such as IV bags and catheters should be seized and carefully processed for prints or touch DNA of the caregiver.

Neglect

The Scene

- Consider examining a scene in conjunction with a state or local child welfare professional.
- An unkempt home, dirty living conditions, and absence of toys or child furnishings may be indicative of child neglect. Physical abuse and neglect often go hand in hand.

General Living Conditions

- Dirty living environment
- Evidence of poor housekeeping
- Overcrowded living conditions
- Inadequate child safety measures
- Lack of items normally associated with child care
- Infestation by roaches, other insects, and vermin

Child's Sleeping Area

- Dirty living environment
- Lack of or inappropriate bed or bedding
- Lack of or inappropriate clothing
- Failure to properly dispose of soiled diapers and clothing
- Presence of roaches, insects, or vermin: turn off the lights; wait about 10 minutes; turn the lights back on; photograph insects or vermin present

Food Preparation and Eating Area

- Dirty food preparation and eating environment
- Unclean dishes and cooking equipment
- Leftover food not properly discarded
- Presence of roaches, insects, or vermin
- Kitchen cupboards, pantries, refrigerator:
  - Lack of or inappropriate food supplies
  - Dirty food storage areas
  - Spoiled or rotting food
- Consider seizing relevant items to demonstrate victim's living conditions.

Child Sexual Abduction and Murder

28

Child abduction for the purpose of sexual assault is often followed by murder. In rare cases, a child is abducted for the purpose of serving as a long-term sexual captive of the perpetrator. This chapter will focus on the abduction scene, the site of the sexual assault, the scene of the murder, and the scene where the body was discovered.

The expertise of a sexual assault response team (SART) at the scene of these deaths may be very valuable during the body process phase. The SART must stay under the control of the lead DSI when examining the body. It is best if prior contact, training, and coordination are accomplished between the death investigation unit and the SART, as their training has focused on living victims.

Worksheets and Documentation

The following documentation guides, forms, logs, and worksheets are provided in Section VIII, "Death Investigation Checklist and Worksheets," and may be used in documenting this scene. Additional forms, other than those noted, may also be used as dictated by your scene. These forms may be preprinted from the publisher's website (www.crcpress.com/cw/maloney) or photocopied from this procedural guide.

- *Death Investigation Checklist*
  - Section 1: Crime Scene Information
  - Section 2: Civilians Who Entered the Death Scene
  - Section 3: Death Scene
  - Section 4: Coroner/Medical Examiner Notification
  - Section 9: Wounds/Weapons/Drugs/Medications
  - Section 10: Identification/Notification
  - Section 11: Scene Processing
  - Section 12: Death Scene Release Information
  - Section 13: Narrative Report
  - Section 14: (appropriate forms and logs)

- *Worksheets*
  - Worksheet 1: Postmortem Indicators
  - Worksheet 2: Death Scene Entry Log
  - Worksheet 3: Photography Head Slate
  - Worksheet 4: Photography Log
  - Worksheet 7: Entomology Recovery
  - Worksheet 8: Biological Evidence Worksheet
  - Worksheet 9: Trace Evidence
  - Worksheet 10: Friction Ridge Evidence
  - Worksheet 11: Impression Evidence
  - Worksheet 14: Bullet Defects
  - Worksheet 15: Bloodstain Patterns

Abduction

Often a kidnapping or missing person report will not involve an identifiable scene. The act may have taken place on a city street, playground, or other public area. In such cases, thorough neighborhood canvassing and interviews may provide the only details about the act. If a struggle was suspected, the area of the struggle should be processed in the same manner as any violent assault scene.

- It is critical to canvass for any surveillance camera coverage of the suspected abduction site as well as routes of egress from the area.
- Consider canvassing public areas for individuals who may have been recording video or taking photographs on smart phones or other devices. They may have inadvertently recorded the abduction or perpetrator in the background.
- If a park or other public area is suspected as the abduction site, others present during the suspected time frame may have video coverage that inadvertently shows the victim or perpetrator.

Missing Child Report

- A child death case may start as a missing child investigation. Check the residence, neighborhood, and surrounding areas for potential hiding spots.
- In a missing person investigation, a note of intent to leave home or run away may be present. Any notes should be collected and processed as questioned documents to ascertain their authenticity.

- A thorough search of the victim's personal effects, residence, and place last seen should be conducted to locate leads and evidence and identify friends and relatives of the victim, telephone numbers, and places frequented.
- Obtain the most recent photograph of the victim.
- Consider collecting the toothbrush of the victim and known samples of head hair from a hairbrush or pillow at the residence. Such evidence should be taken and packaged for possible future DNA identification. If this step is not handled tactfully, it may produce adverse emotional impacts on the victim's relatives.

Missing Adolescent Report

- Should the child have developed to adolescence or teen/late teen years, the possibility of a planned departure with or without notice or note is a possibility.
  - A thorough search of social media may indicate a planned meeting or departure.
  - Searching the bedroom may result in the discovery of a journal or diary, which may provide information that is useful to the investigation.
  - When in the bedroom, take the opportunity to seize a toothbrush or other item that could later be used as a DNA exemplar if required.
  - Thorough interviews of friends may indicate if the departure was planned.
  - AMBER alert should be immediately considered if criteria are met.
- In adolescent, teen, or late teen disappearance, the possibility of suicide must also be considered.
  - A thorough search of social media may indicate a planned intention to take their own life.
  - An Internet history search may indicate if suicide websites were visited and possibly the planned method of suicide.
  - Searching the bedroom may result in the discovery of a journal or diary, which may provide information that is useful to the investigation.
  - When in the bedroom, take the opportunity to seize a toothbrush or other item that could later be used as a DNA exemplar if required.

- Thorough interviews of friends may indicate if there were indications that the person was depressed or suicidal.
- AMBER alert should be immediately considered if criteria are met.

Scene

- In a confirmed stranger abduction case, immediately consult agency policy for issuance of an AMBER alert.
- All available videotapes of the suspected abduction location and avenues of approach and egress from the scene must be immediately seized and reviewed.
- Through scene analysis and a review of videotapes, determine whether the suspect may have handled objects at the scene; process such objects for latent prints and touch DNA testing.
- Through scene analysis and a review of videotapes, determine whether the suspect may have left evidence suitable for DNA processing (cigarette butts, chewing gum).
- Through scene analysis and a review of videotapes, determine whether the suspect left two- or three-dimensional footwear impressions or tire marks.
- Through scene analysis and a review of videotapes, determine whether the suspect dropped or discarded in waste cans or elsewhere any items that might aid in his or her identification.

Sexual Assault

If a scene where the victim was suspected to be held, sexually assaulted, and/or murdered is identified, follow the Chapter 5 guidelines for homicide scene processing and

- Thoroughly search for biological stains, particularly semen and blood.
- Identify any item that may have been used to restrain the child and may yield DNA, fingerprint, or trace evidence.
- Identify any item that may have been used as a gag and may yield DNA, fingerprint, or trace evidence.
- Search for age-inappropriate items (toys, children's clothing) at the scene if all the primary residents are adults.
- Search for cameras and recording devices.
- Search for a hidden area containing souvenirs from victims.

Searches Related to Pedophilia

Search the location where the sexual assault occurred. Also search outbuildings, sheds, garages, automobiles, attics, basements, storage facilities, post office boxes, and work spaces. Look for the following types of evidence:

- Cameras and video equipment intended for taking, producing, or reproducing photographic images: cameras (instant developing, 35 mm, digital), video production equipment, photographic printing equipment, lenses, enlargers, photographic papers, films, and developing chemicals.
- Phone books, phone registers, calendars, correspondence, lists of names, addresses, or phone numbers that identify the victim and other juveniles. This information may be found on computer hard drives or disks or may be encrypted on a computer. Remember, common gaming consoles may be used to store digital data.
- Photographs, movies, slides, videotapes, computer images, negatives, drawings, and undeveloped films that identify the victim and other juveniles and adults. Such information may be encrypted on storage media.
- Computers, thumb drives, storage devices, and disks intended for recording, producing, or transferring photographic images, data, or correspondence related to the victim. Remember, almost all gaming devices have the ability to store data and their purpose may have been suborned for this purpose.
- Correspondence, diaries, calendars, and other writings; tape recordings; letters relating to juveniles or adults that reveal identities and show sexual conduct between juveniles and/or adults. This information may be saved on computer hard drives or disks or encrypted on storage media.
- Magazines or books depicting nudity or sexual activities; collections of newspaper, magazine, and other clippings of juveniles that demonstrate the particular sex and age preferences of the suspect; child erotica; "art" collections; dance, ballet, gymnastics, and cheerleading photos. Such information may be encoded on a computer.
- Sexual aids such as rubber penises, dildos of various sizes and types, vibrators, lubricants, condoms, and bondage gear.
- Articles of personal property (locks of hair, panties, barrettes), toys, drawings, and other items belonging to or made by the victim.
- Safe deposit box keys, bank statements, billings, and checks that show the locations of safe deposit boxes and storage facilities of

any person involved in the sexual exploitation of children through molestation, pornography, or prostitution. The items may be found in file cabinets, mailing envelopes, or delivered mail.

- Indicators of occupancy such as personal property that establishes the identity of the person or persons in control of the premises where the sexual assault occurred. Examples are rent receipts, delivered mail, keys, and utility bills. This evidence is important when occupancy is questioned or disputed.
- Evidence of pedophile organization membership such as the North American Man–Boy Love Association (NAMBLA), Rene Guyon Society, Diaper Pail Fraternity (DPF), and others. Examples are newsletters, check stubs, credit card receipts for dues payments, bills for memberships, applications, and phone records.
- Evidence of computer site visitations to areas depicting or advertising adult pornography meant to simulate child pornography. This investigation requires a qualified computer forensic investigator!
- Evidence of the suspect's participation in legitimate youth organizations and activities.
- The suspect's work and attendance records.
- Peepholes, drop ceilings, and hidden cameras and compartments.

Murder

Specific guidance for steps in securing the scene, photography, and initial death scene procedures are covered in Section I ("Death Scene Investigations").

- Consider processing for perishable evidence and then securing the scene and delaying its processing (after processing perishable evidence) until results of medicolegal examination are available.
- Begin documentation via notes, sketching, and photography. Documentation should be ongoing.
- If the suspect is not a member of the household, examine paths of entry, exit, and the area of the incident for two- and three-dimensional footwear and/or tire impressions.
- Clothing, bed linens, rugs, and car seats may contain hair, blood, semen, and fiber evidence. Process these areas for biological and/or trace evidence.
- If the suspect does not live at the death scene and items of clothing and bedding were laundered, consider examining the lint from the washer and dryer for trace evidence.
- Use an ALS to detect biological evidence and fibers.

- Pay special attention to bathrooms since a suspect may clean up after a sexual assault. Washcloths, towels, and tissues may contain biological evidence residue.
- Any clothing, particularly underwear or diapers worn by the victim, should be seized.
- If the suspect is not a member of the household, process logical areas for impression and latent print evidence.
- Search for all evidence that corroborates or refutes witness or suspect statements.

Body Recovery

The search for and recovery of the body should follow the procedures discussed in Section III ("Recovery of Human Remains").

Evidence on Body

- If the body is still at the scene of the death, request attendance by a SART and a medical examiner.
- Inform the medical examiner of allegations, suspicions, or scene indications of vaginal or anal penetration (penile, digital, or other), recent oral penetration, fondling, and biting or other physical injuries. Physical evidence on the body should be shown to the examiner.
- Discuss swabbing for touch DNA analysis on areas of the body likely to have been handled to facilitate the sexual assault, murder, and disposal of the body. This must be done before substantial manipulation of the body by the medical examiner's staff.
- Request an examination of the body with and without clothing, using an ALS to detect biological fluids and other trace evidence such as lubricants, lotions, fibers, and hairs. Refer to Chapter 41 ("Biological Evidence").
- If an ALS is not available, use an ultraviolet light. Such lights are commonly used at medical facilities and are called *Woods lamps*.
- Discuss the sexual assault examination with the medical examiner before the examination proceeds; ensure that a prepared victim sexual assault evidence recovery kit approved by the servicing crime laboratory is used.
- Evidence associated with a sexual assault is perishable and should be collected as soon as possible.
- Ensure that the victim's clothing is collected, protected for trace evidence, and separately packaged.

- An examination using a colposcope may help locate microscopic injuries in the vagina and anus. This instrument can be used to better view bruises, tears, and scars. A camera can be attached to the colposcope to produce excellent documentation.
- If vaginal penetration is alleged or suspected, have the condition of the hymen evaluated and documented.

Examination of Suspect

- Appropriate authorization should be requested to conduct a physical examination of a suspect for evidence purposes.
- Generally, if fewer than 72 hours have elapsed since the reported incident, arrange for a medicolegal examination of the suspect using a prepared sexual assault examination kit approved by the servicing crime laboratory. This should include, at a minimum, combed and plucked pubic and head hairs, blood, saliva, penile swabs, and fingernail scrapings. All physical injuries should be completely documented.
- Generally, if more than 72 hours have elapsed since incident was reported, arrange for a medicolegal examination of the suspect using a prepared sexual assault examination kit approved by the servicing crime laboratory. This should include, at a minimum, combed and plucked pubic and head hairs, blood, and saliva.
- Any statements made to medical personnel about the incident should be thoroughly documented.
- Collect the clothing the suspect was wearing during the incident. Use the procedure described for processing clothing of victims.

Sexual Activities Resulting in Death

29

This chapter covers noncriminal consensual and solo sexual activities that may result in death. The expertise of a sexual assault response team (SART) at the scene of suspicious deaths may be very valuable. The SART must stay under the control of the lead DSI when examining the body. It is best if prior contact, training, and coordination is accomplished between the death investigation unit and the SART, as their training has focused on living victims.

Worksheets and Documentation

The following documentation guides, forms, logs, and worksheets are provided in Section VIII, "Death Investigation Checklist and Worksheets," and may be used in documenting this scene. Additional forms, other than those noted, may also be used as dictated by your scene. These forms may be preprinted from the publisher's website (www.crcpress.com/cw/maloney) or photocopied from this procedural guide.

- *Death Investigation Checklist*
  - Section 1: Crime Scene Information
  - Section 2: Civilians Who Entered the Death Scene
  - Section 3: Death Scene
  - Section 4: Coroner/Medical Examiner Notification
  - Section 9: Wounds/Weapons/Drugs/Medications
  - Section 10: Identification/Notification
  - Section 11: Scene Processing
  - Section 12: Death Scene Release Information
  - Section 13: Narrative Report
  - Section 14: (appropriate forms and logs)
- *Worksheets*
  - Worksheet 1: Postmortem Indicators
  - Worksheet 2: Death Scene Entry Log
  - Worksheet 3: Photography Head Slate
  - Worksheet 4: Photography Log
  - Worksheet 8: Biological Evidence Worksheet
  - Worksheet 9: Trace Evidence

- Worksheet 10: Friction Ridge Evidence
- Worksheet 11: Impression Evidence

Death during Coitus

The rigors of sexual activities may have an adverse effect on those that do not possess the stamina or health necessary to actively participate. If a fragile medical condition exists such as cardiac disease or cerebrovascular disease, to include the increase in plaque in supplying blood vessels, the rigors of sexual activity may be sufficient to cause a cardiac or cerebral incident leading to death. It cannot be determined if this is a natural death due to an underlying medical condition until after the autopsy. The scene should be documented and processed as a suspicious death.

The Scene

- No indication of forced entry into location.
- Location of sexual activity is logical for circumstances.
- Consider if location is logical within the confines of voyeurism or seeking the excitement of a possible disclosure.
- Consider if the location is logical if the partner is not the spouse or significant other of the victim.
- Consider if the location is logical due to the home, financial circumstances, and age of the participants.
- No indications of violence.
- No indication of restraints or bindings.
- If apparent consensual activities involve light bondage, gags, or other devices, equipment, or toys, consideration should be given that this death may be accidental as a result of positional asphyxia or suffocation.
- If apparent consensual activity involves heavy bondage, gags, restraints, or other devices, consideration should be given that this death is the result of homicide through direct intent or failure to exercise reasonable safety precautions.
- Any devices, restraints, clamps etc... on the body should be thoroughly photographed. They should remain on the body for review by the medical examiner. Any surface used in a device's application should be carefully sampled for touch DNA without its removal from the body.
- Items near the body or within the scene should be seized as evidence and preserved for friction ridge, DNA, and touch DNA.

- Documented medical history of condition that could explain the death.
- Medications, paraphernalia, and documentation that support the medical condition.
- Statements consistent with physical findings.

The Victim

- Documentation at the scene should involve the sexual assault protocol.
- The victim should undergo a sexual assault protocol during examination to include a victim sexual assault evidence recovery kit.

The Intimate Partner

If autopsy results are inconclusive for the presence of disease that would account for a natural death, then the intimate partner (and any other identified intimate partners for the 72 hours prior to death) should be taken to a medical facility for the completion of a suspect or partner sexual assault evidence recovery kit.

Hypoxic Deaths (Consensual, Breath Play)

Hypoxyphilia (breath play) involves restricting the oxygen available to the brain, which reportedly increases the intensity of the orgasm on the part of the practitioner. This may be practiced consensually with a partner in the form of face sitting (when the partner sits on the face of the practitioner restricting their ability to breathe), through soft suffocation (a pillow or towel), or manual strangulation. The intent in these acts is not to cause the practitioner's death but rather to enhance the sexual experience. If excessive pressure, duration, or inadequate judgment as to when to relieve pressure is exercised, it may result in the death of the practitioner. This is a suspicious death.

This practice may also be self-administered; this is referred to as *auto-erotic asphyxiation* and is detailed later in this chapter.

The Scene

- No indication of forced entry into location.
- Location of sexual activity is logical for circumstances.
- Consider if location is logical within the confines of voyeurism or seeking the excitement of a possible disclosure.

- Consider if the location is logical if the partner is not the spouse or significant other of the victim.
- Consider if the location is logical due to the home, financial circumstances, and age of the participants.
- Evidence and scene are consistent with intimate partner's statement.
- The scene has not been altered post-incident.
- Often the intimate partner may make superficial attempts to remove or hide those items that they feel would be embarrassing. This may include sex toys, bondage restraints, etc. These items should be seized as evidence and preserved for friction ridge, DNA, and touch DNA evidence.
- There may be inconsistencies in the statements, scene, and body's appearance. A skilled investigator generally overcomes these discrepancies.
- No indications of violence.
- No indication of restraints or bindings.
- If consensual activities involve light bondage, gags, or other devices, equipment, or toys, consideration should be given that this death may be accidental as a result of positional asphyxia or suffocation. These items should be seized as evidence and preserved for DNA evidence including touch DNA.
- If apparent consensual activity involves heavy bondage, gags, restraints or other devices, consideration should be given that this death is the result of homicide through direct intent or failure to exercise reasonable safety precautions. These items should be seized as evidence and preserved for DNA evidence including touch DNA.
- Any devices, restraints, clamps, etc... on the body should be thoroughly photographed. They should remain on the body for review by the medical examiner. Any surface used in a device's application should be carefully sampled for touch DNA without its removal from the body.
- Items near the body or within the scene should be seized as evidence and preserved for friction ridge, DNA, and touch DNA.
- Hypoxic methodology is supported by scene findings and evidence.
- Face sitting: seize intimate partner's panties, photograph for saliva stains on exterior area consistent with buttocks/crotch. Protect for DNA, to include touch DNA. Sample for DNA.
- Smothering object (pillow, towel, etc.): seize item and photograph for saliva stains on exterior area consistent with buttocks/crotch. Sample for touch DNA of intimate partner and DNA of victim in saliva stain and on object.
- Strangulation: fully document any marks on the neck of the victim. Fully document the hands of the intimate partner, including finger spread.

The Victim

- Documentation at the scene should involve the sexual assault protocol.
- The victim should undergo a sexual assault protocol during examination, to include a victim sexual assault evidence recovery kit.

The Intimate Partner

The intimate partner (and any other identified intimate partners for the 72 hours prior to death) should be taken to a medical facility for the completion of a suspect or partner sexual assault evidence recovery kit.

- Request appropriate authorization to conduct a physical examination of an intimate partner for purposes of finding evidence.
- If fewer than 72 hours have elapsed since the reported incident, arrange for a medicolegal examination of the suspect using a prepared sexual assault examination kit approved by the servicing crime laboratory (combed and plucked pubic and head hairs, blood, saliva, penile swabs, and fingernail scrapings). All physical injuries should be completely documented.
- If more than 72 hours have elapsed by the time additional partners are identified and examined, collected evidence may be limited to combed and plucked pubic and head hairs, blood, and saliva.
- All statements made to medical personnel about the incident should be thoroughly documented.
- Collect the clothing the suspect was wearing during the incident. Use the procedure described for processing clothing of victims.

Hypoxic Deaths (Nonconsensual)

During BDSM (bondage, domination, sadism, masochism) sexual encounters with the use of a gag, either commercially procured (ball gag, bit gag, ring gag, inflatable gag, etc.) or expedient (panties, scarves, handkerchief, etc.), the device may shift position or become saturated with saliva and no longer allow air to pass. An inattentive or inexperienced dominant partner may fail to recognize the respiratory distress until it is fatal.

The Scene

- No indication of forced entry into location.
- Location of sexual activity is logical for circumstances.

- Consider if location is logical within the confines of voyeurism or seeking the excitement of a possible disclosure.
- Consider if the location is logical if the partner is not the spouse or significant other of the victim.
- Consider if the location is logical due to the home, financial circumstances, and age of the participants.
- Evidence and scene are consistent with intimate partner's statement.
- The scene has not been altered post-incident.
- Often the intimate partner may make superficial attempts to remove or hide those items that they feel would be embarrassing. This may include sex toys, bondage restraints, etc. These items should be seized as evidence and preserved for DNA evidence, including touch DNA.
- There will be inconsistencies in the statements, scene, and body's appearance. A skilled investigator generally overcomes these discrepancies.
- No indications of violence beyond the scope of the consensual activities. These are generally limited to spanking, whipping, slapping, nipple clamps, genital clamps, and pinching (often through clothespins applied to various parts of the body).
- Check that bondage is consistent with BDSM activities. This may run from light recreational gear such as cuffs, silk ties, soft whips, and gags to heavy lifestyle bondage with leather restraints, chains, ropes, and gags.
- Any devices, restraints, clamps, etc... on the body should be thoroughly photographed. They should remain on the body for review by the medical examiner. Any surface used in a device's application should be carefully sampled for touch DNA without its removal from the body.
- Items near the body or within the scene should be seized as evidence and preserved for friction ridge, DNA, and touch DNA.
- The object that obstructed breathing must be fully photographically documented in place. It should not be removed prior to autopsy. Its condition should be noted, unusual placement, alignment, or saturation with saliva. Any surface used in the device's application should be carefully sampled for touch DNA without its removal from the body.
- Computers, tablets, and other devices will often demonstrate a history of sites associated with BDSM. These should be seized and documented.
- Visitation to violent BDSM, snuff films, or similar websites may speak to intentional rather than accidental misadventure.

The Victim

- Documentation at the scene should involve the sexual assault protocol.
- Gag should be thoroughly documented and photographed. If visible, comment on degree of saliva saturation.
- If inflatable gag is in place, thoroughly document and attempt to note degree of inflation (in case of valve leakage so that information is available at autopsy).
- Do not deflate any device in any body opening; leave in place and thoroughly document.
- Any restraint, devices, clamps, or penetrating objects should be thoroughly documented and remain affixed to or within the body.
  - Any surface used in the device's application should be carefully sampled for touch DNA without its removal from the body.
- Items that have disassociated from the body should be photographed and documented in the context of their relationship to the body. They should be seized as evidence and preserved for friction ridge, DNA, and touch DNA.
- The victim should undergo a sexual assault protocol during examination, to include a victim sexual assault evidence recovery kit.

The Intimate Partner

The intimate partner (and any other identified intimate partners for the 72 hours prior to death) should be taken to a medical facility for the completion of a suspect or partner sexual assault evidence recovery kit.

- Devices worn or used by the intimate partner (strap-on dildo or other penetration devices) should be carefully removed and seized, preserving DNA and touch DNA evidence.
- Request appropriate authorization to conduct a physical examination of an intimate for purposes of finding evidence.
- If fewer than 72 hours have elapsed since the reported incident, arrange for a medicolegal examination of the suspect using a prepared sexual assault examination kit approved by the servicing crime laboratory (combed and plucked pubic and head hairs, blood, saliva, penile swabs, and fingernail scrapings). All physical injuries should be completely documented.
- If more than 72 hours have elapsed before additional partners are identified and examined, collected evidence may be limited to combed and plucked pubic and head hairs, blood, and saliva.
- All statements made to medical personnel about the incident should be thoroughly documented.

- Collect the clothing the suspect was wearing during the incident. Use the procedure described for processing clothing of victims.

Autoerotic Asphyxiation

Autoerotic asphyxiation occurs during self-practice of hypoxic sexual acts. This may involve simple to elaborate restraints, cross-dressing, leather wear, gags, and the use of clamps on the nipples or genitals as well as the anal insertion of objects. The practitioner's intention is not to die but rather to increase the effect of his or her sexual experience/orgasm.

General

- Autoerotic asphyxiation is typically a male masturbation practice, although female autoerotic deaths have been documented.
- Death may involve ligature strangulation, hanging, asphyxiating gases, or suffocation.
- Death results when unconsciousness occurs before the victim releases the asphyxiating device.
- These deaths are distinguished from suicides by the presence of an escape mechanism and/or indications of repeated practice.

The Scene

- No indication of forced entry into location.
- Location of sexual activity is generally isolated or private: a garage, workshop, etc.
- Document scene indicators that show the victim sought privacy (closed blinds, locked doors, remote location, etc.).
- Look for signs of repeated activity, such as multiple abraded areas at the suspension point and elsewhere. Examine fixed suspension points such as anchor points in overhead beams.
- There are often indications of repeated episodes with eyehooks established in beams/walls for bondage or areas on beams abraded smooth by the frequent rubbing of ropes.
- Any of the following indicators may be present at the scene: nudity, cross-dressing, pornographic materials, lubricants, receptacle for ejaculate (rag or tissue), strategically placed mirrors for self-viewing, cameras, and bondage paraphernalia.
- Search for a cache of sexual paraphernalia or clothing associated with autoerotic practices.

- A scene may be altered by those who discovered the body due to the implications of this type of death.
- Bindings, suspension mechanisms, and escape mechanisms must be thoroughly examined and documented. They may initially appear too elaborate or complex to have been self-applied.
- Do not underestimate the creativity of a practitioner of autoerotic hypoxyphilia in devising complex self-bondage and asphyxiating devices.

The Victim

- Appearance will be consistent with suffocation, hanging, ligature, or other strangulation death.
- A ligature may be wide or padded to prevent marks or contusions.
- Any ligature should be fully documented and remain on the body and be transported with the victim to autopsy.
- Any gag or other device that causes or contributes to suffocation should be thoroughly documented and photographed. If visible, comment on degree of saliva saturation.
  - If inflatable gag is in place, thoroughly document and attempt to note degree of inflation (in case of valve leakage so that information is available at autopsy).
  - Do not deflate any device in any body opening; leave in place and thoroughly document.
- Any restraints, devices, clamps, or penetrating objects should be thoroughly documented and remain affixed to or within the body.
  - Any surface used in the device's application should be carefully sampled for touch DNA without its removal from the body.
- Items that have disassociated from the body should be photographed and documented in the context of their relationship to the body. They should be seized as evidence and preserved for friction ridge, DNA, and touch DNA.
- The victim should undergo a sexual assault protocol during examination, to include a victim sexual assault evidence recovery kit.

Rape and Sexual Assault Resulting in Death

30

This chapter covers death investigations that involve elements of sexual assault, rape, or torture. The death may be planned as a part of the act or not planned and accomplished in response to a particular set of circumstances (unexpected or planned use of deadly force, inability to render the victim compliant, fear of discovery, and other factors). The motive of the offender is often used to categorize these crimes. The classification of the sexual assault and/or death based on suspect motivation and profile is best done during the conduct of the investigation rather than as an initial crime scene approach. This chapter focuses on the scene processing and analysis phase of a sexual death investigation.

The expertise of a SART at the scene of these deaths may be very valuable. The SART must stay under the control of the lead DSI when examining the body. It is best if prior contact, training, and coordination are accomplished between the death investigation unit and the SART, as their training has focused on living victims.

Worksheets and Documentation

The following documentation guides, forms, logs, and worksheets are provided in Section VIII, "Death Investigation Checklist and Worksheets," and may be used in documenting this scene. Additional forms, other than those noted, may also be used as dictated by your scene. These forms may be preprinted from the publisher's website (www.crcpress.com/cw/maloney) or photocopied from this procedural guide.

- *Death Investigation Checklist*
  - Section 1: Crime Scene Information
  - Section 2: Civilians Who Entered the Death Scene
  - Section 3: Death Scene
  - Section 4: Coroner/Medical Examiner Notification
  - Sections 5–7: Appropriate Body Location When Discovered
  - Section 9: Wounds/Weapons/Drugs/Medications
  - Section 10: Identification/Notification
  - Section 11: Scene Processing

- Section 12: Death Scene Release Information
- Section 13: Narrative Report
- Section 14: (appropriate forms and logs)
- *Worksheets*
    - Worksheet 1: Postmortem Indicators
    - Worksheet 2: Death Scene Entry Log
    - Worksheet 3: Photography Head Slate
    - Worksheet 4: Photography Log
    - Worksheet 6: Firearms Recovery
    - Worksheet 7: Entomology Recovery
    - Worksheet 8: Biological Evidence Worksheet
    - Worksheet 9: Trace Evidence
    - Worksheet 10: Friction Ridge Evidence
    - Worksheet 11: Impression Evidence
    - Worksheet 14: Bullet Defects
    - Worksheet 15: Bloodstain Patterns

Scene Context and Considerations

Often the scene and suspect and witness statements may allow the physical evidence to be placed into context within the scene and overall assault. This may allow for prioritizing analysis of certain items of evidence as well as using their context when auditing the veracity of suspect or witness statements. This should be considered during processing but is not meant to limit thorough crime scene processing.

Acquaintance Rape/Sexual Assault

In acquaintance rape, the victim is known to the perpetrator. There has been some prior or present level of social interaction. The victim and the perpetrator may be engaged in some level of consensual social relationship and/or intimate relationship. The perpetrator has legitimately gained a position or location of relative privacy and the victim has accepted the position of privacy. The level of consensual social and/or physical contact in the private setting is withdrawn by the victim or exceeded by the perpetrator. Victim control is maintained through intimidation, verbal threats, coercion, and physical force used as necessary to gain compliance. If physical force is met with increased resistance, it may escalate to the death of the victim. The death may either be the result of this escalating force crossing the threshold to fatal injury or by perceived necessity to avoid discovery.

- Consider safeguarding fragile evidence and then holding the scene until after the statement of the perpetrator is taken.
- This allows the focus to narrow and to emphasize what physical evidence may be used to de-conflict victim's and suspect's statements
- Look for possible souvenirs taken from victim (e.g., panties, a picture, photographs) in the possession of the perpetrator.

Drug-Facilitated Rape/Sexual Assaults

The victim in a drug-facilitated rape may be an acquaintance or stranger. The victim may have already been mildly intoxicated. The effects of the drug may not be as noticeable to bystanders, and often distracted friends. The victim may have been a recreational drug user, lowering their sexual inhibitions. The "date rape drugs" mimic a state of alcohol intoxication, greatly reducing social and sexual inhibitions and ultimately leading to unconscious or muscular paralysis, leading to an inability to physically respond to assault. Death may occur, as the drugs are not administered in any set dosage, may have been adulterated, and those of home manufacture may include toxic impurities. Toxicity aside, overdose may cause fatal central nervous system depression. Additionally, death may occur when positional asphyxia or a compromised airway results in asphyxiation.

- Often photographs or recordings of the assault are taken by the perpetrator(s); look for any media, cameras, or video systems.
- Witnesses may have been present and capture aspects of the assault on personal cameras and phones. These videos may be posted to social media sites.
- Additional drugs may be present on suspect or in his car, home, or clothing.
- Drugs commonly associated with facilitated sexual assaults include GHB, ecstasy, ketamine, rohypnol, and alcohol.

Stranger Rape/Sexual Assault

- May be elaborate stalking of a particular victim based upon "idealized" fantasy by rapist. May be based on body type, hairstyle, hair color, race/ethnicity, clothing, profession/trade, or any other trait or characteristic that is the focus of the perpetrator.
- May be elaborate surveillance based upon "ideal" location and independent of specific victimology. May require a setting by a lake, in an alley, office building after hours, etc.

- May be completely disorganized with little preparation or selection, based upon inability to control impulses. When the impulse becomes irrepressible, he will choose a victim and location with little thought or planning. The victim and location are of convenience.

Victim Control

- Ambush: speed and violence of attack leaves victim little time to mount any level of resistance. Initial force followed rapidly by complete intimidation.
- Deception: allows access to victim in a secluded location, followed by an ambush that is typically fast, violent, and overcomes resistance rapidly through force, threat of force, and intimidation.

Unique Scene Indicators

- Secondary scene: location of ambush.
- Secondary scene: location of surveillance/observation.
- Attacker may have come with prepared kit.

Examination of Victim

If possible, have a SART respond to the scene to process the body for evidence of sexual assault and minimize the opportunity for evidence to be lost during transit or over time. The SART must stay under the control of the lead DSI when examining the body. It is best if prior contact, training, and coordination are accomplished between the death investigation unit and the SART, as their training has focused on living victims.

Sexual Assault Evidence

- If the body is still at the death scene, request that a SART and medical examiner respond.
- Inform the medical examiner of allegations, suspicions, or scene indications of vaginal or anal penetration (penile, digital, other), recent oral penetration, fondling, biting, and other physical injuries. Indicate any physical evidence on the body to the examiner.
- Discuss swabbing for touch DNA testing on body areas likely to have been handled to facilitate the sexual assault, death, and disposal of the body. This must be done before substantial manipulation of the body by medical examiner personnel.

- Request an examination of the body with and without clothing using an ALS to detect biological fluids and other trace evidence such as lubricants, lotions, fibers, and hairs. Refer to Chapter 41, "Biological Evidence," and Chapter 42, "Trace Evidence."
- If an ALS is not available, ultraviolet light should be used. Such lights are commonly used by medical facilities and called *Woods lamps*.
- Discuss the sexual assault examination with the medical examiner before the examination proceeds. Ensure the examination is conducted using a prepared victim sexual assault kit approved by the servicing crime laboratory.
- Sexual assault evidence is perishable and should be collected as soon as possible.
- Ensure that the victim's clothing is collected, protected for trace evidence, and separately packaged.
- An examination using a colposcope may be helpful for finding microscopic injuries in the vagina and anus. This instrument can better view bruises, tears, and scars. A camera can be attached to the colposcope to provide excellent documentation.
- Ask the doctor to microscopically examine vaginal and/or anal swabbing for motile sperm.

Physical Assault Evidence

- Take color photographs (with and without scale) of injuries.
- Use a color card to achieve more accurate color rendition on final prints.
- Photos of individual injuries should also be taken with the camera parallel to the body surface, both midrange to establish the injury location on the body as well as examination quality photographs (with scale) to allow for detailed comparison with possible weapons.
- Consider requesting ultraviolet or infrared photography to enhance the visibility of pattern injuries or older bruising.
- Injuries should be photographed over several hours if possible.
- Ask the doctor what type of weapon may have caused the injuries and whether the injuries are consistent with the victim's account of the assault.
- Bite marks should be processed as soon as possible. Refer to Chapter 44, "Impression Evidence," for processing.
- Obtain copies of all associated medical reports.

Examination of Suspect

- Request appropriate authorization for conduct of a physical examination of a suspect for purposes of finding evidence.

- If fewer than 72 hours have elapsed since the reported incident, arrange for a medicolegal examination of the suspect using a prepared sexual assault examination kit approved by the servicing crime laboratory (combed and plucked pubic and head hairs, blood, saliva, penile swabs, and fingernail scrapings). All physical injuries should be completely documented.
- If more than 72 hours have elapsed since the reported incident, arrange a medicolegal examination of the suspect using a prepared sexual assault examination kit approved by the servicing crime laboratory (combed and plucked pubic and head hairs, blood, and saliva).
- All statements made to medical personnel about the incident should be thoroughly documented.
- Collect the clothing the suspect was wearing during the incident. Use the procedure described for processing clothing of victims.

Examination of Intimate Partner

- Administer a sexual assault evidence recovery kit for any party with whom the victim may have had sexual relations and who may have contributed evidence collected during the victim's physical examination.
- The third party should submit to a medicolegal examination using a prepared sexual assault examination kit approved by the servicing crime laboratory (plucked pubic and head hairs, blood, and saliva).

Scene Considerations

The scene should be processed as a homicide in accordance with the guidance provided in Section I. Any identified mechanism of injury should be cross-referenced to the appropriate chapter in Section IV. Additional issues include the following:

- Consider securing the scene and delaying its processing (except for processing perishable evidence) until results of the medicolegal examination are available.
- Begin documentation by notes, sketching, and photography. Documentation should be ongoing.
- Items such as clothing, bed linens, rugs, and car seats may contain hair, blood, semen, and fibers. Process these areas for biological and/or trace evidence.

- If the suspect does not live in the scene residence and items of clothing and bedding have been laundered, consider removing lint from the washer and dryer to test for trace evidence.
- Use of an ALS is indicated to detect biological evidence and fibers.
- Pay special attention to bathrooms, as a suspect may clean up after a sexual assault. Washcloths, towels, and tissues may contain biological evidence.
- Search for all evidence that corroborates or refutes witness or suspect statements.

Multiple Victim Death Scenes

31

Multiple victim murder may be the result of one or more attackers. The victims may also include the killer themselves, in the form of murder/suicide.

- The scene is often complex, with evidence overlapping between one victim and another. This may be in the form of bloodstain pattern analysis or spent bullet cases that are often difficult to attribute to one bloodletting episode or a single shooter/attacker position.
- The degree of proficiency necessary to sort out patterns of multiple positions is very high and requires an experienced and well-trained crime scene reconstructionist.
- The victims often share a common connection such as familial, employment, or social connection that places them in the same location at the same time for the murders.

Serial Murders

Serial murders are committed by a single person (in most cases), with each incident separated by a passage of time. They may or may not be linked by general location. The motivation in serial crimes is frequently sexual fantasy fulfillment or the need to violently demonstrate power or mastery. If the desire is fantasy fulfillment there is a link and commonality between each of the crimes, though it may be difficult to discover and unfortunately may only become apparent over multiple victims.

- Victimology is critical. Ensure you collect all of the information necessary for VICAP (Violent Criminal Apprehension Program) entry.
- Treat each scene separately; do not force a scene into a serial crime box. Exploit all available evidence and all logical leads.
- If it is believed this is a serial crime, hold the scene after you have processed it. At this point review and assess the serial aspects and determine if there is additional scene work or documentation required.
- Be cautious on press releases; there is generally a critical piece of information common to all of the crimes that is held back. This allows the interrogators to identify the actual killer from those seeking attention or publicity by admitting to the crime.

Spree Killing

Spree killings generally involve multiple victims in single or linked locations. An example would be all killings taking place in a shopping mall, school, or the killing of coworkers or family members at linked locations such as separate homes or offices and outlying offices. The spree killer generally focuses on revenge or hatred toward a group of people from which they feel disassociated or ostracized. The victims do not have to necessarily be those toward whom the hatred is directed but rather representative of that group.

- Spree killings often involve targeting against a group of people who represent an individual or a group that the attacker perceives as causing him or her continual harm or oppression.
- There may be a primary victim who specifically reflects the rage the individual feels, such as a school administrator, psychologist, or other, and that extends to other victims who are associated with that individual.
- These investigations are often contained to one or two locations where the scene boundaries may be demarcated.
- An example would be the primary victim being a specific psychologist in the hospital and then the spree continuing to other psychologists in the hospital, the staff of the psychologists, and culminating in patients at random until the act ends in the death of the perpetrator by law enforcement intervention.
- Another example would be an individual venting anger and rage against a class of people who are associated with a specific shopping mall or other facility, which represents a perceived wrong sometime in the past that has festered into rage on the part of the perpetrator.
- These acts are generally committed by one or two attackers with deep and close personal bonds and are contained over time to a single event or two events (possibly more), separated only by the time necessary to travel between locations.

Scene Considerations

- Based upon how spread out the scene is and the assets on hand, it may be necessary to activate mutual aid protocols for multiple DSI teams. A single DSI scene supervisor/manager should be appointed. See Chapter 32, "Death Scene Management."
- Victims may range from two or three to scores. Each victim is treated as a separate crime scene, in as much as the scene may be delineated.

- Layered evidence is critical in reconstructing the events. If an item of evidence is beneath another item, the relationship and sequence must be documented.
- Body location and position are critical for reconstructing the events. The bodies' relationship to each other and items of evidence may be very useful in sequencing the events. The leg of one victim over the back of another is an example of the layering that must be documented.
- It is only after each death is thoroughly processed that the reconstructionist may apply the techniques of event analysis to sequence the event.

Mass Murder

Mass murder usually involves state-sponsored or terrorist-sponsored activity against an ethnic group, religious group, or citizens of a nation who are perceived as being undesirable or as having caused great harm to the sponsoring organization or state.

- Mass murder scenes generally involve a specific area that allows for the killing of hundreds of victims and includes those routes and means of transportation of the victims to the killing area.
- The killing area may or may not be separated geographically from the burial area or disposal area of the victims.
- Examples of mass murder include, but are not limited to, the pogrom against the Jews during WWII, the execution of Muslims in the former Yugoslavia, and the murder of Kurds under Saddam Hussein's regime.
- As the incidents are generally state or governmentally supported/sponsored, there is little effort beyond mass burial put into hiding the crime.
- In addition, the sheer number of victims effectively precludes the hiding or cleaning of all forensic evidence associated with the murder and the mechanism or mode of murder of these individuals.

Scene Considerations

- There is generally not a rush to exploit these scenes. Once discovered there is generally time to
  - Set an investigative plan and goals with prosecutors
  - Gather appropriate equipment
  - Gather appropriate scene personnel

- Based upon how spread out the scene is and the assets on hand, it may be necessary to activate mutual aid protocols for multiple DSI teams. A single DSI scene supervisor/manager should be appointed. See Chapter 32, "Death Scene Management."
- It is important to understand and set realistic documentation and collection goals. Meet with prosecutors to determine what is required.
- Layered evidence is critical in reconstructing the events. If an item of evidence is beneath another item, the relationship and sequence must be documented.
- Body location and position are critical for reconstructing the events. The bodies' relationship to each other and items of evidence may be very useful in sequencing the events. The leg of one victim over the back of another is an example of the layering that must be documented.
- It is only after each death is thoroughly processed that the reconstructionist may apply the techniques of event analysis to sequence the event.

Death Scene Management: Tasks and Responsibilities

VI

Death Scene Management

32

Processing of a death scene requires certain roles to be filled and tasks to be accomplished no matter what the size and complexity of the scene or response. The management of these tasks as well as the overall approach to the death scene will generally fall to the lead DSI. The primary tasks and roles are described below and then detailed in the following chapters of this section. It is important to note, if one DSI or a team processes the death scene, each of the roles must at some level be fulfilled.

Arrival and Initial Organization

The lead DSI should refer to Chapter 1, "Death Scene Response," for detailed guidance. The lead DSI must

- Exercise overall control of the death scene
- Ensure appropriate legal authority exists to examine the scene
- Establish a death scene entry control point and designate access routes into and through the death scene
- Be responsible for the initial walk-through and formulation of death scene strategy

Task Prioritization

There are a myriad of tasks that must be accomplished at the scene. Some of these, such as rendering aid, securing the scene, and identifying witnesses, have priority, as they are perishable aspects of the incident. Others that present themselves, such as on-scene witness interviews and death notification, must be conducted or initiated through the scene but may not have the same urgency.

The officer in charge of the scene, the responding investigator, and the DSI will have to prioritize tasks and make assignments as additional personnel become available.

- Make assignments to other DSIs, as available, to accomplish death scene observations, photography, sketching, search, processing, and evidence collection. Each of these roles are detailed in the following chapters.

- Ensure required equipment and support are available.
- Ensure safety and comfort (in as far as possible) of DSIs.

As tasking and assignments are made for the completion of the processing of the scene, the following considerations must also be considered. These will often impact the order and prioritization of steps and processes.

- Scene coordination
- Confirming the scope of the scene
- Establishing scene controls
- Legal concerns (search authorization)
- Scene assessment, planning, and strategy
- Establishing investigative direction
- Scene processing

Scene Coordination

It is important to determine who has investigative jurisdiction over the physical location of the death scene, the body of the deceased, the type of offense committed, and interdepartmental responses.

- Determine investigative jurisdiction and what agency will have lead investigative responsibility.
- If matter will be tasked for out-of-jurisdiction response, coordinate with requested agency.
- If an interdepartmental response involving patrol, death scene unit, and/or investigative units is anticipated, coordinate with on-scene patrol supervisor and lead investigator assigned to the case.
- Coordinate with the local medical examiner or coroner. In most jurisdictions, the body is theirs! Coordinate your scene work and processing of the body, or follow prescribed standard operating procedure.
- If the victim has been transported to a medical facility, remember, the victim *is* a part of the primary death scene, even if removed physically from the death scene proper; responding to the bodies location is a priority!
- If the initial scope and description of the death scene indicate a need for interagency assistance, begin coordination with appropriate agencies or departments. For example, a scene involving unstable ground, a building requiring lighting, or an underwater death scene may need assistance from the fire department, rescue squad, or other crime scene investigation units.

Confirming the Scope of the Scene

Primary Scene: Inner Perimeter

- The inner perimeter should be extended to include all areas associated with the primary scene in which evidence is expected to be found. Determine if the scene has been adequately identified and its perimeter secured. If not, enlarge perimeter as necessary (Figure 32.1).
- Determine the likely areas a perpetrator would have entered or exited the scene and any subsequent paths of travel. If noted, ensure they are within the inner perimeter.

Primary Scene: Outer Perimeter

- This is a clearly marked border around the inner perimeter that allows access to locations within the inner perimeter without having to constantly traverse the scene.
- This includes a DSI staging area for donning Tyvek suits and gathering equipment if needed.

Identifying Ancillary Scenes

- Determine if the initial information would indicate the possibility of ancillary, or secondary, death scenes.

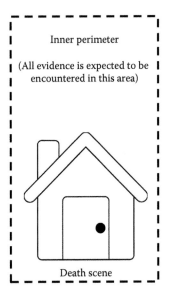

Figure 32.1 Establishing death scene inner perimeter.

- See specific guidance under chapter 2. natural, 3. accidental, 4. suicidal, and 5. homicidal deaths.
- Properly secure these areas until they can be processed.

Establishing Scene Controls

- Identify a point of entry and exit for those working the scene and establish an entry control point and a controller (preferably someone from law enforcement) using a Death Scene Entry Log (Worksheet 2).
- Determine the level of security required and task appropriate personnel.
- Determine what level of PPE is required for the scene and establish PPE guidelines for entry (Appendix A).
- Once a scene's perimeter is established, designate an area outside of the perimeter for DSIs to work in (e.g., sketching, on-scene evidence processing, changing PPE, trash collection, and/or for breaks) (Figure 32.2).
- DSIs or other law enforcement personnel should never take food, drinks, or tobacco products into a death scene area!

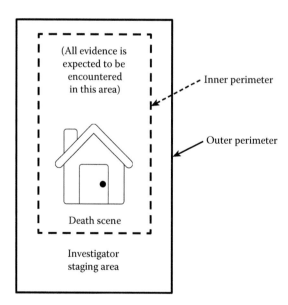

Figure 32.2 Establish death scene outer perimeter.

Major Scene Control Considerations

On major scenes where departmental, governmental, and media interests are expected, the following should be established as soon as possible.

Media Area

- Designate a media area for news personnel to have indirect access to the scene.
- This area prevents direct access but provides a visual site of interest that allows them to capture video of an area of interest (e.g., DSIs moving in and out of the scene with equipment or the front entrance of the structure). At the same time, it should be positioned in such a way as to prevent them from filming the critical investigative area.
- This location should also be far enough removed from the command briefing area as to preclude any chance of the media capturing, recording, or hearing any part of command briefs.
- A failure to designate a media area may result in the media having 360-degree access to the death scene perimeter.
- The media will be either be in a designated area or where they want to be; the choice rests on how quickly the DSI designates an area that provides the media what they need while containing the flow of case-sensitive information (Figure 32.3).

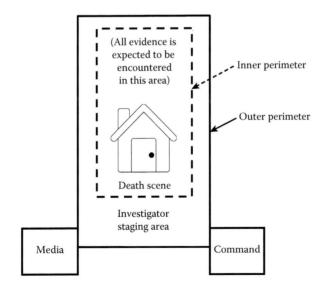

Figure 32.3 If required establish media and command areas. Media area should be afforded a camera angle that allows for them capturing interesting but non-critical scene details such as DSI's approach into scene. Command should be separated from the media area.

Command Briefings

- Designate an area for command briefings.
- This area should be outside of the death scene perimeter and allow easy access for death scene supervisors to hold briefings.
- The location should also be sufficiently isolated to limit law enforcement command personnel from becoming involved in routine death scene investigation decisions and direction. This will help avoid any appearance of unusual influence over the processing procedure (Figure 32.3).

Legal Concerns

The initial response to the death scene, the possible need for emergency medical care, and the search for the possible perpetrator were all covered under the "exigent circumstances" clause of search and seizure law. By this point in the investigation, most likely the exigent circumstances have been satisfied and it is now necessary to reassess the legal authority to continue with the scene. A death scene investigation is basically the *search* for evidence and properly documenting, preserving, and collecting this evidence. The key word is *search*; the DSI must ensure that a person's Fourth Amendment rights against unreasonable search and seizure are protected. It is incumbent upon the DSI to ensure that he or she has the legal authority to be present conducting the scene investigation.

The key legal premise to determine is who has a *reasonable expectation of privacy* in the area where the death scene investigation is being conducted. This may not necessarily be the titleholder of a piece of property. Lawfully rented property requires the authority of the lawful renter, not necessarily the property owner. A roommate may allow a search, but that authority is limited to his or her personal area and any shared area (such as the kitchen and living room); such consent would not extend to the other roommate's bedroom. The individual that has a reasonable expectation of privacy in the area to be searched either grants approval or a judge with appropriate jurisdiction may grant permission to search through a search warrant.

- Consult with appropriate legal counsel if there is any question as to the DSI's authority to be present conducting a death scene investigation.
- *Public lands and property* hold no expectation of privacy for the individual that chooses to be present on the public land. Individuals do not have a reasonable expectation of privacy in public parks, public

wooded areas, streets, etc. A warrant is generally not required in these areas; seek legal counsel to determine if there is a specific need in your jurisdiction.

- *Exigent circumstances* apply to the initial uncertainty surrounding an emergency response. It includes searching for victims, ensuring no threat to safety remains at the scene (e.g., searching for suspects). Exigent circumstances do not allow for the routine law enforcement function of processing a death scene. That said, during the execution of the duties called for under exigent circumstances, the law enforcement officer does not have to ignore evidence of a crime that is in plain view. If exigent circumstances required an initial law enforcement presence, that authority expires when
  - The search for additional victims is complete.
  - The search for an immediate threat from a perpetrator is complete.
  - All emergency aid to the injured is complete and they are removed from the scene.
  - Threat to public safety (gas leaks, structural collapse, etc.) is resolved.
- A *permissive search* is perhaps the easiest method to obtain authority to conduct the death scene investigation. A permissive search is easily invoked when the victim is also the one that has a reasonable expectation of privacy for the property or area in question. Most departments maintain a standard form for the individual to grant a permissive search.
- A *search warrant* is obtained by providing probable cause to a judge that there is evidence of a crime on the property, what the nature of that evidence is, and generally where it is. The judge will then decide if a warrant will be issued. This is by far the legally safest method of conducting a search. Anytime the search involves an area where a potential suspect exercises a reasonable expectation of privacy, a warrant should be considered.

Scene Assessment, Planning, and Investigative Strategy

At the conclusion of the walk-through (detailed in Chapter 1), the evidence and body within the context of the scene are assessed. The videotape from the walk-through (or pictures) may be helpful during this process. The Death Scene Investigation Decision Tree (inside of back cover) will aid the investigator in making an evidence-based decision on initially handling the scene as a homicide, suicide, accident, or natural death. This method defaults in ambiguous situations to the more conservative investigative approach.

- For natural death, refer to Chapter 2 for detailed processing guidance.
- For accidental death, refer to Chapter 3 for detailed processing guidance.
- For suicidal death, refer to Chapter 4 for detailed processing guidance.
- For homicidal death, refer to Chapter 5 for detailed processing guidance.

This is an opportunity to *slow down* and determine investigative priorities, tasking, and assignments. Once an investigative direction is developed, it should remain sufficiently flexible to allow for unforeseen developments.

NOTE: As the scene manager, it is critical that you do not allow the information flow to only support the investigative direction chosen. You must remain open to contradictory information and to reassessing the investigative direction when it is encountered!

Scene Considerations

- Consider tasks at hand and manpower available and make appropriate assignments.
- Consider any unique equipment requirements such as auxiliary lighting, side scanning sonar, or safety equipment.
- Consider the need for support through specialists such as explosive ordnance disposal, underwater evidence unit, computer forensics, fire cause and origin, or search and recovery teams.
- Consider unique weather or terrain requirements. The area may be on a steep grade or unstable ground that would require rope work, in a tidal area, or along a busy roadway that requires traffic control.
- For outdoor scenes, consider any pending weather challenges.

Available Personnel

The following tasks are routinely completed during the investigation of a death scene. A team approach may be conducted when a coordinated and trained death investigation team responds to the scene. In many instances one or two DSIs will be the only available assets. If this is the case, they are responsible for filling each of the following roles.

- *Scene observation:* Refer to Chapter 36, "Death Scene Notes and Observations," for detailed guidance on the tasks and responsibilities.
- *Videography:* Refer to Chapter 35, "Death Scene Videography," for detailed guidance on the tasks and responsibilities.

- *Photography:* Refer to Chapter 34, "Death Scene Photography," for detailed guidance on the tasks and responsibilities.
- *Sketching:* Refer to Chapter 33, "Death Scene Sketching," for detailed guidance on the tasks and responsibilities.
- *Searching the scene:* Refer to Chapter 10, "Searching for Human Remains" for detailed guidance on the tasks and responsibilities.
- *Processing/collecting evidence:* Refer to Section VII, "Death Scene Evidence Processing," for detailed guidance on the tasks and responsibilities.

Scene Documentation

- The Death Investigation Checklist included as Section VIII is an excellent source for documenting the scene.
- Ensure documentation of the scene through appropriate notes, photography, and sketches.
- Ensure each DSI is taking notes appropriate for their tasks. The supplemental worksheets should be used to document the investigative actions at the scene.
- Ensure all items of evidence are properly collected, preserved, and entered into the evidence custody system.

Integrating with the Investigation (Information Flow)

A critical function of death scene analysis is placing the evidence within the context of the scene to assist the lead detective in determining investigative direction and developing investigative leads.

- Frequent communication between the lead DSI and lead detective or medical examiner is critical to ensure that information developed during scene processing may be integrated into the investigative and interview strategies.
- Information from the lead detective can often be used at the scene to focus or refine searches and processing strategies.

Command Functions

- Brief organizational command structure as appropriate.
- Establish command post if necessary.
- Establish media control point if necessary.
- Coordinate information for the media with the public affairs officer.

Scene Completion and Post-Scene Activities

Before Releasing the Scene

- Prior to release of the crime scene, coordinate with detectives, medical examiner/coroner, and the prosecutor's office.
- Determine the appropriate time to release the scene and ensure the scene is secured and turned over to an appropriate responsible person.
- Have a fresh set of eyes go through the scene to determine if anything has been missed, collect any gear that may have been left at the scene and act as a confidence check of the processing methodology and procedures used.

Releasing the Scene

- Release the scene to a responsible party or ensure scene is secured.
- If an inventory of items removed is required, provide it to the responsible party.
- If a search warrant was used, ensure that you complete and turn in the return of service.

Post-Scene Activities

Personnel Issues

- If any injuries occurred during the scene response, ensure that appropriate notifications, treatment, and claims (worker's compensation) have been initiated.
- If any unintentional exposure to blood-borne pathogens occurred, ensure that proper notification, treatment, and claims (worker's compensation) have been initiated.

Evidence and Laboratory Issues

- Ensure all evidence has been turned in to the evidence facility.
- Ensure all evidence is screened for forensic value and sent to the appropriate forensic laboratory for analysis.
  - Coordinate preparation of lab requests.
  - Assist in prioritizing evidence for analysis.
  - Coordinate shipping or transportation of the evidence to the laboratory.

Reports and Follow-Up Analysis

- Ensure all death scene reports are completed.
- Request forensic reconstruction if appropriate.
  - Bloodstain pattern analysis
  - Shooting reconstruction/trajectory analysis
  - Event analysis (who was where and positioned how during the dynamic event)

Death Scene Sketching 33

The death scene sketch(es) document spatial relationships between items of evidence and the scene. A series of sketches may be required when documenting a death scene. An overall sketch shows the location where the death occurred; an area sketch shows the relationship of the room or area within a structure to the floor plan. Additional sketches showing the location of specific evidence categories such as bloodstain patterns or trajectories through the scene may be required.

Rough Sketch

- The original sketch that is drafted at the scene is the rough sketch. It may be drafted onto graph paper and is generally done in pencil with a straight edge and other simple drawing tools or perhaps a template (Figure 33.1).
- Advances in technology allow for tablet or smart phone devices using applications such as MagicPlan CSI to provide a rough sketch with measurements. This is done through augmented reality: the DSI stands in the center of the room, views the scene on the screen of the tablet or smart phone, and tags the corners and doorframes of the room. An overhead sketch with measurements is then created by the application.

Finished Sketch (Final Diagram)

- From the rough sketch, a finished sketch will be prepared. It will be the sketch attached to the death scene report and quite likely will be used in court. It needs to be a professional-looking product.
- The finished sketch may be simply prepared by using templates, ink pen, and straight edges.
- Computer software or advanced CAD programs may also be used to prepare the sketch (Figure 33.2).
- Sketches may also be prepared from laser and photographic mapping systems (Figure 33.3).

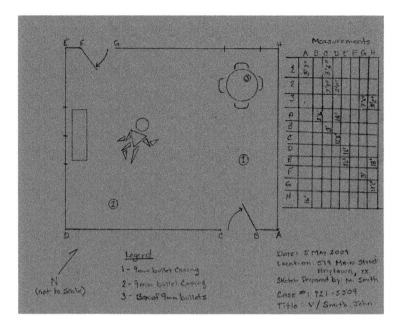

Figure 33.1 Rough sketch of death scene.

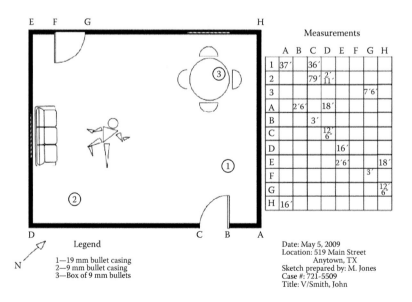

Figure 33.2 CAD finished sketch of death scene.

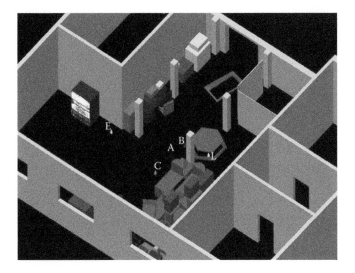

Figure 33.3 Laser mapping.

General Components of a Sketch

- A north arrow is placed on the sketch showing orientation. In certain instances (a ship or boat on the water, an airplane in flight), a north arrow would serve no purpose. In these instances, the sketch should be oriented to a logical feature of the craft such as the bow of a boat or ship and the flight deck/nose of an aircraft.
- The sketch should be marked "not to scale," unless an actual scale is used. The latter is not recommended, unless agency protocol requires it. If used, the scale must be very accurate, or the DSI risks having the opposing counsel make an issue at trial of any minor error.
- A title block should be included indicating the case title, location, dates, and who prepared the sketch.
- Measurements: Overall measurements of the room or space should be provided. Important room features, such as doors, windows, and furnishings should also be measured in relation to room corners, walls, and/or each other. Of course, individual items of evidence need to be measured from two points to place them in their location within the scene. Measurements need to be made in a straight line. If used, tape measures need to be held taut, and the plane used to measure distances should be the same plane as the items being measured. For example, if measuring the distance from the corner of the room to an item on the floor, the

tape measure or other device should be held parallel to the level of the floor, not at an indiscriminate angle, which would add to the actual distance involved.

Depictions

- An area sketch depicts the general location or area of the death scene. It would include surrounding homes and properties, street names, and any other pertinent area features the DSI considers important.
- A scene sketch includes all areas where evidence is located.
- A detailed sketch shows the spatial relationship of specific items of evidence and their immediate surroundings.
- Additional sketches may be prepared that show specific evidentiary findings such as all bloodstain patterns or bullet defects and trajectories (Figure 33.4).

Types of Sketches

- A bird's-eye view (overview or plan view) provides the perspective of looking down onto the area being sketched (Figure 33.5).

Figure 33.4 Supplemental sketch: Bloodstain pattern mapping.

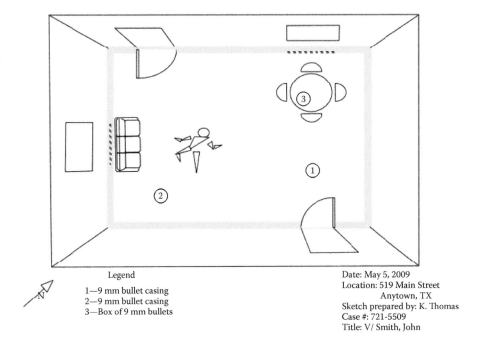

Legend

1—9 mm bullet casing
2—9 mm bullet casing
3—Box of 9 mm bullets

Date: May 5, 2009
Location: 519 Main Street
Anytown, TX
Sketch prepared by: K. Thomas
Case #: 721-5509
Title: V/ Smith, John

Figure 33.5 Overhead sketch (bird's-eye view).

- Exploded (cross-projection) is a way of adding walls and ceilings to the floors by laying down adjacent surfaces onto a 2D format (Figure 33.6).
- Elevation usually shows a side view, such as the perspective of looking at a vertical wall from the side.

The Body

- When fixing the body to the sketch, triangulation is generally used. The body is triangulated at the following points (Figure 33.7):
  - Nose if face up; center mass back of head if face down
  - Umbilicus
  - Elbows
  - Wrists
  - Knees
  - Ankles
- Stick figure drawings of bodies are not appropriate. A simplified body may be depicted using a circle for the head and triangles to represent the body and limbs (Figure 33.8).

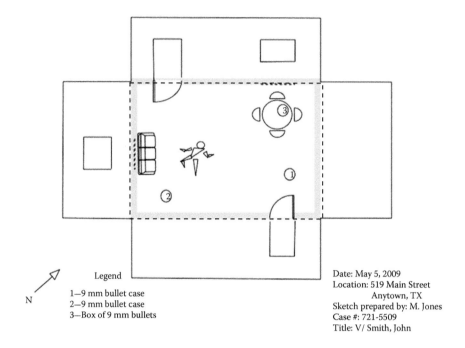

Date: May 5, 2009
Location: 519 Main Street
Anytown, TX
Sketch prepared by: M. Jones
Case #: 721-5509
Title: V/ Smith, John

Legend

N

1—9 mm bullet case
2—9 mm bullet case
3—Box of 9 mm bullets

Figure 33.6 Cross projection sketch (exploded view).

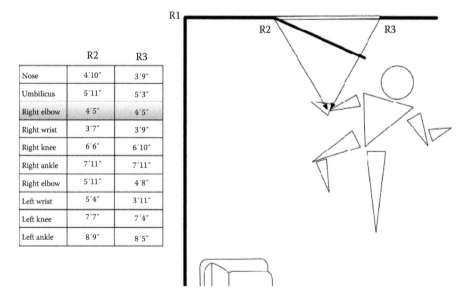

	R2	R3
Nose	4′10″	3′9″
Umbilicus	5′11″	5′3″
Right elbow	4′5″	4′5″
Right wrist	3′7″	3′9″
Right knee	6′6″	6′10″
Right ankle	7′11″	7′11″
Right elbow	5′11″	4′8″
Left wrist	5′4″	3′11″
Left knee	7′7″	7′4″
Left ankle	8′9″	8′5″

Figure 33.7 Measuring the body.

Figure 33.8 Using triangles to depict the body.

Scene Measurements

- Measurements are taken to identify general scene dimensions and specific locations of evidence where the crime occurred. A standard tape measure or an electronic/laser tape measure may be used.
- Evidence measurements are generally made to the nearest 1/4 inch. If a greater degree of precision is required to document a specific spatial relationship, a smaller unit of measure on the scale may be used. For instance, in showing extreme details, the use of the metric system (in centimeters or millimeters) may be more applicable, as used in close-up or examination quality photography.
- In documenting close-up photographs of bloodstain patterns and bullet defects, the most precise unit of measure available should be photographically depicted. These measurements are generally represented using a metric scale with millimeter demarcations (Figure 33.9).
- Measurements to the evidence may be taken to center mass of the evidence if spatial orientation does not matter. An example would be measuring to the center of a strand of hair on the carpet or an ejected bullet case (Figure 33.10).
- At least two separate sets of measurements to two different points on the evidence may be taken if spatial orientation is important.

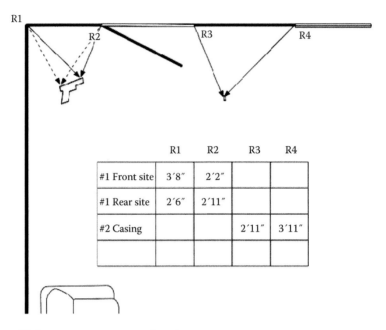

Figure 33.9 Measuring items of evidence.

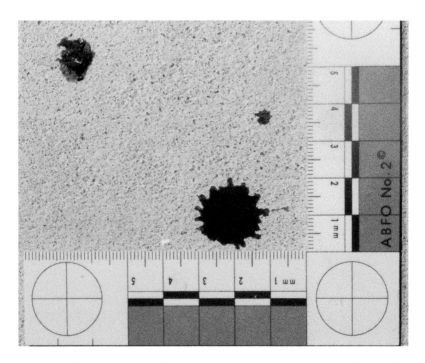

Figure 33.10 Documenting individual bloodstain patterns or bullet defects with ABFO scale.

An example would be measuring to both the handle and the tip of the blade of a knife, or to the front sight, rear sight, and tip of the trigger on a handgun.

- Permanent features of the area, such as walls, door openings, or room corners, are the primary reference points. Additional reference points can be established on such features (e.g., Reference Point 1 is located on the west wall 2' north of the SW corner of the room). Reference points are usually designated by an upper case "R" followed by a number (R1, R2, R3).
- If there are very limited items of evidence, the measurements may be depicted on the primary sketch with straight lines and the measurement represented beside them.
- Representing all measurements on the primary sketch very quickly becomes confusing and difficult to decipher. A table may be prepared (on the sketch or a supplemental page) that shows the distances between the fixed points, the fixed points and furnishings, and the distance between fixed points and items of evidence (Figure 33.11). An alternative is to create an additional sketch that depicts only the evidence measurements.

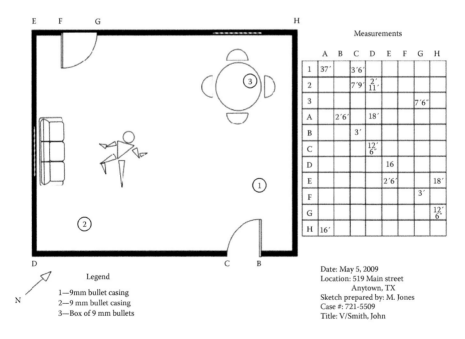

Measurements

	A	B	C	D	E	F	G	H
1	37'		3'6'					
2			7'9'	2'11'				
3							7'6"	
A		2'6'		18'				
B			3'					
C				12'6'				
D				16				
E					2'6'			18'
F						3'		
G								12'6'
H	16'							

Legend

1—9mm bullet casing
2—9 mm bullet casing
3—Box of 9 mm bullets

Date: May 5, 2009
Location: 519 Main street
    Anytown, TX
Sketch prepared by: M. Jones
Case #: 721-5509
Title: V/Smith, John

Figure 33.11 Using a table to represent measurements.

Methods of Measuring

- *Triangulation*: Commonly used to fix furnishing and items of evidence on any surface. Measurements are taken from two fixed points to the item of evidence. The distance between the two fixed points must be known. It is critical that the fixed points are just that; they cannot be moveable. Examples are corners of rooms and the edges of door or window openings (Figure 33.12).
- *Rectangular coordinates*: Commonly used to document the location of any item of evidence and is effective when fixing evidence on a vertical surface such as a wall. This method is used for documenting the location of bloodstain patterns and bullet defects. Measurements are taken at 90 degrees to the floor and the nearest intersecting wall or feature (such as a door frame) (Figures 33.13 and 33.14).
- When items lie adjacent to or flush to a surface, a single measurement from a known point effectively fixes its position when using either triangulation or rectangular coordinates. An example would be that a spent bullet casing is located 6'2" from the south corner along the wall running south to north.
- *Baseline*: Interior baseline is commonly used in large areas where limited reference points exist (e.g., a warehouse). A single baseline is established down the center of the room and measurements are taken at 90 degrees from the baseline and represented as + or – depending on which side of the line the measurement is made from. Baseline is particularly effective when the floor consists of tiles or something

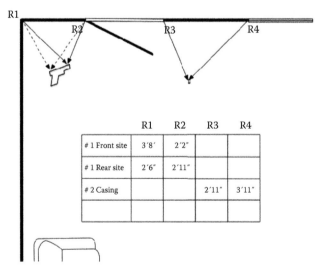

	R1	R2	R3	R4
# 1 Front site	3'8'	2'2"		
# 1 Rear site	2'6"	2'11"		
# 2 Casing			2'11"	3'11"

Figure 33.12 Triangulating items of evidence.

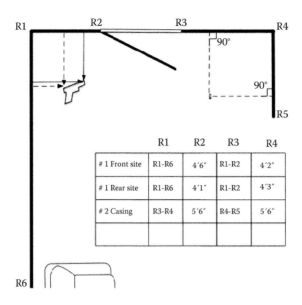

Figure 33.13 Rectangular coordinates method of measuring items of evidence on a horizontal surface.

	R1	R2	R3	R4
# 1 Front site	R1-R6	4′6″	R1-R2	4′2″
# 1 Rear site	R1-R6	4′1″	R1-R2	4′3″
# 2 Casing	R3-R4	5′6″	R4-R5	5′6″

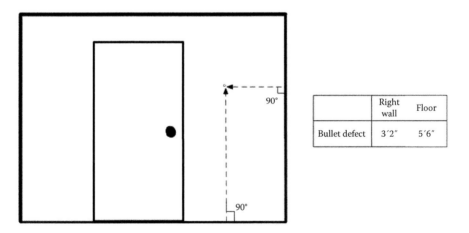

Figure 33.14 Rectangular coordinates method of measuring items of evidence on a vertical surface.

	Right wall	Floor
Bullet defect	3′2″	5′6″

similar with known measurements (for instance, 12-inch floor tiles). The distance out from one wall can be easily measured and the distance from a designated line (created by the tiles) can be determined.

- *Baseline method with an outdoor scene*: Baseline is a form of modified rectangular coordinates. It involves running a long tape measure between two fixed points (telephone poles, trees, or other landmarks) after fixing the two points with a Global Positioning System (GPS). Measurements are then taken at 90 degrees from the baseline and represented as + or – depending on which side of the tape the measurement is from (Figure 33.15). The baseline's fixed points (beginning and end) can be further fixed if required by driving a metal stake or short piece of concrete reinforcing bar (rebar) into the ground at the respective point. This will allow for subsequent location of the fixed points if needed by using a metal detector. This technique is effective if the baseline is located in an area with limited or changing features (e.g., a wooded area). Baseline is also effective if an existing linear permanent feature such as the edge of a road or a sidewalk is present, so long as the feature is straight. The use of curved features (e.g., a roadway with a gradual turn) should not be used as the baseline.

- *Polar coordinates*: In this method, a fixed reference point is established and a compass heading (azimuth) is noted as well as the distance along that azimuth to the evidence. The azimuth is most accurately taken with the use of surveyor's transit, although a lensatic compass may also be used. An example would be that an item of evidence lies 137 degrees and 62' 8" from a reference point (Figure 33.16). This is often used for outdoor scenes that have an obvious center of attention, such as the seat of an explosion.

Figure 33.15 Baseline measurement.

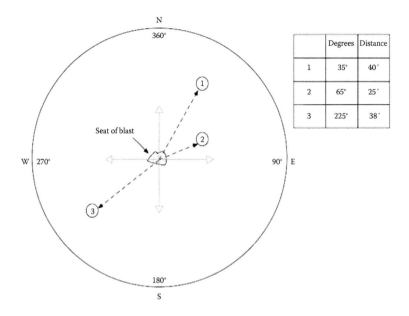

Figure 33.16 Measurements by polar coordinates.

Evidence Identification

- Items of physical evidence that will be removed from the scene are usually represented by numbers (1, 2, 3).
- Pattern evidence, such as two-dimensional footwear impressions, bloodstain patterns, or items of evidence that cannot be taken from the scene, such as a bullet defect in asphalt or concrete, are designated by uppercase letters (A, B, C). If the pattern is collected or sampled as physical evidence, it is co-designated with a number for the evidence custody form.
- The use of either numbers or letters for the evidence is acceptable; however, use the alternative for the patterned evidence.
- A legend (on the sketch or a supplemental page) should be prepared to identify each of the numbers and letters or other symbols used, with a description of the item of evidence they represent.

Death Scene Photography

34

Documentation through proper death scene photography is critical to visually preserve the scene as you see it; maintain a record of the spatial relationships between the body, its wounds, and items of evidence; and to support both notes and sketching.

Equipment

The scene and body should be photographed with the highest quality photographic equipment available. Though the ability to use the camera provided with a smart phone or tablet may be convenient, there are a variety of shots that require a more flexible lighting and exposure system. Though you may be limited by budgetary constraints, every effort should be made to procure the use of a system with the following requirements. A tablet or smart phone should only be used as a supporting system or in critical situations where no other system is available.

- Digital single lens reflex (DSLR) camera
  - Manual and automatic focus
  - Ability to shoot outside of program mode
  - 28–80 zoom lens
  - Threaded lens to accept filters
  - Flash shoe for attaching external flash
- Close-up/macro option
- Aperture priority
- Shutter priority
- UV skylight filter
- Orange, red, yellow (two of each) filters for shooting with an ALS
- Polarizing filter for shooting through glass or water
- Magnifying ring or macro lens for close-up detail
- Off-camera flash unit (Figure 34.1)
- Flash synchronization cord
- Sturdy tripod, preferably with boom capability
- Three memory cards with the maximum gigabytes currently available (capacities improve too frequently to list number of gigs)

Figure 34.1 Digital single-lens reflex (DSLR) camera with off-camera flash and synchronization cord.

- Two sets of spare batteries for each device that uses them
- Complete set of numbered or lettered evidence markers
- A variety of English and metric scales
- Hemostats for holding scale to object without photographing fingers or hand

Setup

- Begin and maintain a photo log. This is often easier when an assistant aids the photographer by filling out the log. Worksheet 4 is a Photography Log.
- The detail required in the photographic log will differ based upon your camera and capture method. At a minimum, exposure/image number and description of the view are necessary.
- Capture digital images in raw format (e.g., NEF format) as well as JPEG.
- If shooting digital with metadata, as long as ISO, (International Standards Organization rating of film speed, sometimes referred to as ASA for American Standards Association film speed rating) f-stop, aperture setting, and flash are recorded as a part of the metadata, they do not need to be recorded on the log.
- The use of any external flash, lighting, or filters that are not recorded on the metadata should be noted in the photography log.
- Ensure date and time stamps on exposures or recorded in metadata are correct.

- If using digital media, ensure that the card or memory stick is new or has been appropriately reformatted. Do not start taking photographs on a partially filled data source.
- If using film, do not start photos on a roll that has already been partially exposed. Use a fresh roll.

Technique

- The first photograph should be of the head slate (identifier card with photographer, date, case title or number, and organization). A template is provided as Worksheet 3, "Photography Head Slate."
- If practical, use the highest resolution image available on your camera.
- RAW images allow for the highest resolution as well as digital documentation that they have not been compressed or altered.
- RAW images should be transferred to an evidence quality CD or agency server at the soonest possible opportunity, prior to viewing or image enhancement.
- Working copies may be made from the RAW images and stored as JPEG or other more portable files. These copies may be enhanced digitally as necessary.
- When working with a program that allows digital enhancement and correction, ensure that each step of alteration to the original image is recorded.
- If working with film instead of digital, it may be necessary to "bracket" your exposures. In other words, expose the same photograph at +/− 1 f-stop to ensure proper exposure. In arson cases, consider bracketing using several f-stops.

General Photography Guidelines

- Keep crime scene processing equipment and investigators out of photographs.
- The evidence should be photographed without scale first, and then with scale (Figure 34.2).
- When slower shutter speeds are used, consider a tripod to ensure sharpness.
- In examination-quality photographs, fill the frame with the evidence and take the photograph with the film/CCD plane at 90 degrees from the portion of the evidence that is of most interest (Figure 34.3).
- If using film, ensure it is appropriate for the lighting. As an example, the surgical lights during autopsy are generally tungsten and will

Figure 34.2 Evidence photographed without and with scale.

Figure 34.3 Examination quality photograph.

not render true color if daylight film is used. A tungsten-type film is recommended.

- Ensure with digital exposures that the white balance is correct for the lighting. This may involve setting the camera for automatic white balance or, in the situation described above, choosing tungsten lighting.

Use of Flash

- Flash should be used on most indoor and many outdoor exposures. The flash will correct for white balance as well as filling in the shadows.
- If using a digital camera, whenever possible set the camera to flash mode; however, some digital cameras may not allow such a setting.

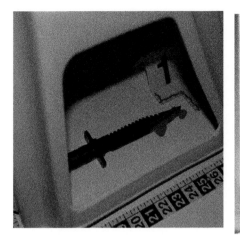

Figure 34.4 Using off-camera flash to fill in shadowed areas (fill flash).

- Shadows often accentuate detail and highlight impressions. Use a detachable electronic flash unit to manipulate or eliminate shadows.
- Front lighting eliminates unwanted shadows and highlights evidentiary details. In some situations, too much light will wash out detail or eliminate accentuating shadows.
- Off-camera flash capability is critical for crime scene photography. This allows for both oblique lighting and fill flash.
- The flash may be angled across the surface being photographed to provide low-level oblique lighting that enhances surface texture. This is an important technique when photographing footwear/fingerprint impressions, tool marks, and bite marks, as well as trace evidence.
- Off-camera flash capability also allows for specifically aiming the flash to fill in shadows naturally created by the scene (Figure 34.4).
- Off-camera flash may also be used to "paint" the background of photographs taken of luminol or other darkened conditions.
- Off-camera flash is also used in the technique to illuminate large areas in the dark called "painting with light."

Use of Filters

- A polarizing filter allows for visibility of objects under shallow water or through windows, diminishing the glare from the water or glass (Figure 34.5).
- A neutral density (ND) 30 filter or series of ND filters may be useful in photographing green laser in daylight conditions.

Figure 34.5 Use of polarizing filters to eliminate reflection and glare.

- A variety of colored filters may be useful in photographing friction ridge detail from colored surfaces. When photographing in black and white, color filters may be used to "drop out" the background color, making the print more readily visible.
- For print photography on multicolored or brightly colored surfaces, color filters closely matching the background will cause that background to drop out, making the print more readily visible.

Scene Photography

- Photograph areas around the scene, including possible points of entry and exit. Remember to include exterior shots of the structure if working inside.
- Consider aerial photography to show spatial relationship within the scene. Aerial photography is accomplished through aircraft, aerial ladder, or an elevated vantage point.
- If strong, natural backlighting conditions exist, use a flash aimed in a direction that would eliminate shadows, or take the photograph from a different angle.
- Avoid taking a photograph that includes the DSI or DSI equipment in it, either directly or as a reflection from any surface. Also avoid taking a photograph where the DSI's shadow is visible.

Overlapping Method/Panographic

- Take a series of photos in a circular, clockwise direction to get 360 degrees of coverage or take photographs from overlapping vantage points (e.g., shooting from the four corners of the room).
- Overlap each photo with items or areas appearing in the preceding photo to permit matching or comparison.
- Be sure to include floors and ceilings in your photographs.

Progressive Method

- Pinpoint a specific item in a scene and show its relationship to other items in the scene.
- Take a series of overall, evidence-establishing (also known as *midrange* or *relationship photographs*), and close-up photographs (without and with scale) from the same angle and from the same perspective (walk into the evidence).
- Micro- or macrophotographs may be needed to show greater detail on close-ups.

Photographing Items of Evidence

- Photograph all evidence before moving it.
- Photograph the item as it is found, with evidence-establishing shot (placing it in context with its surrounding) and close-up shot.
- Repeat the evidence-establishing and close-up shot after placing an evidence placard and scale (if not a part of the placard) by the item.
- Take an examination-quality photograph if required.
- Coordinate with the sketcher, on-scene evidence custodian, and evidence collection team before moving the item.
- At the time of collection, capture all aspects of the item (e.g., photograph the side of a pistol or body that was not visible as it lay in the scene).

Photographic Perspectives

- *Overall:* Shows a general area as found and helps establish the relationship between the area/scene and its surroundings (Figure 34.6).
- *Evidence establishing (midrange/relationship):* Establishes relationship between items of evidence and some known landmark in the

Figure 34.6 Overall photograph.

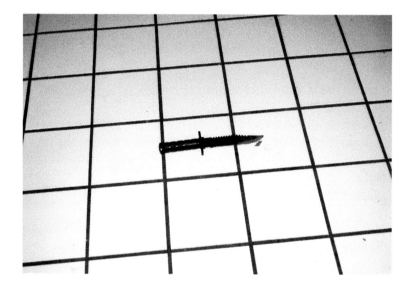

Figure 34.7 Evidence establishing (mid-range) photograph.

scene (Figure 34.7). This photo effectively "establishes" where in the
scene a specific item is.

- *Close-up:* Shows the item of evidence in detail (fill the frame with the
  item). Taken both without and with scale (Figure 34.8).
- *Examination quality:* Used to document evidence that will later
  undergo examination, such as latent prints, bite marks, and tool
  marks (Figure 34.9).

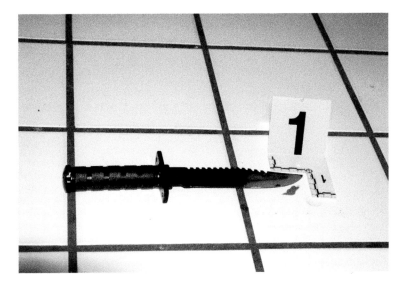

Figure 34.8 Close-up photograph.

Figure 34.9 Examination quality photograph.

Work closely with the sketcher; photographs and sketches must augment each other in accurately depicting the crime scene.

Body at Scene Photography

In-Scene Context

- Take photographs of the body within the context of the scene.
- An overall, or distant, photograph showing the body within the scene.

- Evidence-establishing photographs showing the body in relationship to markers within the scene (wall, carpet, rocks, road, etc.).
- Evidence-establishing photographs showing the body in relationship to associated items of evidence (weapons, bullet cases, discarded wallet, bloodstain patterns, etc.).
- This does not replace thorough scene photography as discussed below.

Identification

- Do not clean or alter the face in any way! Do not move or alter the position of the head! Identification photos will also be taken during the autopsy when the face has been cleaned. These initial identification photos may be necessary for early investigative efforts.
- Photograph of the face.
- Right profile.
- Left profile.
- Photograph any obvious scars, marks, or tattoos.

Overall

Photograph the body as it lies from as high an angle as possible (overhead view).

- Entire body
- Upper half (waist up)
- Head and shoulders
- Chest and abdomen
- Right upper arm
- Right lower arm
- Right hand
- Left upper arm
- Left lower arm
- Left hand

When all photography of injuries and processing are completed for the visible portions of the body, the body is carefully rolled to 90 degrees and rephotographed as detailed above.

Injuries

- All injuries are photographed without scale and with scale. No alterations to the injury or clothing are made at this point. Only what is visible is photographed.
- Each injury is photographed in a mapping technique.

- Each injury is photographed in as much detail as possible with an emphasis on demonstrating any associated defects, bloodstain flow patterns, bruising, or powder residues and their alignment/association with the wound.

Body at Autopsy Photography

Autopsy photography including methodology and suggested photographs are thoroughly covered in Chapter 9, "Autopsy Protocol and the Investigator's Role."

Death Scene Videography 35

MICHAEL MALONEY
AND WADI SAWABINI[1]

Documentation through proper death scene videography is an important step in visually preserving the scene as you see it; maintaining a record of the spatial relationships between the body, its wounds, and items of evidence; and supporting both notes, sketching, and photography.

Equipment

The scene and body should be recorded with the highest quality videographic equipment available. Though the ability to use the video function provided with a smart phone or tablet may be convenient, there are a variety of shots that require a more flexible lighting, focus, and exposure system. Though you may be limited by budgetary constraints, every effort should be made to procure the use of a system with the following requirements. A tablet or smart phone should only be used as a supporting system or in critical situations where no other system is available.

- Camcorder with macro capability.
- On-the-lens manual focusing.
- Auxiliary microphone jack for audio or ability to turn audio off.
- A viewfinder.
- Screw threads on the end of the lens.
- UV (sky filter) to protect the front element of the camcorder's lens.
- Consider the addition of an add-on wide-angle lens for use in shooting interior video.
- Auxiliary lighting for video recording in low light conditions.
  - Attached video lighting tends to be too "hot."
  - Mechanics light sets are affordable and easy to set up.
- A small, fluid head tripod is extremely handy for shooting extreme "macro" close-ups of evidence.
- Orange, red, and yellow (two of each) filters for shooting with an ALS.

---

[1] Wadi Sawabini is the chief instructor with Sawabini & Associates, LLC. He is a pioneer and recognized expert in the application of videography to law enforcement investigations. His assistance in the writing and preparation of this chapter was invaluable.

- Polarizing filter for shooting through glass or water.
- Three memory cards with the maximum gigabyte capacity currently available (capacities improve too frequently to list number of gigs).
- Two sets of spare batteries for each device that uses them.
- Complete set of numbered or lettered evidence markers.
- A variety of English and metric scales.
- Hemostats for holding scale to object without photographing fingers or hand.

Setup

- If date and time stamp is to be recorded, ensure they are correct.
- Synchronize the evidence log with video recorder's time stamp. This may seem unnecessary, but consider a critical item of evidence that based on the camera's time stamp does not appear in the video shot 5 minutes before its recorded collection time.
- Disable audio recording using a 3.5 mm male phone plug (aka a "knock-out" plug) that has been made into a "dead short" and is inserted into the auxiliary microphone jack.
- Your first shot on every evidence video is a slate using an identifier card or your cell phone with the following: photographer, date, case title or number, and organization. Worksheet 3, "Photography Head Slate," may be used. Use macro focus for this shot. Be sure the shot is at least 4 seconds in length.
- Your second shot on every evidence video is a shot of a GPS app, Goggle Map™, or compass app that shows your location. Again, use macro focus for this shot. Again, insure that it is at least 4 seconds in length.

Technique

- Always use manual focus: deep focus, macro focus, and shallow focus.
- Work any crime scene, search warrant, or accident scene from left to right.
- Remove all personnel from the area being recorded and remove all DSI equipment that might appear in the recording.
- Record an establishing shot, a medium shot, a close-up shot, and wherever it is safe to do so, also record a macro shot for each piece of evidence.
- Pause the recording between each shot.
- Change image angle and image size with each shot.
- Link each piece of evidence to the next by using a pan shot.

- Hold each shot for at least 4 seconds before pausing the recording.
- Do not zoom while recording. (The human eye cannot zoom.)
- Do not walk and shoot at the same time. (This is to insure your personal safety.)
- Use pan or tilt shots to establish the overall scene.
- On exterior shots, always try to frame your shot to include a known geographic landmark.

Deep Focus

- Before recording any video, set the camcorder to manual focus.
- Zoom into the point farthest away from you that you want in focus.
- Manually focus the lens and then zoom out to the widest angle.
- Refocus for each shot.

Macro Focus

- Insure the camcorder is set for manual focus.
- Zoom out to the widest angle possible.
- Place the camcorder 2 inches or less from the piece of evidence you wish to video.
- Focus the lens.
- Begin recording and continue recording for at least 4 seconds.
- Consider a second macro shot of any evidence using a scale.
- *Caution*: Only shoot a macro of evidence when it is safe to do so. Do not risk blood-borne contamination or injury to make a macro shot.

Zoom

- Do not zoom while recording video; the human eye does not zoom.
- Zoom (or setting the focal length of the lens) is done prior to recording specifically to optimize the forensic value of the shot.

Panorama Shot (Pan)

- Begin each new scene with a panorama shot (pan shot) from left to right.
- Plan your pan finding a start point and a stop point.
- Having prefocused and with the zoom lens at the widest angle, begin recording, hold the shot for 4 seconds and then pan from left to right in a smooth, nonstop motion. At the stop point, hold the shot steady for 4 seconds before pausing the recording. Do not pan back to the start point.

Vertical Panorama Shot (Tilts)

- *Vertical pans* are called *tilts*: Start at the top of a building, object, or blood spatter and then tilt down. This method follows the natural flow pattern of liquid evidence such as blood.
- Do not combine pans and tilts in one shot.
- Limit motion to either the horizontal or vertical plane.

Use of Auxiliary Lighting

- When low light conditions exist or when evidence must be recorded in the shadows, the use of auxiliary lighting is required.
- Area lighting is best accomplished with commercially available mechanic's halogen light sets.
- If pinpoint lighting is required under objects or shadowed areas that cannot be illuminated through area lighting, a handheld flashlight may be used; caution must be exercised to ensure the recorded subject is properly illuminated through alignment of the auxiliary light.
- Additionally, the texture of a surface, two-dimensional footwear impressions, or trace evidence may be better visualized with strong low angle oblique lighting.

Use of Filters

- A polarizing filter allows for visibility of objects under shallow water or through windows, diminishing the glare from the water or glass.
- An ND 30 filter or series of ND filters may be useful in recording green laser in daylight conditions.
- Orange, red, and yellow filters (two each) for shooting with an ALS. The filter on the lens must match the barrier filter you are using to observe the fluorescence.
- Magnifying ring or macro lens for close-up detail.

The Death Scene

Record the Following

- Record the address of the scene (mailbox, street sign, address on front of house, etc.).
- Record both exterior and interior scenes ASAP upon arrival.
- Record any bystanders or onlookers near the scene.

- Record both general and specific conditions at the scene.
- Record items of evidence and their spatial relationship to the scene and other items of evidence.
- Consider recording the scene again prior to leaving it. This can help to defend the agency in any action the owner of the property may bring against it later.

The Body at the Scene

General

- Set the camcorder to manual focus.
- Insert the knockout plug into the auxiliary microphone jack to silence the camcorder.
- Shoot a macro shot, at least 4 seconds in length, of a slate with the date, time, location, case ID, and operator name and ID number.
- Shoot a macro shot, at least 4 seconds in length, of a GPS or phone app that shows the location.

Scene for Context

Begin by shooting an overall shot of the location. (If the body is inside a structure, a pan shot of the "legal address" front of the building is a good starting point.) If the body is outside, position your first shot with your back to the sun.

The Body (*In Situ*)

- If the body is outside, position your first show with your back to the sun.
- As you face the body, work your way around the body going from left to right.
- *Caution:* Do not record while walking.
- Record the body from above. Use a step stool or ladder if necessary to capture the entire body and its immediate surroundings in the frame. Hold and record for at least 10 seconds.
- Recording the body of the deceased from above, slowly pan from head to feet. This shot should be stopped if necessary to reposition; do not record and move. Hold for at least 4 seconds at each of the following points:
  - Head and shoulders
  - Upper torso

- Upper arms
- Lower arms
- Right hand
- Left hand
- Waist/hips
- Upper legs
- Lower legs
- Feet
- Bottom of feet

- Record again from above, carefully pan the camera to cover the area adjacent to the body.
- Start at the victim's head. A portion of the body should appear in the shot for reference, but 90% of the frame should be the surrounding area.
- Proceed slowly in a clockwise fashion. Pause the pan at the head, shoulder, mid-upper torso, hip, mid-thigh, mid-calf, and feet, and repeat in reverse order as the pan rounds the feet and goes up the other side of the body.
- Use a series of shots, at least 4 seconds in length, to record specific areas of interest. This would include wounds, injuries, scars/marks/tattoos, etc. Record each in this order:
  - Establishing shot, then pause, remove the camcorder from in front of your face, and change image angle and image size.
  - Medium shot, then pause, remove the camcorder from in front of your face, and change image angle and image size.
  - Close-up shot, then pause, remove the camcorder from in front of your face, and change image angle and image size.
  - Macro shot (only if safe to do so).
- If possible, shoot video when the body is moved or rolled to capture anything that comes off the body or was under the body.
- Once the body has been removed, consider reshooting the video of the immediate area around the body.

The Body at Autopsy

Typically, the autopsy is not video recorded without a specific need. When recorded, it must be done with the express permission of the medical examiner. It is generally best to mount the camcorder on a tripod and from above the examination table record down at the body and procedure.

Bindings and Sequencing Issues

- In the case of complex bindings, particularly in suicides when it is believed the victim was self-bound, record the medical examiner untying the bindings.
- This video may then be reversed with specific screen captures to build a step-by-step instruction guide for the bindings.
- In cases with complex sequencing (multiple layers of clothing), the removal of the clothing may be recorded to ensure the proper order/ sequence is maintained.

Death Scene Notes and Observation

36

Scene Observer Duties

The scene observer records all objective data at the crime scene. Each DSI is still responsible for his or her own observations and notes as they relate to their specific assignments. General Death Scene Notes are an excellent resource, available in Section VIII. Worksheets are provided to assist the individual DSI in recording his or her observations and processes. The DSI assigned observation duties is responsible for the following:

- Overall scene documentation
- Recording overall observations

NOTES

Section VIII of this guide contains an extensive series of Death Scene Investigation checklists and supplemental worksheets. These worksheets were developed to ensure the complete documentation of the death scene. These worksheets may be copied from the guide for use in the field; an access code for downloading the worksheets in a digital fill or written fill version is provided with this publication.

- Written notes are the best method for recording observations.
  - Number each page.
  - Initial and date each page.
  - Include case reference on each page.
  - Done in pen.
  - Mistakes are struck through with a single line and initialed.
  - Generally recorded in chronological order.
  - Do not contain extraneous data; limited to facts, observations, logical leads developed from observations.
- An audio recording may be appropriate when time does not allow for written notes in situations such as a hostile area, imminent danger, and heavy blood-borne pathogen contamination.
  - Lead-in narration on the recording should include time, date, location, and case number/name (if available).
  - Recordings must be transcribed at some point.

Observations (Scene Indicators) for Indoor Scenes

Structure Type/Location

Document static nonchanging characteristics of the involved scene, including the following:

- Exact address or location of structure
- Type of structure (e.g., apartment, house, townhouse, commercial building)
- Number of stories (e.g., single-story, two-story)
- Construction (e.g., brick, wood, masonry)
- Entry and exit points (e.g., all doors, windows)

General Appearance

Document specific scene conditions.

- Evidence of criminal activity
- Forced entry or lack thereof
- Evidence of struggle
- Evidence of ransacking
- Evidence suggesting missing items
- Evidence of personal injury, such as blood on floor or other surfaces

Possible Related Video Coverage

- Is there video coverage of avenues of approach to the area?
- Is there on-scene video coverage of the scene itself (e.g., security, nanny cams)?

Entry/Exit

- Are doors open or closed?
- Are doors locked or unlocked?
- What types of locks are on doors?
- Are the doors bolted from inside?
- Is there any evidence of forced entry?
- Who has keys or a passkey, and are all keys accounted for?

Windows

- Are the windows open or closed?
- Are the windows locked or unlocked?

- What types of locks are on the windows?
- Are there screens on the windows? Are the screens in place?
- Is there any evidence of forced entry?
- What window covering (e.g., curtains, blinds, and shades) are in place and what are their positions?
- Continuity aspects of windows and screens (e.g., the presence or absence of cobwebs or dirt on the sill).

Kitchen and Dining Room

- Is there food preparation indicating recent eating before, during, or after crime?
- Are there indications of cleanup after a meal?
- Does food preparation indicate multiple parties present at scene?
- Is the oven on? If so, what is the status of the food within (raw, under-cooked, overcooked, burnt)?
- Are there dated or spoilt foodstuffs in the pantry or refrigerator?

Environmental Controls

- What is the temperature in room?
- What is the thermostat setting? If there is a program mode, how far into the cycle is it?
- Is the thermostat on a timer, and what are the settings?

Laundry and Utility Areas

- Are appliances running or warm (to include washer/dryer)?
- Is there clothing in the washer or dryer, wet or damp?
- If suspect's clothes were believed to be laundered, consider lint trap as evidence.

Lighting (In Each Room as well as Outside Lights)

- Are the lights on or off?
- Are the lights working?

Telephones and Cellular Phones

- Is there any record of incoming and outgoing calls? Attempt to determine those calls.
- Are there any answering machine messages?
- Is there an off-site answering service? What does it take to ascertain those messages?

- Can mapping of cellular towers indicate the location of where a call was made?
- Are there text messages? Ensure charger is included with the mobile phone.

Mail

- What is the date on any outgoing mail?
- Are there any time-dated receipts?
- What is the date of mail outside the home or in mailbox?
- What is the date of mail brought in or opened?

Contents of Wastebaskets and Ashtrays

- Check and document the contents of wastebaskets and trashcans, if appropriate.
- Check ashtrays; if there are indications of multiple parties being present, consider collecting cigarette butts for DNA analysis.

Bath and Toilet Areas

- Are there damp or bloodstained towels or washcloths?
- Is there evidence of recent bathing or washing activity (e.g., wet tubs, towels)?
- If victim is a single female living alone, is the toilet seat raised?
- Is there evidence of suspect cleanup?
- What drugs or medicines are in medicine cabinets?
- What are the dates on prescription medication and number of tablets missing?

Calendars and Planners

- What are the entries on any calendars for the time period before and contemporaneous to the crime?
- What are the diary or day-planner entries for the time period before and contemporaneous to the crime?

Computers and Internet

- When was the victim last on the computer?
- Is there computer activity after the suspected time of crime?
- Is there email, chat, or telephone activity contemporaneous to the time of crime?

Observations for Outdoor Scenes

Environmental Conditions

- What is the temperature?
- What is the humidity?
- Is there an ongoing precipitation or an evidence of recent precipitation?
- What are the past temperatures, precipitation, and humidity covering the time since the crime?
- Is it daylight, nighttime, or evening?
- What time was sunrise, sunset (if applicable)?
- What is the moon phase and cloud cover?
- What is the ambient lighting? Consider streetlights, porch lights, and even city sky glow.

Immediate Area of Crime Scene

- Is there evidence of a struggle?
- Are there footwear impressions, scuff marks, or tire marks?
- Is there any video coverage of the area? Consider ATMs, surrounding store video, and/or traffic surveillance systems.
- Is there evidence discarded in nearby trash receptacles?

Extended Area of Crime Scene

- What are the likely paths of travel to and from the scene?
- Is there evidence discarded in trash receptacles, ditches, underpasses, etc.?
- Is there any video coverage of avenues of approach to the area?
- Are there nearby convenience stores or gas stations that might have video coverage and trash receptacles that could be searched for evidence?

Observations for Motor Vehicle Scenes

Exterior

- Are there signs of damage, particularly signs of recent damage, to include indications of collision, bullet holes, etc.?
- If the vehicle was suspected of being involved in a personal injury, do the mirrors, bumpers, grill, or undercarriage have possible human hairs, fibers, blood, etc., present?

- Are there areas likely handled/touched by suspects that need to be protected for possible latent fingerprint detection/touch DNA recovery?
- Record VIN, plate number, and any other identifying feature of vehicle, to include the vehicle's make, model, color, and distinguishing features.
- For pickups, record contents of the bed.
- Observe tires, rims, and wheel well areas for possible mud, dirt, etc., that would indicate the presence of materials that might be needed for subsequent alibi comparisons.
- Is there a need for later towing and raising the vehicle to search for evidence of the crime deposited on the undercarriage?

Interior

- Is blood or other evidence of personal injury present?
- Are tools present that might have been used in the crime?
- Are items present (mail, written messages, other objects with names on them) that would indicate the identity of passengers/drivers of the vehicle?
- Are items missing from any separate, but related, scene present in the vehicle?
- Are there items in the trunk that are related to the crime or that help identify persons?

Death Scene Evidence Processing

VII

Documenting and Processing Bloodstain Patterns at the Scene

37

Bloodstains in the form of characteristic patterns such as spatter, flows, transfers, and drips are associated with crimes of violence and injury and can be interpreted to help in the reconstruction of bloodshed events. Only a properly trained bloodstain pattern analyst should interpret these patterns. Bloodstain pattern analysis is best accomplished at the scene by an expert; however, if the scene is properly documented and processed, a complete bloodstain pattern analysis can be accomplished at a later date. The basic procedures for the DSI to follow when documenting a bloodstained scene are as follows:

- Assess the scene and detect all bloodstain patterns on the victim, his or her clothing, and at the scene.
- Isolate individual patterns, particularly where they overlap.
- Identify the patterns as far as your training allows.
- Document the patterns through a mapping technique.
- Identify the discrete portion of the pattern that will be sampled for DNA analysis.
- Document and collect that sample.

Detection

- Bloodstain patterns will often be visible on the walls, ceilings, and floors, as well as intermediary objects associated with a violent incident.
- Identification and documentation of these patterns is essential for proper analysis.
- Though many bloodstain patterns are obvious at the scene, subtle transfer patterns or very fine misting patterns are easily overlooked.
- The scene must be thoroughly searched for any and all bloodstain patterns.

Visual

- Strong white light directed at 90 degrees to the surface is the best method that will allow the viewer to recognize the presence of blood, even on a dark surface.

- A strong white light at an oblique angle to the surface is also effective.
- Use of magnification (20×) when examining the surface to prevent missing small submillimeter-sized stains that may be present. This is particularly important when examining clothing items.

Alternate Light Source

- Blood does not fluoresce when exposed to any wavelength of light; rather it absorbs the light, darkening its color.
- Using ultraviolet lighting (350 nm) will not fluoresce blood; however, the blood will darken, creating increased contrast with its background. No goggles are required to view the stains.
- When using wavelengths of 400–520 nm of light, the stains will darken as well. Viewed through yellow or orange goggles, the bloodstain will appear like a dark spot in the background material.

Infrared

- Blood also darkens when exposed to infrared (IR) light, while many dark surfaces tend to be IR reflective, including dark clothing. This combination will make the surface appear lighter, creating significant contrast between the two.
- There are, however, no rules as to what items will be IR reflective or not, so use of IR requires a trial-and-error approach. Sometimes it works in excellent fashion; other times it does not.
- Due to this behavior, IR video or photography of darker colored items is an excellent way to visualize bloodstain patterns.
- Specialized IR cameras are available for forensic work; these are the easiest to use and generally give excellent results.
- Unlike other wavelengths, the use of a normal digital camera with IR light will have no effect. Standard digital cameras are equipped with an internal IR filter that removes all IR light.
- Older digital cameras no longer in use for normal photography can be economically altered to remove the internal IR filter present, making them IR capable.
- IR capable cameras require care in focusing. The IR focal point is different than the visible light. This may cause a slight difficulty with autofocus cameras.

Chemical Enhancement

- In some instances (e.g., a death scene reconstruction or when significant cleanup is suspected), once all other scene processing efforts

are completed, the use of chemical blood enhancement techniques to better visualize the latent blood may prove beneficial.
- There are a variety of chemical blood enhancement products available. These include various forms of luminol (e.g., Bluestar®, Lumiscene) as well as Lueco crystal violet.

Luminol

- Luminol causes minute amounts (latent blood) of blood to fluoresce from a chemical reaction (chemiluminescence). No ALS or UV light is needed.
- It generally does not adversely affect DNA analysis, depending upon the specific formula.
- It will work on surfaces where the blood has been cleaned or in some cases even painted over.
- It is not effective on visible bloodstains; however, it may be used to extend the margins of visible bloodstains if cleanup is suspected.
- It must be used and photographed in near-total darkness. Ambient light will greatly reduce the ability to visualize and photograph the chemifluorescence. Bluestar has the reported advantage of being better photographed in low light conditions.
- It is important to use a small amount of luminol to see if any reaction is present. If a bluish glow is observed, a camera (still and/or video) can be set up with the use of lighting, using a tripod. More luminol can then be used and captured in total darkness with a second application.
- Photograph with time exposure; set the background with a fill flash near the end of the exposure to capture the scene itself.
- *Caution*: Luminol is a suspected carcinogen. As such, proper skin, breathing, and eye protection should be used. Review MSDS (Material Safety Data Sheet) and apply accordingly!
- Luminol is most effective if applied with a commercially available atomizer or compressed paint gun (the system must not contain metal parts that would be exposed to the spray).

Modified Luminol Formulas (Such as BlueStar)

- Luminol-based products.
- Does not adversely affect DNA analysis (caution should still be used to avoid excessive application).
- More sensitive to extreme dilutions of blood.
- Does not require total darkness to be visualized and photographed (ambient lighting should be reduced as much as possible to near darkness).
- Effective after bleach has been used to clean up the blood.

- Apply according to manufacturer's instructions. Be sure to follow safety instructions.
- More effective if applied with a commercially available atomizer or compressed paint gun (must not contain metal parts that would be exposed to the spray).

Fluorescein
- Available as separate ingredients or in kits
- Two part application.
- Longer lasting reaction than with luminol.
- Repeat application is more effective than luminol.
- The reaction is visualized and photographed with an ALS set to 4550–485 nm and viewed through either yellow or orange goggles, depending upon the wavelength used.
- Results can be photographed with a camera using the same type of filter needed by the investigator to visualize the results.
- Does not require total darkness as with luminol

Isolate and Identify Discrete Patterns

The bloodstain pattern taxonomy approach to classifying bloodstain patterns was introduced by Bevel and Gardner in *Bloodstain Pattern Analysis* (see Appendix B for Bevel and Gardner's Bloodstain Pattern Taxonomy BSPA Decision Tree). This allows for a decision-based approach to identifying discrete bloodstain patterns. The classification of patterns should only be done by those with appropriate training. Although it is not imperative, bloodstain documentation is more effective when the DSI has been trained as a minimum in basic pattern recognition. Otherwise, it is sufficient to isolate the patterns based on their general appearance and document them using a mapping technique.

Spatter

Linear spatter (Figure 37.1)

- Spurt (arterial)
- Cast-off
- Drip trail

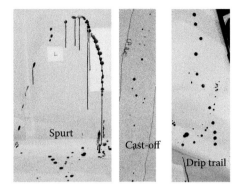

Figure 37.1 Linear spatter patterns.

Figure 37.2 Non-linear spatter patterns.

Nonlinear spatter (Figure 37.2)

- Impact spatter
- Misting spatter
- Expectorate
- Drip

Nonspatter Stains

Irregular margin (Figure 37.3)

- Blood into blood
- Gush
- Smear

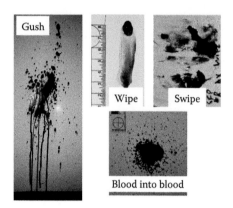

Figure 37.3 Non-spatter patterns irregular margins.

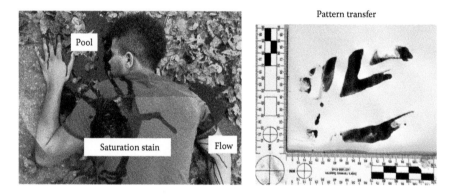

Figure 37.4 Non-spatter patterns—regular margin.

Regular margin (Figure 37.4)

- Pattern transfer
- Flow
- Pool
- Saturation

Documentation through Mapping

Bloodstain patterns are significant in the size and shape of the individual spatter/stain, the appearance of the overall pattern, the location of the pattern, and the location of the pattern in association with the body and other patterns. Toby L. Wolson of the Miami-Dade Police Department's Crime

Laboratory introduced a concept that is now called "road mapping," which effectively places the pattern in context. The technique introduced in this guide for bloodstains, bullet defects, and injuries to the body is based on this technique and referred to as "mapping."

Mapping

This technique works well on all surfaces within the scene, clothing, and bloodstains on the body. Mapping technique is illustrated through figure 37.5.

- Take an establishing photograph of the item of evidence or surface that the bloodstain is on.
- Take an additional photograph with a scale.
- Identify the discrete pattern(s) on the surface with letter markers.
- Bracket the discrete pattern horizontally and vertically with large scaled rulers or ruled tape.
- Take an establishing photograph containing the overall scale and discrete pattern identifiers and scales.
- Take a photograph of each discrete pattern with scale.
- Identify the spatter pattern that will be used for area of origin determination and mark with designators (example: Pattern A, Stains A1, A2, and A3).
- Bracket the discrete spatter pattern with a horizontal and vertical scale. Ensure the vertical arm of the scale is plumb.
- Take a photograph of the bloodstain pattern with the individual stains identified and marked.

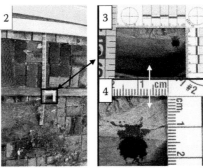

Figure 37.5 Bloodstain pattern mapping. (1) Overall with vertical and horizontal scale demonstrating stain position in scene. (2) Evidence establishing stain location to scale. (3) Close-up showing stain location by scale measurements. (4) Examination quality allowing for measurement of individual stain by scale.

- Take examination-quality photographs of a representative sample of the individual stains that make up the pattern.
  - Divide the pattern into thirds either along the pattern's long axis (if linear or curvilinear) or by rings (think of a bull's-eye target).
  - Photograph at least three individual stains from each third.
  - Sample for DNA a stain adjacent to (and appearing in) the examination quality photograph.
  - This will result in at least nine individual stains being photographed and sampled for each pattern type.
  - This is a recommended minimum number for documentation; additional stains for a radiating impact pattern will further assist in area of origin determination.
- Take a final establishing photograph of the item of evidence or surface that the bloodstain is on with all identifiers and scales.

Mapping Large Area Patterns

- When presented with a large area or surface containing multiple bloodstain patterns, it may be beneficial to divide the surface into grid squares (Figure 37.6).
- Mapping may then be accomplished with the staining identified by the appropriate grid squares.

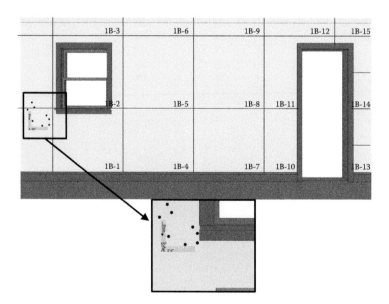

Figure 37.6 Large area mapping.

Clothing

Mapping of bloodstains is also effective on clothing items. The procedure is no different than that described for scene surfaces above. The following is an example of sequential mapping photographs used on an item of clothing (Figure 37.7).

Photography

- Use a high resolution setting on the camera. Maximize the capture of detail (pixels); this will allow enlarging sections of the photograph for examination.
- Mount the camera on a tripod and use a remote shutter release. Ensure that the film plane (or body of the camera) is parallel to the surface being photographed.
- Use a normal or macro lens for the camera. Do not use wide-angle lenses. Overlap the photographs if necessary for full coverage.
- Overall photograph shows the item of clothing in its entirety with scale.
- Establishing photographs of the patterns should demonstrate the relationship to the surface and a recognizable feature or scale.
- All close-up photographs should be examination quality and include a metric scale (preferably L-shaped to show height and width of the stain).

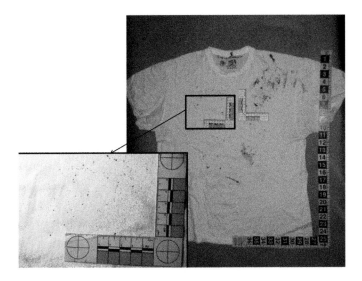

Figure 37.7 Bloodstain pattern mapping on clothing.

- The L-shaped metric scale should be oriented with the vertical leg along the long axis of the clothing and towards midline, the horizontal leg should be parallel with the bottom edge of the clothing.

Sketching

- A rough sketch of the location of all bloodstain patterns should be made using an exploded view.
- The rough sketch should be transposed into a finished drawing including measurements and placements of bloodstain patterns within the scene.

Sampling and Collection

- Use the guidelines contained in Chapter 41, "Biological Evidence."
- Sample, if possible, a minimum of nine stains or spatters within a discrete pattern.
- If practical, remove the wall, carpet, or ceiling sections containing the blood stain pattern.
- Smaller patterns can be lifted using large tape or clear contact paper and placed on panels the same size as the object they were removed from, much like the lifting and preserving of developed fingerprints.

Documenting and Processing a Shooting Scene

38

The fatal shooting scene offers unique challenges for the DSI. Establishing the shooter and victim's locations in a scene and body positions at the time of the shooting may be critical in resolving the investigation. In order to effectively document the scene, it is necessary to be able to identify all bullet defects, to include ricochets and grazes, determine the direction (trajectory) the bullet traveled, and determine logical shooter positions along the trajectory and the victim's position along the trajectory. This can only be accomplished if thorough documentation of the angle of the shot causing the defect as well as the precise location of that defect can be determined.

This documentation and the evidence at the scene should only be interpreted by someone properly trained in shooting incident reconstruction. A properly documented and processed shooting scene may be reconstructed at a later date. The basic procedures for the DSI to follow when documenting a shooting scene are as follows:

- Assess the scene and identify all firearms-related evidence (spent bullet cases, bullets, guns, gunpowder marks, etc.).
- Identify all potential bullet defects, to include ricochet marks and grazes. It may be necessary to chemically test ambiguous marks to increase confidence that they are firearms related.
- Document the patterns through a mapping technique.
- Identify any defects or patterns that will be sampled for gunpowder residue or DNA analysis, or from which a bullet will be recovered.
- Document and collect samples and collect bullets.

Recovery of Firearms Evidence from the Scene

The Weapon

Weapons safety Is of paramount concern
- If the weapon is within an area secured by law enforcement, it should be properly documented and thoroughly photographed in place prior to any manipulation.

- If the crime scene is still dynamic (marginal law enforcement control), the weapon should be expediently documented and made safe, if positive law enforcement control of the area cannot be immediately established.

Documenting the Firearm

- Photograph and place the weapon onto the death scene sketch.
- While completing and documenting initial examination, using Worksheet 6, "Firearms Recovery Worksheet," place the weapon in an unloaded and safe condition.
- Thoroughly photograph the weapon in place. This includes any close-up photography of the serial numbers, unique identifiers, and bloodstains.
- Prior to handling the weapon, if it is safe to do so, process for touch DNA (Chapter 41). Swab the handgrips or other areas you will have to handle in order to safe and collect the weapon.
- The weapon should be handled with a gloved hand on its knurled surface or other area least likely to contain latent prints. **Note:** It is not advisable to place any item into the weapon's barrel to facilitate collection.
- Photograph the surfaces of the weapon that were not visible in its original orientation.

Make the Weapon Safe

- Safe the weapon. It is best not to be tentative in an attempt to minimize handling. Firmly grasp the weapon as you would your own, remove the ammunition source, and remove any rounds remaining in the chamber.
- In the rare instance when a weapon cannot be unloaded at the scene, it must be carefully packaged in as safe a condition as possible, packaged in such a way as to preclude accidental discharge, and the container marked with "Warning, Loaded Firearm." All subsequent personnel and facilities that will handle the evidence must be made aware of the loaded condition of the weapon.

Processing the Weapon On-Scene

- Do not unload the magazine. Note the approximate number of rounds and Superglue™ the magazine with the bullets in place and the round ejected from the chamber.

- Discreetly sample any bloodstains adhering to the weapon after they have been thoroughly documented (Chapter 41, "Biological Evidence").
- If possible, Superglue™ the weapon and any bullets removed from the weapon to preserve latent prints or touch DNA.

Collecting and Packaging the Firearm

- The weapon must be packaged so as to prevent any movement that might obliterate latent print, trace, or biological evidence.
- The weapon may be secured to a piece of cardboard with plastic tie-downs or similarly immobilized in special boxes made for this purpose.
- *Do not* package the weapon with the ammunition.
- If blood, tissue, or other biological evidence is present on the weapon, it must be thoroughly air-dried before final packaging.

Recovery of a Firearm from Water

- The weapon should be left in the water until all packaging materials are ready.
- Without removing the weapon from the water, it should be made safe in the same manner as described above.
- The weapon should be packaged in a container filled with the same water from which it was seized. Minimum exposure to the air should be allowed. This will retard rusting or further deterioration of the weapon.
- The weapon must be transported to the forensic laboratory as soon as possible.

Recovery of Cartridges, Spent Bullet Cases, and Bullets

- The location of cartridges, spent bullet cases, and bullets should be carefully documented.
- Bullets should not be dug from objects, but rather the object or portion of the object containing the bullet should be collected.
- Spent bullets should be placed on the sketch individually and not documented or sketched as a group.
- Bullet cases and bullets should not be marked in any way.

- Cartridges, spent bullet cases, and bullets should be Superglue™ fumed, individually packaged in individual rigid containers, and the packaging marked.
- Weapon, loaded ammunition, and additional loose or boxed ammunition of the same type and lot fired should be collected to assist in range of fire determinations.

Additional Analysis Considerations

- Bloodstain pattern analysis
- Shooting incident reconstruction—trajectory analysis

Documenting Bullet Defects

The bullet may strike, ricochet from, deflect from, travel through, or penetrate a variety of surfaces during its travel. Each of these defects must be thoroughly documented. When multiple defects occur at the scene, they may be documented through Worksheet 14, "Bullet Defect Worksheet."

- Each defect should be placed on the sketch and photographically documented through a mapping technique (Figures 38.1 and 38.2).
- When possible sequential defects should be designated as such: A1, A2, A3 to designate the bullet defect's sequential relationship as it passes through multiple surfaces (Figure 38.3).

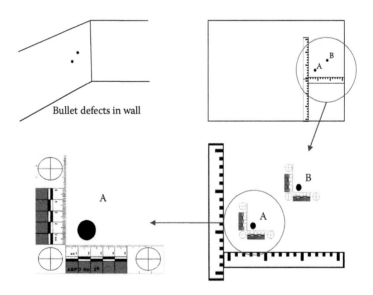

Figure 38.1 Bullet defect mapping.

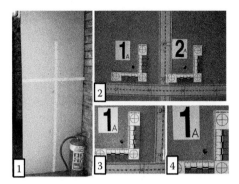

Figure 38.2 Mapping technique. (1) Overall of wall with vertical and horizontal scales. (2) Defects 1 and 2 with reference to scales. (3) Defect 1 with reference to scale. (4) Defect 1 examination quality.

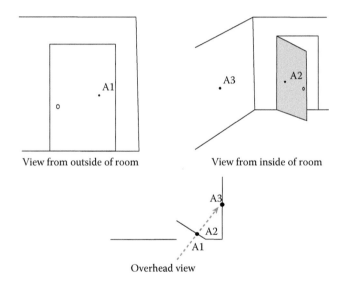

Figure 38.3 Labeling sequential defects from a single shot.

- The bullet's terminal location should be thoroughly documented.
- Lead splash patterns are particularly useful when a bullet is deflected from the surface or ricochets. Latent lead splash can be made visible by reagent testing of the surface. Lead splash may not be visible in ambient light due to low volume or due to being deposited on a dark surface.
- Positive tests for copper and lead not only indicate that the defect was caused by a bullet but also give an indication of the direction of travel. Bullet wipe and lead splash occur on the entry side of a bullet hole.

- Ricochets or low angle defects may demonstrate directionality through the orientation of the lead in mark, pinch point, or bow wave (Figures 38.4 and 38.5).
- A ricochet from a hard, smooth surface may demonstrate an elongated tail in the direction of travel. The orientation of the trail (left or right side of the ricochet) is indicative of the twist of the bullet (Figure 38.6).
- Once documented, a rod and level should be used to demonstrate the elevation angle of the trajectory (Figure 38.7).
- Once documented, a rod and protractor should be used to demonstrate the azimuth angle of the trajectory (Figure 38.8).
- A bullet defect through tempered glass may be marked at the scene with string. This technique preserves the defect location, should the glass fall out of the frame (Figure 38.9).

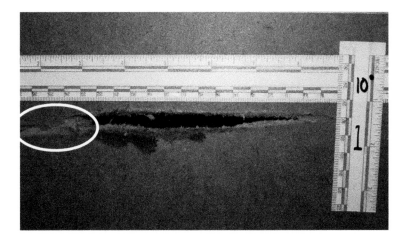

Figure 38.4 Lead-in mark on a 10°-bullet defect to wall board.

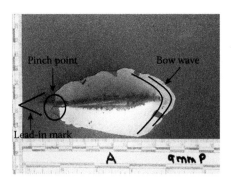

Figure 38.5 Low-angle bullet impact demonstrating pinch point and bow wave.

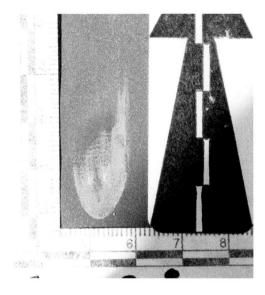

Figure 38.6 Bullet ricochet from a metal surface. The elongated pattern on the right side of the mark indicates the bullet had a right-hand twist.

Figure 38.7 Demonstrating trajectory (elevation) with rods.

Chemical Testing to Determine If It Is a Bullet Defect

When a bullet comes in contact with a surface, minute amounts of metal may transfer from the bullet to the impacted surface. If it is uncertain that a defect was caused by a bullet's passage, chemical testing can be accomplished to detect the copper and/or lead that may have transferred.

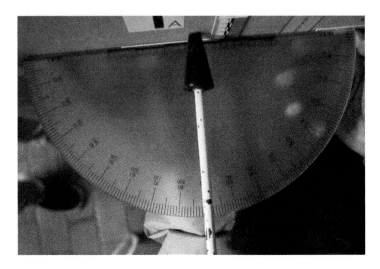

Figure 38.8 Demonstrating trajectory (azimuth) with rods.

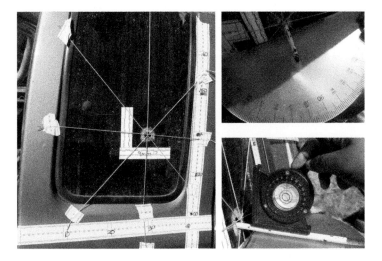

Figure 38.9 Strings are used to "bull's-eye" a bullet defect in tempered glass. Should the glass fall from the frame due to heat expansion or movement of the vehicle analysis may still be accomplished.

Testing for Copper

See Figure 38.10.

- DTO and 2-NN testing for copper must be done before using sodium rhodizonate to test for lead.
- Dithiooxamide (DTO) is a colorimetric reagent that will produce a gray-green color in the presence of copper.

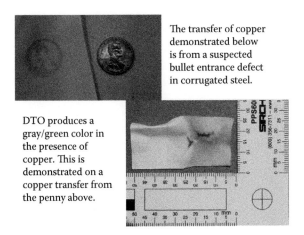

The transfer of copper demonstrated below is from a suspected bullet entrance defect in corrugated steel.

DTO produces a gray/green color in the presence of copper. This is demonstrated on a copper transfer from the penny above.

Figure 38.10 Dithiooxamide (DTO) will produce a gray-green color in the present of copper.

- A solution of ammonium hydroxide is sprayed onto the absorbent side of plastic-backed filter paper.
- The wetted filter paper is then pressed against the suspected bullet defect. The hydroxide will solubilize the copper, which will then be absorbed onto the filter paper.
- The orange DTO solution is then sprayed onto the filter paper. If copper is present, a ring of gray-green color will develop around the lifted defect pattern.
- The results should be photographed and the lift retained as evidence.
- If the ammonium hydroxide lift has a substrate color that would obscure DTO results, 2-nitro-1-naphthol (2-NN) can be used instead of DTO.
- Using 2-NN on a lift containing copper will produce a pink color. DTO is sprayed over the pink and will produce the positive gray-green color if copper is present. Each of the color changes should be photographed and the lift retained as evidence.

Testing for Lead

See Figure 38.11.

- Sodium rhodizonate is a chemical reagent that is used to test for the presence of lead.
- When the surface is dried after testing for copper, rhodizonate testing can be done on the same area for lead.
- This is a nondestructive test, meaning other tests can be done to the same evidence.

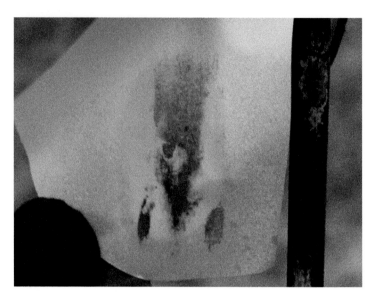

Figure 38.11 Sodium rhodizonate will produce an immediate pink color in the presence of lead. This pattern was transferred onto a piece of filter paper from a suspected bullet ricochet mark and then treated with sodium rhodizonate.

- A colorless tartrate buffer solution is sprayed onto the surface. The buffer will solubilize lead.
- Then the orange-brown sodium rhodizonate solution is sprayed over the same area. If lead is present, an immediate color change to pink will occur.
- The results of this test should be photographed.
- To confirm that a pink color change was caused by the presence of lead, 5% hydrochloric acid can be sprayed over the pink color (or a portion of the pink color). If the pink was produced by the presence of lead, the pink color will change to a purple-blue color.
- The results should be photographed and the lift should be retained as evidence.

Recovery of Firearms Evidence from the Victim

Detection of Gunpowder Patterns

Visual
- Gunpowder patterns can be visible surrounding a bullet defect or on the hands or surface directly adjacent to a weapon when it is fired.
- If visible, these patterns should be photographed.

Infrared

See Figure 38.12.

- Infrared video and photography of darker colored items is an excellent way to visualize gunpowder patterns on darker surfaces patterns.
- Specialized IR cameras are available for forensic work; these are the easiest to use and give excellent results.
- IR filters can be used on digital cameras; less expensive cameras have a built-in IR filter that prevents it from being captured.
- IR filters on digital cameras also require care in focusing. The IR focal point is different than the visible light. This may cause difficulty with autofocus.

Collection and Packaging of Clothing

- Clothing can only be removed at the scene with the permission of the medical examiner. This permission may exist as a preagreed protocol when the bloodstain patterns or gunshot residue would be obscured or degraded by the clothing remaining on the body.
- Always seize the victim's clothing as evidence. While powder may not be readily visible over the outer surface of clothing, microscopic examination may reveal fragments of powder caught in the weave of the material.

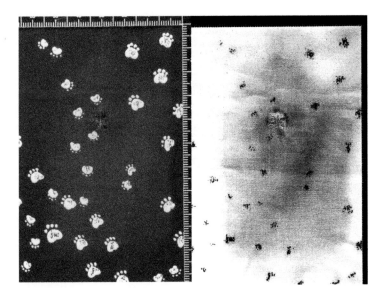

Figure 38.12 Dark print fabric with gunpowder pattern photographed with regular lighting and IR. Photograph courtesy of Jeff Borngasser, Oregon State Central Point Crime Laboratory, Portland, OR.

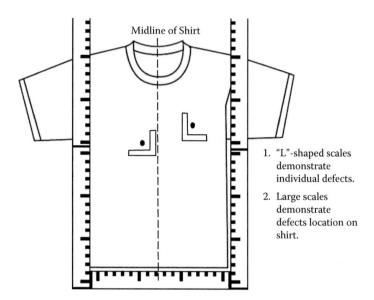

Figure 38.13 Mapping bullet defects in clothing.

- The suspect's clothing (outer clothing worn at the time of the shooting) should also be seized. This should include any gloves he or she may have been wearing.
- Clothing with visible defects, gunshot residue, or bloodstain patterns should be photographically documented through a mapping technique (Figure 38.13).
- All clothing collected should be thoroughly air-dried. If a bloodstain is present, a piece of heavy paper between layers of fabric can prevent blood pattern transfer.
- Clothing items should be packaged separately in paper containers.
- Weather and environmental conditions, at the scene such as air movement and precipitation, should be documented to assist in range of fire determination.

Documentation and Collection of Gunshot Residue

- Gunshot residue testing should be conducted on the hands of anyone believed to have handled the firearm.
- The victim of a possibly self-inflicted wound should have their hands sampled for gunshot residue. This may be done at the scene with the medical examiner's approval or the hands may be bagged at the scene and the samples taken at autopsy.

- Use GSR analysis to help evaluate whether a person handled or fired a weapon.
  - Questions for subjects of GSR examination and collection:
  - "When was the last time you handled a firearm?"
  - "When was the last time you fired a weapon?"
  - "When was the last time you were present when a weapon was fired, and what was your proximity to the weapon?"
  - "When was the last time you washed your hands?"
  - "Are you right- or left-handed?"

Documenting and Processing Post-Blast (Explosive Incident) Scenes

39

The interpretation of explosive scenes is highly specialized and requires special training. Working in conjunction with a trained post-blast investigator or with the ATF is highly recommended.

NOTE: It is highly recommended that an explosive ordnance detachment (EOD) team be present to inspect and make safe all such devices prior to processing and collection. Worksheet 5, "Post-Blast Scene Management," is provided for documentation of the scene using the polar coordinates method.

Initial Actions

Caution: It should always be assumed that secondary explosive devices have been set to attack first responders. Extreme caution must be exercised. All explosive scenes should be cleared by EOD personnel.

Establishing a Perimeter

- The perimeter of the explosive scene must be set at a minimum of one and one half times the distance from the center of the explosion (seat of blast) to the furthest piece of debris identified.
- This is not necessarily the furthest area of damage; the blast wave and shock damage will likely far exceed the distance to the furthest debris from the seat of blast.
- It may be necessary to establish a secondary safety perimeter to ensure the safety of responders and bystanders. The area contained inside this secondary perimeter will include areas that have falling glass, debris, or demonstrate structural instability.

Legal Concerns

- Determine the legal authority to be present and to conduct a crime scene examination. At some point, the exigent circumstances for responding to the scene (e.g., caring for victims) will be over.

- What is the continued authority to remain on scene and collect evidence (e.g., search warrant, consent authorization, no reasonable expectation of privacy)?
- See Chapter 32, Death Scene Management: Legal Concerns, for a detailed explanation of search and processing legal concerns.

Establishing Context

- The context of the scene may provide indicators as to the nature of the bomber, which may be apparent during the initial walk-through or scene survey.
  - A *juvenile bomber* circumstance may involve the accidental or experimental (curious) making of devices that result in destruction and damage far beyond that intended. Gunpowder, matches, PVC pipe, combustible materials, and a relatively unsophisticated detonation method are generally observed, and the location of the origin may be an outside area isolated from observation or in a garage, basement, or other area where the device is constructed.
  - The *juvenile vandal/delinquent bomber* will often target schools or other properties that have meaning to them as representing the establishment or the social order that they are rebelling against. Their devices may resemble that of the juvenile bomber or be more sophisticated. Web searches on bomb manufacture or the presence of books such as the *Anarchist Cookbook* may be present in written or digital format.
  - An *explosion to commit fraud* by the owner or one with a financial interest in a property may be indicated when items of furnishing, office equipment, high-dollar, or personal items have been removed from the location prior to the fire explosion. Lower-cost items may have been placed in the scene to replace the more expensive items to give the appearance of an "undisturbed" scene. Additionally, examination of insurance records, tax records, legal liens, bankruptcy, and foreclosure notices affecting the property may provide indications of arson for profit.
  - An *extremist bomber* uses explosive devices to advance a political, religious, or social agenda. This may include acts of terrorism, burnings during civil unrest/riots, and other circumstances.
  - A *serial bomber* may be juvenile or adult. The explosions will seldom involve theft or removal of property, as the explosion itself is the motivation for this crime. Patterns as to the physical locations of the bombings and the construction of the device itself may suggest an offender profile.

- There are a variety of motivations involved in constructing and detonating bombs; the cited examples are emphasized only as they may be indicated from the appearance of the physical scene.

Crime Scene Processing Guidelines

Specific guidance for steps in securing the scene, photography, and initial crime scene procedures covered in Section VI, "Death Scene Management, Tasks, and Responsibilities," is applicable to all crime scenes and should be reviewed to ensure no steps are missed. Worksheet 5, "Post-Blast Scene Management," allows for documenting the evidence at the scene through polar coordinates.

Initial Briefing

If possible, seek and debrief someone responsible and objective who witnessed or heard the event. Discuss this information with first responders and investigators, who might have additional information about the event.

- Determine when the incident reportedly occurred.
- Determine who had control over the site of the bomb when it went off.
- Determine if other secondary devices are present.
- Determine whether or not anyone videotaped the smoke plume and/ or other effects of the explosion.
- Determine if commercial or government video devices might have recorded the explosion.
- Determine what parties all have already been through the scene (e.g., first responders, witnesses, neighbors).
- Determine if the area has open access to the public or visitors or if access is generally limited, such as private/guarded property.

Initial Walk-Through

Conduct a scene walk-through, avoiding paths of travel likely used by the perpetrators.

- Note any perishable evidence and document/collect or safeguard it.
- Note any obvious items missing or disturbed.
- Determine area of primary activity to commit the crime.
- Limit the scene through logical progression to determine specifically where the individual might have been to trigger the blast and what they would have had to touch.

Blast Scene Mapping (Searching and Evidence Recovery)

A thorough crime scene search must be made for portions of the detonating devices and explosive containers. These are often difficult to identify and may still pose an explosive hazard. The use of an explosives expert is highly recommended.

Any items that seem strange or foreign to the setting should be documented and collected.

Items closest to the origin of the blast may contain explosive residues. These should be documented and collected.

- The most effective method for documenting the location of evidence within a blast scene is using polar coordinates (Figure 39.1).
- The seat of blast is searched first and rendered safe.
  - Note any material and its construction found near the seat of blast.
  - Note the size and depth of the crater at the seat of the blast.
  - Dirt and debris should be sifted using a 1/2-inch screen first, then a 1/4-inch screen, in an attempt to locate remnants of the device.
- The blast area should be broken down into four 90-degree quadrants covering the full 360 degrees surrounding the seat of the blast.
- Quadrants with the most evidence are processed first. All quadrants, however, must be thoroughly searched!

NOTE: Blasts resulting from exploding dust, gas, and/or chemicals that are not under pressure may not leave an identifiable seat of blast. If noted early in the scene investigation, the lack of a distinct crater may assist in discerning this type of explosion is involved.

Procedure for Mapping

- A surveyor's transit or similar device is set up at the seat of blast. (A lensatic compass may be used if necessary; see Figure 39.2.)
  - Designate magnetic north as 0 degrees.
  - Zone 1: 0–90 degrees
  - Zone 2: 90–180 degrees
  - Zone 3: 180–270 degrees
  - Zone 4: 270–360 degrees
- Search teams examine the quadrants and mark all items of evidence. It is easiest at this point to use a standard evidence placard.
- Designate each item of evidence on the sketch using the evidence number inside of the following symbols:
- Record the azimuth and distance from the seat of the blast for each item of evidence.

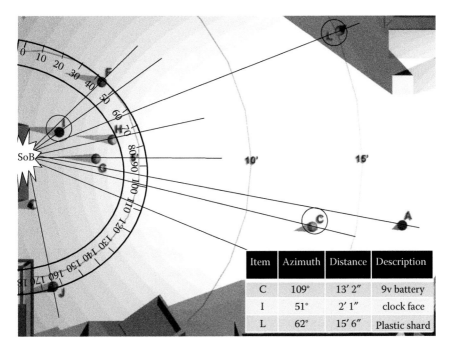

Item	Azimuth	Distance	Description
C	109°	13′ 2″	9v battery
I	51°	2′ 1″	clock face
L	62°	15′ 6″	Plastic shard

Figure 39.1 Example of polar coordinates method on a post-blast scene.

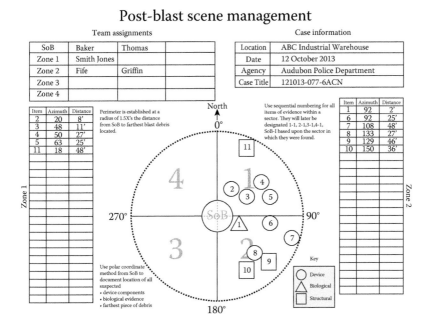

Figure 39.2 Example of a completed post-blast worksheet.

- It is preferable to measure distance from the seat of the blast using a sonic or laser measuring device that has been calibrated at the scene.
- Photograph the evidence with an evidence marker.

Collecting the Evidence

- Evidence is collected and grouped by category and zone number.
- Significant evidence is bagged separately. This includes the following:
  - Body parts/biological material
  - Suspected device components, which are subdivided into
    - Electrical
    - Wiring
    - Mechanical
- General debris may be packaged together in a bag marked for the zone/quadrant.
- The guidelines provided in Section "Collection of Explosives Residue Materials" in Chapter 42, "Trace Evidence" should be followed when collecting and sampling explosive residues and other trace evidence.

Commonly Encountered Evidence

The following evidence is commonly found at explosive scenes.

Identified Device and Component Parts

- Friction ridge evidence (be sure to consider any tape used to build the device)
  - Patent prints
  - Latent prints
- Biological evidence
  - Touch DNA
  - Hairs
- Impression evidence
  - Tool marks

Post-Blast Debris

- Timing devices
- Explosive devices
- Electrical devices
- Explosive containers
- Wiring and connectors
- Batteries

- Circuit boards
- Body parts
- Unidentified biological material

Evidence of an accelerated fire or explosive residue must be handled carefully. It is best to detect, sample, and collect in conjunction with a trained post-blast or fire investigator. Liquids or solids may still be highly flammable, shock sensitive, and/or toxic.

Explosive Evidence Collection Guidelines

- Use only clean, unlined paint or lined (keep control sample) cans or glass jars without rubber liners or seals.
- Nylon collection bags may be used for solid objects or objects of unusual shape or size.
- Never fill a container more than 2/3 full.
- An adhesive-backed activated charcoal strip may be secured to the inside lid of the container. This strip will absorb a sample of any volatile fumes coming from the sample.

Sampling for Explosive Residue

- Sample any area where an explosives detector or bomb K-9 indicates the possible presence of explosives.
- Take soil and other samples for potential explosive residue near the seat of the blast.
- Sample both from the seat of the blast and just outside of the seat of the blast.
- Remaining vertical surfaces near the seat of the blast sometimes retain blast residues and should be checked and sampled.
- Sampling may be conducted by either seizing the item on which the residue is deposited or by swabbing the surface vigorously with several swabs moistened with distilled water.

Collecting and Packaging

Liquids

- Using a syringe, eyedropper, or pipette, draw a liquid samples from the surface of the liquid and place in a clean unlined metal can. Seal tightly.
- The sample may also be soaked into a clean, untreated gauze pad or cotton swabbing and packaged as above.

Solids

- Solid materials that may have absorbed liquid evidence or been exposed to explosive residue should be collected in an unlined or lined sealed can.
- Solid samples of accelerant explosive residue are potentially corrosive and should be placed in a glass jar without a glued cap liner or rubber seal.
- Large or irregularly shaped objects may be collected and sealed in nylon bags.
- Always collect a control sample relating to any item of evidence taken.

Entomological Evidence 40

MICHAEL MALONEY AND
DONALD HOUSMAN

The use of insect life cycles and insect succession (the order in which various species colonize necrotic tissue and fecal waste) can provide helpful investigative indicators. Though more traditionally used to determine the postmortem interval of the deceased, it may be very valuable in both fatal abuse and neglect cases. In cases of severe neglect, the diapers, creases surrounding the buttocks and anal cleft, and any area with open sores may also be infested with insect eggs or larvae. These may aid in documenting the extent and duration of the neglect. Additionally, foodstuff left in the room of the victim and other garbage may show signs of infestation that may be used to determine the time they have been present at the scene. Entomological evidence may be documented through Worksheet 7.

Terminology

Larvae: The immature form of an insect. With flies, the larval form is commonly referred to as *maggots*.

Maggot: The larval form of flies.

Necrotic tissue: Tissue most commonly at a wound site, injury site, or area where blood flow is cut off for a sustained period and where the tissue has died. It is no longer viable and is decomposing or "rotting."

Pupa: An insect in an inactive immature stage between larvae and adult.

Pupal casing: The case that encloses the pupa. These are abandoned by the emerging adult insect. They may contain traces of drugs or substances from the original food source (i.e., the victim).

Insect succession: Insects colonize an infestation site in a relatively ordered progression. First are those drawn by the scent of decomposing flesh. They are followed by those that feed on the larval forms of the first invading species and lastly those that make use of the dried or desiccated remains.

General Guidelines

A forensic entomologist should be able to provide a good estimate of the amount of time that the infestation site has been active. It is incumbent upon the investigator to understand the following:

- Certain species of insects (often flies) will begin to colonize necrotic tissue or fecal waste within minutes of the site being exposed if the right temperature and other conditions (such as daylight) are present. Additionally, early infestation may be limited by movement of the victim, brushing away flies and other insects as they land on the necrotic tissue.
- Flies usually choose areas of the body that provide protection, moisture, and food for their eggs. In neglect cases, this often includes open wound sites, fecal material adhering to the skin, or in advanced stages the nares (nose), mouth, eyes, and exposed genital area of a victim.
- Most insects that choose to colonize human tissue go through a complete life cycle consisting of egg, larva (maggot), pupa, and finally adult. The larvae themselves usually go through two to three stages called *instars* before becoming pupae.
- Using the known times it takes for specific insects to develop from one stage to another under nominal conditions, entomologists can tell how long the insects have been feeding on the tissue. Environmental factors affecting this estimation include temperature, humidity/moisture, amount of sun versus shade, and related conditions.
- Some of the resulting adult insects are seen as flies; even after they have gone through a complete life cycle to adulthood entomologists can continue to make good estimate of the time since infestation using the succession of arrival of other types of insects that come to the body at various intervals.
- It is therefore important to collect a sample of as many different species of adult flies as observed on and around the victim, as well as beetles on or around the victim and flying insects other than flies.
- With many species, only the adults are used to verify the species. This does not preclude analysis if adults are not present! Immature insect forms may be collected and raised to adulthood by the forensic entomologist.
- Often, the largest larvae at the scene will be the oldest of that particular species present.
- If present, pupae can be found. For example, larvae crawl off the body and bury themselves in the carpet or soil under or near the body,

or they may migrate en masse to a nearby shady/protected area and develop a protective shell around themselves.
- In outdoor scenes, soil samples need to be taken to see if any pupae exist, and if so what species they are. With indoor scenes, pupae may be found under the body, in bedding, or nearby carpeting.

Collection of Samples

Scene collection may be accomplished from clothing removed from the victim at the scene, the bedclothes of the victim, or the victim himself or herself. Expedient methods may cause the DSI to greatly abbreviate the steps and process listed below in order to capture this perishable evidence. Worksheet 7, "Entomological Recovery," provides a mechanism for capturing the data.

Adult and Flying Insects
- Using a figure-eight motion, collect flying insects with an insect net from the area immediately around and above the victim.
- Place immediately into a 70% ethanol or isopropyl (rubbing) alcohol solution that has been further diluted 1:1 with water. Small glass vials make the best collection container for these samples.

Crawling Adult Insects
- Collect any crawling insects from the surface of the wound site or body opening using forceps or gloved fingers.

NOTE: Do not probe the wound, infestation site, or body opening.

- Very small insects may be collected with an artist brush moistened with the preservative solution.
- Place the collected specimens immediately into a 70% ethanol or isopropyl alcohol solution that has been further diluted 1:1 with water.

Maggots, Pupae, and Other Immature Insect Forms
- Record the temperature of any maggot mass on the victim.
- Record the air temperature at body level for the victim.
- Record the surface temperature of the surface near the body (e.g., not at the body's interface with the bed).
- Collect the largest maggots visible from the surface of and from within the body using forceps or gloved fingers. Just a few of these largest ones will be needed *from each of the separate infestation sites on the body.*

NOTE: Do not probe the wound site or body opening, and be careful not to damage the larvae.

- Place the collected specimens immediately into a 70% ethanol or isopropyl alcohol solution that has been further diluted 1:1 with water.
- *Live specimens*: Place about 15–30 of the specimens collected from the same areas of the body in a breathable container with a lid. The container should hold a piece of raw liver that is placed on top of a layer of clean sand, vermiculite (or potting soil), or dampened paper towel. Place the specimens directly on the liver.
- Punch very small holes into a plastic lid, or use an oversized piece of material cut from a pair of ladies' hosiery and held in place over the container with a rubber band to allow air to exchange within the container.
- Fill the remaining space of the container with a clean, damp paper towel that will serve to keep the container moist and minimize the movement of meat and maggots during transport.
  - These insects will be raised to maturity by the forensic entomologist for species identification.
- Mark each container with the investigator's initials and date/time of collection. Also mark containers that are associated with each other (e.g., such as live and dead samples from the same areas of the body—above) in such a manner that the specimens can be associated with each other at the lab.
- Transport all samples (dead and live) to a forensic entomologist as soon as practical.

NOTE: Do not mix different live species in the same container. For example, carrion beetles will eat fly maggots.

Insects in Soil

- Handful-sized samples can be collected from under (head, body, and extremities), adjacent to, and up to 3 feet from the victim's location in both directions, noting the position of each sample in relation to where the body had been located.
- Scoop soil samples into a locking plastic bag and chill. Transport to a forensic entomologist as soon as practical.
- Carefully examine the surrounding soil and soil beneath the body for insects, pupae, and pupae casings. These should be collected and preserved as stated above.

Documentation of Entomological Evidence

- Include a complete set of scene photographs insuring that the surrounding area is depicted. This information should be forwarded to the forensic entomologist, who will complete the analysis.
- Obtain and record climatic conditions including minimum and maximum temperatures for the 2-week period preceding the discovery of the body, any precipitation during this period and amount, wind speed and direction, relative humidity, and cloud cover. This information may be obtained from the National Weather Service. Worksheet 7, "Entomology Recovery," can be used to record the type of information needed by the servicing entomologist.

Contact with the Servicing Forensic Entomologist

- Before transporting the collected samples, it is advisable to contact the entomologist who will be conducting the analysis.
- Explain your collection and preservation process and ask for any additional guidance he or she can give.
- The entomologist often has a collection questionnaire that explains all observations and recordings required for the analysis. If a singular entomologist is utilized by the DSI, it is beneficial to coordinate with him or her in advance of need.
- Discuss an estimate of cost, method of payment, and related business issues and arrange for transportation of the collected samples.
- Insect samples should be treated as evidence in that any changes in custody should be noted and recorded in case this becomes an issue in court.

Biological Evidence

41

Biological evidence is found on the body and clothing of the victim or perpetrator and at the scene. Biological evidence is a valuable source in determining physical presence or contact as well as actions within a scene. Handling biological fluids and stains is hazardous due to blood-borne pathogens. Hepatitis B virus and human immunodeficiency virus are of particular concern. Treat all biological fluids as sources of blood-borne pathogens. See Appendix A for safety instructions and the use of universal precautions. Worksheet 8, "Biological Evidence Notes," provides a mechanism to document processing efforts.

Touch DNA

Touch DNA refers to an incidental transfer of genetic material (DNA) when an object is handled, touched, or brushed up against. The DNA of the person may be transferred through shed skin cells or body fluids.

Detection

- The "touch" transfer is latent, not visible to the naked eye.
- Its possible location, and therefore collection point, is determined through an analysis of the body and evidence in context of the dynamics of movement within the scene.
- Touch DNA should be expected to co-reside with latent or patent fingerprint impressions. Obvious locations at the scene would be at points of entry or where items of physical evidence had to be manipulated by the perpetrator.
- Obvious locations on the deceased may include the upper arms, wrists, or ankles of a victim that was dragged, or the inner thighs or breasts of a sexual assault victim.
- Other locations may be less obvious, but all possible locations of touch DNA on the victim should be thoroughly examined.
- Nothing precludes collection of both DNA and fingerprint evidence.
- Touch DNA can be sampled from areas associated with latent fingerprints transfer by swabbing areas that lack *any* ridge detail. Swab the

areas surrounding the print or areas of relief (e.g., edges, textured aspects of the object that will not hold ridge detail). If the investigator can see a fingerprint impression but it is obviously smeared and lacks ridge detail, there is strong possibility that touch DNA could be retrieved from that surface.

Preservation and Collection on Items of Evidence

- Cyanoacrylate (Superglue™) fuming for the preservation of latent prints serves a dual purpose, as it also preserves touch DNA. This is an ideal method for preserving both possible prints and DNA on weapons.
- Touch DNA may be collected by swabbing the suspected transfer area with multiple swabs moistened with distilled or sterile water. The swabs should be rubbed over the suspected area for at least 15 seconds.
- Do not use standard cotton swabs for touch DNA collection. As the swab is rubbed against the area, the cotton tends to degrade and fall off. This is the very area of the swab that most likely holds the genetic material. Swabs made of rayon or polyester are the better collection method.
- Alternatively, typical small tape tabs (e.g., Post-it sticky flags) can be used if the area to be sampled is dry. The tabs are pressed against the area to be sampled and submitted for evaluation. The adhesive has no known detrimental effect on the DNA itself.

Biological Fluids and Stains

Biological fluids such as blood, semen, saliva, and urine may be left on the body of the deceased or at the scene. These stains may be either wet or dry, or in some cases pooled.

Detection

See Figure 41.1.

- Visual detection may be supplemented with strong oblique lighting. This is the least effective method.
- Ultraviolet lighting (100–400 nm) often fluoresces semen, urine, and occasionally saliva. Use caution when exposing any area believed to contain DNA to extended exposure to ultraviolet light,

Figure 41.1 Searching for biological evidence may require scans with various light sources. Strong white light, UV light (pictured here) and an ALS light.

as UV light does have a detrimental effect on genetic material. Long wave (315–400 nm) UV is preferred over short wave (100–280 nm) UV light.

- Semen, saliva, and urine will fluoresce when exposed to an ALS tuned to 450–485 nm and viewed through orange goggles.
- Blood, however, does not fluoresce when exposed to alternate wavelengths of light. It absorbs all light and appears black or dark. Blood is best visualized when exposed to 415 nm of light and viewed through yellow goggles. The appearance of the stain will be like a dark hole in the background material and the resulting contrast should allow the investigator to visualize and photograph the blood better.

The Body and Scene Analysis

- Typically, the presence of a stain in the appropriate scene context is sufficient to indicate it is biological. If a stain looks like biological staining and is in an area where biological staining would be expected, it should be processed and collected. A presumptive test is not necessary.
- Occasionally stains may appear in such a context that their biological origin or forensic significance is questioned.

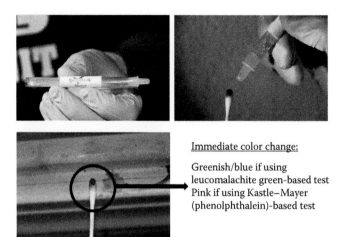

Figure 41.2 Presumptive blood test.

- Presumptive test kits are available that may be used on scene to establish a stain is blood, semen, or saliva. This does not confirm that it is a human sample, but it may assist the DSI in deciding what stains should be sampled (Figure 41.2).
- Human-specific test kits are also available for field use. These allow the stain to be confirmed as human blood, human semen, or human saliva at the scene (Figure 41.3).

Collection of Biological Stains

Biological evidence is usually encountered in one of four conditions:

- *Dry*: contains no moisture, crusty
- *Wet*: a damp stain or area of biological staining
- *Liquid*: a pooled area of biological fluid
- *Tissue*: an actual piece or fragment of tissue

General

- All stains should be thoroughly documented and photographed prior to collection. Include close-up photography, both without and with scale. *Note: If you are illuminating with UV light, remove any skylight or UV protective filter from the lens or the camera will not capture the image.*
- For biological stains on the body, use the injury mapping technique discussed in Chapter 34, "Death Scene Photography."

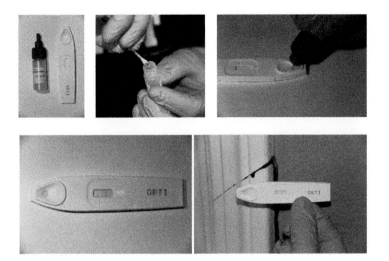

Figure 41.3 Presumptive blood test, human (primate) specific. Positive indicated by parallel blue lines, one at the control (C) position and the other at the test (T) position.

- As collection efforts move from one stain to the next, the potential for cross contamination should be minimized. Either use disposable instruments for collection or instruments that have been cleaned in a 10% household bleach solution for 5 minutes. In addition, two pairs of gloves should be worn, with the outer pair being changed between unassociated stains or samples.
- With prior approval from the medical examiner or coroner, use an indelible marker pen and draw a discreet arrow to any suspected wet semen observable on the body. Once dry, stains that were visible at the scene may not be visible.
- Use an indelible marker pen and circle any suspected wet semen observable on sheets, items of clothing, or other objects. Once dry, stains that were visible at the scene may not be visible.
- If the stains are located on bedding, mark the side that was exposed during the assault and indicate which end was at the head and which was at the foot of the bed. Allow wet stains to air-dry before folding.
- If collecting and submitting the object itself, no control sample is required. Otherwise, obtain a sample from an uncontaminated area on the surface where the stain was found.
- Before folding an item, place a clean piece of paper over stains to prevent cross transfer of the stain to other portions of the item. Do not fold the item through a stain.

Dry Stains

See Figure 41.4.

The Body
- If a dry semen stain is located on the body, discreetly indicate the location with an indelible pen.
- Use the injury mapping technique to photograph the stain as outlined in Chapter 9, "Autopsy Protocol and the Investigator's Role."
- Photograph the stain using UV and ALS.
- Lightly moisten a sterile swab(s) with distilled or sterile water (do not use saline solutions) and swab the stain.
- Saturate the sterile swab(s) with as much of the sample as possible. It is important not to dilute the stain too much.

The Scene
- Submit item if practical or cut out the section containing the stain.
- Collect as much of the stain as possible.
- If the item cannot be seized or the stain cut out, collect dried stains with clean, moistened sterile swabs.
- Lightly moisten a sterile swab with distilled or sterile water (do not use saline solutions) and swab the stain.
- Saturate the sterile swab with as much of the sample as possible. It is important not to dilute the stain too much.
- Continue to saturate swabs with the stain until the swab comes away clean or until six to eight swabs have been collected.

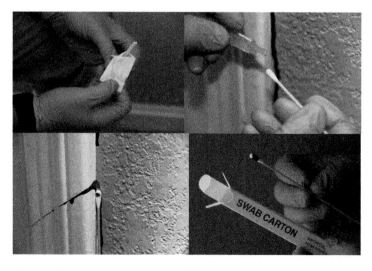

Figure 41.4 Collecting a dry sample of blood after moistening the swab with distilled water.

- Air-dry the swabs.
- Take a control sample with an additional swab, identically moistened, swabbed on an adjacent unstained area of the substrate, and also air-dried. Package separately as "control sample."

Wet Stains

See Figure 41.5.

The Body
- If a wet semen stain is located on the body, discreetly indicate the location with an indelible pen.
- Use the injury mapping technique to photograph the stain as outlined in Chapter 9, "Autopsy Protocol and the Investigator's Role."
- Photograph the stain using UV and ALS.
- Using a sterile swab(s) (lightly moisten if necessary), collect the stain.
- Saturate the sterile swab(s) with as much of the sample as possible.

The Scene
- Submit item if practical, or cut out the section containing the stain.
- Collect as much of the stain as possible.
- Allow stain to thoroughly air-dry prior to packaging.
- If the item cannot be seized or the stain cut out, collect wet stains with clean, dry cotton swabs.
- Saturate the cotton swab with as much of the sample as possible.
- Continue to saturate swabs with the stain until the swab comes away clean or until six to eight swabs have been collected.
- Air-dry the swabs.
- Take a control sample, as described above, using an additional swab, and collect separately as "control sample."

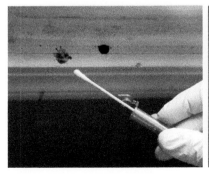

Figure 41.5 Collection of a wet sample of blood using a swab fitted with integrated swab cover to allow for drying and prevent contamination.

Liquid Stains

See Figure 41.6.

The Scene

- Withdraw a sample from the depth of the stain (not at the surface or at the bottom) using a pipette or syringe.
- Place sample in an EDTA test tube (purple top) for DNA testing. Gently mix by rocking test tube back and forth several times.
- Place sample in an ACD test tube (yellow top) for serology and alcohol testing. Gently mix by rocking test tube back and forth several times.
- Refrigerate sample and send to lab as soon as practical.
- An alternate, but less preferred, method is to collect liquid stains with a clean cotton swab.
- Saturate the sterile swab with as much of the sample as possible.
- Saturate and collect six to eight swabs. Let dry before packaging.

Packaging

- Swabs suspected to be from different stains or contributors must never be packaged together!
- All swabs should be thoroughly air-dried and placed in labeled swab boxes. The swab boxes are then packaged in a porous container (bag or box).

Figure 41.6 Collecting a liquid sample of blood with a disposable pipette. The sample is then placed in the appropriate collection tube.

- Swabs from the same collection sample must be packaged in separate swab boxes and containerized; they may be placed in the same secondary package.
- Individual swabs can be marked by the use of tape wrapped around the shaft onto itself, well away from the substance being sampled, where the collector's initials, date, and time (and possibly the location from where the sample was taken) can be recorded.
- Items of clothing or bedding that contain biological stains must be thoroughly allowed to air-dry before being packaged in a porous container.
- Biological stains should never be permanently packaged in nonporous containers (e.g., plastic bags). The only exception would be using plastic as a temporary container for the purpose of transporting the item to a drying area.
- The time biological materials are allowed to stay in nonporous packaging should not exceed 2 hours.
- All items of evidence should be noted on the proper evidence custody document and entered into the evidence custody system.

Trace Evidence

42

Trace evidence is evidence that exists in small quantities or size and may be very difficult to see on the body or at the scene. This includes hair, fibers, paint chips, glass, building materials, and soil. A "Trace Evidence Notes" provided as Worksheet 9 will assist in keeping trace evidence recovery efforts organized and better documented. Trace evidence is unlikely to be detected without a concerted effort and search. At the scene, this often entails the investigator using a deliberate, time-consuming, "hands and knees" approach to searching, as well as the use of technology aids such as ALS. A similarly painstaking search must be conducted on the body of the deceased.

The Body

Hairs, fibers, building materials, explosive residue, glass, and GSR are examples of trace evidence that may be associated with the body of the deceased.

- On the initial body search, perishable trace evidence is noted and immediately safeguarded or processed.
  - Loose hairs or fibers and air currents or precipitation that might move them.
  - GSR on clothing that might be effected by precipitation in an outdoor scene.
  - Any trace item that would be disturbed as the body is moved (rolled) for detailed photography.
- After a body surface is photographed, it should be examined with UV and ALS for trace evidence.
- When the body is rolled and photographed, it should again be searched for trace evidence using UV and ALS.
- When trace evidence is identified, it should be photographed, processed, collected, and packaged in accordance with the procedures outlined below based on their general category.

The Scene

General Processing Guidelines

- Trace evidence is usually searched for and collected prior to processing a scene for fingerprints.
- Trace evidence is easily overlooked. Its discovery requires a meticulous search.
- Avoid cross contamination of trace material by thoroughly cleaning collection gear between samples and changing gloves.

Detection

- Magnification
  - The use of a magnifying glass can greatly assist in the search for trace materials.
  - Magnifiers come in various forms, including headband devices that leave the hands free.
- Oblique lighting
  - The use of a handheld flashlight or other source of white light, such as that from an ALS, can also assist the investigator in seeing possible trace evidence.
  - The light should be held at a very low angle (obliquely) to the surface being examined, under darkened or dimly lit conditions.
  - Moving the light from various directions will often assist in visualizing trace evidence better.
- Ultraviolet lighting
  - Some trace materials will fluoresce under UV light (100–400 nm).
  - Using the UV light after the white light may allow the investigator to see material that was not observable under white light alone.
  - The UV light should be held at various angles to the surface but not as low (obliquely) as the white light was used.
- Alternate light source
  - Some trace materials will fluoresce when excited by various wavelengths (400–800 nm) of light higher than that produced by UV light.
  - The ALS offers a larger range of wavelength options, and it should be used similar to the way the UV light was used, after attempts have been made with white and/or UV light.
  - There are no specific guidelines regarding what wavelengths to utilize, and a broad range of wavelengths should be considered.

General Collection

- Photograph the trace evidence with an evidence-establishing photograph to place it in context with the scene (Figure 42.1).
- Photograph the trace evidence so that it fills the frame of the camera. This might require close-up rings, or a macrophotography lens and settings.
- Trace evidence at the scene can be seized with the item that it is deposited on, as long as it is certain it will not be dislodged or lost in packaging or transit.
- If there is any potential the trace material may be dislodged, collect it immediately.
- When collecting trace materials, always follow the rule: Bring the container to the evidence, not the evidence to the container. This will prevent inadvertent loss during collection.
- Post-it notes may be quickly used to collect perishable trace hairs and fibers. Mark the post-it note with the collection information and then use the adhesive strip to collect the evidence. The note may then be folded over on itself to protect the trace evidence and placed in an envelope or other suitable container (Figure 42.2).

Figure 42.1 Evidence establishing photograph of trace material (hairs) on panties in scene.

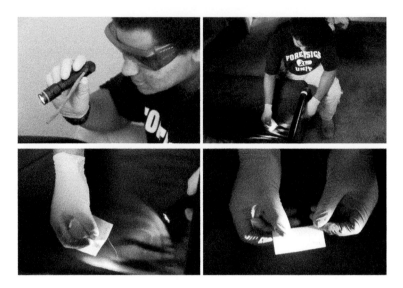

Figure 42.2 Expedient collection of perishable trace evidence using a yellow sticky note.

- Trace evidence such as hairs and fibers are often collected with a gloved hand.
- Trace evidence may also be collected with rubber-tipped or disposable plastic forceps (Figure 42.3).
- Trace evidence may be tape-lifted from a surface. Once collected, the tape is placed against a clear plastic surface such as a clean document protector (Figure 42.4).
- An evidence vacuum is used only as a last resort and only after other techniques have resulted in the collection of the obvious trace evidence.

Packaging

Trace evidence must always be double packaged. The primary (inner) packaging should coincide with the most effective packaging for the particular lifting method used.

- Double package trace evidence.
  - A druggist fold (Appendix C) or glassine envelope is the best primary packaging for most trace material.
  - A standard envelope will work effectively for the outer packaging.
- *Avoid* plastic bags, as static electricity often builds on their surfaces. This makes them inadvisable for primary packaging.

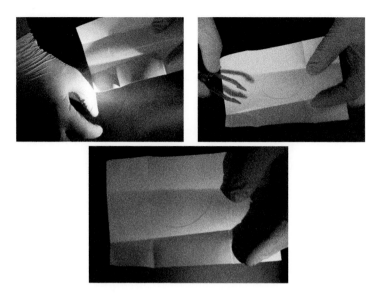

Figure 42.3 Collection of trace evidence with gloved hand and forceps with a druggist fold for primary packaging.

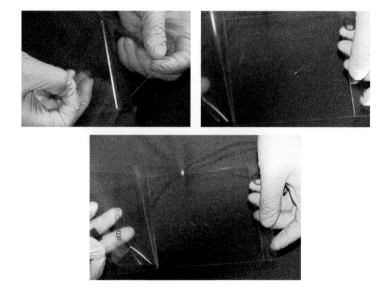

Figure 42.4 Tape lift of trace evidence using a clear adhesive sheet.

- Paint chips should be packaged so as to protect their edges for possible fracture matching. Do not package in cotton.
- Whenever trace evidence is seized from an item, control samples of that material should be taken from potential donor sources.

Hairs

Hairs may be evaluated to determine animal versus human, region of body from which it came (head, pubic), how the hair was removed (cut, pulled, shed), dyes, and treatments.

- DNA (both DNA and mDNA) testing may be possible to determine the source of the hair.
- Unique dyes or treatments may be present that are consistent with a possible donor source.
- Hairs may often be tested for drug toxicology or longer-term heavy metal poisoning.
- Control samples from possible contributors should include about 20 pulled hairs from the head and pubic region. This may be best accomplished by using the appropriate sections of a sexual assault evidence recovery kit. Under almost all circumstances the collection should be done by medical personnel as a part of a sexual assault response team examination.

Fibers

Fibers can be evaluated for determination of the general category of fiber: animal (e.g., wool, mink, fox), vegetable (e.g., cotton, linen), mineral/metallic (e.g., fiberglass insulation), or synthetic and blends.

- The treatments and unique origin of the fibers may allow for determining the source or potential sources of the fiber.
- Control samples should be taken from carpeting, ropes, etc., that may have come in contact with the victim or suspect.

Paint

Chips and transfers frequently occur when two objects come in contact with each other and where one, or both, have painted surfaces.

- Fracture matches of dried paint may allow a paint fragment to be matched to its origin. The layers, which build up with repeated paintings, may also be sufficiently unique to determine an origin.
- Paint evidence may be present in breaking and entering cases where a tool is used to pry open doors or windows.
- Remember, paint from the scene may also be found on tools recovered from suspects.

Collection

- Collect paint chips.
- Collect small objects containing paint transfers.
- Cut out a section of larger objects containing transfers.

Control Sample

- Take control samples from an unmarked surface near the damaged area.
- Take the control sample all the way down to the unpainted surface.

Known Sample

- Collect any item or paint from the suspected source of the transfer.
- On vehicles, take paint samples from several places around the damaged area.
- It is important to take the full thickness of the paint, all the way down to the metal or body of the car.

Packaging

- Double pack chips in a pillbox or druggist fold; then place them in a plastic bag or sealable box.
- Do not allow objects containing paint smears to contact other evidence.
- Seal known paint samples in separate containers.

Glass

Glass is frequently broken or shattered during the commission of crimes. Glass can be evaluated for the general characteristics of the sample and compared with known sources of glass from the scene. Close examination of the edges of broken window pane glass may indicate whether the glass was broken from inside or outside of the building. "Staged" breaking and entering scenes can sometimes be identified through a direction-of-force evaluation.

- Glass evidence at a scene may provide information such as fracture matching, latent prints, direction of force, sequence of impacts, velocity of impacts, and angle of impact.
- When glass is broken, microscopic fragments travel backwards towards the direction of force. The fragments may be found in the hair or on the clothing of the suspect.

- If glass fragments are potentially present on clothing, seize the clothing of the suspect and package it securely.
- Have the suspect comb his or her hair over a clean sheet of paper.

On-Scene Examination

The primary radial (long, not circular) fractures on window pane glass may be used to determine which side of the glass received the force that broke it. This may be important when it is believed a scene is staged.

- Glass both within the frame (not displaced) and loose in the scene (displaced) may be examined. The edge of the primary radial fracture is examined for the presence of a wavelike pattern created by small concordial fractures. These waves will run parallel to the surfaces of the glass and then at one point turn towards the front or back surface at about 90 degrees.
- This evaluation is only valid on primary radial fractures, fractures that originated at the point of impact. Fragments may be present with secondary fractures, but these are not functional for direction of force determinations.
- The rule to follow is the four R's: Ripples on Radial fractures are at a Right angle to the Rear (direction away from force) (Figure 42.5).
- Compare residues on in-place fragments (fragments still in the frame) to displaced fragments to determine which side of the displaced fragment was inside or outside. Look for oily deposits on interior aspects and/or dirt on exterior aspects.

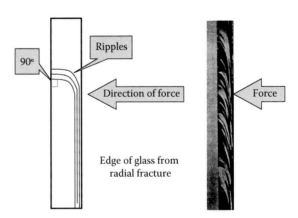

Figure 42.5 Determining directionality in glass fractures. Four "R" rule: "Ripples on Radial cracks are at Right angles to the Rear."

Collection

- Photograph and document the location of glass and glass fragments on the crime scene sketch.
- Collect the clothing of suspects and all glass present at the scene, including any glass in the window or doorframe.
- Mark pieces removed from the frame to indicate which side faced inside.

Known Sample

- Collect a known sample of glass when needed for comparison with glass fragments recovered from a suspect.

Packaging

- Wrap large pieces separately in cotton, a clean paper bag, or butcher-type paper.
- Pack small fragments together in a small container, such as a druggist fold. Prevent shifting during transit.
- Mark "Fragile" and "Sharp Hazard."
- Control samples from broken glass should include glass from the window pane. The glass should be marked as to its orientation in the window (inside, outside, up, down, etc.).

Building Materials

Collection

- Collect suspect's clothing.
- Collect hair combings from suspect.
- Collect samples from suspected tools used (wood chips, saw dust, metal filings).

Known Sample

- Collect a control sample from each layer the suspect would have had to pass through to gain entry to the area.

Soil Evidence

Soil samples may be critical in linking a suspect to the victim, scene, or conveyance (such as automobile). In some cases, it is helpful to determine if the soil on clothes, tools, or automobiles could have come from a particular location. Soil examinations by a qualified person may be helpful in such cases. Send a sketch to the lab with your evidence, showing where each sample was collected.

Collection

- Collect any small items on which soil is found (shoes, tools, tires, floor mats, clothing, etc.).
- Scrape soil from larger items into a container using a clean instrument, such as a razor blade. On large objects, if only trace amounts are available, collect sample with adhesive tape.
- Samples should be taken from the area of interest as well as 3 and 15 feet from the area of interest and repeated along N, S, E, and W coordinates.
- Collect only from the depth at which the activity occurred such as surface collection (down to about 1 inch), or at the various depths if evidence is buried.
- Samples should be placed individually in canisters, jars, or plastic urine cups.

Known Sample

- Take at least eight soil samples from each area you want compared with the questioned soil. These should be taken from 3 and 15 feet from the area of interest and repeated along N, S, E, and W coordinates.
- Collect only from the depth that the suspected sample was found.
- Samples should be placed individually in canisters, jars, or plastic urine cups.

Alibi Sample

- If a suspect offers an alibi location, where they "really" were when the crime was committed, sample the soil from the area they identify.
- These samples may then be compared to any soil samples taken from the suspect's footwear, tire tread, wheel wells, etc., and may indicate they were not at the alibi location.

Packaging

- Dry all soil samples before final packaging.
- Wrap small items separately to prevent losing any soil.

- Pack scraped samples from larger items into film canisters, clean baby food jars, or plastic urine cups.
- Pack known and questioned samples in separate shipping containers.

Trace Metals Evidence

Trace metal examinations of suspected bullet ricochets, suspected bullet holes or defects, tool marks, etc., often yield valuable information. Field chemical testing of possible bullet defects may be warranted in order to appropriately process the scene.

Field Testing for Lead and Copper for Bullet Defects

Testing for Copper

- DTO and 2-NN testing for copper must be done before rhodizonate testing for lead.
- Dithiooxamide (DTO) is a colorimetric reagent that will produce a gray-green color in the present of copper.
- A solution of ammonium hydroxide is sprayed onto the absorbent side of plastic-backed filter paper.
- The wetted filter paper is then pressed against the suspect bullet defect. The hydroxide will solubilize the copper, which will then be absorbed onto the filter paper.
- The orange DTO solution is then sprayed onto the filter paper. If copper is present, a ring of gray-green color will develop around the lifted defect pattern.
- The results should be photographed and the lift retained as evidence.
- If the ammonium hydroxide lift has a substrate color that would obscure DTO results (e.g., something that will not provide sufficient contrast to the green/gray positive color response of DTO), 2-nitro-1-naphthol (2-NN) may be used instead of DTO.
- Using 2-NN on a lift containing copper will produce a pink color. DTO is then sprayed over the pink and will produce the positive gray-green color if copper is present. Each of the color changes should be photographed and the lift retained as evidence.

Testing for Lead

- Sodium rhodizonate is a chemical reagent that is used to test for the presence of lead.
- When the surface has dried after testing for copper, rhodizonate testing can be done on the same area for lead.

- This is a nondestructive test, meaning other tests can be done to the same evidence.
- A colorless tartrate buffer solution is sprayed onto the surface. The buffer will solubilize lead.
- Then the orange-brown sodium rhodizonate solution is sprayed over the same area. If lead is present, an immediate color change to pink will occur.
- The results of this test should be photographed.
- To confirm that a pink color change was caused by the presence of lead, 5% hydrochloric acid can be sprayed over the pink color (or a portion of the pink color). If the pink was produced by the presence of lead, the pink color will change to a purple-blue color.
- The results should be photographed and the lift should be retained as evidence.

Collection

- Take items on which the trace metal is believed to be present.

Control Sample

- Collect samples of the material on which the trace metal is present, from a location away from the area containing the evidence.

Known Sample

- Take any tools, bullets, or materials that may have made the mark.

Packaging

- Pack to protect against accidental transfers or contact with the area in question.

Trace Explosives Evidence

The collection of trace explosives evidence is a rather unique situation involving attempts to identify the materials used to produce the bomb itself. It comes in the form of explosives residues as well as very small pieces of component materials (wiring, container, trigger mechanisms, wrappers, fragmentation pieces, batteries, etc.) made of plastic, paper, metal, or other materials. The search for trace materials stemming from blasts should be conducted in conjunction with the processing guidelines found in Chapter 39. It is highly recommended that the general crime scene investigator, unless trained specifically in this type of search and collection effort, enlist the assistance of someone specially trained in this field.

Collection of Explosives Residue Materials

This involves the deliberate search and collection of possible trace amounts of explosives materials used in making the bomb. These can be residues from primary or secondary explosives.

- These residues may be located in the crater/seat of the blast, on other recovered bomb component parts, or on nearby surfaces, including preexisting vertical or horizontal surfaces.
- Preexisting surfaces include street signs, vehicles, sides of buildings left standing, and other nonporous and porous objects.
- Priority should be given to charred or deformed surfaces and porous substrates such as wood, textiles/clothing. These surfaces retain the smaller particles of explosives residues better.
- When surfaces possibly containing explosives residues can be reasonably collected and preserved, they should be recovered and placed in clean, sealed metal cans or containers used for fire/arson materials.
- When these surfaces do not lend themselves to being seized, they should be swabbed for residues. Control samples of the substrate from areas that do not appear to hold explosives residues should also be taken, either by seizing the object or swabbing a clean area.

Collection of Trace Components Parts

This involves the hands and knees approach to searching what may later be identified as smaller pieces of the component materials of the explosive device.

NOTE: *Tools used to excavate and search for or screens used to sieve post-blast material should be made of brass, which will not spark when in contact with other metals. This is preferable when practical.*

- The use of 1/2-inch and 1/4-inch sieves made of hardware cloth will assist in this search.
- The search should begin in the crater/seat of the explosion, and it should involve the removal of soil well below what is simply observed on top.
- The search and collection of these trace materials should continue through the entire area covered by the crime scene search aided by the use of magnification.

- The search must be slow and methodical. All potential trace material must be identifiable to the sector of the scene from which it was recovered.
- All trace materials collected must be packaged in a manner that ensures their integrity and prevents cross contamination.
- In some cases, explosives residues can be attached to these smaller items, and it is imperative that they be preserved in a manner that allows subsequent laboratory analysis.

Hazardous Materials Evidence

- Before collecting hazardous evidence, obtain advice from the local hazmat team. In many cases, they will collect, package, and store the evidence.
- Work closely with hazmat to ensure the proper chain of custody is maintained throughout the process.
- In cases where hazardous materials are seized, follow the guidance of the local environmental specialists for collection, storage, and shipping/transport.

Friction Ridge Evidence 43

Latent prints consist of friction ridge prints from fingerprints, palm prints, and/or footprints located at the scene of a crime. They are generally processed by chemical or physical means to allow for visualization, photography, and collection. Any chance friction ridge prints found at a scene are often referred to as *latent prints*; technically it is correct to categorize them as follows:

- *Latent* (not readily visible): This category makes up the bulk of prints at a scene. They require physical or chemical development to make them visible.
- *Patent* (visible): These prints can be seen because they are made in some sort of contaminant (e.g., blood, dust, ink, oil, etc.), which contrasts with the substrate on which they are found.
- *Plastic* (three-dimensional): These prints are impressed into items such as putty, soap, or other pliable material.

  A "Friction Ridge Evidence" is provided in Worksheet 10. It will assist in keeping friction ridge recovery efforts organized and properly documented.

Prints on the Body/on Skin

Latent or patent prints on the skin in a homicide investigation are most often associated with the victim. Whenever the perpetrator grasps the body with ungloved hands, there is the opportunity for prints to be transferred. It should also be noted that this type of interaction may also leave transfer (touch) DNA from the perpetrator to the victim. Touch DNA is covered in detail in Chapter 41.

Patent (Visible) Prints on the Skin

- If the print is patent (visible), it should be immediately photographed. Examination-quality photographs with scale are critical!
- The contaminant that made the print should be identified if possible. This might include blood, grease, oil, lotions, paint, etc.

- Oil-based contaminants are not likely to dry and flake, but they are prone to smearing with handling.
- Bloody prints may dry and become subject to flaking, or they may be obscured or destroyed during movement and transportation or by continued blood flow.

Latent Prints on the Skin

Detection

- Latent prints on the body are very difficult to visualize even with oblique lighting or the use of an alternate light source.
- If sufficient force was used, bruising or discoloration patterns may indicate likely areas. This might include visible finger marks on the neck of someone who was strangled.
- The bruising or discoloration from these types of injury may also be visible through infrared video or photography.
- These prints are generally located by using a lifting technique on the most likely area for deposition and recovery.
- The most likely area for deposition is determined by examining the body in the context of the scene.
- If the victim has been moved or dragged, determine the most likely area that would have been grasped by the perpetrator.
- The most likely surface for recovery is smooth, hairless surfaces such as the neck, inner arms, thighs, and inner ankles.

Transfer Lift Method
See Figure 43.1.

- The area identified as the most likely to have prints that could be recovered must be cooled to approximately 75°F. This may be accomplished with a small battery-operated fan blowing across the skin's surface.
- The transfer medium may be a thick piece of glass, polished metal, or metal mirror. The transfer medium is warmed to approximately 85°F. This may be accomplished by placing a medical quick-heat pack against its surface or a commercially available hand warmer pack.
- The transfer medium is then rocked across the cooled surface with firm pressure. It is important not to smear the area where a print might be located.
- The transfer medium may then be manipulated under a light to see if the image of a print transferred to its surface.
- If the image of a print is visible (with or without visible ridge detail), the transfer medium should be Superglue™ fumed to preserve the print as well as any touch DNA that may have been transferred.

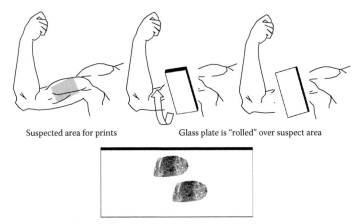

Suspected area for prints   Glass plate is "rolled" over suspect area

Plate is held up to light to visualize any transferred prints.

Figure 43.1 Transfer lift method for suspected latent fingerprints on skin.

Superglue™ Fuming of Human Skin

- In the case of a deceased victim, human skin can be superglued just like other surfaces.
- This can be done on scene or under more controlled conditions at the morgue.
- Obtain authority from the medical examiner before attempting any Superglue™ effort of a deceased victim whether on scene or at the morgue.
- *Superglue™ fuming cannot be attempted on live victims!*

Prints at the Scene

General

- It is usually necessary to photograph and sketch the scene prior to examining items for prints, as the processing for prints may involve the moving of items.
- It is generally best to process for prints after biological and trace evidence has been processed.
- It is best to use a systematic search for prints. Do not skip from one area to another.
- Remember to examine items inside other items found at the scene (e.g., the batteries inside a flashlight left behind, the magazine inside a weapon, or food and containers inside a refrigerator from which prints are developed on the door).
- Elimination prints should be taken from persons with legitimate access to the area.

Detecting Prints

Oblique Lighting

- The use of reflected light (such as that from a flashlight) held at a low oblique angle is helpful in locating prints (Figure 43.2).
- Varying the angle and direction of the light will assist in locating prints.

NOTE: Even if prints are not readily visible when using reflected light, they may still be present, and the area should still be dusted or further processed for prints.

Reflected Ultraviolet Imaging System

- Utilizes a short wave UV light source combined with an imaging system that enhances UV light.
- The reflected ultraviolet imaging system (RUVIS) can see the reflected UV even in bright ambient light.
- May be able to visualize undeveloped prints on nonporous surfaces.
- RUVIS is a nontouch technology. Visualized prints must be photographed through the RUVIS imager; they cannot be lifted, as they are in effect unprocessed. After imaging, the print can be processed using standard techniques and a lift attempted (Figure 43.3).

Alternate Light Sources

- Occasionally fingerprints will inherently fluoresce.
- A general crime scene search wavelength of about 450 nm with orange goggles is appropriate for this search.

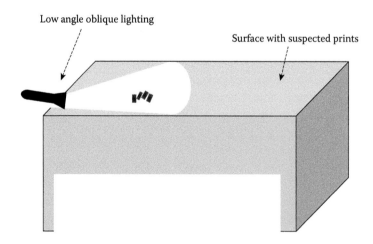

Figure 43.2 Locating latent prints with oblique lighting.

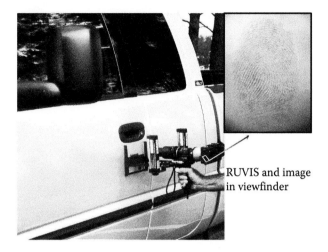

Figure 43.3 Searching for prints with RUVIS. Photograph courtesy of Sirchie®.

Photography of Prints

See Figure 43.4.

- Always photograph a print as soon as it becomes visible. Do not overpower the print.
- Fill the frame of the camera viewfinder with the print; 1:1 photography is preferred.
- Use a scale in the photograph.

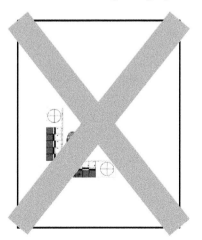

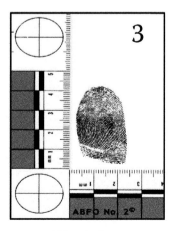

Filling the frame

Figure 43.4 For examination-quality photograph, fill the frame.

- Be sure to take the photograph with the film/CCD plane of the camera oriented parallel to the surface where the print is located.
- Be aware of depth of field problems associated with prints on items with curved surfaces or other three-dimensional surfaces.

DNA Considerations

- Be aware of the potential for cross contamination of touch DNA through the use of reusable fingerprint brushes and powders.
- The issue can be resolved through two approaches:
  - Ensure all DNA collection efforts precede any fingerprint recovery efforts. In this instance, there is no requirement for disposable fingerprint brushes.
  - Use disposable fingerprint brushes, always use fresh fingerprint powder from the container, and never return used powder to the container.

Prints on Nonporous Surfaces

Items that do not absorb moisture, such as plastics, glass, metal, etc., are considered nonporous and can generally be processed at the scene.

Print Stabilization with Superglue™ Fuming (Cyanoacrylate)

See Figure 43.5.

- Superglue™ fuming on scene is the most effective way to stabilize a latent print before processing and lifting. Superglue™ also stabilizes any touch DNA that may be present in the print.
- Portable items may be fumed on-scene in a portable fuming chamber or surfaces can be covered and glued in place (e.g., using a makeshift plastic chamber to cover a door knob and fuming inside it).
- Entire rooms, vehicle interiors, vehicle exteriors, or larger surfaces may be fumed with creative larger makeshift containers.
- Commercial portable fuming chambers may be used at the scene. An expedient chamber may also be constructed for on-scene processing of large items of evidence. As an example, larger items of evidence may be fumed in a large plastic trashcan with locking lid.
- The size of the fuming chamber, ambient temperature, and humidity will affect how much glue is applied. The amount used and the

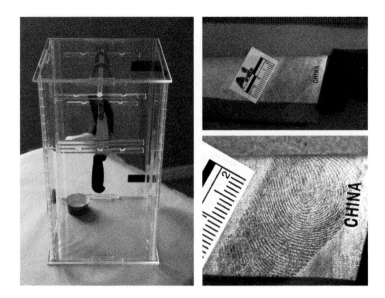

Figure 43.5 Superglue™ fuming of evidence in portable chamber. Polymerized print may then treated with powders or dye stains.

time the item is exposed to fumes in field applications is based on experience.

- Cotton balls soaked in a solution of baking soda and water (1 lb of baking soda dissolved in 1 gal of water) and then thoroughly air-dried will act as a catalyst and accelerate the reaction. These are prepared ahead of time and stored in a large plastic bag with the crime scene supplies.
- A small aluminum tin is placed in the bottom of the chamber and several cotton balls are placed in the tray. At least 10–15 drops of Superglue™ are dripped onto the cotton balls. The reaction should be visible within moments, as the cotton balls will begin to emit visible fumes. The chamber is then sealed.
- A black fingerprint card with a print applied to its surface is placed in the chamber where it can be readily viewed as a test print.
- Items of evidence should never be overfumed. As soon as the test print is lightly visible as a white print on the black fingerprint card, stop the fuming. Remove the evidence from the fuming chamber, allow the items to set up for a few minutes, then photograph any visible prints and package the evidence.
- *Caution*: Superglue™ fumes are very irritating to the eyes and lungs. Be cautious when working near the fumes. Do not utilize field-fuming techniques if wearing contact lenses. Ensure good ventilation when using Superglue™!

Developing

- Generally, nonporous items at the scene will be processed with fingerprint powders either before or after Superglue™ fuming.
- Once a technique is chosen, if possible place a test print on the item and attempt to develop it. Place the test print on an area not considered likely to contain fingerprint evidence (e.g., confronted with a coffee mug of unknown composition, obtain a similar mug from the back of a cabinet, place prints on it, and process it as a test).
- *Contrast*: Choose a color of powder that will contrast with the color of substrate being examined (dark powder on light surfaces, light powder on dark surfaces).
- *Surface*: Standard powders applied with a fiberglass brush can be used on most nonporous surfaces.
- Magnetic powders applied by a magnetic brush should be used on nonferrous items.

NOTE: A surface may be checked for magnetic properties by touching it with the magnetic wand in an area less likely to damage any potential print, prior to the application of powder.

- If in doubt about how to process an item, consider the following:
  - Contacting the servicing forensic laboratory for guidance.
  - Removing the item and forwarding it to a laboratory for processing.

Recovering Latent Prints from Nonporous Surfaces

- Photograph prints once they become visible; do not overpowder. Once photographed, use standard lifting tape to lift the developed print from the surface. Recover the tape and lift and secure as evidence.
- Prints on curved and textured surfaces may be recovered using standard tape, but gel lifters and polyethylene tape generally recover more ridge detail.
- The tape with the lifted print is placed on a white or black card, contrasting with the color of powder used.
- The card should be annotated with the time, date, and investigator's initials; the item from which the print was taken and a sketch of its relative location on the item should be noted on the backside of the card.

NOTE: If the print is not successfully lifted, the photograph may become your evidence.

Packaging

- When seizing items that have not yet been processed and/or stabilized with Superglue™ techniques, it will be necessary to secure them in such a way that they cannot move within a container and no other items can rub against them in transit. Always consider protecting the print by Superglue™ fuming the item on scene.
- Do not place unprocessed items in plastic bags or containers.
- Clearly label the container or tag "Preserve for Latent Prints."

Prints on Porous Surfaces

Items that would absorb moisture, such as paper, unfinished wood, etc., are best photographed, seized, protected, and forwarded to a lab for further processing, as they may require advanced chemical means to develop prints.

Packaging

- When seizing items that have not yet been processed, it is necessary to secure them in such a way they cannot move within a container and no other items can rub against them in transit.
- Papers that are being preserved for both latent prints and questioned document examination may be placed in a clear document protector or paper envelope. The advantage to the document protector is that the document may be photographed or photocopied without having to handle it in and out of the envelope.
- Clearly label the container or tag "Preserve for Latent Prints."

Chemical Development of Latent Prints

Prints on Wet Surfaces

- If possible, wet surfaces should be air-dried and processed in the manner recommended for that particular surface.
- If a wet, nonporous surface must be processed for prints immediately, MOS_2 (Wet Print) may be used.
- MOS_2 (Wet Print) is sprayed on the wet surface, allowed to stand for about a minute, and then gently rinsed off.
- The print is then photographed; be sure to include examination-quality photographs.
- Once the print is thoroughly dried, it can then be lifted with standard lifting tape.

- If the surface cannot be dried, use standard lifting tape and squeegee it across the print with the edge of a credit-type card. The print is then lifted and applied to a white backing card.

Prints in Blood

- Patent prints in blood on nonporous surfaces may be treated with various dye stains.
- The print is photographed before any development; be sure to include examination-quality photographs.
- Biological sampling of the blood in the print can be accomplished in any area of the stain where ridge detail is obscured.

Amido Black
See Figure 43.6.

- Amido Black is available as either an aqueous (water-based) dye stain or an alcohol-based dye stain. The alcohol-based dye stain is the more effective treatment; however, the aqueous-based is easier to travel with and mix at the scene.
- The bloody prints are treated with a fixing solution. This solution is sprayed or washed over the print and allowed to stand for about a minute. On a vertical surface an absorbent paper towel may be taped over the suspected print and saturated.
- The Amido Black is mixed according to instructions and either sprayed on or washed over the surface with the bloody prints. On a vertical surface, an absorbent paper towel may be taped over the suspected print and saturated.

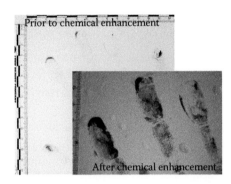

Figure 43.6 Enhancing prints in blood. Print in blood before and after treatment with amido black.

- Ensure areas around the print where continued ridge detail or impression is possible are covered. The dye will stain visually undetectable quantities of blood and often develop considerably more of the print than was originally visible.
- The dye stain is allowed to saturate the blood for about a minute.
- The excess Amido Black is gently rinsed with water.
- The print is allowed to completely dry.
- The print is photographed again; be sure to include examination-quality photographs. Photography is the best method of documentation.
- If at all possible, collect the object or surface containing the print (ex: drywall can be cut out, tiles from the floor can be lifted).
- If this is not possible, attempt to lift the print with a gel lifter.

Hungarian Red

- Hungarian Red is an aqueous-based dye. The dried, stained print may show further detail if excited with a green ALS.
- The bloody prints may be treated with a fixing solution. This solution is sprayed or washed over the print and allowed to stand for about a minute. On a vertical surface, an absorbent paper towel may be taped over the suspected print and saturated.
- The Hungarian Red is mixed according to instructions and either sprayed on or washed over the surface with the bloody prints. On a vertical surface, an absorbent paper towel may be taped over the suspected print and saturated.
- Ensure areas around the print where continued ridge detail or impression is possible are covered. The dye will stain visually undetectable quantities of blood and often develop considerably more of the print than was originally visible.
- The dye stain is allowed to saturate the blood for about a minute.
- The excess Hungarian Red is gently rinsed with water.
- The print is allowed to completely dry.
- The print is photographed again; be sure to include examination-quality photographs. The best method of documentation is photography using a green (520–560 nm) ALS. Use of the ALS may show enhanced detail.
- If at all possible, collect the surface.
- If this is not possible, attempt to lift the print with a gel lifter.

Leucocrystal Violet

- Leucocrystal Violet (LCV) is available as alcohol based and uses hydrogen peroxide to cause a reaction with the heme molecule in blood. LCV may be mixed at the scene from a prepackaged kit.

- The shelf life, once mixed, is relatively short, and the solution should be used within a day or two and then discarded.
- The advantage of LCV over Amido Black is that it does not require rinsing after application.
- The LCV is mixed according to instructions and either sprayed on or washed over the surface with the bloody prints. On a vertical surface, an absorbent paper towel may be taped over the suspected print and saturated.
- Ensure areas around the print where continued ridge detail or impression is possible are covered. The dye will stain visually undetectable quantities of blood and often develop considerably more of the print than was originally visible.
- The excess LCV may be blotted from the surface with an absorbent paper towel.
- The print is allowed to completely dry.
- The print is photographed again; be sure to include examination-quality photographs.
- If at all possible, collect the surface.
- If this is not possible, attempt to lift the print with a gel lifter.

Prints in Oil or Grease

- Patent prints in oil or grease on nonporous surfaces may be treated with Sudan Black in either an aqueous (water-based) or mixed ethanol (alcohol) based preparation.
- The dye will stain the fatty components of sebaceous sweat and produce a blue/black image. It is less sensitive than other stains but is recommended for prints in oil or grease.
- The item with potential oily or greasy prints is immersed in a tray filled with the Sudan Black/ethanol mixture.
- For surfaces that cannot be immersed in a tray, the following procedure applies:
  - The Sudan Black is mixed according to instructions and either sprayed on or washed over the surface with the prints. On a vertical surface, an absorbent paper towel may be taped over the suspected print and saturated.
  - Ensure areas around the print where continued ridge detail or impression is possible are covered. The dye will stain visually undetectable quantities of blood and often develop considerably more of the print than was originally visible.
  - The dye stain is allowed to saturate the print for about a minute.
  - The excess Sudan Black is gently rinsed with water.
- The print is allowed to completely dry.

- The print is photographed again; be sure to include examination-quality photographs. This is the best method of documentation.
- If at all possible, collect the surface.
- The use of Sudan Black is a messy process and can interfere with other subsequent forensic examinations.

Impression Evidence

44

Impression evidence is categorized in two major categories, two-dimensional impression evidence and three-dimensional impression evidence. Three-dimensional evidence is what we generally consider when we think of footwear or footprints in soil or tire tread marks. It may also include bite marks and tool marks. Two-dimensional evidence is often referred to as *residue prints*. It includes contaminants that are either left on or removed from a surface by footwear, feet, tire treads, etc. The contaminants may include blood, oil, grease, paints, wax, etc.

Impression evidence processing may be documented through Worksheet 11, "Impression Evidence Notes."

The Body

Bite Marks in Skin

Bite marks in skin may appear on the deceased, the living, or on other soft surfaces such as food. The deceased may have been bitten by the attacker, particularly in sexual assault cases. The victim may have bitten the attacker during the attack or the victim or attacker may have bitten food in the area of the death. Each of these bite marks may be of significance in relating the attacker, victim, and scene. Bite marks should be considered as fragile and processed expeditiously, as they may quickly fade.

Photographing Bite Marks

- Using an ABFO® scale and wound mapping techniques, photograph the bite marks (Figure 44.1).
  - Take an establishing photograph to identify the location on the body where the bite appears.
  - Take a close-up photograph showing the bite mark.
  - Take an examination-quality shot maximizing the bite mark framed by the ABFO scale within the image.
- Repeat the examination-quality photograph using UV light if available. Keep in mind that short wave UV light in particular can be harmful to human skin and degrade DNA evidence; long wave

407

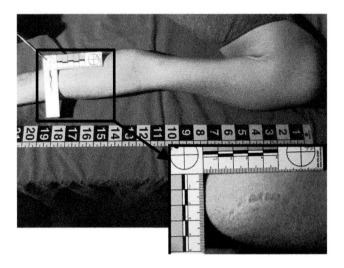

Figure 44.1 Mapping the bitemark. Using the same mapping techniques used in injuries and bloodstains the bitemark is photographed in relationship to anatomical markers and examination quality.

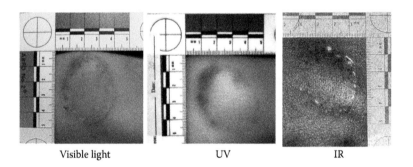

Visible light   UV   IR

Figure 44.2 Visible, UV and IR photography of bite marks. Photographs courtesy of Greg Golden, DDS, Chief Odontologist, San Bernardino County Sheriff's/ Coroner Division.

UV (300–400 nm) is preferred and even then at short intervals (Figure 44.2).

- Repeat the examination-quality photograph using an alternate light source with appropriate filter.
- Repeat the examination-quality photograph with IR photography, if available. IR photography generally yields the best results when documenting bite marks (Figure 44.2).
- It may be advisable to repeat these techniques at autopsy, as the pattern may become more distinct or show additional detail over time.

Processing Bite Marks: Special Considerations

- If the mark is in a food item, do not allow the item to dry out. Photograph and cast it as soon as possible.
- For bite marks on the skin of a living individual, in which the skin is broken, seek medical attention.
- Bite marks in living individuals are perishable and will fade quickly; process as soon as possible.
- For bite marks on the deceased, make arrangements with the medical examiner before casting. It may be best to cast at the autopsy.
- Swab both the inside of and outside of the dental arch for possible DNA from the suspect (Figure 44.3).
- Casting should be done with silicone rubber casting compound such as Mikrosil® following the directions supplied by the manufacturer (Figure 44.4).

Tool Marks in Bone

In sharp force, chopping, blunt force, or even sawing injuries, tool marks may be left in the bone underlying the injury. Teeth marks from animal bites or predation may also be visible on the bones. The skeletal remains should be thoroughly examined by a forensic anthropologist for any tool marks. If necessary, on a cadaver that is not completely defleshed, a forensic anthropologist can deflesh the area so that tool marks may be casted and preserved.

During autopsy or anthropological examination:

- Photograph the tool mark as soon as it is visible.
- Examine the tool mark with white, UV, and alternate light.
- Photograph any trace evidence associated with the tool mark.
- Have the medical examiner or anthropologist isolate the tool mark from the surrounding flesh.

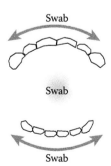

Figure 44.3 Swabbing dental arch of a bite mark for DNA evidence.

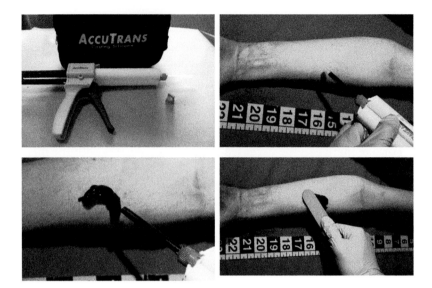

Figure 44.4 Casting the bitemark with a silicon-based casting compound. This particular method self-mixes the compound with the catalyst as it travels to the tip of the dispenser gun. The bitemark is covered with casting compound which is then smoothed and pressed into the bitemark with the tongue depressor. The casting is dry when it easily peels off.

- Photograph the tool mark with scale.
- If possible, have the bone section seized isolated, if necessary, and seized as evidence.
- Casting should be done with silicone rubber casting compound such as Mikrosil® following the directions supplied by the manufacturer.

Two-Dimensional Residue Impressions on Skin

Kick or Stomps to the Body

- Stomping and kicks to the body may leave two-dimensional impressions on the victim's skin and/or clothing.
- The Stati-Lift self-charging metallic film works well on clothing and skin, as it does not require a variable charge.
- A standard electrostatic dust print lifter may also be used under the guidance of the medical examiner. Care is required to use the minimum charge necessary to get the film to adhere to the surface without damaging the skin.
- The techniques for both the Stati-Lift and the electrostatic dust print lifter are detailed in Processing Dry Impressions:
  - Electrostatic Dust Print Lifter, later in this chapter.

The Scene

Tool Marks (Three-Dimensional Impression Evidence)

These are three-dimensional impressions that result when a hard object (e.g., tool—screwdriver, hammer, wire cutters, or teeth) comes into contact with a softer substance. The resulting marks may yield both class and individualizing characteristics of the object that made them. Bite marks may be associated with assaults, sexual assault, on gags or items forced into a victim's mouth or on food eaten at the scene. Tool marks may be present at locations of any forced entry. An "Impression Evidence Notes" is provided as Worksheet 11 and will assist in keeping impression evidence recovery efforts organized and properly documented.

General
- Impressions also yield the possibility of transfer of trace evidence such as saliva, paint, metal chips, etc.
- *Caution*: The tool suspected of causing an impression should never be placed into the mark to see if it fits. This will create a potential for cross contamination of trace evidence and likely alter the impression itself.

Detection
- At the scene, carefully examine areas of forced entry or damage where tools may have come into contact with softer objects.
- Oblique lighting may assist in locating subtle, shallow marks.

Photography
See Figure 44.5.

- Tool marks should be photographed in place prior to any processing. Subsequent processing and recovery of these impressions may destroy/alter them.
- The camera should be tripod mounted with a shutter remote and the film/CCD plane of the camera parallel to the impression.
- The impression should fill the frame of the viewfinder.
- If in bright sunlight, the impression may need to be shaded for proper photography.
- The initial photographs should be without scale.
- Place an appropriate scale (e.g., ABFO, L-scale) adjacent to the impression for subsequent photographs. Ensure the scale is on the same plane as the impression.

Figure 44.5 Toolmark photography.

- After the initial photographs, large items of trace evidence such as paint chips or metal fragments that are not imbedded in the impression may be carefully removed and seized as trace evidence (Chapter 42).
- Low angle oblique lighting will assist in highlighting the impression.
- Using an off-camera flash or strong flashlight, direct the light at a low angle across the impression. Use a flashlight first to help determine the most effective flash angle.
- Photograph the impression with the oblique lighting from each side of the impression.
- Be aware of depth of field requirements for three-dimensional impressions.

Processing/Casting Tool Marks

See Figure 44.6.

- Whenever possible, the item containing the impression should be seized if it would not damage the impression.
- If this is not practical, after detailed photography, the impression may be cast.
- Casting should be done with a silicone rubber casting compound such as Mikrosil®, following the directions supplied by the manufacturer.

Figure 44.6 Processing toolmarks.

Footwear and Tire Impressions (Three-Dimensional Impression Evidence)

General

- It is important to keep in mind that law enforcement actions on scene may obscure impression evidence left by the suspect. All attempts should be made to use paths of travel not likely used by the suspect until those areas have been examined.
- It is advisable to keep nonessential personnel out of the scene and to wear protective footwear while processing the scene. The use of new clean "booties" by crime scene personnel each time they enter or reenter the scene will minimize further contamination.
- Thorough measurements and documentation of the distances between impressions, as well as their relationship to each other, may provide valuable information as to the gait of the individual, wheel base or axle length of the vehicle, etc.
- Casting impressions in mud, sand, snow, or underwater requires specialized techniques. Learn and practice appropriate methods for the local area in advance of any need.

  Caution: Do not reapproximate the item suspected of having made the impression to the impression itself. This will create the potential for cross contamination of trace evidence and likely alter the impression itself.

Detection

- Three-dimensional prints should be fairly obvious on initial inspection of likely areas in the scene.
- Oblique lighting may be helpful in locating more shallow impressions.

Photography

See Figure 44.7.

- Impressions should be photographed in place prior to any processing. Subsequent processing and recovery of these impressions will destroy/alter them.
- The camera should be tripod mounted with a shutter release remote and the film/CCD plane of the camera parallel to the impression.
- The impression should fill the frame of the viewfinder.
- If in bright sunlight, the impression may need to be shaded for proper photography.
- Initial photographs should be without scale.
- Place an appropriate scale (e.g., L-scale) adjacent to the impression for subsequent photographs. Ensure the scale is on the same plane as the impression.
- After initial photographs, large items (twigs, leaves, etc.) that are *clearly* not embedded in the impression and appear nonevidentiary may be carefully removed. If there is any doubt if they are or are not embedded, leave them in place and cast as is.

Figure 44.7 Photographing footwear impression evidence.

- Low angle oblique lighting will assist in highlighting the impression.
- Using an off-camera flash or strong flashlight, direct the light at a low angle across the impression. Use a flashlight first, to help determine the most effective flash angle.
- Photograph the impression with the oblique lighting from each side of the impression.
- Be aware of depth of field requirements for three-dimensional impressions.

Processing/Casting

See Figure 44.8.

- Whenever possible, the item containing the impression should be seized if it would not damage the impression. If this is not practical, after detailed photography, the impression may be cast.
- Dental stone or die stone is recommended as a casting agent. These substances require no reinforcement, show better detail than plaster of Paris, do not shrink, and will set up even under water.
- The casting material is typically mixed in a large (gallon size) Ziploc® bag.

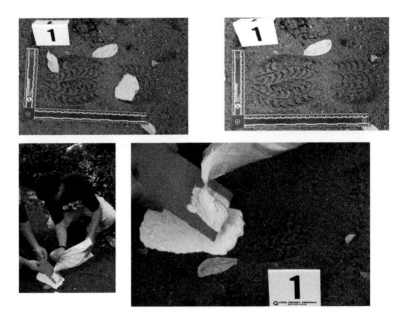

Figure 44.8 Casting footwear impressions. (1) Photograph impression. (2) Remove obvious (non-embedded) contaminants. (3) Pour dental or dye stone using a buffer to help direct the spread and prevent impacting the impression with the pouring stone.

- The Ziploc bags should be prepackaged with approximately 2 lbs of casting material. One bag should be sufficient for one footwear impression. Much larger quantities are required for tire marks.
- Add 12 oz. of water (a clean soda can full) to the powder and mix thoroughly by kneading the bag (this is a general guideline; refer to manufacturer's instructions for exact mixing directions).
- The resulting mixture should be adjusted until it is about the consistency of pancake batter.

NOTE: Framing is not necessary with these materials unless unusual terrain conditions exist (e.g., impression on an inclined surface like a hillside).

- The mixture should be poured to the side of the impression and allowed to run into the impression. Alternatively, an item can be used to act as a baffle, allowing the mixture to flow gently onto the impression.
- The impression should be completely covered in the first pour. An additional mixture may be added to the first in order to obtain a thickness of about 3/4 to 1 inch.
- Once the cast sets, an indelible marker is used to mark the castor's initials, the date/time, and a north arrow directly on the back of the cast.
- The cast should be allowed to set completely before removal. This should take approximately 30 minutes.
- Once removed, leave all adhering sand, dirt, or other particles on the cast surface. Cleaning will be done at the laboratory.
- Allow the cast to air-dry for 24–48 hours before preparing it for transport to the lab.

Casting Underwater

See Figure 44.9.

- Impression evidence under standing or slow-moving water may be cast in place.
- Impressions should be photographed with a scale at the same depth as the impression.
- A polarizing filter for the lens will reduce reflection from the surface of the water.
- A strong waterproof flashlight (or dive light) may be used to apply oblique lighting. *Note:* Any excessive movement of the water may stir up the bottom and obscure the print.
- Using a flour sifter, the dental/die stone is sifted so that it floats down and covers the print.
- Several layers are built up this way and allowed to partially harden.

Figure 44.9 Casting footwear impressions underwater. Powdered dental stone is poured down the PVC pipe and deposited at impression level or, using a flour sifter dental stone is dispersed over the surface of the water and allowed to drift down into the impression.

- Once the initial layer is set, place a frame around the existing cast.
- Once several sifted layers are built up, mix dental/die stone in a slightly thinner mixture than normal.
- Pour this mixture through the water so it settles within the frame and onto the hardening cast.
- Allow to completely dry; this may take several hours!
- Carefully work your fingers under the edge of the cast.
- Slowly and carefully work back and forth and along the length of the cast until it is free.
- Do not clean off any mud or other matter adhering to the cast!
- If casting in shallow saltwater, be aware that the dental stone will harden and set up more quickly.

Impressions in Snow
- *Primary method*: Spray the snow with commercially available spray wax. This fixes the impression in the snow, provides a contrasting color, and insulates it from the casting material.
- *Secondary method*: Using a flour sifter, sift two or three light coatings of dry dental/die stone into the impression and moisten each coating with a fine mist of water.

- Casts in very cold weather may take a considerable time to harden. If in an open area that will not be disturbed, vehicles may be moved over the cast to protect it while drying. The catalytic converter/exhaust system will provide warmth to help set the cast.

Impressions in Sand/Dust

- It is very easy to damage the detail of a three-dimensional footwear impression in sand or dust.
- The impression should be photographed first.
- The impression is then "fixed" by spraying hair spray or a substance sold commercially for this purpose. The can is held in such a way to allow the sprayed material to fall onto the impression via gravity instead of the force of the spray being applied directly to the impression.
- The spray should be allowed to set up/harden.
- After being photographed, the impression can be processed as ordinary three-dimensional impressions in dirt, as above. The use of a baffle or allowing the casting material to flow slowly and indirectly onto the impression is of utmost importance.
- Use a thinner mix of casting material for the initial layer to ensure the material flows easily across the loosely bound sand.

Special Considerations for Tire Marks

Follow the same procedures as for footwear impression but with the following considerations:

- Tire marks should be cast in approximately one-and-a-half-foot sections and encompass a length of about 6 feet (for standard car tires) to 9 feet (for larger/truck tires) to ensure the entire circumference of the tire is cast.
- The full depth of a tire mark should be cast, as important detail is often contained on the sidewall.
- Due to the volume of casting material used, be cautious and ensure the cast is completely dry before removal. The cast will be warm to the touch while drying. Use this as an indicator; do not attempt to lift until the cast is completely cool!
- The cast is marked with initials, date, item number, and north indicated with an arrow prior to lifting.
- Carefully work your fingers under the edge of the cast.
- Slowly and carefully work back and forth and along the length of the cast until it is free.
- Do not clean off any dirt or other matter adhering to the cast!

Packaging
- Package in separate cardboard containers.
- Ensure the cast is secured and will not slide back and forth within the container.

Footwear and Tire Impressions
(Two-Dimensional Impression Evidence)

Two-dimensional impressions, or dust prints, occur when the dust or contaminants on a suspect's footwear or tire are transferred to the surface being walked upon. They may also be present on the clothing or body of the victim when a stomping occurs. These prints are very fragile and should be considered as perishable evidence and receive priority processing.

Detection
- As with fingerprints, areas likely used by the suspect should be examined. Start with the point of entry; areas to, around, and from the point(s) where physical evidence is found and points of exit should all be examined with oblique lighting.
- Likewise, hard outdoor surfaces may also contain two-dimensional impressions. These may need to be processed quickly to avoid loss due to environmental factors (rain, snow, etc.).
- The use of powerful oblique lighting (at very low angles to the surface) will greatly assist in locating two-dimensional impressions.
- Impressions that may not be readily visible or even made visible by oblique lighting may still actually exist. If there is any reason to believe dust prints are present, consider screening the area with an electrostatic dust print lifter.

Oblique Lighting Visualization
- Darken the room or dim the lights, if possible.
- A strong white light is held at about a 10–15 degree angle so it skims across the floor or other surface being searched.
- Starting at the doorway or entrance to the scene, search your way in.
- Mark the location of all two-dimensional evidence as it is revealed to avoid its accidental obliteration.

Mirror and Oblique Lighting
Clear a path by the oblique lighting method, or make access to the scene from opposite side.

- Using a long rectangular mirror, hold it at the far end of the search area with the longest edge of the mirror perpendicular to the floor.

- Lean the mirror forward towards the search area at about a 5–10 degree angle. The best angle may be found by moving it back and forth while visualizing for prints.
- The searcher uses the same oblique lighting technique discussed above but looks into the mirror to visualize the two-dimensional prints.
- Once this technique is practiced and mastered, it is very effective for visualizing two-dimensional prints.

Photography
See Figure 44.10.

- Impressions should be photographed in place as soon as they are visualized. The subsequent processing and recovery of these impressions may destroy/alter them.
- The camera should be tripod mounted with the film/CCD plane of the camera parallel to the print.
- The print should fill the frame of the viewfinder.
- Low angle oblique lighting will assist in highlighting the print.
- Photograph both without and with scale.
- Seize the item if possible.
- An electrostatic dust print lifter, gelatin lifters, or wide tape may be used to lift the print from a hard surface.

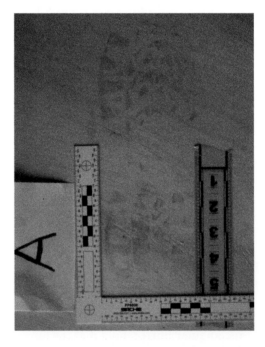

Figure 44.10 Photographing two-dimensional-impression evidence.

Processing Dry Impressions

Electrostatic Dust Print Lifter See Figure 44.11.

- The metallic film from the dust print lifter is placed black side down over the suspected two-dimensional impression.
- The unit's charging lead is placed onto the metallic top surface of the film. Follow manufacturer's instructions for safety and procedure.
- The unit's grounding lead is placed on a metal ground plate that is near, but not touching, the metallic film.
- Do not touch any part of the grounding plate or film during operation!
- The unit is powered up starting at the lowest setting, gradually increasing power until the film begins to adhere to the surface. Continue increasing power until the film is tightly adhered to the surface.
- Using the wooden handled rubber roller (provided with the kit), gently roll out the film across the suspected print, ensuring tight contact.
- Reduce power.
- Turn the unit off and remove it from film.
- Release any residual static charge (if provided with a static wire) or allow the film to lay in place for a minute, then carefully lift the film from the surface.
- Turn the film over carefully and inspect with oblique light for two-dimensional impression.

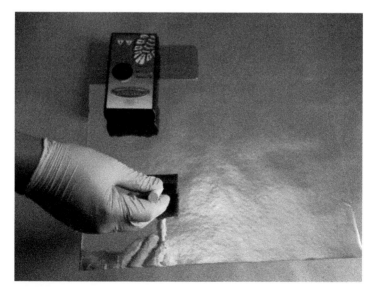

Figure 44.11 Use of the electrostatic dust print lifter.

- Photograph any evident impressions in darkness with the camera on a tripod. Fill the viewfinder frame with the impression and use timed exposures of 5, 10, 15, and 20 seconds.
- During exposure time, move the beam from a flashlight completely across the image at a very low angle of oblique lighting (Figure 44.12).
    - Do not pivot the flashlight back and forth; this will cause a hotspot where the light originates.
    - Make certain when moving the light back and forth that the beam comes completely off the film as it passes from left to right; this will prevent the edges from becoming burned out.
    - It is possible, though not recommended, to secure the completed metallic film in a box. As the static charge dissipates over time, the dust impression may no longer adhere to the film. The best method for preservation is photography.

Stati-Lift® Dust Print Lifter
- This is similar to the electrostatic dust print lifter in that it uses static electricity; however, the metallic film comes with a static charge already present. It does not require a power source and may be safely used on a living body (e.g., stomp marks, tire marks).
- The film is pulled away from its plastic cover sheet; this creates the static charge and exposes the black film surface.
- The black side of the film is laid carefully over the suspected impression.
- The film is carefully rolled out with a 4-inch rubber roller.
- The film is turned over and immediately photographed; do not replace the plastic cover sheet yet!

 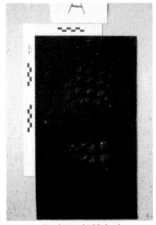

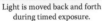

Light is moved back and forth   Results in a highlighted
during timed exposure.   2-dimensional impression.

Figure 44.12 Photographing dust print lifts by painting with light.

- Turn film over carefully and inspect with oblique light for two-dimensional impression.
- It should be photographed the same as with the electrostatic dust print lifts.
- After photography, replace the plastic cover sheet.

Gel Lifter

See Figure 44.13.

- Choose a gel lifter that will contrast in color with the suspected contaminant.
- A plastic cover sheet protects the gel. Carefully pull off the plastic cover sheet and expose the gel.
- The gel side of the matrix is laid carefully over the suspected impression.
- The film is carefully pressed into the surface with a 4-inch rubber roller.
- The gel is then lifted and turned over for inspection. Do not replace the plastic cover sheet yet!
- Carefully inspect for impressions. If an impression is evident, photograph it.
- If not readily apparent, search with oblique light for the two-dimensional impression.

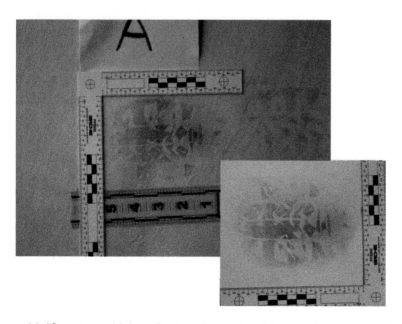

Figure 44.13 Using gel lifters for two-dimensional-impression evidence developed with black magnetic power.

Tape Lift

- If other means are not available, the two-dimensional impression may be lifted with tape and placed on a contrasting card.
- Apply a base layer of tape below the short axis of the impression.
- Carefully, using the widest tape available, run a strip of tape overlapping the base layer the full length of the impression.
- Repeat as many times as necessary, allowing each piece of tape to overlap at least 1/4 inch with the piece beside it.
- When the entire impression has been taped, gently lift the tape, starting with the base tape at the side of the overlapping run that was laid first.
- Lift all of the tape as a single piece and apply it to a contrasting surface card.

Processing Moist Impression

Two-dimensional moisture impressions occur when the impressing surface moves something wet (e.g., puddles, dew on grass) and then comes in contact with a dry, firm surface. This print is very transitory and should be photographed immediately upon discovery (Figure 44.14). The print will only be visible as long as the moisture has not evaporated. These prints are very

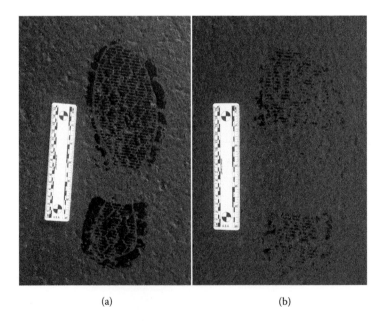

(a)   (b)

Figure 44.14 Documenting highly perishable moisture prints for two-dimensional-impression evidence. Photograph (a) Expediently photographed with iPhone Camera (b) taken two minutes after photograph (a).

fragile and should be considered as perishable evidence and receive priority processing.

- *Caution*: If the print is believed to have been made by a transfer of blood or oily contaminant, collect a sample and use a chemical staining method such as Amido Black or Sudan Black. Refer to latent print chemical enhancement in Chapter 43, "Friction Ridge Evidence."
- In all other cases, immediately photograph the print to demonstrate the spatial relationship and orientation of the print to the scene.
- Immediately photograph the print at 90 degrees, filling the frame of the viewfinder with the impression.
- Depending upon the nature of the surface the print is found on, it can be processed either wet or dry.
  - If the surface is smooth and nonporous, utilize a dry processing method.
  - If the surface is rough or textured, utilize a wet processing method.

Processing: Dry
- Continue to photograph the print with scale, as the print disappears.
- Once the print is dry, process the surface like a latent print, with contrasting powder.
- After development with fingerprint powder, photograph without and with scale.
- Lift the developed print with gelatin lifter or wide tape.

Processing: Wet
- Using a good contrasting fingerprint powder, lightly powder the wet print. Do not overpowder.
- Once developed, cast the area in the same manner as a three-dimensional cast, using dental stone. This will require placing a small tab (e.g., a piece of strong tape, a tongue depressor) at one edge of the cast. This tab is used to assist in levering up the dental stone after it is dry.

Packaging
- If the item itself is collected, it must be packaged in such a manner as to avoid having the print contact any item of packaging, etc.
- The gel lift or tape lift should be secured in a cardboard box.

Death Investigation Checklist and Worksheets

VIII

Dick Warrington with
Michael Maloney

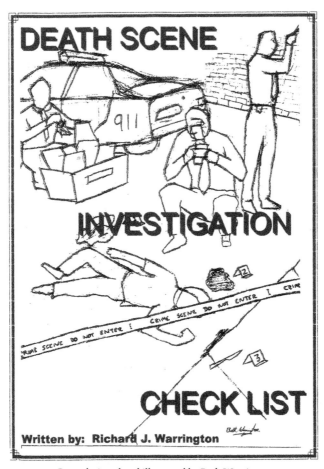

Cover designed and illustrated by Beth Warrington
Original Copyright 1998 By Richard J. Warrington Topeka, Kansas 66611

Dick Warrington's Death Scene Investigation Checklist has been an industry standard for over two decades. It is used by local, state, and federal Crime Scene Investigation Units and Forensic Laboratories to ensure the scene and evidence is thoroughly documented. I have personally used the checklist since its first publication. Dick has graciously allowed me to publish his checklist in full, as well as to make the checklist in digital fill-in format available with the publication of this procedural guide. For ease in transition, some changes in wording were made in order to remain consistent with the procedural guide. For example, "crime scene" has been replaced with "death scene" as the audience of this procedural guide includes those that investigate noncriminal deaths.

Added to the end of the Checklist is a series of Supplemental Worksheets specific to the Death Scene Investigation Procedural Guide, 2nd Edition.

Michael Maloney
2017

Author

Richard J. Warrington is a crime scene consultant, educator, author, and inventor. He retired from the Shawnee County (Kansas) Sheriff's Department in 1996 after a 25-year career in law enforcement. His career included more than 19 years of direct involvement with crime scene investigation as a supervisor and as the lead crime scene officer for the Major Case Squad. He served on the board of directors of the International Crime Scene Investigators Association, as well as a member and past president of the Kansas Division of the International Association for Identification (IAI).

Mr. Warrington remained active in the field of crime scene investigation as an instructor. He taught basic fingerprinting techniques, developing and lifting latent off unusual surfaces, and basic crime scene investigation throughout the United States and Canada at conferences and also for the IAI.

His website (www.csigizmos.com) consists of cost-effective tools and techniques applied in crime scene investigation. He has written numerous articles on crime scene technology and procedures as well as a column titled "Who Says You Can't Do It" in *Forensic Magazine*. He has also written articles for *Popular Science* magazine and the *IAI Forensic Journal*. In 1994, Mr. Warrington wrote and published the Death Investigation Check List Manual.

Forward

The Death Scene Investigation Check List has been a standard for over two decades in thoroughly documenting the death scene. Dick Warrington has provided timely updates to the forms to embrace emerging technologies and cutting edge techniques to death scene investigators whether they are law enforcement, medico-legal, or judicial investigators. These forms have been adopted by many local, state, and federal agencies as their standard documentation protocol at the scene. You may have seen these forms used at scenes and wondered what their source was.

In the first edition of the Death Scene Investigation Procedural Guide, I included a number of worksheets for assisting in documenting evidence at the scene. I had thought to expand on this considerably for the second edition, built, the bottom line is for over 20 years I have used Dick's Death Scene Investigation Checklist. Dick has enthusiastically updated and allowed his checklist to be added to this procedural guide as well as providing for the digital download with form fill capabilities.

The Death Scene Investigation Checklist is designed to help officers in their investigation at a crime scene. It will allow them to thoroughly document the scene and their efforts at the scene in an organized manner. By using these forms, the information is easy to refer back when necessary. It is no longer necessary to sort through pages of notes to find the vehicle VIN number or the address of the person who discovered the body. This checklist and the supplemental worksheets serve as both a source of information as well as a reminder of what needs to be done. This checklist jogs the investigator's memory on those observations that should be made at the scene.

Timely documentation is critical in working a death scene but many times an officer relies on memory alone. With so many things going on at one time, even the best forget. Once the scene is released, it is hard to get back into the scene to collect additional evidence and have it admitted into court.

This section contains the blank forms and supplemental worksheets of the Death Scene Check List. You will need several copies of some of the forms in the Check List, such as the Officer Entry Log, Evidence Recovery Log, Photographic Log, to name a few. You can make copies of these forms as needed. When copying a 33% enlargement will allow the form to fill standard printer paper. The crime scene officer or investigator who does the scene should have a copy of the Death Scene Check List in his/her vehicle so it will be readily available when needed. In addition, the forms may be filled from a tablet or Smartphone or from your desktop computer. Instructions for downloading the form fill version are detailed below.

The website and login supplied with this book has the Death Scene Investigative Check List fill-in forms and logs you will need. It will give you the ability to put the Death Scene Check List on your tablet or Smartphone and fill in at the scene. This site also has a downloadable version of the full instructions for using the checklist.

Death Scene Investigation
Check List Fill-In Forms

SECTION 1	DEATH SCENE INFORMATION	(SEC. 1-A)

DEPARTMENT:		
OFFENSE:	DATE:	CASE #:
LOCATION:		
CITY:	COUNTY:	STATE:

TIME NOTIFIED:	TIME ARRIVED:
NOTIFIED BY:	AUTHORIZED BY:
OFFICER IN CHARGE:	DEPT.:
FIRST OFFICER AT SCENE:	DEPT.:

SCENE SECURITY	(SEC. 1-B)

WAS SCENE SECURED: YES ☐ NO ☐
METHOD: OFFICERS ☐ BARRIER TAPE ☐ OTHER ☐
DESCRIBE:
SCENE SECURITY LOG STARTED: YES ☐ NO ☐ STARTED BY:
OFFICER ENTRY LOG STARTED: YES ☐ NO ☐ STARTED BY:

SEARCH WARRANT INFORMATION	(SEC. 1-C)

SEARCH WARRANT NEEDED: YES ☐ NO ☐		
OBTAINED BY:	DATE:	TIME:
COUNTY/DISTRICT ATTY.:	JUDGE:	
COUNTY/DISTRICT ATTY. AT SCENE: YES ☐ NO ☐		
COUNTY/DISTRICT ATTY.:		
TIME ARRIVED:	TIME DEPARTED:	

REMARKS

COMPLETED BY:	
CASE #:	DATE:

SECTION 2	PERSONS AT THE DEATH SCENE	(SEC.2-A)

FIRST RESPONDERS		
NAME	**TOWNSHIP/DEPARTMENT**	**PHONE NUMBER**

MEDICAL PERSONNEL		
NAME	**COMPANY**	**PHONE NUMBER**

FAMILY AT SCENE		

NAME:	RELATIONSHIP:	
ADDRESS:		PHONE #:
NAME:	RELATIONSHIP:	
ADDRESS:		PHONE #:
NAME:	RELATIONSHIP:	
ADDRESS:		PHONE #:
NAME:	RELATIONSHIP:	
ADDRESS:		PHONE #:

REPORTING PERSON(S)		
NAME	**ADDRESS**	**PHONE NUMBER**

COMPLETED BY:	
CASE #:	DATE:

PERSONNEL AT SCENE		
NAME	DEPARTMENT/ADDRESS	PHONE NUMBER

REMARKS

COMPLETED BY:	
CASE #:	DATE:

SECTION 3	CRIME SCENE	(SEC.3-A)

OFFENSE:	
LOCATION:	
DEATH SCENE SUPERVISOR:	DEPT.:
SKETCH/DIAGRAM:	DEPT.:
PHOTOGRAPHER:	DEPT.:
VIDEOGRAPHER:	DEPT.:
OBSERVER:	DEPT.:
EVIDENCE COLLECTION:	DEPT.:
EVIDENCE CUSTODIAN:	DEPT.:

OFFICERS ASSISTING / SPECIALIST		(SEC.3-B)

NAME	DEPARTMENT	ASSIGNMENT

WEATHER CONDITIONS		(SEC.3-C)

SCENE TEMP:	OUTSIDE TEMP:	SKY:
WIND DIRECTION:	WIND SPEED:	PRECIPITATION:

SCENE DESCRIPTION	(SEC.3-D)

BRIEFLY DESCRIBE THE SCENE AS YOU FOUND IT:

COMPLETED BY:	
CASE #:	DATE:

SECTION 4   MEDICAL EXAMINER /CORONER NOTIFICATION (SEC. 4-A)

DATE:		TIME:	NOTIFYING PERSON:	
ME/C INVESTIGATOR NOTIFIED:				
ME/C ARRIVED: DATE:			TIME:	
ME/C DEPARTED: DATE:			TIME:	
ASSISTING ME/C:			AGENCY:	
ASSISTING ME/C:			AGENCY:	

REMARKS FROM CORONER

BODY REMOVAL   **(SEC. 4-B)**

COMPANY NOTIFIED FOR REMOVAL:		
DATE:	TIME:	NOTIFIED BY:
AUTHORIZED BY:		
TIME ARRIVED:		TIME DEPARTED:
PERSONNEL:		

BODY BAG SEALED: YES ☐ NO ☐ SEALED WITH TAPE ☐ LOCKING TAG ☐	
TAG # :	OTHER: ☐
DESCRIBE:	
BODY TRANSPORTED TO:	
AUTHORIZED BY:	
BODY ESCORTED: YES ☐ NO ☐	
ESCORTED BY:	DEPT.:

REMARKS

COMPLETED BY:	
CASE #:	DATE:

INFORMATION OF DECEASED		(SEC. 4-C)

LAST:	FIRST:	MIDDLE:
ADDRESS:	CITY:	STATE:
PHONE #:	MARITAL STATUS:	D.O.B.:
AGE: RACE:	SEX: HEIGHT:	WEIGHT:
HAIR COLOR:	EYE COLOR:	FACIAL HAIR: YES ☐ NO ☐
DESCRIBE:		
SCARS/MARKS/TATTOOS: YES ☐ NO ☐		
DESCRIBE:		

REMARKS

DECEASED FOUND BY		(SEC. 4-D)

LAST:	FIRST:	MIDDLE:
ADDRESS:	CITY:	STATE:
D.O.B.:	PHONE #:	
LAST:	FIRST:	MIDDLE:
ADDRESS:	CITY:	STATE:
D.O.B.:	PHONE #:	
DATE FOUND:	TIME FOUND:	

REMARKS

COMPLETED BY:	
CASE #:	DATE:

AREA WHERE BODY WAS FOUND

CHECK THE PROPER SECTION AND PAGE NUMBER BELOW FOR THE BODY LOCATION OF YOUR CASE AND REFER TO THAT SECTION TO CONTINUE FOR PROPER DOCUMENTATION

☐ BODY IN STRUCTURE	SECTION 5	PAGE # 8
☐ BODY IN WATER	SECTION 6	PAGE # 12
☐ BODY IN VEHICLE	SECTION 7	PAGE # 15
☐ BODY IN OPEN AREA	SECTION 8	PAGE # 19

UPON COMPLETION OF THE APPROPRIATE BODY LOCATION SECTION, PROCEED TO SECTION 9 PAGE 22 TO CONTINUE THE DEATH SCENE CHECK LIST

REMARKS

COMPLETED BY:	
CASE #:	DATE:

SECTION 5	BODY FOUND IN STRUCTURE

LOCATION / TYPE OF STRUCTURE	(SEC. 5-A)

APARTMENT ☐   DUPLEX ☐   HOUSE ☐   GARAGE ☐   OUTBUILDING ☐   OTHER ☐

DESCRIBE:

ADDRESS:	CITY:	STATE:
TELEPHONE #:		

NUMBER OF ROOMS: | BASEMENT: YES ☐   NO ☐   IF YES: FULL ☐

PARTIAL ☐   OTHER ☐

CONDITIONS OF SURROUNDINGS	(SEC. 5-B)

ENTRANCE BY: DOOR FORCED ☐   KEY ☐   CUTTING CHAIN ☐   WINDOW ☐

UNDETERMINED ☐   OTHER ☐

DESCRIBE:

EVIDENCE OF ROBBERY OR THEFT: YES ☐   NO ☐   NOT DETERMINED ☐

DESCRIBE:

CONDITION OF DOORS: OPEN ☐ CLOSED ☐ LOCKED ☐ UNLOCKED ☐ FORCED ☐

DESCRIBE:

GARAGE DOOR(S): YES ☐ NO ☐ IF YES: LOCKED ☐ UNLOCKED ☐ OPEN ☐

CLOSED ☐   FORCED ☐

CONDITION OF WINDOWS: OPEN ☐ CLOSED ☐   LOCKED ☐

COMBINATION BROKEN ☐ FORCED ☐

DESCRIBE:

CONDITION OF INTERIOR: NEAT AND ORDERLY ☐ DISARRAY ☐ RANSACKED ☐

DESCRIBE:

LIGHTS ON: YES ☐ NO ☐ COMBINATION ☐

IF YES, LIST LIGHTS AND LOCATION:

COMPLETED BY:	
CASE #:	DATE:

APPLIANCES ON: TV ☐ RADIO ☐ STEREO ☐ RANGE ☐ MICROWAVE ☐
DISH WASHER ☐ CLOTHES DRYER ☐ CLOTHES WASHER ☐ OTHER ☐
DESCRIBE:
COMPUTER: YES ☐ NO ☐ IF YES: ON ☐ OFF ☐

TELEPHONE: YES ☐ NO ☐ PHONE #:	WORKING: YES ☐ NO ☐

ANSWERING MACHINE: YES ☐ NO ☐ IF YES: ON ☐ OFF ☐
CHECK MESSAGES AND DESCRIBE:
TABLET: YES ☐ NO ☐ IF YES: ON ☐ OFF ☐
CHECK MESSAGES AND DESCRIBE:
CELL PHONE: YES ☐ NO ☐ IF YES: ON ☐ OFF ☐
CHECK MESSAGES AND DESCRIBE:
HEATER: ON ☐ OFF ☐   AIR CONDITIONER: ON ☐ OFF ☐

TEMPERATURE INSIDE:	THERMOSTAT SETTING:
ANIMALS PRESENT: YES ☐ NO ☐	

IF YES, DESCRIBE CONDITION AND DISPOSITION:
DATED MATERIAL: YES ☐ NO ☐ IF YES, LIST BELOW:
MAIL:
NEWSPAPERS:
RECEIPTS:
OTHER DATED MATERIAL:
EVIDENCE OF LAST FOOD PREPARATION: YES ☐ NO ☐
BREAKFAST ☐ LUNCH ☐ DINNER ☐ SNACK ☐
IF YES, TYPE OF FOOD AND LOCATION:
EVIDENCE OF LAST MEAL CLEANUP: YES ☐ NO ☐
BREAKFAST ☐ LUNCH ☐ DINNER ☐ SNACK ☐
IF YES, TYPE OF FOOD AND LOCATION:
ALCOHOL PRESENT: YES ☐ NO ☐ OPENED ☐ SEALED ☐
IF YES, TYPE AND LOCATION:

COMPLETED BY:	
CASE #:	DATE:

LOCATION OF BODY IN STRUCTURE	(SEC. 5-C)

LOCATION: LIVING ROOM ☐   DINING ROOM ☐   KITCHEN ☐   MUDROOM ☐
MASTER BEDROOM ☐   MASTER BATHROOM ☐   BEDROOM ☐   BATHROOM ☐
FAMILY ROOM ☐   HALLWAY ☐   BASEMENT ☐   ATTIC ☐   GARAGE ☐
OTHER ☐
DESCRIBE:
LOCATION IN ROOM:

POSITION OF BODY	(SEC. 5-D)

POSITION: SUPINE ☐   PRONE ☐   RIGHT SIDE ☐   LEFT SIDE ☐   SITTING ☐
HANGING ☐   OTHER ☐
DESCRIBE:
BODY DIAGRAMED: YES ☐ NO ☐   BODY PHOTOGRAPHED: YES ☐ NO ☐

CLOTHING AND JEWELRY ON BODY	(SEC. 5-E)

CLOTHING: FULLY CLOTHED ☐   PARTIALLY CLOTHED ☐   NUDE ☐
DESCRIBE:
JEWELRY ON BODY: YES ☐ NO ☐   IF YES, PHOTOGRAPH ON BODY: YES ☐ NO ☐   BLANCHING ☐ NO ☐
IF YES, DESCRIBE JEWELRY:

CONDITION OF BODY	(SEC. 5-F)

PRESERVATION: WELL PRESERVED ☐   PARTIALLY DECOMPOSED ☐
DECOMPOSED ☐   SKIN SLIPPAGE ☐   SKELETAL REMAINS ☐
DESCRIBE:

COMPLETED BY:	
CASE #:	DATE:

ESTIMATE RIGOR: COMPLETE ☐ NECK ☐ ARMS ☐ LEGS ☐
DESCRIBE:
LIVIDITY: FRONT ☐ BACK ☐ LOCALIZED ☐ BLANCHING: YES ☐ NO ☐
DESCRIBE:
BODY COLOR:
BLOOD: ABSENT ☐ PRESENT ☐
IF PRESENT, LIST LOCATION:
ANYTHING TIED TO BODY: YES ☐ NO ☐
IF YES, DESCRIBE:
LIGATURE MARKS: YES ☐ NO ☐
IF YES, DESCRIBE:
USE POST MORTEM INDICATORS WORKSHEET

REMARKS

WHEN COMPLETED WITH THIS SECTION CONTINUE TO SECTION 9

COMPLETED BY:	
CASE #:	DATE:

SECTION 6	BODY FOUND IN WATER

LOCATION	(SEC. 6-A)

WATER TYPE: POND ☐   LAKE ☐   RIVER ☐   CREEK ☐   TIDAL POOL ☐

OCEAN ☐   POOL ☐   OTHER ☐

IF LAKE, RIVER OR CREEK, GIVE NAME:

LOCATION:

NEAREST STRUCTURE WITH WATER ACCESS (MAY BE BRIDGE OVER WATER):

TYPE:

NEAREST ROAD TO SCENE:	NAME OF ROAD:
DISTANCE FROM SCENE:	DIRECTION:

AIR TEMP:	WATER TEMP:	WATER DEPTH:
WIDTH:	CURRENT: YES ☐ NO ☐	DIRECTION:

WATER CLARITY: MUDDY ☐   CLOUDY ☐   CLEAR ☐

LAST PRECIPITATION IN AREA:	AMOUNT:

LOCATION OF BODY : IN WATER ☐   PARTIALLY IN WATER ☐   ON BANK ☐

IN WATER, DISTANCE FROM SHORE / BANK:

SHORE / BANK TYPE: SAND ☐   ROCK ☐   GRAVEL ☐   DIRT ☐   GRASS ☐

SHORE / BANK HEIGHT:	NEAREST BOAT RAMP:	NONE: ☐

BODY POSITION	(SEC. 6-B)

BODY POSITION: FLOATING ☐   PARTIALLY SUBMERGED ☐

ON BACK ☐   FACE DOWN ☐   RIGHT SIDE ☐   LEFT SIDE ☐   OTHER ☐

DESCRIBE:

CONDITION OF BODY	(SEC. 6-C)

PRESERVATION: WELL PRESERVED ☐   PARTIALLY DECOMPOSED ☐

DECOMPOSED ☐   SKIN SLIPPAGE ☐   SKELETAL REMAINS ☐

WITHIN MARINE PREDATOR ☐

DESCRIBE:

COMPLETED BY:	
CASE #:	DATE:

ESTIMATE RIGOR: COMPLETE ☐   NECK ☐   ARMS ☐   LEGS ☐
DESCRIBE:

LIVIDITY: FRONT ☐   BACK ☐   LOCALIZED ☐   BLANCHING: YES ☐   NO ☐
DESCRIBE:

BODY COLOR:

BLOOD: ABSENT ☐   PRESENT ☐
IF PRESENT, LIST LOCATION:

ANYTHING TIED TO BODY: YES ☐   NO ☐
IF YES, DESCRIBE:

LIGATURE MARKS: YES ☐   NO ☐
IF YES, DESCRIBE:

USE POST MORTEM INDICATORS WORKSHEET

BODY DIAGRAMED: YES ☐   NO ☐   BODY PHOTOGRAPHED: YES ☐   NO ☐

CLOTHING AND JEWELRY ON BODY	**(SEC. 6-D)**

CLOTHING: FULLY CLOTHED ☐   PARTIALLY CLOTHED ☐   NUDE ☐
DESCRIBE CLOTHING:

JEWELRY ON BODY: YES ☐   NO ☐   IF YES, PHOTOGRAPH ON BODY: YES ☐   NO ☐
IF YES, DESCRIBE JEWELRY:

CLOTHING FOUND IN AREA: YES ☐   NO ☐
IF YES, LOCATION / DESCRIBE:

COMPLETED BY:	
CASE #:	DATE:

SEARCH BY DIVERS	(SEC. 6-E)

AREA SEARCHED BY DIVERS: YES ☐ NO ☐		
DATE:	TIME STARTED:	TIME ENDED:

AREA SEARCHED:

DIVER'S NAME	AGENCY / DEPARTMENT

ITEMS RECOVERED: YES ☐   NO ☐

DESCRIBE:

LOCATION OF RECOVERED ITEMS (INCLUDE DEPTH AND GPS COORDINATES):

REMARKS

WHEN COMPLETED WITH THIS SECTION CONTINUE TO SECTION 9

COMPLETED BY:	
CASE #:	DATE:

SECTION 7	BODY FOUND IN VEHICLE

VEHICLE LOCATION	(SEC. 7-A)

SPECIFIC VEHICLE LOCATION:

ROADWAY ☐ DRIVEWAY ☐ PARKING LOT ☐ FIELD ☐ OTHER ☐
DESCRIBE:

SURFACE CONDITION: CONCRETE ☐ ASPHALT ☐ GRAVEL ☐ DIRT ☐
GRASS ☐ ROCK ☐ OTHER ☐
DESCRIBE :

NEAREST RESIDENCE / BUSINESS:

NEAREST ROAD TO SCENE:	NAME OF ROAD:
DISTANCE FROM SCENE:	DIRECTION:

VEHICLE INFORMATION	(SEC. 7-B)

VEHICLE TYPE: CAR ☐   VAN ☐   PICKUP TRUCK ☐   LARGE TRUCK ☐
MOTOR HOME ☐   BUS ☐   TRAILER ☐   OTHER ☐
DESCRIBE:

NUMBER OF DOORS: 2DR ☐ 3DR ☐ 4DR ☐ 5DR ☐ HATCHBACK ☐ OTHER ☐
PICKUP TRUCK: SHORT BED ☐ LONG BED ☐ FLAT BED ☐ NO BED ☐
CAMPER ☐   TOPPER ☐ OTHER ☐
DESCRIBE:

VEHICLE MAKE:	MODEL:		YEAR:
TAG #:	STATE:	VIN #:	
COLOR TOP:	COLOR BOTTOM:		
ODOMETER READING:		TRIP METER READING:	
REGISTERED OWNER:			PHONE #:
ADDRESS:		CITY:	STATE:
LIEN HOLDER:			

REMARKS

COMPLETED BY:	
CASE #:	DATE:

VEHICLE LOCATION	(SEC. 7-C)

DOORS: OPEN ☐ CLOSED ☐ LOCKED ☐ UNLOCKED ☐ OTHER ☐
DESCRIBE:

WINDOWS: OPEN ☐ CLOSED ☐ BROKEN ☐ OTHER ☐
DESCRIBE:

DAMAGE TO VEHICLE: YES ☐ NO ☐
IF YES, DESCRIBE:

KEYS IN IGNITION: YES ☐ NO ☐
DESCRIBE:

IGNITION ON: YES ☐ NO ☐
ENGINE RUNNING: YES ☐ NO ☐
RADIO ON: YES ☐ NO ☐   CHANNEL TUNED IN:
DESCRIBE:

TRANSMISSION: STANDARD ☐ AUTOMATIC ☐ FLOOR SHIFT ☐ COLUMN SHIFT ☐
IN GEAR: YES ☐ NO ☐   IF YES, WHICH GEAR:
LIGHTS ON: HEADLIGHTS ☐ PARKING LIGHTS ☐ TURN SIGNAL ☐ DOME LIGHT ☐
DESCRIBE:

BATTERY CONDITION: GOOD ☐ BATTERY DEAD ☐
TIRES: NO FLATS ☐ TIRE(S) FLAT ☐ TIRE(S) MISSING ☐
DESCRIBE:

GAS GAUGE READING: EMPTY ☐ 1/4 ☐ 1/2 ☐ 3/4 ☐ FULL ☐ PAST FULL ☐
ASHTRAY CONTENTS:

VEHICLE INVENTORIED:	YES ☐	NO ☐
SEE VEHICLE INVENTORY SHEET:	YES ☐	NO ☐
VEHICLE DIAGRAMED:	YES ☐	NO ☐
SEE VEHICLE PROCESSING SHEET:	YES ☐	NO ☐

REMARKS

COMPLETED BY:	
CASE #:	DATE:

VEHICLE LOCATION	(SEC. 7-D)

BODY LOCATION: FRONT SEAT ☐   BACK SEAT ☐   TRUNK ☐   DRIVER'S SIDE ☐
PASSENGER'S SIDE ☐   FRONT FLOOR ☐   REAR FLOOR ☐   PICKUP BED ☐
OUTSIDE OF VEHICLE ☐   PARTIALLY IN/OUT ☐   OTHER ☐
DESCRIBE:

BODY POSTION: SITTING ☐   LYING DOWN ☐   SUPINE ☐   PRONE ☐
RIGHT SIDE ☐   LEFT SIDE ☐
DESCRIBE:

BODY DIAGRAMED: YES ☐   NO ☐   BODY PHOTOGRAPHED: YES ☐   NO ☐

CONDITION OF BODY	(SEC. 7-E)

PRESERVATION: WELL PRESERVED ☐   PARTIALLY DECOMPOSED ☐
DECOMPOSED ☐   SKIN SLIPPAGE ☐   SKELETAL REMAINS ☐
DESCRIBE:

ESTIMATE RIGOR: COMPLETE ☐   NECK ☐   ARMS ☐   LEGS ☐
DESCRIBE:

LIVIDITY: FRONT ☐   BACK ☐   LOCALIZED ☐   BLANCHING: YES ☐   NO ☐
DESCRIBE:

BODY COLOR:

BLOOD: ABSENT ☐   PRESENT ☐
IF PRESENT, LIST LOCATION:

ANYTHING TIED TO BODY: YES ☐   NO ☐
IF YES, DESCRIBE:

LIGATURE MARKS: YES ☐   NO ☐
IF YES, DESCRIBE:

USE POST MORTEM INDICATORS WORKSHEET

COMPLETED BY:	
CASE #:	DATE:

CLOTHING AND JEWELRY ON BODY	(SEC. 7-F)

CLOTHING: FULLY CLOTHED ☐   PARTIALLY CLOTHED ☐   NUDE ☐

DESCRIBE CLOTHING:

JEWELRY ON BODY: YES ☐ NO ☐   IF YES, PHOTOGRAPH ON BODY: YES ☐ NO ☐

IF YES, DESCRIBE JEWELRY:

CLOTHING FOUND IN AREA: YES ☐   NO ☐

IF YES, LOCATION / DESCRIBE:

REMARKS

WHEN COMPLETED WITH THIS SECTION CONTINUE TO SECTION 9

COMPLETED BY:

CASE #:   DATE:

SECTION 8	BODY FOUND IN OPEN AREA

LOCATION	(SEC. 8-A)

SPECIFIC LOCATION:

TYPE OF AREA: ROADWAY ☐ DITCH ☐ PARKING LOT ☐ DRIVEWAY ☐

FIELD ☐ OTHER ☐

DESCRIBE:

AREA CONDITION: PAVED ☐　GRAVEL ☐　DIRT ☐　GRASS ☐

WOODED AREA ☐　ROCKY ☐

WATER IN AREA: YES ☐　NO ☐

IF YES, DESCRIBE:

NEAREST RESIDENCE / BUSINESS:

NEAREST ROAD TO SCENE:	NAME OF ROAD:
DISTANCE FROM SCENE:	DIRECTION:

NEAREST POINT OF REFERENCE:

AREA DIAGRAMED: YES ☐ NO ☐

POSITION OF BODY	(SEC. 8-B)

POSITION: ON BACK ☐ FACE DOWN ☐ RIGHT SIDE ☐ LEFT SIDE ☐ SITTING ☐

HANGING ☐ OTHER ☐

DESCRIBE:

BODY DIAGRAMED: YES ☐ NO ☐　　BODY PHOTOGRAPHED: YES ☐ NO ☐

REMARKS

COMPLETED BY:	
CASE #:	DATE:

CONDITION OF BODY	(SEC. 8-C)

PRESERVATION OF BODY: WELL PRESERVED ☐   PARTIALLY DECOMPOSED ☐

DECOMPOSED ☐   SKIN SLIPPAGE ☐   SKELETAL REMAINS ☐

DESCRIBE:

ESTIMATE RIGOR: COMPLETE ☐   NECK ☐   ARMS ☐   LEGS ☐

DESCRIBE:

LIVIDITY: FRONT ☐   BACK ☐   LOCALIZED ☐   BLANCHING:

DESCRIBE:

BODY COLOR:

BLOOD: ABSENT ☐   PRESENT ☐

IF PRESENT, LIST LOCATION:

ANYTHING TIED TO BODY: YES ☐   NO ☐

IF YES, DESCRIBE:

LIGATURE MARKS: YES ☐   NO ☐

IF YES, DESCRIBE:

USE POST MORTEM INDICATORS WORKSHEET

REMARKS

COMPLETED BY:	
CASE #:	DATE:

CLOTHING AND JEWELRY ON BODY	(SEC. 8-D)

CLOTHING: FULLY CLOTHED ☐   PARTIALLY CLOTHED ☐   NUDE ☐

DESCRIBE CLOTHING:

JEWELRY ON BODY: YES ☐   NO ☐   IF YES, PHOTOGRAPH ON BODY: YES ☐   NO ☐

IF YES, DESCRIBE JEWELRY:

CLOTHING FOUND IN AREA: YES ☐   NO ☐

IF YES, LOCATION / DESCRIBE:

REMARKS

WHEN COMPLETED WITH THIS SECTION CONTINUE TO SECTION 9

COMPLETED BY:	
CASE #:	DATE:

SECTION 9	WOUNDS / WEAPONS / DRUGS / MEDICATION

APPARENT WOUNDS	(SEC. 9-A)

APPARENT WOUNDS VISIBLE: YES ☐   NO ☐

TYPE OF WOUND: ASPHYXIAL ☐   SHARP FORCE ☐   BLUNT FORCE ☐   CHOP ☐

FIRE ARMS ☐   EXPLOSIVE ☐   THERMAL ☐   ELECTRICAL ☐

DEFENSIVE WOUNDS ☐   UNDETERMINED ☐   HESITATION ☐   OTHER ☐

DESCRIBE WOUND(S):

MARKS ON BODY: YES ☐   NO ☐

DESCRIBE:

LOCATION OF MARKS / WOUNDS: HEAD ☐   NECK ☐   CHEST ☐   ABDOMEN ☐

BACK ☐   ARMS ☐   HANDS ☐   FEET ☐   BUTTOCKS ☐

DESCRIBE:

SEE BODY DIAGRAM: YES ☐   NO ☐   SEE PHOTOGRAPH: YES ☐   NO ☐

WEAPONS PRESENT	(SEC. 9-B)

WEAPONS PRESENT: YES ☐   NO ☐

TYPE OF WEAPON: GUN ☐   KNIFE ☐   OTHER TYPE WEAPON ☐

DESCRIBE:

GUN TYPE: HANDGUN ☐   RIFLE ☐   SHOTGUN ☐   OTHER ☐

DESCRIBE:

BRAND:	MODEL:	SERIAL #:

BULLET CASE: YES ☐   NO ☐   SPENT ROUNDS: YES ☐   NO ☐

DESCRIBE / LOCATION:

USE FIREARMS DOCUMENTATION WORKSHEET

COMPLETED BY:	
CASE #:	DATE:

KNIFE: YES ☐   NO ☐

DESCRIBE / LOCATION:

BRAND:	TYPE:	BLADE LENGTH:

OTHER TYPE WEAPON: YES ☐   NO ☐

DESCRIBE / LOCATION:

BLOOD ON WEAPON: YES ☐ NO ☐

DESCRIBE:

MEDICATIONS / DRUGS   (SEC. 9-C)

EVIDENCE OF DRUG USE: YES ☐   NO ☐

PRESCRIPTION DRUGS: YES ☐   NO ☐

MEDICATION NAME	DOCTOR	RX#	PHARMACY	DATE

LOCATION OF MEDICATION:

REMARKS

COMPLETED BY:

CASE #:	DATE:

ILLEGAL DRUGS PRESENT: YES ☐ NO ☐

DRUG PARAPHERNALIA PRESENT: YES ☐ NO ☐

TYPE / DESCRIBE:

LOCATION:

REMARKS

EVIDENCE OF SEXUAL ACTIVITY AT TIME OF DEATH: YES ☐ NO ☐

DESCRIBE:

EVIDENCE OF SEXUAL ACTIVITY: YES ☐ NO ☐

DESCRIBE:

REMARKS

COMPLETED BY:

| CASE #: | DATE: |

SECTION 10	IDENTIFICATION / NOTIFICATION

IDENTIFICATION OF DECEASED	(SEC. 10-A)

POSITIVE IDENTIFICATION OF DECEASED: YES ☐   NO ☐

HOW WAS IDENTIFICATION ACCOMPLISHED:

IF NO, HOW IS IT TO BE ACCOMPLISHED:

NAME IF YES, LAST:		FIRST:	MIDDLE:
ADDRESS:	CITY:		STATE:
D.O.B.:	SOCIAL SECURITY NO.:		
NEXT OF KIN: YES ☐ NO ☐			
PERSON NOTIFIED:		PHONE #:	
ADDRESS:	CITY:		STATE:
NOTIFIED BY:		DATE:	TIME:

REMARKS

COMPLETED BY:	
CASE #:	DATE:

SECTION 11	SCENE PROCESSING

EVIDENCE RECOVERED	(SEC. 11-A)

EVIDENCE RECOVERED AT THE CRIME SCENE:	YES ☐ NO ☐
SEE EVIDENCE RECOVERY LOG:	YES ☐ NO ☐
SEE PHYSICAL EVIDENCE CUSTODY RECEIPT:	YES ☐ NO ☐

ITEMS PROCESSED AT THE CRIME SCENE	(SEC. 11-B)

LOCATION WHERE PROCESSED:

DATE:	TIME BEGAN:	TIME ENDED:

ITEMS PROCESSED	(SEC. 11-C)

ITEMS PROCESSED FOR LATENT PRINTS: YES ☐   NO ☐

USE FRICTION RIDGE EVIDENCE WORKSHEET

ITEM	LOCATION	METHOD	RESULTS

SEE ATTACHED LIST OF ADDITIONAL ITEMS PROCESSED: YES ☐   NO ☐

COMPLETED BY:	
CASE #:	DATE:

TRACE EVIDENCE	(SEC. 11-D)

USE TRACE EVIDENCE NOTES
USE BIOLOGICAL EVIDENCE NOTES
BLOOD: YES ☐   NO ☐
IF YES, DESCRIBE / LOCATION:
HAIR: YES ☐   NO ☐
IF YES, DESCRIBE / LOCATION:
FIBERS: YES ☐   NO ☐
IF YES, DESCRIBE / LOCATION:
STAINS: YES ☐   NO ☐
IF YES, DESCRIBE / LOCATION:
GLASS FRAGMENTS: YES ☐   NO ☐
IF YES, DESCRIBE / LOCATION:
SOIL / DIRT: YES ☐   NO ☐
IF YES, DESCRIBE / LOCATION:
TOOL MARKS: YES ☐   NO ☐
IF YES, DESCRIBE / LOCATION:
LIQUID: YES ☐   NO ☐
IF YES, DESCRIBE / LOCATION:
OTHER: YES ☐   NO ☐
IF YES, DESCRIBE / LOCATION:

COMPLETED BY:	
CASE #:	DATE:

SHOE / TIRE TRACKS AND CASTING INFORMATION	(SEC. 11-E)

SHOE TRACKS AT SCENE: YES ☐ NO ☐ SEE SHOE TRACK DIAGRAM: YES ☐ NO ☐

LOCATION / DESCRIBE:

CASTING: YES ☐ NO ☐	ELECTRO-STATIC LIFT: YES ☐ NO ☐
PHOTOGRAPHS: YES ☐ NO ☐	DIAGRAMED: YES ☐ NO ☐
OFFICER:	DATE:	TIME:

REMARKS

TIRE TRACKS AT SCENE: YES ☐ NO ☐

LOCATION / DESCRIBE:

CASTING: YES ☐ NO ☐	ELECTRO-STATIC LIFT: YES ☐ NO ☐
PHOTOGRAPHS: YES ☐ NO ☐	DIAGRAMED: YES ☐ NO ☐
OFFICER:	DATE:	TIME:

REMARKS

COMPLETED BY:	
CASE #:	DATE:

VEHICLE INFORMATION	(SEC. 11-F)

VEHICLES AT THE CRIME SCENE

VEHICLE(S) AT THE CRIME SCENE: YES ☐ NO ☐ IF YES, LIST VEHICLE INFO.

VEHICLE(S) PROCESSED: YES ☐ NO ☐

VEHICLE INFORMATION	(SEC. 11-G)

VEHICLE #1

MAKE:	MODEL:	YEAR:	TAG:	ST.:

VIN#:   OWNER:

VEHICLE LOCATION:

VEHICLE PROCESSED: YES ☐ NO ☐

SEE VEHICLE PROCESSING SHEET: YES ☐ NO ☐

VEHICLE #2

MAKE:	MODEL:	YEAR:	TAG:	ST.:

VIN#:   OWNER:

VEHICLE LOCATION:

VEHICLE PROCESSED: YES ☐ NO ☐

SEE VEHICLE PROCESSING SHEET: YES ☐ NO ☐

VEHICLE #3

MAKE:	MODEL:	YEAR:	TAG:	ST.:

VIN#:   OWNER:

VEHICLE LOCATION:

VEHICLE PROCESSED: YES ☐ NO ☐

SEE VEHICLE PROCESSING SHEET: YES ☐ NO ☐

SEE ATTACHED SHEET FOR ADDITIONAL VEHICLES: YES ☐ NO ☐

REMARKS

COMPLETED BY:

CASE #:	DATE:

SECTION 12	CRIME SCENE RELEASE INFORMATION

RELEASE INFORMATION	(SEC. 12-A)

SCENE RELEASED AUTH. OF:		DATE:	TIME:
CLEARED BY: DETECTIVE YES ☐ NO ☐	D.A. / CO. ATTY. YES ☐ NO ☐		
SCENE SECURED AT TIME OF RELEASE: YES ☐ NO ☐			
IF YES, METHOD USED:			
SCENE RELEASED BY:		DATE:	TIME:
SCENE RELEASED TO:		PHONE #:	
ADDRESS:	CITY:		STATE:

REMARKS

COMPLETED BY:	
CASE #:	DATE:

SECTION 13	CRIME SCENE RELEASE INFORMATION	(SEC.13-A)

Death Scene Investigation
Check List: Logs and Forms

CRIME SCENE ENTRY LOG				(Section 14-A)
CASE #:		LOCATION :		DATE:
DATE	TIME ENTERED	TIME EXITED	OFFICER	REASON

REMARKS

COMPLETED BY:

CRIME SCENE SECURITY LOG				(Section 14-B)
CASE #:		LOCATION :		DATE:

DATE	TIME STARTED	TIME ENDED	OFFICER	LOCATION

REMARKS

COMPLETED BY:	
CASE #:	DATE:

PHOTOGRAPHIC LOG	(Section 14-C)

LOCATION:

Photographer:		Date:	

Camera:	Lens:	Macro:	Filter:
Digital SLR ☐	Digital point & shoot ☐	Film SLR ☐	Point & shoot ☐
Film type: Color print ☐	Color slide ☐	Black and white ISO ☐	Digital ☐

NO.	Photograph Description	Location

Page: **of**

COMPLETED BY:

EVIDENCE RECOVERY LOG			(Section 14-D)
Item No.	Description:	Location:	Date / Time Collected Hrs.
Photos: YES NO ☐ ☐	Diagram: YES NO ☐ ☐	Collected by:	
Item No.	Description:	Location:	Date / Time Collected Hrs.
Photos: YES NO ☐ ☐	Diagram: YES NO ☐ ☐	Collected by:	
Item No.	Description:	Location:	Date / Time Collected Hrs.
Photos: YES NO ☐ ☐	Diagram: YES NO ☐ ☐	Collected by:	
Item No.	Description:	Location:	Date / Time Collected Hrs.
Photos: YES NO ☐ ☐	Diagram: YES NO ☐ ☐	Collected by:	
Item No.	Description:	Location:	Date / Time Collected Hrs.
Photos: YES NO ☐ ☐	Diagram: YES NO ☐ ☐	Collected by:	
Item No.	Description:	Location:	Date / Time Collected Hrs.
Photos: YES NO ☐ ☐	Diagram: YES NO ☐ ☐	Collected by:	
Item No.	Description:	Location:	Date / Time Collected Hrs.
Photos: YES NO ☐ ☐	Diagram: YES NO ☐ ☐	Collected by:	
Item No.	Description:	Location:	Date / Time Collected Hrs.
Photos: YES NO ☐ ☐	Diagram: YES NO ☐ ☐	Collected by:	
Item No.	Description:	Location:	Date / Time Collected Hrs.
Photos: YES NO ☐ ☐	Diagram: YES NO ☐ ☐	Collected by:	
Item No.	Description:	Location:	Date / Time Collected Hrs.
Photos: YES NO ☐ ☐	Diagram: YES NO ☐ ☐	Collected by:	

Page: of

COMPLETED BY:

SCENE DIAGRAM FORM	(Section 14-E)

CASE #:	LOCATION :	DATE:

COMPLETED BY:

DIRECTION

THREE-DIMENSIONAL DIAGRAM WORKSHEET											(Section 14-F)
Case #		Date:		Address:					Room:		

Item No.	Description	Left - Right	Front - Back	Top - Bottom	Floor - Top	Back - Wall	Side - Wall	Room Location		Room Location	
A	Sofa	72″	36″	34″	38″	6″	32″	106″	N	39″	W

REMARKS

COMPLETED BY:

SHOE TRACK DIAGRAM FORM	(Section 14-G)

CASE #:	LOCATION :	DATE:

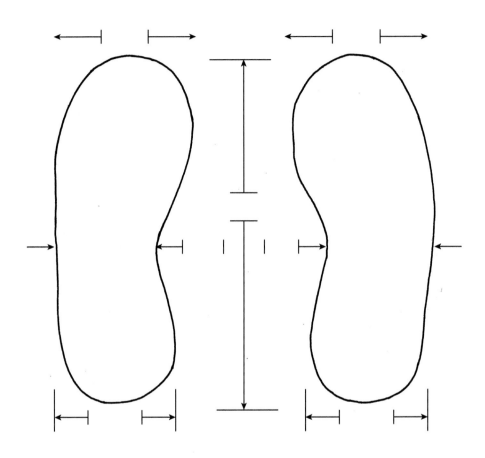

REMARKS

COMPLETED BY:

VEHICLE DIAGRAM SHEET	(Section 14-H)

CASE #:	DATE:

VEHICLE INFORMATION			
MAKE:	MODEL:	YEAR:	COLOR:
VIN#:		TAG:	
RECORDING OFFICER:			

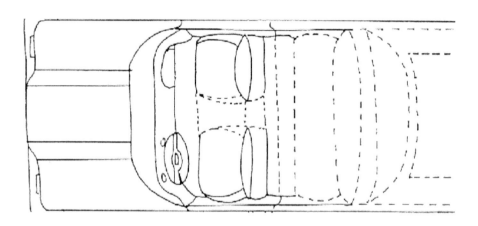

REMARKS

COMPLETED BY:

VEHICLE SEARCH FORM	(Section 14-I)

CASE #:	DATE:	TIME STARTED:	TIME ENDED:

PERSON IN CHARGE:	CO. ATTY. / D.A. PRESENT:
LOCATION:	DESCRIPTION:

OFFICERS PRESENT	
NAME:	AGENCY:
NAME:	AGENCY:
NAME:	AGENCY:
NAME:	AGENCY:
NAME:	AGENCY:

VEHICLE INFORMATION					
OWNER:			PHONE NUMBER:		
ADDRESS:			CITY:		STATE:
MAKE:	MODEL:	YEAR:	TAG #:		STATE:
VIN#:			2 DR: ☐ 4 DR: ☐ CAR ☐ TRUCK ☐		
COLOR: TOP:		BOTTOM:	EVIDENCE SEIZED: YES ☐ NO ☐		
SEE EVIDENCE RECOVERY LOG: YES ☐ NO ☐			VEHICLE INVENTORIED: YES ☐ NO ☐		

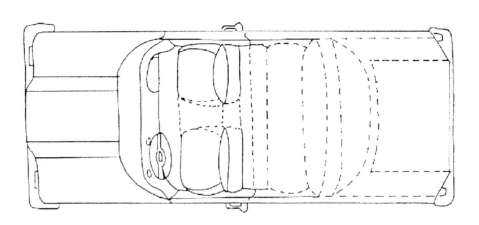

COMPLETED BY:

VEHICLE INVENTORY SHEET		(Section 14-J)

CASE #:	DATE:	

VEHICLE INVENTORIED: MAKE:		MODEL:
YEAR:	TAG #:	VIN #:
VEHICLE LOCATION:		

ITEM DESCRIPTION	ITEM LOCATION	COLLECTED YES	NO
		☐	☐
		☐	☐
		☐	☐
		☐	☐
		☐	☐
		☐	☐
		☐	☐
		☐	☐
		☐	☐
		☐	☐
		☐	☐
		☐	☐
		☐	☐
		☐	☐
		☐	☐
		☐	☐
		☐	☐
		☐	☐
		☐	☐
		☐	☐
		☐	☐
		☐	☐
		☐	☐
		☐	☐
		☐	☐
		☐	☐
		☐	☐
		☐	☐
		☐	☐
		☐	☐
		☐	☐
		☐	☐
		☐	☐

COMPLETED BY:	
CASE #:	DATE:

| BODY DIAGRAM (MALE) | (Section 14-K) |

VICTIM:

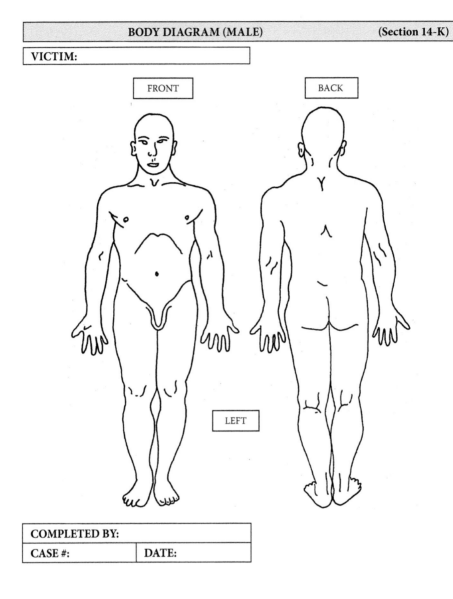

FRONT

BACK

LEFT

| COMPLETED BY: | |
| CASE #: | DATE: |

BODY DIAGRAM (FEMALE) (Section 14-L)

VICTIM:

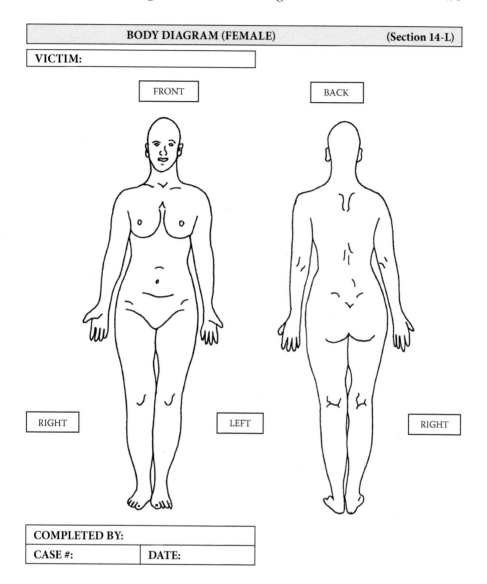

FRONT

BACK

RIGHT

LEFT

RIGHT

COMPLETED BY:

CASE #: DATE:

| BODY DIAGRAM (SIDE VIEW) | (Section 14-M) |

VICTIM:

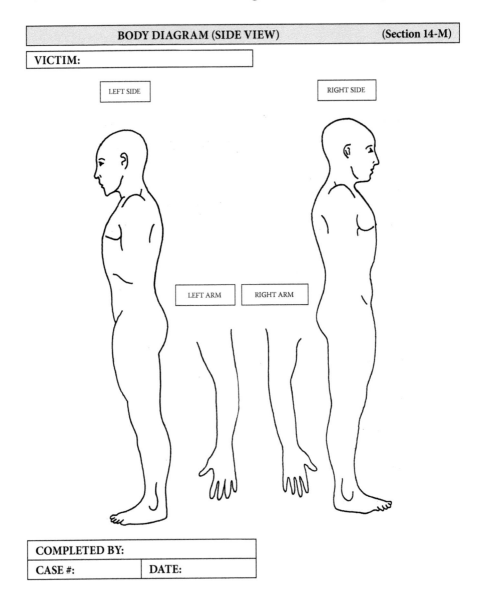

LEFT SIDE

RIGHT SIDE

LEFT ARM

RIGHT ARM

| **COMPLETED BY:** | |
| **CASE #:** | **DATE:** |

BODY DIAGRAM HEAD (SIDE VIEW) (Section 14-N)

VICTIM:

RIGHT

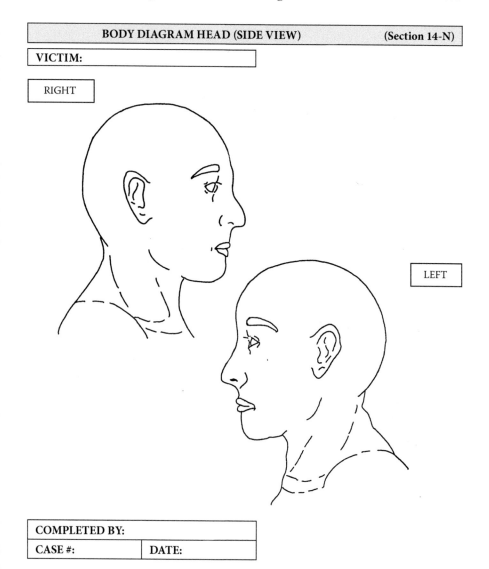

LEFT

COMPLETED BY:

CASE #: **DATE:**

BODY DIAGRAM HEAD (FRONT-REAR)   **(Section 14-O)**

VICTIM:

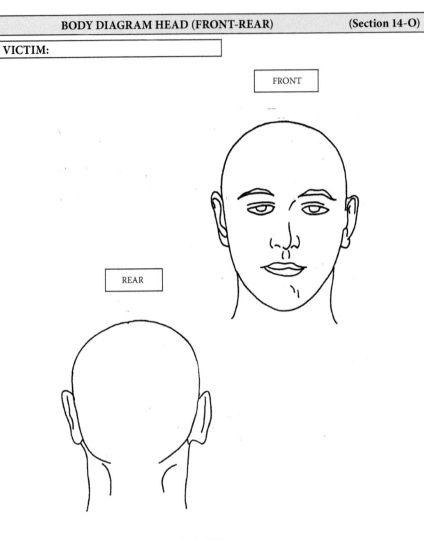

COMPLETED BY:	
CASE #:	DATE:

BODY DIAGRAM (HEAD & SHOULDERS) (Section 14-P)

VICTIM:

TOP VIEW HEAD AND SHOULDERS

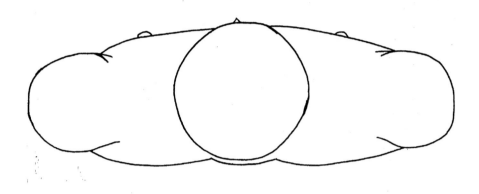

COMPLETED BY:	
CASE #:	DATE:

Supplemental Death Scene Worksheets

DEATH SCENE NOTES

TITLE: _____ DATE: _____

CASE NUMBER: _____ INVESTIGATOR: _____

TIME OF NOTIFICATION: _____ TIME OF ARRIVAL: _____ TIME OF DEPARTURE: _____

1. DEATH SCENE SURVEY - NOTES:

_____
_____
_____
_____
_____
_____
_____
_____
_____
_____
_____
_____
_____

3. SUPPLEMENTAL REPORTS:

[ ] DEATH SCENE ENTRY LOG   [ ] BIOLOGICAL EVIDENCE
[ ] PHOTOGRAPHY LOG   [ ] FRICTION RIDGE EVIDENCE
[ ] DEATH SCENE SKETCH   [ ] TRACE EVIDENCE
[ ] IMPRESSION EVIDENCE   [ ] TOOLMARK EVIDENCE
[ ] FIREARMS EVIDENCE   [ ] BITEMARK EVIDENCE
[ ] IMMERSION BURN WORKSHEET   [ ] BLOODSTAIN DOCUMENTATION
[ ] POST BLAST WORKSHEET   [ ] SHOOTING DOCUMENTATION

4. MISCELLANEOUS COMMENTS:

_____
_____
_____
_____
_____
_____
_____

Supplemental Notes:

_____
_____
_____
_____
_____
_____
_____
_____
_____
_____
_____
_____
_____
_____
_____
_____
_____
_____
_____
_____
_____
_____
_____
_____
_____
_____
_____
_____
_____
_____
_____
_____
_____
_____

Worksheet 1: Post Mortem Indicator (PMI)

Time (Hourly)	Livor Mortis			Rigor Mortis			Algor Mortis		
	Visible (Y or N)	Fixed (Y or N)	Consistent with Position (Y or N)	Present (Y or N)	Full or Partial (F or P)	Consistent with Position (Y or N)	Body Temp	Air Temp	Surface Temp

Method of Recording Temperature: [ ] Liver [ ] Rectal [ ] Axillary [ ] forehead scan [ ] eardrum

Title: _____   Date: _____

Case: _____   Investigator: _____

Worksheet 2: Death Scene Entry Log

Title: _____ Date: _____

Case Number: _____ Investigator: _____

Location: _____

Time Log Opened: _____ Opened By: _____

Already On-Scene:

_____

_____

_____

_____

_____

NAME	ORGANIZATION	TIME IN	TIME OUT

Worksheet 3: Photographic Head Slate

Photographic Head Slate

Department/Agency: _____

Case/Incident #: _____

Photographer: _____

Location: _____

Date: _____

0%	10%	20%	30%	40%	50%	60%	70%	80%	90%	100%

Worksheet 4: Photography Log

Title: _____ Date: _____

Case Number: _____ Investigator: _____

Camera: _____ Lens: _____

Filters: _____ Macro Lens: _____

[ ] Digital SLR   [ ] Digital Point & Shoot   [ ] Smartphone/Tablet _____

Accessories: [ ] Macro Lens   [ ] Off Camera Flash [ ] Filters _____

1. _____ _____

2. _____ _____

3. _____ _____

4. _____ _____

5. _____ _____

6. _____ _____

7. _____ _____

8. _____ _____

9. _____ _____

10. _____ _____

11. _____ _____

12. _____ _____

13. _____ _____

14. _____ _____

15. _____ _____

16. _____ _____

17. _____ _____

18. _____ _____

19. _____ _____

20. _____ _____

PAGE ___of ___

Worksheet 5: Post-Blast Scene Management

Team Assignments

SoB		
Zone 1		
Zone 2		
Zone 3		
Zone 4		

Case Information

Location	
Date	
Agency	
Case Title	

Item	Azimuth	Distance

Use sequential numbering for all items of evidence within a sector. They will later be designated 1-1, 2-1,3 -1,4-1, SoB-I based upon the sector in which they were found.

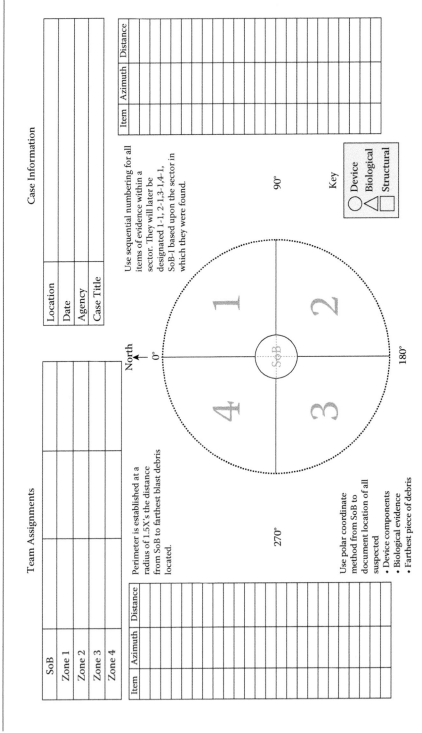

North

0°

90°

180°

270°

SoB

1

2

3

4

Key
○ Device
△ Biological
□ Structural

Perimeter is established at a radius of 1.5X's the distance from SoB to farthest blast debris located.

Use polar coordinate method from SoB to document location of all suspected
• Device components
• Biological evidence
• Farthest piece of debris

Item	Azimuth	Distance

Worksheet 6: Firearms Recovery Worksheet

TITLE: _____ DATE: _____

CCN: _____

Circumstances Of Recovery: _____

_____

WEAPON:

Handgun: ☐Automatic ☐Semi-Automatic ☐Revolver ☐Bolt Action ☐Break Action: ☐ Single shot ☐ Double shot

Rifle: ☐Automatic ☐Semi-Automatic ☐Magazine Fed ☐Tube Fed ☐Lever Action ☐ Break Action ☐Pump

Shotgun: ☐Automatic ☐Semi-Automatic ☐Pump ☐Break Action: ☐Single Barrel ☐Double Barrel ☐Bolt Action ☐Double Action ☐Single Action

Manufacturer: _____ Model: _____ Serial Number: _____

Other: _____

Safety: ☐On ☐pff ☐Left Handed ☐Right Handed

Decock Lever: ☐Left Handed ☐Right Handed

Magazine Release: ☐Left Handed ☐Right Handed

Magazine: ☐Fully Seated ☐Partially Seated ☐Removed Manufacturer: _____

Slide: ☐Forward ☐Locked to the Rear

Hammer: ☐Fully Cocked ☐3/4 Cocked ☐1/2 Cocked ☐1/4 Cocked ☐Not Cocked

AMMUNITION TYPE

Note: If ammunition differs, designate by cylinder number, magazine number or evidence item number.

☐Ball ☐Hollow Point ☐ Wad Cutter ☐Specialty: _____

☐Not Jacketed ☐Jacket ☐Semi-Jacketed ☐Other: _____

Caliber: ☐.22 ☐.25 ☐.32 ☐.38/357 ☐.380 ☐.41 ☐.44 ☐.45

Millimeter: ☐9mm ☐10mm

Gauge: ☐12 ☐16 ☐20 ☐28 ☐.410 Shot Size: _____

Manufacturer:_____ Make: _____ Lot Number: _____

Begin #1 with cylinder chamber which is in line with the barrel. Continue numbering clockwise or counterclockwise based upon the direction the cylinder turns. Package each round separately

1. ☐Fired ☐Misfire ☐Not Fired ☐Empty HeadStamp: _____
2. ☐Fired ☐Misfire ☐Not Fired ☐Empty HeadStamp: _____
3. ☐Fired ☐Misfire ☐Not Fired ☐Empty HeadStamp: _____
4. ☐Fired ☐Misfire ☐Not Fired ☐Empty HeadStamp: _____
5. ☐Fired ☐Misfire ☐Not Fired ☐Empty HeadStamp: _____
6. ☐Fired ☐Misfire ☐Not Fired ☐Empty HeadStamp: _____
7. ☐Fired ☐Misfire ☐Not Fired ☐Empty HeadStamp: _____
8. ☐Fired ☐Misfire ☐Not Fired ☐Empty HeadStamp: _____

Worksheet 7: Entomology Worksheet

Victim/Case Title: _____

Date/time neglect reported: _____/_____ Reported by: _____

Location of neglect:_____

Description of bldg/residence:_____

Condition/Injuries to victim's body:_____

Temperatures of victim's living area taken at various times around the clock (Ex: 3 hours)

Time:_____ Temp:_____ Time:_____ Temp:_____ Time:_____ Temp:_____

Time:_____ Temp:_____ Time:_____ Temp:_____ Time:_____ Temp:_____

Time:_____ Temp:_____ Time:_____ Temp:_____ Time:_____ Temp:_____

Description of Insect Infestation on victim:_____

_____

Description of Adult Insects Observed in Living Area:_____

_____

Insect Collection:

Largest larvae observed (live sample + kill sample)

Adult flies and other insects (sample of each placed in kill jar)

Pupae located in carpet, bedding, or other nearby area (live sample + kill sample)

Additional Information Needed:

Complete photographic coverage and sketch of living space

Status of Doors and Windows: (open/closed), broken screens, etc.

Observations about insects in other parts of the residence and their food sources

Area daily weather as reported by National Weather Service for time interval involved

Presence/absence of dirty diapers/underwear or other soiled clothing

Recovery of bedding, clothing, or other items used to cover victim before discovery

Presence/absence of open food in living space and other areas of residence

Humidity level of the main living area

Worksheet 8: Biological Evidence Notes

TITLE: _____ DATE: _____

CASE NUMBER: _____ INVESTIGATOR: _____

[ ] **SAMPLE**   LOCATION:
[ ] **Dry**   [ ] **Wet**   [ ] **Liquid**   [ ] **Tissue**

DETECTION METHOD:
[ ] Visible   [ ] Oblique   [ ] UV   [ ] FLS

COLLECTION METHOD:
[ ] Swab   [ ] Pipette   [ ] Swatch
[ ] Scraping   [ ] Forceps   [ ] Seize Item

PACKAGING METHOD:
Test Tube: [ ] Purple Top   [ ] Druggist Fold
                     [ ] Yellow Top   [ ] Envelope
                     [ ] Gray Top   [ ] Other _____

PRESUMPTIVE TEST:
[ ] Positive   [ ] Negative   [ ] Type: _____

[ ] **SAMPLE**   LOCATION:
[ ] **Dry**   [ ] **Wet**   [ ] **Liquid**   [ ] **Tissue**

DETECTION METHOD:
[ ] Visible   [ ] Oblique   [ ] UV   [ ] FLS

COLLECTION METHOD:
[ ] Swab   [ ] Pipette   [ ] Swatch
[ ] Scraping   [ ] Forceps   [ ] Seize Item

PACKAGING METHOD:
Test Tube: [ ] Purple Top   [ ] Druggist Fold
                     [ ] Yellow Top   [ ] Envelope
                     [ ] Gray Top   [ ] Other _____

PRESUMPTIVE TEST:
[ ] Positive   [ ] Negative   [ ] Type: _____

[ ] **SAMPLE**   LOCATION:
[ ] **Dry**   [ ] **Wet**   [ ] **Liquid**   [ ] **Tissue**

DETECTION METHOD:
[ ] Visible   [ ] Oblique   [ ] UV   [ ] FLS

COLLECTION METHOD:
[ ] Swab   [ ] Pipette   [ ] Swatch
[ ] Scraping   [ ] Forceps   [ ] Seize Item

PACKAGING METHOD:
Test Tube: [ ] Purple Top   [ ] Druggist Fold
                     [ ] Yellow Top   [ ] Envelope
                     [ ] Gray Top   [ ] Other _____

PRESUMPTIVE TEST:
[ ] Positive   [ ] Negative   [ ] Type: _____

Worksheet 9: Trace Evidence Notes

TITLE: _____ DATE: _____

CASE NUMBER: _____ INVESTIGATOR: _____

[ ] **SAMPLE**   **LOCATION:**
[ ] **Hair**   [ ] **Fiber**   [ ] **Soil**   [ ] **Building Material**
[ ] **Explosive Residue**   [ ] **Fire Residue**

DETECTION METHOD:
[ ] Visible   [ ] Oblique   [ ] UV   [ ] FLS
[ ] Hydrocarbon Detector   [ ] Aromatic   [ ] Canine

COLLECTION METHOD:
[ ] Swab   [ ] Pipette   [ ] Swatch
[ ] Scraping   [ ] Forceps   [ ] Seize Item

PACKAGING METHOD:
[ ] Test Tube   [ ] Druggist Fold   [ ] Paint Can
[ ] Envelope   [ ] Tape Lift   [ ]Other _____

[ ] **SAMPLE**   **LOCATION:**
[ ] **Hair**   [ ] **Fiber**   [ ] **Soil**   [ ] **Building Material**
[ ] **Explosive Residue**   [ ] **Fire Residue**

DETECTION METHOD:
[ ] Visible   [ ] Oblique   [ ] UV   [ ] FLS
[ ] Hydrocarbon Detector   [ ] Aromatic   [ ] Canine

COLLECTION METHOD:
[ ] Swab   [ ] Pipette   [ ] Swatch
[ ] Scraping   [ ] Forceps   [ ] Seize Item

PACKAGING METHOD:
[ ] Test Tube   [ ] Druggist Fold   [ ] Paint Can
[ ] Envelope   [ ] Tape Lift   [ ]Other _____

[ ] **SAMPLE**   **LOCATION:**
[ ] **Hair**   [ ] **Fiber**   [ ] **Soil**   [ ] **Building Material**
[ ] **Explosive Residue**   [ ] **Fire Residue**

DETECTION METHOD:
[ ] Visible   [ ] Oblique   [ ] UV   [ ] FLS
[ ] Hydrocarbon Detector   [ ] Aromatic   [ ] Canine

COLLECTION METHOD:
[ ] Swab   [ ] Pipette   [ ] Swatch
[ ] Scraping   [ ] Forceps   [ ] Seize Item

PACKAGING METHOD:
[ ] Test Tube   [ ] Druggist Fold   [ ] Paint Can
[ ] Envelope   [ ] Tape Lift   [ ]Other

Worksheet 10: Friction Ridge Evidence

TITLE: _____ DATE: _____

CASE NUMBER: _____ INVESTIGATOR: _____

[ ] **PRINT**   LOCATION:
[ ] **Finger**   [ ] **Palm**   [ ] **Lip**   [ ] **Foot**
[ ] **Partial**   [ ] **Unknown**

DETECTION METHOD:
[ ] Visible   [ ] Oblique   [ ] UV   [ ] FLS

PROCESSING METHOD:
[ ] Standard Powder   [ ] Magnetic Powder   [ ] Fluorescent   [ ] Black
[ ] White/Gray   [ ] Bichromatic   [ ] Fluorescent
[ ] Cyanoacrylate Fuming

COLLECTION METHOD:
[ ] Photograph   [ ] 35mm   [ ] 1:1   [ ] Polaroid
[ ] Tape   [ ] Gel Lift   [ ] Mikrosil   [ ] Seize Item

[ ] **PRINT**   LOCATION:
[ ] **Finger**   [ ] **Palm**   [ ] **Lip**   [ ] **Foot**
[ ] **Partial**   [ ] **Unknown**

DETECTION METHOD:
[ ] Visible   [ ] Oblique   [ ] UV   [ ] FLS

PROCESSING METHOD:
[ ] Standard Powder   [ ] Magnetic Powder   [ ] Fluoresce   [ ] Black
[ ] White/Gray   [ ] Bichromatic   [ ] Fluorescent
[ ] Cyanoacrylate Fuming

COLLECTION METHOD:
[ ] Photograph   [ ] 35mm   [ ] 1:1   [ ] Polaroid
[ ] Tape   [ ] Gel Lift   [ ] Mikrosil   [ ] Seize Item

[ ] **PRINT**   LOCATION:
[ ] **Finger**   [ ] **Palm**   [ ] **Lip**   [ ] **Foot**
[ ] **Partial**   [ ] **Unknown**

DETECTION METHOD:
[ ] Visible   [ ] Oblique   [ ] UV   [ ] FLS

PROCESSING METHOD:
[ ] Standard Powder   [ ] Magnetic Powder   [ ] Fluorescent   [ ] Black
[ ] White/Gray   [ ] Bichromatic   [ ] Fluorescent
[ ] Cyanoacrylate Fuming

COLLECTION METHOD:
[ ] Photograph   [ ] 35mm   [ ] 1:1   [ ] Polaroid
[ ] Tape   [ ] Gel Lift   [ ] Mikrosil   [ ] Seize Item

PAGE ___of ___   INITIALS ____

Worksheet 11: Impression Evidence Notes

TITLE: _____ DATE: _____

CASE NUMBER: _____ INVESTIGATOR: _____

[ ] **IMPRESSION**

| [ ] **Foot Print** | [ ] **Foot Wear** | [ ] **Tire Print** | [ ] **Toolmark** | [ ] **Bitemark** |
| [ ] **Soil** | [ ] **Sand** | [ ] **Mud** | [ ] **Underwater** | [ ] **Snow** |

PHOTOGRAPHY: [ ] Without Scale [ ] With Scale

CASTING METHOD:

| [ ] Dental Stone | [ ] Alginate | [ ] Tape | [ ] Stair-lift |
| [ ] Mikrosil | [ ] Silicon Rubber | [ ] Snow Print Wax | [ ] Electro-Static Print Lifter |

[ ] **IMPRESSION**

| [ ] **Foot Print** | [ ] **Foot Wear** | [ ] **Tire Print** | [ ] **Toolmark** | [ ] **Bitemark** |
| [ ] **Soil** | [ ] **Sand** | [ ] **Mud** | [ ] **Underwater** | [ ] **Snow** |

PHOTOGRAPHY: [ ] Without Scale [ ] With Scale

CASTING METHOD:

| [ ] Dental Stone | [ ] Alginate | [ ] Tape | [ ] Stair-lift |
| [ ] Mikrosil | [ ] Silicon Rubber | [ ] Snow Print Wax | [ ] Electro-Static Print Lifter |

Worksheet 12: Immersion Burn Worksheet

CASE NUMBER: _____ DATE: _____

TITLE: _____ TIME: _____

VICTIM: _____

LOCATION: _____

TYPE OF BASIN: ☐Bathtub ☐Bathroom Sink ☐Kitchen Sink ☐Other:

MEASUREMENTS: Width _____ Length _____ Depth _____ Other _____

MATERIAL: ☐Porcelain ☐Fiberglass ☐Steel ☐Iron ☐Plastic ☐Other_____

MANUFACTURER: _____ MODEL: _____

TYPE OF FIXTURES: ☐Single Temperature Control ☐Dual Temperature Control
☐Spray Attachment ☐Shower Head ☐Bathtub Spout
☐Single Spout ☐Separate Hot/Cold Spouts

MANUFACTURER: _____ MODEL: _____

HOT WATER HEATER:

MANUFACTURER: _____MAKE: _____ MODEL: _____

SERIAL NUMBER: _____ CAPACITY: _____

THERMOSTAT SETTING: Upper _____ Lower _____

RUNNING WATER TEMPERATURES			
HOT WATER		COLD WATER	
seconds	temperature	seconds	temperature
0		0	
5		5	
10		10	
20		20	
30		30	
40		40	
50		50	
60		60	
70		70	
80		80	
90		90	
100		100	
110		110	

STANDING WATER - FULL HOT			
Temperature recorded from mid-basin at mid-depth			
FILL TIME		TEMPERATURE	
Measured from time			
water is turned off			
depth	time	minutes	temperature
1		0	
2		1	
3		5	
4		10	
5		15	
6		20	
7		25	
8		30	
9		35	
10		40	

_____ ran a separate basin of water at my request. The temperature was _____ degrees at a depth of _____ inches one minute after the water was turned off. Measurements were made at mid-basin, mid-depth.

Thermometer: Make:_____ Model: _____ Size: _____ Range: _____

Worksheet 13: SIDS/SUIDS (sudden infant death)

Sudden Unexplained Infant Death Investigation

SUIDI
Reporting Form

INVESTIGATION DATA

Infant's Information: Last _____ First _____ M. _____ Case # _____

Sex: ☐ Male ☐ Female   Date of Birth ___/___/___   Age _____   SS# _____
                                    Month Day Year   Months

Race: ☐ White ☐ Black/African Am. ☐ Asian/Pacific Islander ☐ Am. Indian/Alaskan Native ☐ Hispanic/Latino ☐ Other

Infant's Primary Residence Address:
Address _____ City _____ County _____ State _____ Zip _____

Incident Address:
Address _____ City _____ County _____ State _____ Zip _____

Contact Information for Witness:

Relationship to the deceased: ☐ Birth Mother ☐ Birth Father ☐ Grandmother ☐ Grandfather
☐ Adoptive or Foster Parent ☐ Physician ☐ Health Records ☐ Other: _____

Last _____ First _____ M. _____ SS # _____

Home Address _____ City _____ State _____ Zip _____

Place of Work _____ City _____ State _____ Zip _____

Phone (H) _____ Phone (W) _____ Date of Birth ___/___/___
                                                    Month Day Year

WITNESS INTERVIEW

1 Are you the usual caregiver? ☐ Yes ☐ No

2 Tell me what happened: _____

3 Did you notice anything unusual or different about the infant in the last 24 hrs? ☐ No ☐ Yes ⇨ Describe:

4 Did the infant experience any falls or injury within the last 72 hrs? ☐ No ☐ Yes ⇨ Describe:

5 When was the infant *LAST PLACED?* .... ___/___/___ : _____ _____
                                                        Month Day Year Military Time Location (room)

6 When was the infant *LAST KNOWN ALIVE(LKA)?* ___/___/___ : _____ _____
                                                        Month Day Year Military Time Location (room)

7 When was the infant *FOUND?* .... ___/___/___ : _____ _____
                                                        Month Day Year Military Time Location (room)

8 Explain how you knew the infant was still alive. _____

9 Where was the infant - (P)laced, (L)ast known alive, (F)ound (circle P, L, or F in front of appropriate response)?

P L F Bassinet	**P L F** Bedside co-sleeper	**P L F** Car seat	**P L F** Chair
P L F Cradle	**P L F** Crib	**P L F** Floor	**P L F** In a person's arms
P L F Mattress/box spring	**P L F** Mattress on floor	**P L F** Playpen	**P L F** Portable crib
P L F Sofa/couch	**P L F** Stroller/carriage	**P L F** Swing	**P L F** Waterbed
P L F Other _____			

WITNESS INTERVIEW (cont.)

10 In what position was the infant *LAST PLACED*? ☐ Sitting ☐ On back ☐ On side ☐ On stomach ☐ Unknown
Was this the infant's usual position? ☐ Yes   ☐ No ⇨ What was the infant's usual position? _____

11 In what position was the infant *LKA*?   ☐ Sitting ☐ On back ☐ On side ☐ On stomach ☐ Unknown
Was this the infant's usual position? ☐ Yes   ☐ No ⇨ What was the infant's usual position? _____

12 In what position was the infant *FOUND*? ....☐ Sitting ☐ On back ☐ On side ☐ On stomach ☐ Unknown
Was this the infant's usual position? ☐ Yes   ☐ No ⇨ What was the infant's usual position? _____

13 FACE position when *LAST PLACED*? ..... ☐ Face down on surface   ☐ Face up   ☐ Face right ☐ Face left

14 NECK position when *LAST PLACED*?..... ☐ Hyperextended *(head back)* ☐ Flexed *(chin to chest)* ☐ Neutral ☐ Turned

15 FACE position when *LKA*? .... ☐ Face down on surface   ☐ Face up   ☐ Face right ☐ Face left

16 NECK position when *LKA*?...................... ☐ Hyperextended *(head back)* ☐ Flexed *(chin to chest)* ☐ Neutral ☐ Turned

17 FACE position when *FOUND*?................. ☐ Face down on surface   ☐ Face up   ☐ Face right ☐ Face left

18 NECK position when *FOUND*?................. ☐ Hyperextended *(head back)* ☐ Flexed *(chin to chest)* ☐ Neutral ☐ Turned

19 What was the infant wearing? *(ex. t-shirt, disposable diaper)* _____

20 Was the infant tightly wrapped or swaddled? ☐ No ☐ Yes ⇨ Describe: _____

21 Please indicate the types and numbers of layers of bedding both over and under infant (not including wrapping blanket):

Bedding UNDER Infant	None	Number	Bedding OVER Infant	None	Number
Receiving blankets	☐	____	Receiving blankets	☐	____
Infant/child blankets	☐	____	Infant/child blankets	☐	____
Infant/child comforters *(thick)*	☐	____	Infant/child comforters *(thick)*	☐	____
Adult comforters/duvets	☐	____	Adult comforters/duvets	☐	____
Adult blankets	☐	____	Adult blankets	☐	____
Sheets	☐	____	Sheets	☐	____
Sheepskin	☐	____	Pillows	☐	____
Pillows	☐	____	Other, specify: _____		
Rubber or plastic sheet	☐	____			
Other, specify: _____					

22 Which of the following devices were operating in the infant's room?
☐ None ☐ Apnea monitor ☐ Humidifier ☐ Vaporizer ☐ Air purifier ☐ Other _____

23 What was the temperature of the infant's room? ☐ Hot ☐ Cold ☐ Normal ☐ Other _____

24 Which of the following items were near the infant's face, nose, or mouth?
☐ Bumper pads ☐ Infant pillows ☐ Positional supports ☐ Stuffed animals ☐ Toys ☐ Other _____

25 Which of the following items were within the infant's reach? ☐ Blankets   ☐ Toys   ☐ Pillows
☐ Pacifier   ☐ Nothing   ☐ Other_____

26 Was anyone sleeping with the infant? ☐ No   ☐ Yes ⇨ Name these people.

Name	Age	Height	Weight	Location in Relation to Infant	Impaired *(intoxicated, tired)*

27 Was there evidence of wedging?   ☐ No   ☐ Yes ⇨ Describe: _____

28 When the infant was found, was s/he: ☐ Breathing ☐ Not breathing
If not breathing, did you witness the infant stop breathing? ☐ No ☐ Yes

WITNESS INTERVIEW (cont.)

29 What had led you to check on the infant? _____

30 Describe infant's appearance when found.

	Unknown	No	Yes	Describe and specify location:
a) Discoloration around face/nose/mouth	☐	☐	☐ ⇨	_____
b) Secretions *(foam, froth)*	☐	☐	☐ ⇨	_____
c) Skin discoloration *(livor mortis)*	☐	☐	☐ ⇨	_____
d) Pressure marks *(pale areas, blanching)*	☐	☐	☐ ⇨	_____
e) Rash or petechiae *(small, red blood spots on skin, membranes, or eyes)*	☐	☐	☐ ⇨	_____
f) Marks on body *(scratches or bruises)*	☐	☐	☐ ⇨	_____
g) Other	☐	☐	☐ ⇨	_____

31 What did the infant feel like when found? *(Check all that apply.)*

☐ Sweaty ☐ Warm to touch ☐ Cool to touch
☐ Limp, flexible ☐ Rigid, stiff ☐ Unknown
☐ Other ⇨ Specify: _____

32 Did anyone else other than EMS try to resuscitate the infant? ☐ No ☐ Yes ⇨ Who and when?

Who _____   ___/___/___   ___:___
Month Day Year   Military Time

33 Please describe what was done as part of resuscitation:
_____
_____

34 Has the parent/caregiver ever had a child die suddenly and unexpectedly? ☐ No ☐ Yes ⇨ Explain
_____

INFANT MEDICAL HISTORY

1 Source of medical information: ☐ Doctor ☐ Other healthcare provider ☐ Medical record
☐ Mother/primary caregiver ☐ Family ☐ Other: _____

2 In the 72 hours prior to death, did the infant have:

	Unknown	No	Yes			Unknown	No	Yes
a) Fever	☐	☐	☐	h) Diarrhea		☐	☐	☐
b) Excessive sweating	☐	☐	☐	i) Stool changes		☐	☐	☐
c) Lethargy or sleeping more than usual	☐	☐	☐	j) Difficulty breathing		☐	☐	☐
d) Fussiness or excessive crying	☐	☐	☐	k) Apnea *(stopped breathing)*		☐	☐	☐
e) Decrease in appetite	☐	☐	☐	l) Cyanosis *(turned blue/gray)*		☐	☐	☐
f) Vomiting	☐	☐	☐	m) Seizures or convulsions		☐	☐	☐
g) Choking	☐	☐	☐	n) Other, specify _____				

3 In the 72 hours prior to death, was the infant injured or did s/he have any other condition(s) not mentioned?

☐ No ☐ Yes ⇨ Describe: _____

4 In the 72 hours prior to the infants' death, was the infant given any vaccinations or medications?
(Please include any home remedies, herbal medications, prescription medicines, over-the-counter medications.)

☐ No ☐ Yes ⇨ List below:

Name of vaccination or medication	Dose last given	Date given (Month Day Year)	Approx. time (Military Time)	Reasons given/ comments:
1.		___/___/___	___:___	
2.		___/___/___	___:___	
3.		___/___/___	___:___	
4.		___/___/___	___:___	

INFANT MEDICAL HISTORY (cont.)

5 At any time in the infant's life, did s/he have a history of?

	Unknown	No	Yes	Describe:
a) Allergies *(food, medication, or other)*	☐	☐	☐	⇨ _____
b) Abnormal growth or weight gain/loss	☐	☐	☐	⇨ _____
c) Apnea *(stopped breathing)*	☐	☐	☐	⇨ _____
d) Cyanosis *(turned blue/gray)*	☐	☐	☐	⇨ _____
e) Seizures or convulsions	☐	☐	☐	⇨ _____
f) Cardiac *(heart)* abnormalities	☐	☐	☐	⇨ _____
g) Metabolic disorders	☐	☐	☐	⇨ _____
h) Other	☐	☐	☐	⇨ _____

6 Did the infant have any birth defects(s)? ☐ No ☐ Yes

Describe: _____

7 Describe the two most recent times that the infant was seen by a physician or health care provider:
(Include emergency department visits, clinic visits, hospital admissions, observational stays, and telephone calls)

	First most recent visit	Second most recent visit
a) Date	___/___/___ Month Day Year	___/___/___ Month Day Year
b) Reason for visit	_____	_____
c) Action taken	_____	_____
d) Physician's name	_____	_____
e) Hospital/clinic	_____	_____
f) Address	_____	_____
g) City	_____	_____
h) State, ZIP	_____	_____
i) Phone number	(___) - _____	(___) - _____

8 Birth hospital name: _____

Street _____

City _____ State _____ Zip _____

Date of discharge ___/___/___
Month Day Year

9 What was the infant's length at birth? _____ inches **or** _____ centimeters

10 What was the infant's weight at birth? _____ pounds _____ ounces **or** _____ grams

11 Compared to the delivery date, was the infant born on time, early, or late?
☐ On time ☐ Early—How many weeks early?_____ ☐ Late—How many weeks late?_____

12 Was the infant a singleton, twin, triplet, or higher gestation?
☐ Singleton ☐ Twin ☐ Triplet ☐ Quadruplet or higher gestation

13 Were there any complications during delivery or at birth? *(emergency c-section, child needed oxygen)*
☐ No ☐ Yes ⇨ Describe the complications: _____

_____

_____

14 Are there any alerts to pathologist? *(previous infant deaths in family, newborn screen results)*
☐ No ☐ Yes ⇨ Specify: _____

_____

_____

INFANT DIETARY HISTORY

1 On what day and at what approximate time was the infant last fed?

_____ / _____ / _____   _____ : _____
Month   Day   Year   Military Time

2 What is the name of the person who last fed the infant? _____

3 What is his/her relationship to the infant? _____

4 What foods and liquids was the infant fed in the <u>last 24 hours</u> (include last fed)?

	Unknown	No	Yes	Quantity	Specify: (type and brand if applicable)
a) Breast milk (one/both sides, length of time)	☐	☐	☐	⇨ _____ ounces	_____
b) Formula (brand, water source - ex. Similac, tap water)	☐	☐	☐	⇨ _____ ounces	_____
c) Cow's milk	☐	☐	☐	⇨ _____ ounces	_____
d) Water (brand, bottled, tap, well)	☐	☐	☐	⇨ _____ ounces	_____
e) Other liquids (teas, juices)	☐	☐	☐	⇨ _____ ounces	_____
f) Solids	☐	☐	☐	⇨	_____
g) Other	☐	☐	☐	⇨	_____

5 Was a new food introduced in the 24 hours prior to his/her death?

☐ No   ☐ Yes ⇨ Describe (ex. content, amount, change in formula, introduction of solids)

_____
_____
_____

6 Was the infant last placed to sleep with a bottle?

☐ Yes   ☐ No ⇨ Skip to question **9** below

7 Was the bottle propped? (i.e., object used to hold bottle while infant feeds)

☐ No   ☐ Yes ⇨ What object was used to prop the bottle? _____

8 What was the quantity of liquid (in ounces) in the bottle? _____

9 Did death occur during?   ☐ Breast-feeding   ☐ Bottle-feeding   ☐ Eating solid foods   ☐ Not during feeding

10 Are there any factors, circumstances, or environmental concerns that may have impacted the infant that have not yet been identified? (ex. exposed to cigarette smoke or fumes at someone else's home, infant unusually heavy, placed with positional supports or wedges)

☐ No   ☐ Yes ⇨ Describe concerns: _____

_____
_____
_____

PREGNANCY HISTORY

1 Information about the infant's birth mother:

First name _____   Middle name _____

Last name _____   Maiden name _____

Date of Birth: _____ / _____ / _____   SS # _____ - _____ - _____
              Month Day Year

Current Address: _____   City _____   State _____   Zip _____

How long has the birth mother been a resident at this address? _____ and _____   Previous Address _____   City _____   State _____
                                                              Years Months

2 At how many weeks or months did the birth mother begin prenatal care?

_____ Weeks   _____ Months   ☐ No prenatal care   ☐ Unknown

3 Where did the birth mother receive prenatal care? (Please specify physician or other health care provider name and address.)

Physician/provider _____   Hospital/clinic _____   Phone (_____) _____

Street _____   City _____   State _____   Zip _____

PREGNANCY HISTORY (cont.)

4 During her pregnancy with the infant, did the birth mother have any complications?
(ex. high blood pressure, bleeding, gestational diabetes)
☐ No ☐ Yes ⇨ Specify: _____

5 Was the birth mother injured during her pregnancy with the infant? *(ex. auto accident, falls)*
☐ No ☐ Yes ⇨ Specify: _____

6 During her pregnancy, did she use any of the following?

	Unknown	No	Yes	Daily consumption		Unknown	No	Yes	Daily consumption
a) Over the counter medications	☐	☐	☐	_____	d) Cigarettes	☐	☐	☐	_____
b) Prescription medications	☐	☐	☐	_____	e) Alcohol	☐	☐	☐	_____
c) Herbal remedies	☐	☐	☐		f) Other	☐	☐	☐	_____

7 Currently, does any caregiver use any of the following?

	Unknown	No	Yes	Daily consumption		Unknown	No	Yes	Daily consumption
a) Over the counter medications	☐	☐	☐	_____	d) Cigarettes	☐	☐	☐	_____
b) Prescription medications	☐	☐	☐	_____	e) Alcohol	☐	☐	☐	_____
c) Herbal remedies	☐	☐	☐		f) Other	☐	☐	☐	_____

INCIDENT SCENE INVESTIGATION

1 Where did the incident or death occur? _____

2 Was this the primary residence? ☐ Yes ☐ No

3 Is the site of the incident or death scene a daycare or other childcare setting?
☐ Yes ☐ No ⇨ Skip to question **8** below.

4 How many children were under the care of the provider at the time of the incident or death? _____ *(under 18 years old)*

5 How many adults were supervising the child(ren)? _____ *(18 years or older)*

6 What is the license number and licensing agency for the daycare?
License number: _____ Agency: _____

7 How long has the daycare been open for business? _____

8 How many people live at the site of the incident or death scene?
_____ Number of adults *(18 years or older)* _____ Number of children *(under 18 years old)*

9 Which of the following heating or cooling sources were being used? *(Check all that apply.)*

☐ Central air   ☐ Gas furnace or boiler   ☐ Wood burning fireplace   ☐ Open window(s)
☐ A/C window unit   ☐ Electric furnace or boiler   ☐ Coal burning furnace   ☐ Wood burning stove
☐ Ceiling fan   ☐ Electric space heater   ☐ Kerosene space heater
☐ Floor/table fan   ☐ Electric baseboard heat   ☐ Other ⇨ Specify: _____
☐ Window fan   ☐ Electric (*radiant*) ceiling heat   ☐ Unknown

10 Indicate the temperature of the room where the infant was found unresponsive:
_____ Thermostat setting _____ Thermostat reading _____ Actual room temp. _____ Outside temp.

11 What was the source of drinking water at the site of the incident or death scene? *(Check all that apply.)*
☐ Public/municipal water source   ☐ Bottled water   ☐ Other ⇨ Specify: _____
☐ Well   ☐ Unknown

12 The site of the incident or death scene has: *(check all that apply)*

☐ Insects   ☐ Mold growth   ☐ Odors or fumes ⇨ Describe: _____
☐ Smoky smell *(like cigarettes)*   ☐ Pets   ☐ Presence of alcohol containers
☐ Dampness   ☐ Peeling paint   ☐ Presence of drug paraphernalia
☐ Visible standing water   ☐ Rodents or vermin ☐ Other ⇨ Specify: _____

13 Describe the general appearance of incident scene: *(ex. cleanliness, hazards, overcrowding, etc.)*
_____
_____
_____

INVESTIGATION SUMMARY

1 Are there any factors, circumstances, or environmental concerns about the incident scene investigation that may have impacted the infant that have not yet been identified?

_____

_____

2 **Arrival times:** Law enforcement at scene: _____:_____   DSI at scene: _____:_____   Infant at hospital: _____:_____
                          Military Time   Military Time   Military Time

Investigator's Notes
Indicate the task(s) performed.

☐ Additional scene(s)? (forms attached)   ☐ Doll reenactment/scene re-creation   ☐ Photos or video taken and noted
☐ Materials collected/evidence logged   ☐ Referral for counseling   ☐ EMS run sheet/report
☐ Notify next of kin or verify notification ☐ 911 tape

If more than one person was interviewed, does the information differ?
☐ No   ☐ Yes ⇨ Detail any differences, inconsistencies of relevant information: *(ex. placed on sofa, last known alive on chair.)*

_____

_____

_____

_____

INVESTIGATION DIAGRAMS

1 Scene Diagram:

2 Body Diagram:

SUMMARY FOR PATHOLOGIST

Case Information

Investigator Information: Name _____ Agency _____ Phone _____

Investigated: ___/___/___ _____:_____ Pronounced Dead: ___/___/___ _____:_____
Month Day Year Military Time — Month Day Year Military Time

Infant's Information: Last _____ First _____ M. _____ Case # _____

Sex: ☐ Male ☐ Female   Date of Birth ___/___/___   Age _____ Months
Month Day Year

Race: ☐ White ☐ Black/African Am. ☐ Asian/Pacific Islander ☐ Am. Indian/Alaskan Native ☐ Hispanic/Latino ☐ Other

1 Indicate whether preliminary investigation suggests any of the following:

Yes No

Sleeping Environment

☐ ☐ Asphyxia (ex. overlying, wedging, choking, nose/mouth obstruction, re-breathing, neck compression, immersion in water)
☐ ☐ Sharing of sleep surface with adults, children, or pets
☐ ☐ Change in sleep condition (ex. unaccustomed stomach sleep position, location, or sleep surface)
☐ ☐ Hyperthermia/Hypothermia (ex. excessive wrapping, blankets, clothing, or hot or cold environments)
☐ ☐ Environmental hazards (ex. carbon monoxide, noxious gases, chemicals, drugs, devices)
☐ ☐ Unsafe sleep condition (ex. couch/sofa, waterbed, stuffed toys, pillows, soft bedding)

Infant History

☐ ☐ Diet (e.g., solids introduced, etc.)
☐ ☐ Recent hospitalization
☐ ☐ Previous medical diagnosis
☐ ☐ History of acute life-threatening events (ex. apnea, seizures, difficulty breathing)
☐ ☐ History of medical care without diagnosis
☐ ☐ Recent fall or other injury
☐ ☐ History of religious, cultural, or ethnic remedies
☐ ☐ Cause of death due to natural causes other than SIDS (ex. birth defects, complications of preterm birth)

Family Info

☐ ☐ Prior sibling deaths
☐ ☐ Previous encounters with police or social service agencies
☐ ☐ Request for tissue or organ donation
☐ ☐ Objection to autopsy

Exam

☐ ☐ Pre-terminal resuscitative treatment
☐ ☐ Death due to trauma (injury), poisoning, or intoxication

☐ ☐ Suspicious circumstances
☐ ☐ Other alerts for pathologist's attention

Any "Yes" answers should be explained and detailed.

Investigator Insight

Brief description of circumstances: _____
_____
_____
_____
_____
_____
_____
_____

Pathologist

2 Pathologist Information:

Name _____ Agency _____

Phone (_____) _____-_____ Fax (_____) _____-_____

Worksheet 14: Bullet Defect Worksheet

Case: _____
Examiner: _____

Designation	Perforating		Cartesian Coordinates		Trajectory			Penetrating			
	Entry	Exit	X (from Left)	Y (from floor)	Azimuth	Elevation	Gamma	Width	Length	Incident Angle

Worksheet 15: Bloodstain Pattern Worksheet

Case: _____

Examiner: _____

Pattern Designation	Stain Designation	Cartesian Coordinates		Individual Spatter				Distance to Convergence
		X (from Left)	Y (from floor)	Gamma Angle	Width	Length	Incident Angle	

Appendix A: Universal Precautions for Bloodborne Pathogens

Universal precaution—All biological materials are assumed to be contaminated.

Potentially infectious materials—A variety of harmful microorganisms can be transmitted through body fluids, including the hepatitis B virus (HBV) and the human immunodeficiency virus (HIV). Both HBV and HIV are transmitted through broken skin or mucous membrane contact but not via casual contact. Be alert for infectious materials at all death scenes.

Occupational Safety and Health Administration (OSHA) requirements—Your organizational protocols should comply with 29 CFR 1910.1030 (Bloodborne Pathogens), particularly for death scene investigators who face occupational exposure risks. Contact your local public health office for guidance.

Personal protective equipment (PPE)—Determine the appropriate combination of protective equipment. Consult medical specialists if you are unsure about appropriate PPE.

- Wear double gloves when handling infectious materials or infectious material containers.
- Wear full-body overgarments when the splashing or spread of contaminated materials or body fluids is possible (scenes involving large amounts of blood, body fluids, or tissues). Full-body coverage requires wearing a hood, surgical mask, and eye protection in contaminated areas.
- Use disposable booties if boots are not attached to the overgarment. Use disposable shoe coverings to prevent transport of contaminated fluids to vehicles, offices, and homes.
- Wear double latex gloves when processing a scene.
- Wrap duct tape or other suitable tape around wrists and ankles to secure sleeves to glove tops and overgarments to booties.
- Remove PPE before leaving an immediate death scene for any reason. Wash hands thoroughly with water and germicidal soap when leaving. Put on fresh or decontaminated PPE before reentering the scene.

Evidence collection safety—Presume all blood, body fluids, body tissues, sexual assault kits, used medical supplies, biological wastes, and drug paraphernalia are infectious. Other evidence at sexual assault, drug, assault, bodily injury, arson, and death scenes may also be infectious. Attach biohazard labels to all containers of potentially infectious materials.

- Control access to death scenes that contain potentially infectious materials. Limit access to only those who have an official need to enter.
- Pregnant investigators should not process death scenes where potentially infectious materials are present.
- Liquid blood, body fluids, and body tissue samples should be put into in leak-proof containers. Place the containers in sealable plastic bags for secondary containment. Some body fluids, especially blood and saliva, may need to be collected by a different method and air-dried (see Chapter 37).
- Be alert for sharp objects. Exercise extreme caution when handling needles, syringes, knives, razors, broken glass, nails, and other sharp objects. Mark "SHARP HAZARD" on containers for these items. Attach biohazard labels if required.
- If you are cut or your skin is punctured by a contaminated item, immediately cleanse the wound with an appropriate antiseptic and seek medical assistance.
- After processing a potentially infectious death scene, release the scene to the appropriate authorities responsible for decontamination of such scenes.

PPE removal and decontamination—Before leaving a scene, place a large piece of paper or plastic or a bed sheet on the floor of an unaffected area of the death scene near the perimeter. Stand in the center of the paper, plastic, or sheet. Remove each piece of PPE in the following order and ensure it remains on the paper, plastic, or sheet:

- Duct tape if worn
- Outer gloves if gloves are doubled
- Booties if separate from overgarment
- Surgical mask
- Eye protection
- Inner gloves (grasp wrist edge of first glove and pull it off inside out; remove second glove by sliding two fingers beneath the wrist of the second glove and pulling it off inside out: the two fingers should only touch the inside of the second glove)

- Decontaminate reusable PPE and equipment by hand washing the surfaces of each item with a solution of water and chlorine bleach (1 cup bleach to 1 gallon water). Let items air dry.
- Place disposable PPE in a biohazard bag for disposal (bags are usually red or orange and designated with a biohazard symbol on the fronts). Wear protective gloves and eye protection when decontaminating.
- Dispose of reusable PPE as infectious waste if it becomes damaged, saturated with infectious material, or otherwise unusable.
- Ask medical specialists to dispose of infectious waste such as pens, pencils, gowns, gloves, masks, and shoe covers by incineration.

Appendix B: Bloodstain Pattern Decision Tree

Nonspatter Stains

Version 2.4a 11/04/2013 Copyright Bevel, Gardner and Associates, Inc.

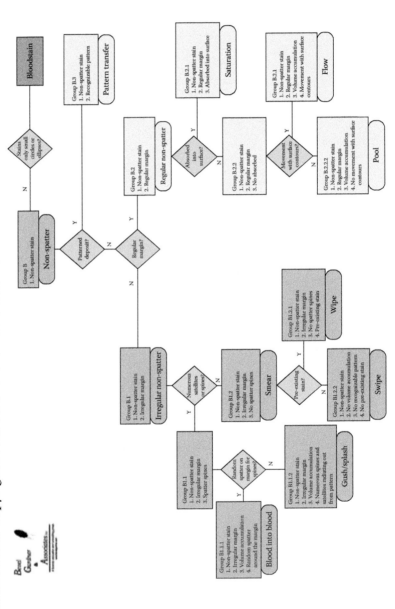

Spatter Stains

Version 2.4a 11/04/2013 Copyright Bevel, Gardner and Associates Inc.

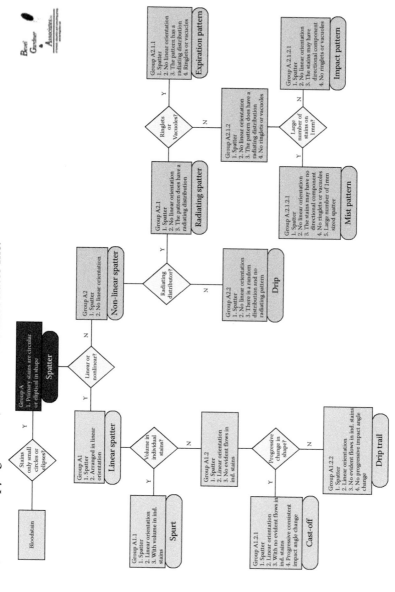

Appendix C: Druggist Fold

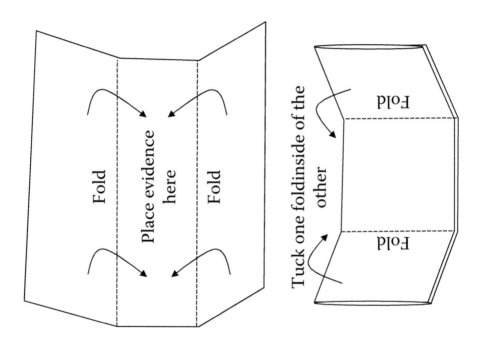

Index

A

Abdominal injuries, 240
Absorption of drugs, 220
Accidental deaths, 10, 25–38, 80
    death notifications, 37–38
    death scene interviews, 36
    death scene processing, 27–34
    definition of, 25
    evidence commonly associated with, 35
    examination of body, 34
    initial scene response, 26–27
    legal determination of death, 29
    outdoor death scenes, 34–35
    plan development, 29
    poisoning, 214–215
    related searches, 35
    review of operator training and
        certification, 35
    scene considerations, 27
    staged, 236–237
    team briefing, 29
    worksheets and documentation,
        25–26, 33
Acquaintance rape, 264–265
Adipocere development, 150
Adolescents, missing, 247–248
Aerial search, for human remains, 138
Algor mortis, 8, 149–150
Alibi sample, 388–389
Alternate light source (ALS), 267, 380
Amido Black, 402–403
Ancillary scenes, identification of,
    9, 279–280
Angled contact wounds, 185–187
Aquatic recovery, of human remains,
    137–145
    body processing, 145
    drift and, 140
    general principles, 137
    locating remains, 138–143
    marine predators and, 145
    scene processing, 143–145
    worksheets and documentation, 137–138

Arrival, at death scene, 5
Ashtray content, 326
Asphyxiation, 155–169
    autoerotic, 161–162, 255, 260–261
    chemical, 155, 165–168
    choking, 162
    drowning, 168–169
    hangings, 155
    hypoxic deaths, 255–260
    infant, 226
    mechanical, 155, 164–165
    smothering, 163–164
    strangulation, 155, 156–162
    worksheets and documentation, 155
Autoerotic asphyxiation, 161–162, 255,
    260–261
Automobile injuries, 180
Autopsy
    buried remains, 136
    in child deaths, 240–241
    circumstances requiring, 82, 87
    custody of evidence form, 100–101
    equipment, 88
    external examination, 89–90
    forensic, 82–84
    internal examination, 90, 98–99
    investigator's responsibilities at, 88–92
    medicolegal, 240–241
    outbrief, 101
    photography, 92–100, 313
    procedures in lieu of, 84, 87–88
    protocol, 87–101
    report, 84, 85
    videography of, 320

B

Baseline measurements, 298–300
Bathrooms, 326
Biological evidence, 369–377
    body and scene analysis, 371–372
    collection of, 370, 372–376
    fluids and stains, 370–376

packaging, 376–377
preservation of, 370
touch DNA, 369–370
Bite marks, 241, 407–409
Bites, 214
Blast lung, 199
Blast wave effect, 199
Bleach, 165
Blood
    detection of, 370–371
    prints in, 402–404
Bloodstain patterns, 331–340
    clothing, 339
    detection of, 331–334
    documentation of, through mapping,
        336–340
    isolate and identify discrete, 334–336
    nonspatter, 335–336
    photographing, 339–340
    sampling and collection, 340
    spatter, 334–335
Blows, blunt force, 178–180
BlueStar, 333–334
Blunt force injuries, 177–180, 197
Body. See Dead body; Human remains
Body temperature, 82, 149–150
Bondage, domination, sadism, masochism
        (BDSM), 257–260
Botanists, 108, 122, 127
Breath play, 255–257
Bruises, 182
Building materials, 387
Bullet defects
    chemical testing to determine, 347–350,
        389–390
    documentation of, 344–347
Bullets, recovery of, 343–344
Buried remains
    establishing grid, 129–130
    evidence recovery, 128
    exhumation of, 135–136
    general principles, 123
    grave excavation, 131–133
    impression evidence, 134
    indicators, 124–125
    locating remains, 124–128
    recovery of, 123–136
    sifting site, 130–131, 133
    soil evidence, 134
    surface documentation, 128
    surface preparation, 128–129
    worksheets and documentation, 123–124

Burns, 202–203, 236
    cigarette, 238–239
    contact, 238–239
    first-degree, 202
    fourth-degree, 203
    immersion, 236, 238–239
    second-degree, 202
    third-degree, 203

C

Cadaver dogs, 105, 114, 125–126, 140–141
Calendars, 326
Carbon dioxide, 212
Carbon monoxide, 165, 166, 167–168, 212
Cartridges, recovery of, 343–344
Cause of death, establishment of, 74–75, 80
Cell phones, 325–326
Central nervous system injuries, 239–240
Chemical asphyxia, 155, 165–168
Chemical enhancement, to detect
        bloodstain patterns, 332–334
Chest injuries, 240
Child abuse, physical, 236–241
Child deaths, 235–243
    body, 237–240
    medical record review, 241
    medicolegal autopsy, 240–241
    Munchausen syndrome by proxy, 242
    neglect, 243
    physical abuse and violence, 236–241
    questions for medical examiner in, 241
    worksheets and documentation, 235–236
Child neglect, 228
Child sexual abduction and murder,
        245–252
    abduction, 246
    body recovery, 251–252
    examination of suspect, 252
    missing adolescent report, 247–248
    missing child report, 246–247
    murder, 250–251
    pedophilia-related searches, 249–250
    scene processing, 248
    sexual assault, 248
    worksheets and documentation,
        245–246
Chlorine gas, 165, 212
Choking, 162
Chopping injuries, 171–175, 181–182
Cigarette burns, 238–239
Close range wounds, 194–195

Clothing, victim's, 350–351
Cocaine, 218, 219
Colored filters, 308, 318
Command briefings, 282
Command functions, 285
Commercial power sources, 205–206
Computers, 326
Confirmatory identification, 74, 79–80
Contact burns, 238–239
Contact gunshot wounds, 184–187
Contact shotgun wounds, 193–194
Control injuries, 31, 179–180
Contusions, 182
Coordination
  en route, 4
  on-scene, 5–6
Copper testing, 348–349, 389
Coroner, 15
  coordination with, 278
  death notifications by, 76–77
  at death scene, 75–77
  role of, 73–77
Coroner's inquest, 77
Criminal homicides, 80
Cutting injuries, 171–175
Cyanoacrylate, 370, 398–401

D

Date rape drugs, 265
Dead body
  See also Human remains
  child deaths, 237–240, 251–252
  chopping injuries, 182
  decomposition of, 150
  drug-related deaths, 221
  examination of, 20, 34, 46–48, 62
  explosive injuries, 198
  initial approach to, 6
  lightning strikes and, 207
  photographing, 19, 32–33, 45–46, 59–60,
    92–100, 311–313
  postmortem changes, 147–152
  postmortem indicators, 7–8
  prints on, 393–395
  processing, 19, 32, 45, 59, 81–82, 116, 145
  sharp force injuries, 172–175
  sketching, 19, 33, 46, 60, 293–295
  stomach contents of, 151
  trace evidence on, 379
  transportation of remains, 70
  videography of, 45–46, 319–320

Death
  accidental, 25–38, 80
  child, 235–243
  determining time of, 147–148
  drug-related, 217–221
  establishing cause of, 74–75, 80
  establishing manner of, 75, 80
  examining mechanism of, 31–32
  homicidal, 53–66, 80
  infant, 225–233
  initial notification of, 3–4
  legal determination of, 17, 29, 43, 57
  medically attended, 73
  medically unattended, 73
  natural, 13–23, 80
  preliminary determination of, 7
  rape and sexual assault resulting in,
    263–269
  sexual activities resulting in, 253–261
  suicidal, 39–51, 80
  undetermined, 80
Death notifications
  accidental deaths, 37–38
  by coroner, 76–77
  general guidelines, 22, 37, 65, 71, 76
  homicidal deaths, 65–66
  natural deaths, 22–23
  procedure, 23, 37–38, 65–66, 71–72,
    76–77
  suicidal deaths, 49–51
Death scene interviews
  accidental deaths, 36
  homicidal deaths, 63–64
  natural deaths, 21–22
  suicidal deaths, 49
Death Scene Investigation Checklist, 3
Death Scene Investigation Decision Tree, 10
Death scene investigators (DSIs)
  notification and response for, 3–11
  preparation by, 4
  role of, during autopsy, 87–101
Death scene management, 277–287
  ancillary scene identification, 279–280
  arrival and initial organization, 277
  available personnel, 284–285
  command functions, 285
  confirming scope of scene, 279
  control considerations, 281–282
  establishing scene controls, 280
  integrating with investigation, 285
  investigative strategy, 283–284
  legal concerns, 282–283

planning, 283–284
post-scene activities, 286–287
reports and follow-up analysis, 287
scene assessment, 283–284
scene completion, 286
scene considerations, 284
scene coordination, 278
scene documentation, 285
task prioritization, 277–278
team briefing, 18
Death scene photography. *See* Photography
Death scene processing, 15–16, 18
accidental deaths, 27–34
aquatic recovery, 143–145
drug-related deaths, 221
homicidal deaths, 55–57, 58
natural deaths, 15–16
suicidal deaths, 41–46
surface recovery of human remains, 116
Death scene response, 3–11
arrival at scene, 5
assessment, planning, and investigative
strategy, 10–11
coordination en route, 4
documentation of postmortem
indicators, 7–8
establishment of perimeter, 5, 8–9
homicidal deaths, 53–66
identification of ancillary scenes, 9
initial approach to body, 6
initial notification, 3–4
initial scene response, 14, 26–27, 40–41,
54–55, 355–357
legal concerns, 10, 14, 26–27, 41, 54–55,
355–356
natural deaths, 14–17
preliminary determination of death, 7
preparation for, 4
scene controls, 10
on-scene coordination, 5–6
suicidal deaths, 39–51
Death scenes
accidental deaths, 25–38
ancillary, 9
arrival at, 5
assessment, planning, and investigative
strategy, 10–11
child deaths, 236
chopping injuries, 182
considerations, 15
coordination en route to, 4
coroner's role at, 75–77

documentation, 3–4
drug-related deaths, 220–221
establishment of control of, 10
establishment of perimeter at, 5
explosive, 198, 355–362
general guidelines, 50
initial evaluation of, 6
lightning strikes, 206–207
medical examiner at, 81–82
multiple victim, 271–274
natural deaths, 13–23
notes and observations, 323–328
organization of, 16–17, 29, 42–43, 56–57
outdoor, 20, 34–35, 48, 62
primary, 15–16, 28, 42, 55–56
prints at, 395–398
procedure, 50–51
releasing, 286
on-scene coordination, 5–6
scene indicators, 152, 324–328
secondary, 16, 28, 42, 55–56
sharp force injuries, 172
shooting scenes, 341–353
taking control of, 16, 28–29, 42, 56
thermal injuries, 201–202
Death scene sketching. *See* Sketching
Death scene videography. *See* Videography
Deceased, establishing identity of, 74, 79–80
Decedent's physician, interview of, 22
Deceleration injuries, 179
Decomposition, 150
Defensive injuries, 173
Dermal absorption, of poisons, 214, 217, 220
Diaper Pail Fraternity (DPF), 250
Dining rooms, 325
Distant gunshot wounds, 188–189
Distant shotgun wounds, 196
Dithiooxamide (DTO), 348–349, 389
DNA evidence, 369–370, 398
Documentation
See also Worksheets and documentation
accidental deaths, 33
bloodstain patterns, 336–340
of bullet defects, 344–347
of entomological evidence, 367
firearms, 342
of gunshot residue, 351–352
postmortem indicators, 7–8
shooting scenes, 341–353
Drift, aquatic recovery and, 140
Drowning, 168–169
Drug-facilitated rape/sexual assault, 265

Drug-related deaths, 217–221
    absorption, 217, 220
    death scenes, 220–221
    evidence, 221
    insufflation/inhalation, 219–220
    intravenous, subdermal, and
        intramuscular injection, 218
    oral ingestion, 217, 218
    worksheets and documentation, 217–218
Dry drowning, 168
Dry stains, 374–375

E

Electrical injuries, 205–209
Electrical sensitivity, 127
Electrostatic dust print lifter, 421–422
Emergency medical services, 5
Entomological evidence, 363–367
Entrance wounds
    gunshot, 183–184
    shotgun, 191–193
Entries/exits, 324
Envenomation, 214
Environmental conditions, 327
Environmental controls, 325
Evidence
    associated with accidental deaths, 35
    associated with homicides, 62–63
    associated with suicide, 48
    from autopsy, custody of, 100–101
    biological, 369–377
    bloodstain patterns, 331–340
    of buried remains, 128
    buried remains, 134
    collecting and packaging, 361–362
    collection of, 7, 360–362, 370, 372–376,
        381–382
    DNA, 398
    documentation of, 7
    drug-related deaths, 221
    entomological, 363–367
    explosive scenes, 360–361
    friction ridge, 393–405
    hazardous materials, 392
    identification, 301
    impression, 134, 407–425
    liquids, 361
    packaging, 376–377, 382–383
    pattern, 301
    photographing, 100, 309
    physical assault, 267

post-scene activities, 286
    preservation of, 6, 7
    processing, 285
    recovery, in surface recovery of human
        remains, 119–120
    searching for, legal concerns, 282–283
    sexual assault, 266–267
    from shooting scenes, 341–343
    soil, 121, 134
    solids, 362
    trace, 379–392
    victim's clothing, 350–351
Exhumation, 123, 125, 135–136
Exigent circumstances, 10, 14, 26–27, 41,
    54–55, 282, 283
Exit hood/bag, 166–167
Exit wounds, 190, 196
Expedient graves, 117, 123, 124
Explosion to commit fraud, 356
Explosive incident scenes, 355–362
    blast scene mapping, 358–360
    commonly encountered evidence, 360–361
    establishing context, 356–357
    evidence collection, 360–362
    initial briefing, 357
    initial scene response, 355–357
    initial walk-through, 357
    processing guidelines, 357
Explosive injuries, 197–199
Explosive residue sampling, 361
Extremist bombers, 356

F

Failure to thrive, 227–228
Falling injuries, 236–237
Falls from a height, 179
Family members, interview of, 21–22
Fibers, 384
Filters, photographic, 307–308, 318
Final autopsy report, 85
Fingerprints, 90, 91, 393–404
Finished sketch, 289–291
Firearm evidence, 341–343
    recovery from victim, 349–353
Firearm injuries, 183–196
    pistols and rifles, 183–190
    shotguns, 191–196
    worksheets and documentation, 183
Firearms
    collecting and packaging, 343
    documentation of, 342

recovery from water, 343
recovery of cartridges, spent bullet cases, and bullets, 343–344
on-scene processing of, 342–343
Fire injuries, 201–204
First-degree burns, 202
First responders, interview of, 21, 36, 49, 63–64
Flash photography, 306–307
Flies, 151, 364
Fluorescein, 334
Follow-up activities, 287
Footwear impressions, 413–425
Forensic anthropologists, 107–108, 121, 127–128
Forensic autopsy, 82–84
Forensic entomology, 151, 367
Forensic pathologist, 82, 87
Forward-looking infrared (FLIR), 105, 115, 127, 141
Fourth-degree burns, 203
Fraud, explosion to commit, 356
Friction ridge evidence, 393–405
    chemical development of, 401–405
    on nonporous surfaces, 398–401
    on porous surfaces, 401
    prints at scene, 395–398
    prints on body/skin, 393–395
    Superglue fuming on skin, 395
    transfer lift method, 394–395
Fulgurate, 209

G

Garroting, 155, 157–158
Gel lifter, 423
Glass, 385–387
Global Positioning System (GPS), 300
Graves
    excavation of, 131–133
    expedient, 117, 123, 124
    shallow, 123, 124
Grid search, 110
Ground lightning strikes, 208–209
Ground search, for human remains, 105–111
    general guidelines, 108
    grid search, 110
    isolating search area, 105–107
    point-to-point search, 108–110
    scientific assistance, 107–108
    specific guidelines, 108
    spiral search, 111

GSR examination and collection, 36, 49, 64, 81, 351–352
Gunpowder patterns, 349–350
Gunshot residue, 351–352
Gunshot wounds, 183–196
    contact, 184–187
    distant, 188–189
    effects of distance on, 184–189
    entrance wounds, 183–184, 191–193
    exit wounds, 190
    intermediate range, 187–188
    near contact, 187
    pistols and rifles, 183–190
    rifle entrance, 189
    shotguns, 191–196
    worksheets and documentation, 183

H

Hairs, 384
Hands, bagging at scene, 47, 60, 82
Hanging, 155, 158–160
Hard contact head wounds, 193
Hard contact wounds, 184–185
Hazardous materials evidence, 392
Head injuries, 239–240
Heaters, carbon monoxide poisoning, 167
Helium, 166–167, 212
Heroin, 218
Hesitation wounds, 173
Hilt marks, 173, 174
Homicidal deaths, 11, 53–66, 80
    child, 250–251
    death notifications, 65–66
    death scene interviews, 63–64
    death scene processing, 55–57, 58
    definition of, 53
    evidence commonly associated with, 62–63
    examination of body, 62
    initial scene response, 54–55
    legal determination of death, 57
    mass murder, 273–274
    multiple victim, 271–274
    note taking, 60–61
    outdoor death scenes, 62
    photographing body, 59–60
    plan development, 57
    poisoning, 214
    processing the body, 59
    from rape and sexual assault, 263–269
    related searches, 63

scene considerations, 55
scene indicators, documenting, 59
scene organization, 56–57
serial murders, 271
sketching body, 60
spree killings, 272
taking control of scene, 56
team briefing, 57
worksheets and documentation, 53–54
Huffing, 165, 213, 219
Human remains
    See also Dead body
    aquatic recovery of, 137–145
    evidence on, 251–252
    exhumation of, 135–136
    interment of, 123
    locating, 138–143
    postmortem changes, 147–152
    recovery of buried, 123–136
    searching for, 105–111
    surface recovery of, 113–122
Hungarian Red, 403–404
Hydrogen sulfide, 212
Hypoxic deaths
    consensual, 255–257
    nonconsensual, 257–260

I

Identification
    confirmatory, 74, 79–80
    of deceased, 74, 79–80
    presumptive, 74, 79
Immersion burns, 236, 238–239
Impression evidence, 407–425
    bite marks, 407–409
    casting underwater, 416–417
    footwear, 413–425
    processing dry impressions, 421–424
    processing moist impressions, 424–425
    in sand/dust, 418
    in snow, 417–418
    three-dimensional, 411–412, 413–419
    tire, 413–425
    tool marks, 411–412
    tool marks in bone, 409–410
    two-dimensional, 410, 419–425
Incomplete contact wounds, 187
Infant deaths, 225–233
    asphyxial, 226
    dietary history, 231–232
    failure to thrive, 227–228

medical history, 232–233
mother's pregnancy history, 233
neglect causes, 228
shaken baby syndrome, 226–227, 240
sudden unexplained, 228–233
violent, 226
worksheets and documentation, 225–226
Information flow, 285
Infrared (IR) light
    to detect bloodstain patterns, 332
    to detect gunpowder patterns, 350
Ingested poisons, 213–214
Inhalation, 217, 219–220
Inhaled poisons, 212–213
Initial notification, 3–4
Initial scene evaluation, 6
Initial scene response, 277
    accidental deaths, 26–27
    homicidal deaths, 54–55
    natural deaths, 14
    suicidal deaths, 40–41
Injuries
    abdominal, 240
    automobile, 180
    blunt force, 177–180, 197
    burn, 238–239
    central nervous system, 239–240
    chest, 240
    chopping, 181–182
    control, 179–180
    deceleration, 179
    defensive, 173
    electrical, 205–209
    explosive, 197–199
    falls, 179
    firearm, 183–196
    head, 239–240
    penetrating, 199
    photographing, 96–98, 312–313
    sharp force, 171–175
    skeletal system, 237
    skin, 237–238
    thermal, 197, 201–204
    traumatic brain, 199
Injury mapping, 96–98, 173
Injury photographs, 96–98, 312–313
Inner perimeter, 8, 9, 15, 279
Insect infestation, 151, 365–366
Insects, 105, 363–367
    sample collection, 365–366
    in soil, 366
Insect succession, 363

Instars, 364
Insufflation, 217, 219–220
Intermediate range wounds, 187–188, 194–195
Interment of remains, 123
Internal examination, 90, 98–99
Internet, 326
Intimate partner
  examination of, 268
  in sexual activity-related deaths, 255, 257, 259–260
Intraoral wounds, 193–194
Intravenous ingestion, 217, 218
Investigative jurisdiction, 278
Investigative strategy, 10–11, 283–284

J

Juvenile bombers, 356
Juvenile vandal/delinquent bombers, 356

K

Ketamine, 218
Kidnapping, 246
Kitchens, 325

L

Laboratory issues, 286
Lacerations, 182
Langer's lines, 173, 175
Larvae, 363
Latent prints, 393–405
  chemical development of, 401–405
  from nonporous surfaces, 400
  on skin, 394
Laundry areas, 325
Lead testing, 349–350, 389–390
Legal concerns, 10, 14, 26–27, 41, 54–55, 282–283, 355–356
Lichtenberg figure, 206
Ligature strangulations, 155, 157–158
Lighting, 325
Lightning strikes, 206–209
Liquid evidence, 361
Liquid stains, 376
Liver temperature, 149
Livor mortis, 7, 147, 148
Locating remains
  aerial search, 138
  in aquatic recovery, 138–143

  cadaver dogs for, 140–141
  drift and, 140
  surface search, 138
  technological search, 141–143
  underwater search, 138–140
Loose contact wounds, 185
Luminol, 333–334

M

Maggots, 151, 363, 365
Magnetometry, 127, 143
Magnification, to detect trace evidence, 380
Mail, 326
Mammalogists, 122
Manner of death, establishment of, 75, 80
Manual strangulation, 156–157
Mapping
  blast scene, 358–360
  bloodstain patterns, 336–340
  bullet defects, 344–347
Marijuana, 219
Marine predators, 145
Mass murder, 273–274
ME. *See* Medical examiner
Measurement methods, 298–301
Mechanical asphyxia, 155, 164–165
Mechanism of death, examination of, 31–32
Media area, 281
Medical examiner (ME), 15, 69
  autopsy by, 82–84, 87–101
  coordination with, 278
  at death scene, 81–82
  outbrief with, 101
  questions for, in child deaths, 241
  reports by, 84–85
  role of, 79–85
Medically attended death, 73
Medically unattended death, 73
Medical record review, 241
Medicolegal autopsy, 240–241
Medicolegal death investigators
  body and scene processing by, 70
  certification of, 69
  death notifications by, 71–72
  role of, 69–72
  transportation of remains and, 70
Methamphetamine, 218
Methane gas detection, 126–127, 141
Missing adolescent report, 247–248
Missing child reports, 246–247
Modified luminol formulas, 333–334

Morphine, 218
Motor vehicle scenes, 327–328
Multiple victim death scenes, 271–274
    mass murder, 273–274
    scene considerations, 272–274
    serial murders, 271
    spree killings, 272
Mummification, 151
Munchausen syndrome by proxy, 242
Murder. *See* Homicidal deaths

N

Natural deaths, 10, 13–23, 80
    common indicators of, 21
    death notifications, 22–23
    death scene interviews, 21–22
    death scene processing, 15–16
    definition of, 13
    examination of body, 20
    initial scene response, 14
    legal determination of death, 17
    outdoor death scenes, 20
    photographing body, 19
    plan development, 17
    primary scene, 15–16
    processing the body, 19
    related searches, 21
    scene considerations, 15
    scene organizations, 16–17
    scene processing, 18
    secondary scene, 16
    sketching body, 19
    taking control of scene, 16
    team briefing, 18
    worksheets and documentation, 13–14
Near contact wounds, 187, 194
Near-drowning incidents, 168
NecroSearch International, 107, 115, 128
Necrotic tissue, 363
Neglect, 243
Neutral density (ND) filters, 307, 318
Next of kin, death notification to, 22–23
Nitrogen, 166–167
Non-criminal homicides, 80
Nonspatter bloodstains, 335–336
North American Man-Boy Love
        Association (NAMBLA), 250
Note taking, 6, 323–328
    accidental deaths, 33
    homicidal deaths, 60–61
    suicidal deaths, 46

O

Oblique lighting, 380, 396, 419–420
Observations, 323–328
On-scene body processing, 81–82
On-scene coordination, 5–6
Opiates, 218
Oral ingestion, 217, 218
Ornithologists, 122
Outbrief, 84, 101
Outdoor death scenes
    accidental deaths, 34–35
    homicidal deaths, 62
    natural deaths, 20
    observations, 327
    suicidal deaths, 48
Outer perimeter, 9, 15, 279

P

Paint, 384–385
Panographic photography, 309
Panorama shots, 317–318
Patent prints, 393–394
Pattern evidence, 301
Pedophilia, 249–250
Penetrating injuries, 199
Perimeter
    establishment of, 5, 8–9, 355
    inner, 8, 9
    outer, 8, 9
Perishable evidence
    collection of, 7
    documentation of, 7
    preservation of, 6, 7
Permissive search, 283
Personal protective equipment (PPE), 6
Personnel, 284–285, 286
Photography, 6, 285, 303–313
    accidental deaths, 32–33
    autopsy, 92–100, 313
    of bite marks, 407–408
    bloodstain patterns, 339–340
    of body, 311–313
    chopping injuries, 182
    equipment, 303–304
    of evidence, 309
    evidence, 100
    filters, 307–308
    footwear and tire impressions, 414–415
    general guidelines, 305–306
    homicidal deaths, 59–60

identification, 312
identification photographs, 95
impression evidence, 420
of injuries, 96–98, 312–313
internal examination, 98–99
natural deaths, 19
overlapping method/panographic, 309
photographic perspectives, 309–311
of prints, 397–398
progressive method, 309
scene, 308
setup, 304–305
sharp force injuries, 173
techniques, 305
tool marks, 411–412
of trace evidence, 381
use of flash, 306–307
Physical assault evidence, 267
Physical child abuse, 236–241
Physicians, interview of, 22
Pistol injuries, 183–190
Planners, 326
Plastic prints, 393
Point-to-point search, 108–110
Poisoning, 211–215
    accidental, 214–215
    bites and envenomation, 214
    body and scene, 214–215
    general considerations, 211
    intentional, 214
    methods of exposure, 212–214
    worksheets and documentation, 211–212
Polar coordinates, 300
Polarizing filters, 307, 318
Porous surfaces, prints on, 401
Post-blast debris, 360–361
Post-blast scenes, 355–362
Postmortem changes, 147–152
    algor mortis, 8, 149–150
    documentation of, 7–8
    early, 148
    immediate, 148
    late, 150–151
    livor mortis, 7, 147, 148
    rigor mortis, 7–8, 147, 148–149
    rule of twelves, 148
    time of death and, 147–148
    worksheets and documentation, 147–148
Postmortem cooling, 8, 149–150
Postmortem interval, 81, 147
Postmortem lividity, 7, 147, 148
Postmortem rigidity, 148–149

Post-scene activities, 286–287
Power sources, 205–206
Pregnancy history, 233
Preliminary autopsy reports, 84
Preparation, 4
Prescription pills, 218
Presumptive identification, 74, 79
Primary death scenes, 15–16, 28, 42,
        55–56, 279
Prints
    in blood, 402–404
    on body/skin, 393–395
    chemical development of, 401–405
    detection of, 396
    DNA considerations, 398
    on nonporous surfaces, 398–401
    in oil and grease, 404–405
    photographing, 397–398
    on porous surfaces, 401
    at scene, 395–398
    Superglue fuming, 398–401
    on wet surfaces, 401–402
Privacy, reasonable expectation of,
        282–283
Probing method, of locating remains, 125
Public lands and property, 282–283
Pulmonary barotrauma, 199
Pupa, 363, 365
Pupal casing, 363

R

Rape
    acquaintance, 264–265
    drug-facilitated, 265
    evidence, 266–267
    intimate partner examination, 268
    resulting in death, 263–269
    scene context and considerations, 264
    scene processing, 268–269
    stranger, 265–266
    suspect examination, 267–268
    victim examination, 266–267
    worksheets and documentation,
        263–264
RAW images, 305
Reasonable expectation of privacy,
        282–283
Rectangular coordinates, 298
Reflected ultraviolet imaging system
        (RUVIS), 396
Rene Guyon Society, 250

Reports
    See also Documentation
    by medical examiner, 84–85
    post-scene, 287
Residential power sources, 205–206
Retinal hemorrhages, 227
Rib fractures, 240
Ricochets, 346–347
Rifle entrance wounds, 189
Rifle injuries, 183–190
Rigor mortis, 7–8, 147, 148–149
Rough sketch, 289
Rule of twelves, 148

S

Saliva, 370–371
Scalds, 236
Scanning sonar, 141–142
Scavenger activities, 105
Scene coordination, 278
Scene documentation, 285
    See also Worksheets and
        documentation
Scene indicators, 152, 324–328
Scene measurements, 295–301
Scene observation, 284
Scene observer duties, 323
Scene photography, 308
    See also Photography
Scientific assistance
    in search for human remains, 107–108,
        127–128
    in surface recovery, 121–122
Scuba scene, 169
Search warrants, 283
Secondary death scene, 16, 28, 42, 55–56
Second-degree burns, 202
Semen, 370–371
Serial bombers, 356
Serial murders, 271
Sexual activities resulting in death,
        253–261
    autoerotic asphyxiation, 161–162, 255,
        260–261
    death during coitus, 254–255
    hypoxic deaths, 255–260
    worksheets and documentation,
        253–254
Sexual assault, 248–250
    acquaintance, 264–265
    drug-facilitated, 265

evidence, 266–267
intimate partner examination, 268
resulting in death, 263–269
scene considerations, 268–269
scene context and considerations, 264
stranger, 265–266
suspect examination, 267–268
victim examination, 266–267
worksheets and documentation,
        263–264
Sexual assault response team (SART),
        245, 263, 266
Shaken baby syndrome, 226–227, 240
Shallow graves, 123, 124
Sharp force injuries, 171–175
    body in, 172–175
    general issues, 171
    scene in, 172
    worksheets and documentation, 171
Shooting scenes, 341–353
    analysis considerations, 344
    bullet defect documentation, 344–347
    chemical testing to determine bullet
        defects, 347–350
    firearms evidence, 349–353
    recovery of evidence from, 341–343
Shored exit wounds, 190
Shotcup, 191–192
Shotgunning, 219
Shotgun wounds, 191–196
    close and intermediate range, 194–195
    contact, 193–194
    distant, 196
    effects of distance on, 193–196
    entrance wounds, 191–193
    exit wounds, 196
    near contact, 194
    worksheets and documentation, 191
Side flash (splash), 208
Side scanning sonar, 142
Site datum, 116–117, 128–129
Skeletal system injuries, 237
Skeletonization, 151
Sketching, 285, 289–301
    accidental deaths, 33
    bloodstain patterns, 340
    body, 293–295
    depictions, 292
    evidence, 301
    finished sketch, 289–291
    general components of sketch, 291–292
    homicidal deaths, 60

natural deaths, 19
rough sketch, 289
scene measurements, 295–301
suicidal deaths, 46
types of, 292–293
Skin exposure, to poisons, 214
Skin injuries, 237–238
Smoking, 219
Smooth bore weapons, 191–196
Smothering, 163–164
Snorting, 219
Sodium rhodizonate, 349–350, 389–390
Soil
    evidence, 121, 134, 387–388
    sifting, 120–121, 130–131, 133
Solvents, 213
Spatter, 334–335
Spent bullet cases, 343–344
Spiral search, 111
Spree killings, 272
Stabbing injuries, 171–175
Staged accidents, 236–237
Stalking, 265
Stati-Lift dust print lifter, 422–423
Stellate wounds, 193
Stippling, 184
Stomach contents, 151
Stranger rape, 265–266
Strangulation, 156–162
    autoerotic asphyxiation, 161–162
    hanging, 158–160
    ligature (garroting), 155, 157–158
    manual (throttling), 156–157
Subcutaneous skin injuries, 237–238
Sudan Black, 404–405
Sudden unexplained infant death (SUID),
        228–233
Suicidal deaths, 11, 39–51, 80
    death notifications, 49–51
    death scene interviews, 49
    death scene processing, 41–45
    definition of, 39
    documenting with notes, 46
    evidence commonly associated
        with, 48
    examination of body, 46–48
    initial scene response, 40–41
    legal determination of death, 43
    outdoor death scenes, 48
    photographing body, 45–46
    plan development, 43

by poisonous gas, 165–167
processing the body, 45
related searches, 48
scene considerations, 41
scene indicators, documenting, 45
sharp force injuries, 173
sketching body, 46
team briefing, 43–44
worksheets and documentation, 39–40
Superglue fuming, 370, 395, 398–401
Surface documentation, 119–120, 128
Surface preparation, 128–129
Surface recovery, of human remains,
        113–122
    body processing, 116
    establishing datum, 116–117
    establishing grid, 117–119
    general principles, 113
    locating remains, 114–115
    recovery of evidence, 119–120
    recovery of remains, 120
    scene processing, 116
    scientific assistance, 121–122
    sifting soil, 120–121
    soil evidence, 121
    surface documentation, 119–120
    worksheets and documentation,
        113–114
Surface search, for human remains, 138
Suspect
    alibis of, 388–389
    examination of, 252, 267–268

T

Tape lift, 424
Task prioritization, 277–278
Team briefing
    accidental deaths, 29
    homicidal deaths, 57
    natural deaths, 18
    suicidal deaths, 43–44
Technological method, of locating remains,
        126–127
Technological search, 141–143
Teeth, 198
Telephones, 325–326
Temperature, 149–150
Terrorism, 273–274
Thermal injuries, 197, 201–204
Thermal tomography, 107, 115, 127, 141

Third-degree burns, 203
Three-dimensional impression evidence, 411–412, 413–419
Throttling, 156–157
Time of death, 147–148
Tire impressions, 413–425
Toilet areas, 326
Tool marks, 411–412
Tool marks in bone, 409–410
Touch DNA, 369–370
Toxicology report, 85
Trace evidence, 379–392
    alibi sample, 388–389
    on body, 379
    building materials, 387
    collection of, 381–382
    detection of, 380
    fibers, 384
    glass, 385–387
    hairs, 384
    hazardous materials, 392
    packaging, 382–383
    paint, 384–385
    at scene, 380–382
    soil, 387–388
    trace explosives, 390–392
    trace metals, 389–390
Trace explosives, 390–392
Trace metals, 389–390
Transfer lift method, 394–395
Transportation of remains, 70
Traumatic brain injuries, 199
Triangulation, 298
Two-dimensional impression evidence, 410, 419–425
2-NN testing, 348–349, 389

U

Ultraviolet lighting, 370–371, 380, 396
Underwater search, for human remains, 138–140
Undetermined death, 80
Urine, 370–371
Utility areas, 325

V

Vehicles, carbon monoxide poisoning, 167
Vertical panorama shots, 318
Victims, 278

Videography, 284, 315–321
    bindings and sequencing issues, 321
    of body, 319–320
    death scene, 318–319
    equipment, 315–316
    setup, 316
    suicidal deaths, 45–46
    techniques, 316–318
    use of auxiliary lightning, 318
    use of filters, 318
Video recordings, 6
Violent Crime Apprehension Program (VICAP), 271
Violent deaths
    See also Homicidal deaths
    infant, 226
Visual techniques, for locating human remains, 114

W

Wadding effect, 191–192
Walk-through, during initial scene evaluation, 6
Wastebasket content, 326
Weapons
    blunt force blows with, 178–179
    child abuse deaths, 236
    documentation of, 342
    recovery from scene, 341–343
    safety, 341–342
    on-scene processing of, 342–343
Wet stains, 375
Windows, 324–325
Witnesses, interview of, 36, 64
Wood lamps, 267
Worksheets and documentation, 285
    accidental death, 25–26
    aquatic recovery of human remains, 137–138
    asphyxiation, 155
    blunt force injuries, 177–178
    buried remains, 123–124
    child abduction and murder, 245–246
    child deaths, 235–236
    chopping, 181
    drug-related deaths, 217–218
    electrical injuries, 205
    explosive injuries, 197–198
    firearm injuries, 183
    homicidal deaths, 53–54

infant deaths, 225–226
natural deaths, 13–14
poisoning, 211–212
postmortem changes, 147
rape and sexual assault, 263–264
sexual activities resulting in death,
        253–254
sharp force injuries, 171
shotgun wounds, 191

suicidal deaths, 39–40, 45, 46
surface recovery of human remains,
        113–114
thermal injuries, 202
Wounds. *See* Injuries

Z

Zoologists, 122